The recent financial crisis has had a dev
Thousands of businesses have closed, m
many people have lost their homes. *Capi*
key economies have fallen into a 'debt
to the real economy, and looks into alternatives to the constant stream of
financial bubbles and shocks. Overlooked by many, cooperatives across the
world have been relatively resilient throughout the crisis. Through four case
studies, this book explores their strategies, providing an in-depth analysis
within a broader debate on wealth generation and a sustainable future. To
all those interested in political economy, enterprise governance, development studies and cooperatives, *Capital and the Debt Trap* opens up new ways
of thinking.

Capital and the Debt Trap

Learning from Cooperatives in the Global Crisis

Claudia Sanchez Bajo

and

Bruno Roelants

Foreword by

Ian MacPherson

First published 2013 by
PALGRAVE MACMILLAN

Palgrave Macmillan in the UK is an imprint of Macmillan Publishers Limited,
registered in England, company number 785998, of Houndmills, Basingstoke,
Hampshire RG21 6XS.

Palgrave Macmillan in the US is a division of St Martin's Press LLC,
175 Fifth Avenue, New York, NY 10010.

Palgrave Macmillan is the global academic imprint of the above companies
and has companies and representatives throughout the world.

Palgrave® and Macmillan® are registered trademarks in the United States,
the United Kingdom, Europe and other countries.

ISBN 978–0–230–25238–7 hardback
ISBN 978–1–137–37235–2 paperback

This book is printed on paper suitable for recycling and made from fully
managed and sustained forest sources. Logging, pulping and manufacturing
processes are expected to conform to the environmental regulations of the
country of origin.

A catalogue record for this book is available from the British Library.

A catalog record for this book is available from the Library of Congress.

Typeset by MPS Limited, Chennai, India.

Contents

List of Boxes, Figures and Tables

Boxes

Figures

Tables

Foreword

As a form of economic organization, the cooperative has been around for over two centuries. Today, it has been widely adopted within all major cultures and in virtually every country; the United Nations estimates that it helps approximately one half of the world's population meet at least one important need. People involved with cooperatives have engaged in lengthy and often fascinating discussions over their potential economic contributions, their underlying values and principles, and their operating practices and distinctive qualities. Because of these discussions, as well as the wide diversities in types of cooperatives and the varied contexts within which they exist, cooperatives can appear to be opaque – the great size of the movement unclear – in the popular mind.

Cooperatives and their movements have, in fact, not generally commanded the interest and respect they deserve. They are rarely discussed in general public discourse, even in places and in relation to issues where they could be particularly useful. They are almost entirely ignored in most academic circles, including those in countries where their contributions are obviously significant. They are typically undervalued in the development of public policy, though governments in different times, places, and situations have often found them useful. They have been frequently subjected to questionable, uninformed critiques and, even more seriously, marginalized and trivialized by pundits and advocates for capitalist firms. They have often been taken for granted or co-opted in countries where the state plays aggressive and domineering economic roles.

In contrast to this rather dismal and frustrating situation, this book presents a thoughtful and exciting consideration of the roles cooperatives can play – and should be expected to play – today. From among the many important dimensions that characterize the movement, five are arguably of particular importance. The first is the context within which it is cast. The book begins with a discussion of some of the current major issues confronting the world today and not with an 'internalist' discussion about cooperatives. It provides a strong and stimulating discussion of the financial breakdown of recent years. It examines what the authors consider are the key economic 'traps' of our times – in consumption practice, liquidity capacities, and debt accumulation. This discussion then becomes the context within which the cooperative model and options are then considered.

In other words, the authors' fundamental purpose is to discuss – realistically and precisely – how and why cooperatives should be seen as important players in the international economy today and not just as mere 'add-ons' when 'real business' for whatever reason is not fully effective. The authors do not fall into the trap, all too often evident among writers interested in cooperatives, of being satisfied with presenting pious declarations of the value of cooperation. The book is based on a well informed and carefully argued examination of the current global situation; an examination that in turn makes what they have to say about cooperatives particularly acute and useful.

At the same time, though, the second most obviously important feature of the book is the way in which the authors take seriously the underlying values and principles on which the cooperative movement and its institutions rest. They understand the fundamental importance of that exercise; they realize that the values and principles are central to cooperatives – they are not just inherited window dressing or a pursuit of market advantage in the age when 'social' business is fashionable. Ultimately, they are what makes the cooperative model particularly relevant in the modern era.

Third, the book provides a stimulating discussion of the importance of control over the economy. It describes the ways in which the current financial systems and short-term benefits for the few have shifted control, even in capitalist firms and within the global economy. It shows how that shift has distorted the 'real value' of what people produce and consume. This consideration leads invariably to a debate of the importance of 'control' within cooperatives. The very structure of the cooperative enterprise, which strives for forms of economic democracy, does provide a bed-rock for lodging control in the hands of key stakeholders, normally the consuming or producing members. Maintaining and refining that control, however, will always be a challenge, even in an age of expanding communication possibilities. It is a challenge that cooperators and cooperative organizations need to address constantly and more deeply. It is also a dimension of cooperation that the outside world needs to appreciate more fully.

Fourth, the book provides case studies of quite different types of cooperative organizations in four widely divergent circumstances in Mexico, France, Spain, and Québec. These cases demonstrate the variety of cooperative enterprise. They show differences in approaches, the importance of cultural and local circumstances, and the versatility of cooperative entrepreneurship. They provide much fruit for thought: they are about organizations responding to, and coping with, some of the most important economic and social changes of the times. They show why we need more such research, more inquiry in what might be called Cooperative Studies.

Finally, the book is particularly interesting because it addresses the 'big picture'. It looks at the commanding heights of economic and social change and not just at local accomplishments and victories. This is a refreshing, relatively uncommon, exception in the intensive literature of the cooperative movement. There is always a danger in cooperative writing and in the field of Cooperative Studies to be fascinated with the beginnings of cooperatives, with the successes achieved by small bands of people coping with adversity or seizing opportunities they individually could not grasp; with what one might call the 'Romance of Cooperation'. There is frequently a tendency, within and without the movement, to be suspicious of large organizations, with co-ops that become prominently and powerfully involved in the large economy.

This book is an imaginative and thoughtfully constructed exception to such trends. It dares to postulate the possible centrality of cooperative enterprise today and in the future. It joins with some other recent scholarship in exploring in a rigorous and tough-minded way what the current situation is and suggesting why and how the cooperative model is so important. It deserves to be widely read and discussed within and across the boundaries that have long divided cooperative proponents and the general public. It is an important opening statement, hopefully the first of many that will deepen celebrations of the United Nations Year of Cooperatives in 2012. It raises many of the issues that need to be discussed more fully; it provides a particularly useful framework within which those discussions can take place.

Ian MacPherson
Emeritus Professor of History
University of Victoria
Victoria, British Columbia, Canada

Acknowledgements

Our first acknowledgement goes to our mentors who have already left us: Professor Jorge Schvarzer, who was a PhD thesis examiner for Claudia Sanchez Bajo and supported her teaching project at Kassel University under the German DAAD programme; and Lu Guangmian, Que Bingguang and Yves Régis, who introduced Bruno Roelants to the world of cooperatives.

We then wish to thank the persons whose contributions and initiatives were fundamental in encouraging us to draft this book: first of all, Professor George Irvin at the School of Oriental and African Studies in London; Eva Nothomb and Amad Aminian who invited us to set up a conference on consumption trends at the Omar Khayam Cultural Centre in Brussels that served as the basis for the consumption trap section in Chapter 2 and the consumer function sub-section in Chapter 3; and former deputy regional director for Asia and the Pacific of the International Cooperative Alliance Rajiv Mehta for twice inviting Bruno Roelants to make presentations on cooperatives and the crisis at Asian meetings in 2008 and 2009. This provided us with very useful feedback from representatives from Asian governments and cooperative federations. We are also grateful to Jean Claude Detilleux, Jean-Louis Bancel and Etienne Pflimlin, whose views on the crisis, as key French cooperative bankers, were very helpful. Thanks to Imad Tabet and Marc Spiker for their precious information on the International Financial Reporting Standards and their evolution. We also thank all the anonymous reviewers' feedback during the process and Palgrave editor Taiba Batool for her faith in the project.

The persons who helped us with the empirical case studies deserve special gratitude: concerning the Natividad fishermen's cooperative in Mexico, president Esteban Fraire for the interview and all the information he provided us. For the Ceralep case, Michel Rohart, director of the Rhône-Alpes Regional Union of Worker Cooperatives in Lyon, for organizing all the interviews; Robert Nicaise, president of the cooperative for his warm welcome at the factory and his introduction to the various interviewees, first and foremost the workers; and Dominique Artaud for his accurate re-reading and correction of the chapter. For Desjardins, Ann Lavoie for introducing us to the various interviewees and resource persons; Alban D'amours for his patient re-reading and comments; and Pierre Poulin for all the material he sent us and for the re-reading and correction of all the historical information. For Mondragon, Mikel Lezamiz who helped identify the interviewees and organize the interviews; Adrian Zelaia for his advice and input; and Javier Salaberria for re-reading and correcting the chapter. We also wish to thank very warmly all the interviewed people in the four empirical cases, whose list can be found at the end of this book.

A number of persons provided us with invaluable information on cooperatives. On international sectoral issues, our thanks go to Rodrigo Gouveia and Thomas Van Zwol in the consumer/retail sector, David Rodger for cooperative housing and the whole CICOPA/CECOP staff for industrial and service cooperatives, especially for the two world surveys on the resilience of cooperatives to the crisis. At the national level, many thanks to Yoshiko Yamada for Japan, Hazel Corcoran for Canada, Tian Lihua for China, Antesh Kumar for India, Natasha Pruttskova for Russia, Joana Nogueira for Brazil, Mervyn Wilson for the UK, Caroline Naett and Gérard Leseul for France, Stefania Marcone for Italy, Paul Armbruster and Klaudia Marcus for Germany, and Carlos Lozano for Spain. We also wish to thank Claire Orts for her help in proofreading, and Maria Lopez de Verolo, Odile Van der Vaeren and Albert Carton for the stimulating discussions we have had with them. We are also grateful to our families and friends who encouraged us faithfully in this project.

The authors and publishers wish to thank the following for permission to reproduce copyright material: the Brookings Institution, the Department for Innovation and Skills of the UK Government, the Dow Jones, the EU Observer, the Daily Telegraph, the European Central Bank, the Financial Accounting Foundation, the Nobel Foundation and the United Nations Conference for Trade and Development (UNCTAD). Every effort has been made to trace rights holders, but if any have been inadvertently overlooked please contact the authors or the publisher.

Finally, we want to give our special thanks to the people of the village of Corezzo in the mountains of Tuscany in Italy, for their support in the very final stages of the drafting process and for their human gift in patience, endurance and wisdom.

Acknowledgements for the second edition

We are very grateful for all the interest and appreciation received since the first edition of the book has been written: to Brazilian Secretary of State Paul Singer and Professors Noam Chomsky (MIT), James K. Galbraith (University of Texas at Austin), Jean Ziegler (University of Geneva), George Irvin (School of Oriental and African Studies, University of London), Robin Murray (LSE Global Governance), Anis Chowdhury (Western Sidney University), Yves Cabannes (University College London), Peter Davis (School of Management, University of Leicester), Stephen Yeo (Ruskin College Oxford) and Louis Favreau (Quebec University) for their reviews of the book; as well as for the reviews published on the Midwest Book Review (USA) in November 2011, Compartir (Spain) in April 2012, Le Monde Diplomatique (France) in July 2012, Finansol (Italy) in August 2012, and the Industry Leaders Magazine ranking of the book as number 6 out of the 10 best finance books of the year in 2011.

We thank Carlos Ingaramo (Vice-president of the Board of Sancor Insurance Cooperative, Argentina) and Yang Qian (Director of the Training Center, All-China Federation of Supply and Marketing Cooperatives) whose reviews led to the decision to publish the book in Spanish and Chinese, and the Intercoop (Buenos Aires, Commercial (Beijing) and Modrijan (Maribor, Slovenia) publishing houses for the foreign language versions of the book already published or in preparation.

Thanks also to the persons who invited us to present the book at various conferences: Miqel Miro at the Financoop conference in Barcelona in June 2012; Mervyn Wilson (Co-operative College, UK) at 'Mainstreaming Co-operation' in Manchester in July 2012; Sonja Novkovic and Tom Webb (St Mary's University) at 'Imagine 2012' in Quebec; Stéphane Bertrand and Joanne Lechasseur (Desjardins) at the International Summit of Cooperatives, also in Quebec; Tadej Slapnik, (Slovenian Social Enterprise Forum) at the international conference 'Cooperatives, Vector of Change in Europe' in Ljubljana in October 2012; Peter Utting (UNRISD) at the UNRISD – ILO conference 'Potential and Limits of Social and Solidarity Economy' in Geneva in May 2013 and the Argentinean Confederation of Cooperatives Cooperar and Intercoop at a special presentation of the book at the Bauen Cooperative Hotel in Buenos Aires in June 2013.

Finally, we would like to express our appreciation for the continuous support from Taiba Batool and her team at Palgrave MacMillan, as well as for the many other reviews and comments received so far which, for lack of space, cannot be mentioned here.

CLAUDIA SANCHEZ BAJO
BRUNO ROELANTS

Introduction

What is happening to the global economy? How do we understand the global financial and economic crisis that was still wreaking havoc in the real economy in 2011? Even though we shall probably be discussing it for decades to come, the first explanations coming to mind are the 'sub-prime' housing mortgage crisis in the USA and financial firms that stopped lending to each other.

Following the fall of Lehman Brothers, the fourth biggest US bank, in September 2008, global panic flared up, spreading the crisis beyond the USA. To save the overall system, governments intervened generously, inflating state deficits along the way. While the financial system was saved, the real economy, firms, households and individuals, began to suffer the consequences of the credit crunch. Eventually, many nation-states have had to undergo a monetarist cure, restricting expenses and public services.

To most people, the crisis came as a surprise, as it had become commonplace to say that a new economy was in the making. A new order of things was to relegate economic cycles to the past. This new economy, highly financialized, thrived on structural state reforms, characterized by deregulation, privatization and liberalization policies, while the state rolled back its regulatory powers. Government became small while many key private economic entities, financial institutions and transnational companies (TNCs) in particular, became larger and larger. These policies were framed as part of 'neo-liberalism' or the 'Washington consensus'. Financial and economic globalization ensued, building highly interconnected global chains of finance, production and distribution. A 'lock in' of national reforms was expected, protecting states from ideological cleavages and political pressure. A 'free market' could finally evolve into an upbeat, unilinear and steady trend that would trickle down benefits over time.

In stark contrast, in September 2008, we were faced with an almost instantaneous collapse of financial and economic activity. Many crises in various countries and continents had occurred before but, this time, the highly interlinked globalized economy was overwhelmed in its entirety.

1

Raging debates about responsibility, guilt and punishment were unleashed. Who was responsible for the crisis? Were markets insufficiently regulated, driven towards speculation, including over-the-counter practices and handsome rewards? Was it because of individuals who took advantage of easy credit thanks to lax government policy? States allowing a high dispersion of regulators that lost their oversight capacity? Or perhaps, was it only the consequence of a few traders' greed? What was the recipe for disaster? The prevalent idea seems to be that banks are the ones to be restrained, while all actors should be 'moralized'.

In this book we explore the causes of this global crisis, delving into deeper layers of analysis (three mechanisms building traps and a shift in control patterns as the deepest cause), linking together the macro and the micro levels, the financial institutions and the real economy. Second, we bring forward inspirational elements drawn from the concrete experience of cooperatives and their resilience during the crisis, in the quest for solutions aimed at both preventing future crises and at creating general wealth.

Even though the whole world suffered the consequences of the financial and economic turmoil, this book centres attention on North America and Europe, as these two regions have been at the core of the crisis. Concerning developing and emerging countries, China receives special attention, given its key position in the world economy.

We will first review the timing of the crisis and its still lasting consequences, the extent of wealth destruction in its widest sense, the main issues addressed so far and the incipient strategies for recovery (Chapter 1).

We will then examine the various theoretical explanations that have been formulated on the crisis. While each explanation offers part of the truth, we propose a focus on three key mechanisms in the build-up of the crisis: a consumption trap, a liquidity trap and a debt trap (Chapter 2). These will help us analyse the in-depth causes of the crisis. From different standpoints, we have observed a pattern of debt practices that have led to an unsustainable financial and economic system. Debt practices have linked the financial and real economy together, and are an integral part of a financialized type of capitalism that appears to endanger capital and long-term wealth generation, as they lack a system of checks and balances. Of the three traps, the debt trap thus emerges as the most fundamental.

At an even deeper level, ongoing changes in the roles of producer, consumer and investor reflect an ongoing shift of boundaries between ownership and control in economic entities, together with the strengthening of global chains of production, distribution and finance (Chapter 3). The issue of control, conceptually distinguished from ownership, can then be connected to debt leveraged onto households and firms, linking the crisis, which is commonly regarded as a macro issue, to economic entities at the micro/meso-level.

We argue that the present complexity and interconnectedness of the global economy calls for new organizational patterns to ensure appropriate representation, transparency, timely information and trustworthy behaviour. Systemic risk is not only due to the fact that some economic entities may have become excessively large but also to the difficulty of setting limits to them, or providing opposing best practices, given that those same large entities are directly taking part in co-regulation with governments.

The extent of involvement and responsibility of very large economic entities has led to calls for a change in values: this is definitely very important, but such calls need to be translated into institutionalized practice, otherwise they will remain evanescent. Consequently, we need to rethink the organization of economic entities (banks, firms, etc.) and this global crisis may be a golden opportunity to do so. But where do we find the necessary inspiration? Amongst the many calls for reform, we hear a great deal about individual incentives and the 'too big to fail' debate. The discussion on control mechanisms against deviant behaviour tends to focus on the efficiency of external control and a change of incentives inside the firms, but ignores the key issue of institutional control mechanisms with proper checks and balances.

Among the diverse actors engaged in the economy, we observe that cooperatives, which are characterized by a specific type of control with checks and balances, have been surprisingly resilient to the crisis. In the second part of the book, we will bring to the fore their experience, by first drawing a general picture of their presence in the economy and society, their reactions and practices during the crisis, their underlying rationality, and their evolution from a political economy standpoint (Chapter 4). Then, in Chapters 5 to 8, we will visit four case studies, providing diversity in terms of sectors of the economy (financial services, industry, distribution, fisheries), size (from small and medium-sized enterprises [SMEs] to large business groups), history (from a few years to over a century) and geographical coverage among the parts of the world that are at the core of the crisis: Natividad in Mexico, Ceralep in France, Desjardins in Canada and Mondragon in Spain. We will argue in which way cooperatives can help us rethink the issue of control and steer clear of the debt trap.

More specifically, we will see that cooperatives offer a particularly interesting experience as they:

- are characterized by specific practices, including the systematic building of financial reserves;
- cater for the needs of key and numerically important stakeholders (for example, producers, consumers and users of services such as banking, social services, housing and energy), while being owned and controlled by these same stakeholders;
- always adopt a long-term perspective, do not delocalize, and have an interest in both economic growth and wealth generation;
- and have information flows among the owners–controllers, which tend to be more transparent and timely than those of average firms, providing legitimacy to decision-making and implementation.

In the final chapter, the book discusses which lessons from cooperatives may be useful in order to address the debt trap, in particular by re-equilibrating control in economic entities. We argue that, although many other measures will have to be carried out, this is a key part of the solution and will grow in importance as time goes by.

We decided to co-author this book by drawing on the respective knowledge and experience of both of us: Claudia Sanchez Bajo as political economy researcher and lecturer on globalization, regionalism, economic actors, production and distribution chains, and cooperatives; Bruno Roelants as specialist in development issues and engaged in the world of cooperatives at the European and world level.

Neoliberal-minded policy makers, after having resorted to massive bailouts and even nationalization of key large banks and firms, have returned to 'business-as-usual' with their previous structural reform policies. The causes of the crisis have not yet been sorted out. If we keep falling into the same traps, we may be faced with a new crisis that could destabilize the global economic system to the core, with grave political and social consequences. We argue that if we want to change the present trajectory, we need to become aware of the relationship between control and ownership, so as to to achieve the institutionalization of new values and practices that allow for a sustainable and long-term creation of general wealth.

We invite the reader to observe that, although the book was completed by the end of 2010, new events – some of them dramatic – are continuing to unfold along the lines of what we had written. We analyse this statement and reflect on some fundamental issues brought up by the debates, presentations and evaluations on the book, in the postscript added to this second edition.

1
The Mother of All Crises?

Introduction

There is no doubt that we have been going through a grave global financial-economic crisis, but is this the mother of all crises? Without pretending to cover all aspects and leaving the explanations and analyses to Chapter 2, we here present the facts, as well as the perceptions and reactions of some key actors during the crisis up to the end of 2010. We are not, at this stage, making much reference to previous bubbles and crises, leaving the discussion for the following chapter. We are taking an inductive approach, as a necessary step before engaging in deeper layers of analysis.

When did it all start? For European Central Bank (ECB) President Jean-Claude Trichet, the turmoil started in August 2007.[1] For the Federal Reserve Bank-St Louis (Fed-St Louis),[2] it had begun on 27 February 2007 when Freddie Mac, in view of accounting changes, made the public announcement that it would stop its sub-prime lending mortgages in August 2007.[3] This letter was probably one of the 'butterflies' leading to the financial storm. In the next section, we review how the crisis began, then we observe signs of mounting trouble at the global level and, finally, we see how the global bubble burst.

Starting as a financial disaster, the crisis evolved into an economic one. Financial assets were wiped out, but the real economy was wounded as well. In the 'wealth destruction' section, we try to evaluate the scale of destruction that has occurred in various ways, not only in financial terms. Private sector credit contracted and had to confront the leverage of its debt obligations, namely the debt relative to assets or income, leading to a drastic downturn. Doubtless, the latter would have been far more dramatic without governmental intervention through rescue packages for banks and fiscal stimulus packages. An in-depth modelling study by Moody's chief economist Mark Zandi and Alan Blinder at Princeton University affirmed that, in the United States, these packages amounting to a total of $1.7 trillion had saved 8.5 million jobs and averted a further dip of 6.5 per cent in US economic output.[4]

We then examine the various measures carried out to stem the crisis and review the main strategies to restart growth observed so far.

In August 2010, US Treasury Secretary Timothy Geithner published 'Welcome to the recovery' in the *New York Times*.[5] But pain is long-standing and after a short while trouble returns because the governments' rescue packages have loaded the public sector with debt.

Also in August 2010, John Taylor from Stanford University doubted that a rapid recovery would take place, arguing that the amount of debt was much higher than was thought and causing concern about tax increases.[6] Swayed by an ideologically minded 'deficit-aversion', many nation-states have been rolling back their powers and presence in the national economy as well as various benefits for their population such as pensions, while the economy still suffers from the fall in activity, credit, employment and consumption. By the end of 2010, no one could affirm that we were out of trouble, while calls mounted for further state cuts to maintain states' credit ratings and affordable funding.[7] In the European Union (EU), this 'austerity' may cost Europeans a double-dip recession, or, at the very least, years of stagnation and high unemployment. In 2010, it was already taking a toll on growth with the exception of Germany and France,[8] while the timid US recovery was receding.[9] Through a vicious circle, the uncertainty was making companies shy away from investment and hiring.

How it began: the sub-prime housing market in the USA

The first domino pieces to fall were US home prices. In the USA, according to Bosworth and Flaaen (2009), 'home prices began to rise rapidly in the late 1990s and, by the year 2000, had far exceeded the growth in either incomes or rent value. At their peak in 2006, home prices were nearly 50 per cent above a norm defined by their historical relationship to household income'.[10] In 2002, Dean Baker had confirmed the housing bubble in the United States and warned about its end, with consequences similar to the collapse of the two bubbles in Japan – housing and stock markets – in the late 1980s. Based on the House Price Index from the Office of Federal Housing Enterprise Oversight, house prices had risen between 1995 and 2002 by almost 30 per cent above the overall rate of inflation.[11] Without any regard to this problematic market data, banks engaged heavily in practices leading to indebtedness of poorer citizens,[12] and re-sold the outstanding debts as assets throughout the world. This was accepted as a process of 'securitization' of collateralized debt obligations (CDOs; see definition in Box 1.1). However, with hindsight, it was more of a house built on shifting sand.

Various factors encouraged property investment. The US government encouraged the provision of housing to the low-income sector of the population, mainly non-white. This could lend political support to the government as well as to the American ideal of each citizen having a home and

Box 1.1 Collateralized debt obligations (CDOs)

CDOs were created in 1987 by bankers to move the portfolio of debt off their balance sheets. This was the core motive, with risk transfer and cash raising a secondary, though more publicized, consideration. CDOs became the fastest selling product as they gave high returns compared to both corporate bonds and the low interest rates set by the Federal Reserve after the 2001 dotcom bust.

There are many types of CDOs, so the easiest way to understand them is to look at a CDO balance sheet. Debt is removed off the balance sheet of banks by selling it as a CDO to a Special Purpose Vehicle (SPV) or Special Purpose Entity (SPE), usually an off-shore trust, depositing a cash collateral account and naming a trustee that is also the collateral administrator. The SPE issues the bonds (the CDOs) with the help of underwriters to investors paying the initial purchase price, the investors purchasing the original loans. CDOs, typically originated by banks, are thus a type of structured asset-backed security whose value and payments are derived from a portfolio of fixed-income underlying assets (bonds and loans including mortgages). The CDO portfolio is then cut in three cascading slices or 'tranches' (senior, mezzanine and equity), where payments on the principal and interest are made in order of seniority, the senior one being protected by the others. Furthermore, the top one is covered by a credit default swap (CDS). Investors pay for the 'tranches' of their preference, ranging from investment-grade to very speculative, with the latter enjoying a higher yield. Afterwards, the SPE lends to new borrowers, e.g. homebuyers.

Through the CDOs, investment banks connect the real economy to financial investors around the world. Banks retain an equity tranche, which suffers the first defaults. In case of default, the debt claim turns into a physical asset, e.g. a bank gets the house in the case of a housing mortgage. Another issue is whether the original debts (financial assets) were highly correlated or not. Synthetic CDOs do not own cash assets like bonds or loans; they work without owning those assets through the use of credit default swaps. The Abacus 2007-AC1, subject of the civil suit for fraud brought by the SEC against Goldman Sachs in 2010, was a synthetic CDO.

private property. To achieve this, the US government allowed multifaceted and very diverse types of economic entities to deliver credit, beyond banks. According to Bosworth and Flaaen, 'the marketing of the sub-prime, alt-A, and home equity loans relied on independent mortgage originators who were part of a financial network that developed in parallel to the issuance and securitization of conventional mortgages by the government-sponsored enterprises (GSEs)'.[13] 'Sub-prime' always refers to a high default risk, but there is no consensus on the exact definition of a sub-prime mortgage loan. The latter can ascertain characteristics of the borrower, of the lender, of the projected default rate of which the loan is part, or of the type of mortgage contract. Yuliya Demyanyk and Otto Van Hemert published evidence that the quality of loans had deteriorated during the six years prior to the crisis and that the securitizers knew about it.[14]

A great part of the problem was that the credit system was not only used by the GSEs but also by this parallel system of originators of the loans. In fact, the collateralized debt obligations (CDOs) were the substitute for the GSE guarantees, standardized and jumbled together in a confused mass to be sold in tranches. Junior tranches absorbed the initial defaults while senior tranches were often assigned triple-A rating. The so-called private-label mortgage-backed securities lacked any kind of credit risk protection by the GSEs. What is even more interesting is that, although the quality of loans deteriorated over the six years prior to the crash, the sub-prime–prime mortgage rate spread (sub-prime mark-up), which accounts for their default risk, declined. Instead, the mark-up should have adjusted upwards. And the securitizers knew it.

The Fed-St Louis was not alone in realizing that February 2007 meant the end of the bubble and the beginning of the big fall. On 7 March 2007, Dan Sparks, the chief of Goldman Sachs' mortgage trading, wrote in a message to his girlfriend that the 'business was totally dead, and the poor little sub-prime borrowers will not last so long.'[15] Moreover, large securitizers participate in the International Accounting Standards Board (IASB) and its working groups, setting through the international financial reporting standards (IFRS) the valuation of liabilities, what can be on- and off-balance sheet and the application of fair value instead of book accounting. They thus knew well in advance that implementing the IFRS would bring about difficulties for all economic entities using previous accounting practices. But, as long as everybody believed in it, everything seemed quite fine, and the 'innovative' products kept selling well. Private-label mortgage-backed securities jumped from about 8 per cent in 2001 to 20 per cent in 2006, while the securitized share of the sub-prime mortgage market grew from 54 per cent in 2001 to 75 per cent in 2006.[16]

Danger ahead

At the global level, warning signs were clearly visible as early as 2006 but nobody did much about it and, by 2007, it was already too late. Edwin Truman, director of the Federal Reserve System's Division of International Finance for 20 years, affirmed in May 2007 that there was a 10 to 15 per cent probability of a catastrophic collapse of the financial system.[17]

2006 was the year when house prices peaked and began to fall both in the United States and in Spain. It was also the year when housing mortgage defaults began to multiply. The Spanish housing bubble began to deflate as early as 2004, but it was only in 2006 that the Bank of Spain confirmed the tendency.[18] In the early months of 2006, the increase in funding granted to households remained very high, more than 20 per cent, giving rise to a new increase in the debt ratio and financial burden, increasing the vulnerability to newly hardening monetary conditions.[19] However, nobody paid much attention to this news. Securitizers knew of these trends; they even lost some money in 2006.[20] As we saw above, the quality of mortgage loans in the United States had consistently fallen since 2001,[21] but the spread or mark-up in securitized products did not follow any of these downward trends in price and quality.

As regards international trade, 2006 was the year signalling a limit to the expectations of very high short-term profits for companies in the developed countries. The Doha round of trade liberalization suffered a halt,[22] while global competition led to overcapacity and many sectors were facing highly reduced profit margins. The halt showed that developed countries could no longer obtain easy access to developing and emerging economies. The largest firms were particularly looking forward to the liberalization of services, among which were financial, accounting and logistics – essential to maintain the lead on global markets. Later efforts during the crisis showed that the revival needed accommodation to developing countries' demands.[23]

Another sign of problems ahead was the preference for currency accumulation by developing and emerging countries. Since the 1997 Asian financial crisis, many countries had had to leave behind their pegging to the US dollar, although by doing so they returned to exports and growth. Through a string of painful financial/economic crises, many developing and emerging countries learnt that it was better to avoid a call to the IMF; and that meant accumulating currency reserves at any cost, China being the best example. Some began to invest in foreign assets through government-controlled funds. Equity and savings were in. Countries turned to exports, and in the process escaped IMF recipes that had proved not that helpful after all: they either repaid their debts to the IMF or halted payments altogether.

Indeed, IMF data show that developing countries had raised their official currency reserves by 400 per cent in 10 years, while developed countries had done so only by 150 per cent, reducing their share from nearly 50 to 30 per cent.[24] Picking up pace after the 1997 Asian financial crisis, developing countries had accumulated about 70 per cent of global exchange reserves of which the US dollar represented a 66.5 per cent share, 'a staggering accumulation' according to Lawrence Summers in 2006.[25] Summers feared the shift as it weakened the effectiveness of existing arrangements to influence domestic policy adjustments and the supply of cross-border capital flows, necessary for global stability. Such global imbalances worried economist

Nouriel Roubini, for whom emerging markets, by the purchase of US debt, were contributing to low US long-term interest rates. Yet, for Roubini it had been just one factor among others in the building of the bubble and the following synchronized global recession.[26]

In 2006, Edwin Truman explained the reasons to accumulate currency:

> First, they are insuring themselves against having to turn in emergencies to the West or to the IMF, with their strict loan conditions. Second, many emerging economies use the money to stay competitive by keeping their own currencies' exchange rates from rising. This particularly applies to China, which is expected to hold 1 trillion dollars in reserve by the year's end.

What did US decision makers want to do about it? According to Edwin Truman, 'nothing ... When the dollar declines, investments in the United States, which remains the world's most liquid and transparent market, grow more attractive, the US debt is easier to finance and new exports reduce its trade deficit'.[27] Having competitive production platforms geared to exports, vital to Transnational Corporations (TNCs), was also part of the explanation. The only time China let the yuan revalue, before the financial crisis, was in July 2005, and the US dollar indeed lost ground and interest rates went up.[28] But this time was different because globalization in both the economic and financial spheres had intertwined.

Another sign of danger ahead came from the globalization of the stock market. A seamless system in automatic gear across continents was being tried out. In June 2006, the globalization process led to the first transatlantic equity stock market, led by US institutions buying European ones, when the New York Stock Exchange (NYSE) came to lead the Paris-based Euronext. The NYSE now controls several stock exchanges such as Paris, Brussels, Amsterdam and Lisbon, as well as the London-based futures and options market, Liffe. Shortly after, the Milan stock market Borsa Italiana was also acquired.[29] On the shopping list were Japan's Tokyo Stock Exchange (its CEO and chairman being in favour) and Europe's derivatives markets, as Euronext owned the Liffe exchange.[30] NYSE Euronext is an American holding company, headquartered in New York, headed by John Thain, with eleven directors on the NYSE side and nine from Euronext. Perhaps only Thain could achieve such a goal. In January 2004, he had taken over a NYSE crippled by corporate scandals. Strongly connected to Europe,[31] he worked out the deal with François Bujon de l'Estang, French Ambassador and President of Citigroup France, who hailed it as a transatlantic bridge.[32] Only the UK London stock exchange (LSE) was still going it alone, even though, also in June 2006, Gulf families had become important investors: Borse Dubai with a 20.56 per cent stake and the NASDAQ with a 25.1 per cent stake.[33]

LSE chief executive Clara Furse was seeking to link up with Euronext and Deutsche Börse, the German exchange, when the NASDAQ took over the stakes.[34] In early 2009, former Lehman Brothers executive Xavier Rolet replaced Clara Furse.[35] Deutsche Börse had to change its organizational model to join in the LSE, but that was difficult because trading and settlement operations were vertically integrated. Furthermore, regulatory obstacles may not have allowed it, as Deutsche Börse and Euronext controlled the two main European derivatives exchanges. [36]

Behind the globalization of stock markets, there was the Transatlantic Partnership agreement.[37] In fact, Europe and the United States were getting very close in economic and financial terms, providing between 60 and 75 per cent of foreign investment to each other's market, both economic and financial.[38] As a consequence, they identified corporate accounting scandals such as Enron's and Parmalat's, namely the mispricing and poor valuation, as a key strategic weakness. To tackle the latter, accounting, auditing and governance policies had to be harmonized; otherwise, the aim of a seamless market for stocks, derivatives and firms' acquisitions would be endangered. In hindsight, they were right, but only partly. As their primary goal was to further foreign acquisitions, they had never considered debt practices to be a weakness.

To accompany the stock market globalization drive, radical change was carried out in the field of accounting and financial information. In the late 1990s, the USA had taken the lead in transforming the international accounting standards (IAS) into the international financial reporting standards (IFRS), thus from accounting into reporting for financial interests, through a body based in London, the International Accounting Standards Board (IASB), whose work picked up after 2001. Yet, as will be further discussed in the next section, the United States decided to implement the IFRS only in 2007, a key reason why Freddie Mac stopped guaranteeing the subprime lending.

As we can see, just before the crisis flared up, a series of signs at the global level were telling us of a fragile situation in rapid change and lacking structure. Huge strides towards a single world stock market had been carried out just before the financial crisis. The 'Transatlantic' regulation project between the United States and the EU began to be implemented in early 2006. The first global regulation was transforming the old accounting that focused on the real economy into one geared towards financial reporting and financial needs. For the first time, the world was truly becoming a circular closed system containing transmission of information and pricing across the globe, permanently interconnected, around the clock, all year round. Anything we do can return through the back door in a non-stop process, and can bring about unintended consequences. Thus, risk increases: a closed system can suffer implosion.

At the same time, all these signs of danger bubbling up leading to the crisis were accompanied by customary beliefs based on old assumptions, some 300 years old. They seemed very rational as faith in stability seemed like an eternal upward evolution akin to the nineteenth century idea of 'progress'. Yet, how could people have come to believe in constant financial returns of 15 per cent on the basis of economies growing at GDP 5 per cent or less? Voltaire's literary personage Candide, for whom everything was always for the best, comes to mind.[39] According to this way of thinking, selling debt as capital in order to get ever more liquidity (without keeping the data in the financial reports) was very rewarding. The more the system was opaque, through offshore sites, hedge funds and 'financial vehicles', the better it was. As a result, few knew exactly what the truth was. In case of a shock, a freeze in the inter-bank market was only normal. Mounting signs of an unstable system, which was rapidly restructuring and reaching a seamless type of integration, were disregarded. Some of them were acknowledged but customary beliefs were stronger, marginalizing dissident voices from the public agenda. Voices claiming foul were unable to articulate the warnings into a political agenda. And even those that worried about the global imbalances, such as Nouriel Roubini, could foresee neither the 'butterflies' nor the final trigger in the 'non-performing' CDOs on the balance sheets of the main Western banks and their hedge funds.

Bursting the global bubble

In early 2007, the first bank run in 150 years took place in the UK. The bank was Northern Rock, which in its previous incarnation had been a very secure building society, namely a member-based bank akin to a cooperative. Converted under Margaret Thatcher into a for-profit firm, it was ironic to see it nationalized, costing the country £60 billion in loans and guarantees for its depositors. Then came the turn of French Société Générale, brought to its knees by trader Jérôme Kerviel; it lost $7 billion.[40] Robin Blackburn's account of the beginning of the crisis is concise and clear. The bursting of a great bubble was linked to the securities used in relation to the housing market in the United States. Such securities were a 'major portion of the asset base' of large banks, which, after hoarding cash, were saved either with the support of the US Federal Reserve or sovereign wealth funds from developing countries. Incredible amounts seemed to disappear through a black hole: $175 billion of capital between July 2007 and March 2008. Banks received $75 billion of new capital by January 2008 to no avail.[41]

Van Denbergh and Harmelink observed that:

> [t]he subprime credit market fiasco nearly brought the $28 trillion credit cycle of the US business economy to a complete standstill in August 2007. Major financial players, including Bear Stearns, Fannie Mae and

Freddie Mac, Lehman Brothers and AIG [were] victims to the spreading financial crisis. Only unprecedented Federal Reserve and Treasury Department actions ... kept credit markets from completely freezing up and other major financial institutions afloat.[42]

Their account of the sudden market freeze refers to exactly one year before Lehman Brothers' downfall.

In August 2007, a Merrill Lynch analyst openly stated that the largest US mortgage firm, Countrywide Financial, faced the possibility of having to file for bankruptcy, given the depressed market conditions related to mortgage securities. The scare was averted when Bank of America agreed to acquire Countrywide. Yet, the latter's CEO had claimed in 2006 that sub-prime loans were toxic. The Moody's rating agency waited one year to take notice and downgrade the company.[43]

Financial market conditions only became worse in the remainder of 2007 and the first half of 2008. In March 2008, Bear Stearns avoided a likely complete collapse only through a Federal Reserve-sponsored takeover by J P Morgan Chase.[44] Bear Stearns' top manager James E. Cayne received hundreds of millions of dollars in compensation while the company went bankrupt, leveraged by 40 to 1. In May 2010, Cayne told the US Financial Crisis Inquiry Commission: 'That was the business. That was, really, industry practice. In retrospect, in hindsight, I would say leverage was too high'.[45] The Federal Reserve guaranteed $30 billion in credit to ensure that the rescue was completed before the financial markets opened on Monday, 17 March 2008.

Prior to the Bear Stearns takeover, the US Federal Reserve had announced a $200 billion programme that would allow financial institutions to utilize mortgage-backed securities as collateral for governmental funds.

Meanwhile, Bank of America acquired Merrill Lynch: by March 2008, three out of the five big US investment banks had lost their independence, falling under the control of commercial banks. In 2008, an analyst at Meeschaert New York announced that the 'investment bank model' had broken down and even Goldman Sachs was expected to adapt. Ken Lewis of Bank of America explained that they had already known this for seven years! Commercial banks would end up owning investment banks for liquidity reasons. The crisis brought about consolidation so that they became both larger and fewer in number.[46] Both Citigroup and Bank of America were saved by the US federal government, guaranteeing all their debts.

The stark deterioration in financial markets taking place in mid-2008 could not be overstated. On Sunday, 8 August 2008, the US government took control of Fanny Mae and Freddie Mac, which had a key role as public service providers, although ownership continued to be in the hands of private shareholders. Treasury Secretary Henry Paulson explained that, from then onwards, those enterprises would no longer be managed to maximize dividends, affirming that such strategy had led to systemic risks for the financial system. In the event of liquidation, the Treasury would have the priority over their assets. Their managers were then replaced by new ones designated by the public authorities. The IMF hailed the action.[47] The rest of the world was astonished at the interventionist stand of the USA, which had long claimed to be against a government role in the economy.

The great disaster took place in September 2008, when financial liquidity was nil and credit circulation froze. Between 12 and 15 September, the US government allowed the bankruptcy of Lehman Brothers, causing a domino effect and, more importantly, the lock-in of the crisis at the global level. Only then did the public authorities and the media wake up.

Lehman Brothers filed for bankruptcy on 15 September 2008, the day after a deal to save the firm negotiated over the weekend fell apart. It had more than $600 billion in debt, and was the largest bankruptcy in US history. With the intermediation of the US government, there were negotiations to try to secure Lehman's acquisition by UK bank Barclays. However, the US government refused to guarantee its toxic assets. Neither the UK Chancellor nor the UK Financial Services Authority (FSA) could approve such a deal without the US guarantee. Further, the FSA could not allow the deal to go through without previous shareholders' approval at Barclays. Barclays stepped aside. Henry Paulson, then US Treasury Secretary, was so infuriated that he publicly insulted the British, and only in 2010 apologized for his rage. British citizens were, for their part, happy to escape Lehman's debt and a probable political crisis if the deal had gone through.

Moreover, Lehman Brothers' fall had a second connection with the UK. An examiner was appointed to report on the case to a US Court. Under US law, this can be made if the court finds out that the company's debts exceed $5 million. The 2,200 page report on Lehman Brothers debt and bankruptcy process was made public on 11 March 2010.[48] The US Court-commissioned report showed that London had a key role in Lehman's case. It was the City law firm Linklaters that approved Lehman's Repo 105,[49] since no US firm would do it.[50] Before reporting each quarter, Lehman Brothers had used off-balance sheet mechanisms to reduce the reported net leverage/debt, and had done this without any economic substance. It reported deals as sales when in fact they were transactions for purely financial reporting purposes: deals amounting to 50 billion dollars. Shortly after, Lehman Brothers had the obligation to buy them back. In public testimony to the Financial Crisis Inquiry Commission, Alan Greenspan expressed that in his opinion the buy-back was the troublesome part.[51] The Court-appointed examiner explained that for some time the New York Federal Reserve Bank had helped to hide Lehman's insolvency by accepting the Repos as collateral for short-term loans, which was not apparently legal.

When the US government, against market expectations, did not bail out Lehman Brothers, creditors suddenly worried about the solvency of the banks to which they had lent their money. Although it was clear that banks had incurred significant losses, nobody knew the amount of toxic assets on individual banks' balance sheets. The impossibility to price the assets led the interbank market to an overnight freeze. And banks, which had increasingly used the interbank markets as a means for short-term funding, found themselves unable to roll over their debt. To reduce their leverage, banks had to obtain fresh capital or sell some of their assets. For the same reason that the interbank market dried up, attracting fresh capital was difficult.

Seattle's Washington Mutual (WaMu), the largest US savings and loan firm, took $7 billion from several investors led by private equity group TPG, one founder of which had been a WaMu director between 1996 and 2002. It stopped offering mortgages through brokers, after more than $200 billion of write-downs and credit losses. WaMu was one of at least a dozen large banks looking for cash in late 2007 and early 2008.[52] On 25 September 2008, WaMu was seized by government regulators who brokered an emergency sale to JP Morgan Chase.[53] During a public hearing in April 2010, the US Senate affirmed that its mortgage lending had been threaded with fraud but had yet to decide on criminal prosecution. Loan officers had been paid according to both volume and speed (of sub-prime mortgage loans) and received extras from overcharging borrowers on their loans or levying penalties.[54]

The above-mentioned issue of accounting standards made it worse. The replacement of the IAS by the IFRS was aimed (a) at comparing the value of global companies and at encouraging mergers and acquisitions deemed part and parcel of the competition for global business scales, and (b) at basing the enterprise value on the 'fair value,' namely market assessment of future short-term expectations, and no longer on the system of historic book accounting. In a crisis, the fair value brings about a vicious pro-cyclical circle through which, every three months, a new financial assessment takes place in a context of uncertainty and falling value of the business, leading to further sales of assets in order to keep the enterprise alive. Thus, banks started hoarding cash and reducing their balance sheets by selling assets, leading to fire-sale prices. In addition, banks reduced credit availability, required more collateral and raised interest rates. As a consequence, firms largely depending on credit lines had to cut costs by reducing investment and laying off workers.

Alignment with the IFRS thus brought a pro-cyclical valuation system that contributed to the steep stock market plunge. But the US lead in accounting did not in fact amount to automatically overwriting its own legislation. The US has kept various types of enterprises out of the scope of the IFRS, such as SMEs and cooperatives and, with the crisis, the US government suspended the use of fair value. Besides, as of January 2010, the 'qualified special-purpose entities' (Qs), usually offshore, including mortgage trusts, by which assets owned by banks were not reported but parked in Qs, were also put back onto balance sheets. Before the crisis, 'if a bank set up a Q so that it would operate automatically, with others owning the securities it issued, the bank could get the assets off its own balance sheet'. FASB chairman Robert Herz commented in 2010:[55]

> On 'autopilot', no entity was deemed to be in control of such SPEs (special-purpose entities) ... effected through complex mathematical calculations that often excluded the effect of key risks such as liquidity risk ... it appears that arrangements were structured to achieve the desired outcomes of removing financial assets and obligations from balance sheets and reporting lower ongoing risk and leverage. From an investor's viewpoint, this obfuscated important risks and obligations.[56]

The EU could not do the same. Incredible as it may seem, the European Commission made the IFRS binding as a whole package in 2002,[57] although the EU has no representative as such in the IASB or the IASF – the foundation that owns the IFRS system. A few EU member states represent their own accounting concerns but are in a voting minority. The EU receives fully finalized texts, and, without intellectual property rights, it cannot modify a comma. The European Commission can refrain from implementing an IFRS only when there is negative advice from two advisory bodies, which has almost never happened. With the crisis, the EU threatened to overwrite the IASB rules, the IASB answering that it takes months to draft and consult worldwide if something has to be fixed, much slower than any government or parliament in times of crisis. The two greatest clashes concerned fair value, on which securities regulators sought more disclosure while banking regulators wanted to protect banks to stop the crisis, and the Qs, concerning off balance-sheet practices, which had been so quickly solved in the USA.

In October 2008, the Troubled Assets Relief Programme (TARP) $700 billion bailout was passed by the US Congress. In 2010, both Fannie Mae and Freddie Mac continued to be under public supervision, kept losing money and received additional public support. In December 2009, US President Barack Obama announced that he would cover their projected losses until 2012, going beyond the pledged $200 billion of public funds. On 24 February 2010, however, an important change took place when Freddie Mac did not request public subsidy of its new yearly loss of $21.5 billion. Since their role was to guarantee real estate and housing mortgages, this meant that the loss would be borne by the banks, the ones handing out the original loans.[58] In the UK, Alliance & Leicester, Bradford & Bingley and Dunfermline building societies were taken over.

Bijlsma and Zwart explain:

> How did the shock to the sub-prime mortgage market develop into a worldwide crisis? The increasing level of defaults on sub-prime mortgage payments caused securitized assets based on sub-prime mortgage loans to fall in value. Banks were exposed to this shock because they held

securitized assets on their balance sheets, or because they implicitly or explicitly guaranteed the shadow banks that bought these assets. The corresponding decline in value of bank assets led to a reduction of bank capital.[59]

The first countries to come under IMF supervision saw waves of riots and the fall of governments. Both the Latvian and Hungarian governments resigned in the wake of public anger. During the 1990s, Central and Eastern European countries had gone crazy about foreign exchange denominated mortgages and loans. There was a difference, though. Whereas several countries such as Poland had used credit to promote export capacity and competitiveness, others, for instance Latvia, had invested their borrowed money in houses and shopping malls.[60] The first improved the tradeables sector, the latter not. Besides, as the Danske Bank noted, the Baltic States were heavily exposed to Credit Default Swap (CDS; see definition in Box 1.2) risks.[61]

Latvia was one of the first to suffer, with a fall in GDP of more than 25 per cent. The IMF predicted that the total loss of output would reach 30 per cent, making Latvia's loss proportionately greater than that of the US during the Great Depression. Latvia's policies were part of the European Union's Maastricht requirements to join the Eurozone, but the country was, unfortunately, maintaining the overvaluation of its currency through a fixed exchange rate. Paul Krugman compared it to Argentina.[62] However, Latvia was in a better position than Argentina, as it could export to the richer Eurozone, get European support and its citizens were free to work in other EU countries. But it was at a competitive disadvantage compared to Poland and other countries in Central and Eastern Europe. Deflation was taking place through devaluation of domestic wages and prices, the loss of economic activity, output, investment and entrepreneurship. The IMF imposed its usual medicine: fiscal tightening, rolling back of the state and 10 per cent cuts in all public expenditure. Companies went bankrupt, unemployment soared and investment was reduced; trained people began to emigrate; aid packages to pay the interest added to the heavy public debt principal; and the policy space for generating growth was reduced. The country ensured that, under the terms of the bailout, its deficit would remain within 5 per cent of GDP, against 7.9 per cent in 2007. The projections for Latvia's debt were 74 per cent of GDP for 2010, stabilizing at 89 per cent of GDP in 2014.[63] Latvia's government resigned after widespread rioting in February 2009.

In Hungary, the credit craze began with Austrian banks, and an important part of the debt was in Swiss francs. The craze had taken off in 2003, when the Swiss National Bank dropped interest rates to 0.75 per cent in order to stave off a perceived threat of deflation, resulting in Switzerland becoming the cheapest source of loan capital in Europe. External lending in Swiss francs reached $643 billion in 2006, according to data from the Bank for International Settlements. Around 80 per cent of all new home loans and

Box 1.2 Credit default swap (CDS)

CDSs were a completely unregulated insurance policy on company debt, worth $60 trillion in October 2008, more than the global GDP according to Will Hutton.*

The key element in the crisis was that the CDSs, from being an insurance practice, had become a speculative practice on the default of firms and states, as the investor or protection buyer did not need to own the asset on which it was betting the money.

A CDS is a bilateral contract related to a reference asset between counterparties in which the buyer of protection or investor pays a premium (CDS spread) to the seller of protection on a regular basis for the duration of the contract, usually on a quarterly basis. A reference asset can be anything (a firm, a state or an obligation or bond). In the case of a 'credit event', there can be a cash or physical settlement. In the first case, the default swap seller pays one minus the recovery rate to the protection buyer. The physical settlement is most common, by which the CDS buyer must physically deliver the reference asset to the swap seller, while the seller pays in cash 100 per cent of the face value, the protection being thus totally covered. The International Swaps and Derivatives Association has defined what is a 'credit event', the most controversial being 'restructuring'.

---

* Source: video 'Credit Default Swaps explained clearly in five minutes', posted by thebigscreen, showing the BBC Newsnight feature by Alex Ritson on Credit Default Swaps, 17 October 2008, http://www.youtube.com/watch?v=jHVnEBw93 EA&feature=related.

50 per cent of loans for small businesses and individuals contracted since early 2006 were denominated in Swiss francs.[64]

At the time, interest rates were very low and available information was that everybody in Hungary was doing the same. In October 2008, the craze came to an end, leaving part of the population with local currency assets and income, but with debt in stronger foreign currency and a hike in interest rates. In November 2008, the IMF, the World Bank and the EU granted a $25.1 billion rescue package to Hungary. Devaluation and IMF surveillance meant the same measures as taken later in Greece, with cuts in social welfare, the thirteenth salary month and rising retirement age. The country also closed embassies and consulates.[65] In March 2009, the Prime Minister resigned. Anger was a vector for political polarization. In the 2010 elections, Hungary's extreme right gained the mainstream with almost 17 per cent of the vote and 47 seats in parliament. Fidesz, the right-wing winner with more than half of the votes, promised to award citizenship to people of Hungarian descent in other countries, to link up with 'lost Hungarians', after the country's 72 per cent loss of land as a result of the Trianon Treaty and the end of the Austro-Hungarian Empire after the First World War.

These events in Central and Eastern Europe were not given enough coverage by the media in Western Europe. When the time eventually came for Greece, many Europeans were not fully aware that the IMF was already working within the EU and that stringent policies were to follow those in Eastern Europe. At the start of 2010, leverage was still a major problem and deflationary concerns remained unabated, but the global consulting firms shifted their weight onto the issue of public debt: they upheld that discussing debt in the private sector was open to debate as leverage is often measured in multiple ways according to the economic sector. The focus on public debt, as the outstanding amount of debt in relation to GDP, became the centre of attention.

Wealth destruction

Even though, at the time of writing it is too early to measure the full scale of the damage, we must identify the various consequences of the crisis in order to learn from it. To have a general idea of the wealth destroyed: by early 2010, citizens of the USA had lost 35 per cent of their financial wealth and those of the Eurozone 25 per cent.[66] However, with regard to wealth we should look beyond financial assets:

> As Robert Heilbroner states, 'wealth is a fundamental concept in economics; indeed, perhaps the conceptual starting point for the discipline. Despite its centrality, however, the concept of wealth has never been a matter of general consensus'... We may define the wealth of a nation as the total amount of economically relevant private and public assets including physical (or natural), financial, human, and 'social' capital ... In addition, it is easily ignored that wealth creation involves a distributive dimension, permeating all of its stages from the preconditions to the generation process, the outcome, and the use for and allocation within consumption and investment. In fact, the productive and the distributive dimensions of wealth creation are intrinsically interrelated.[67]

In this section, we therefore deal with some of the various ways in which wealth was affected, related to housing equity, stock markets and trade, jobs and income, enterprise bankruptcies, pensions, public services, cutbacks in investment, training and R&D, trust and lives, social cohesion and the loss of prestige and soft power for some countries.

The initial effects began to make themselves felt at the level of the local and provincial governments (e.g. French and Belgian local authorities with

Dexia bank, UK local authorities with Icesave, US states such as California going bankrupt). It then began to affect large companies such as General Motors in the USA and then thousands of SMEs. As companies began to shed employees, consumption suffered due to fears of job loss. In addition, the losses of pension funds hurt individuals and families, as well as trade unions. Insurance companies were shaken. The energy and transportation companies followed the downward movement. People began to ask whether this was a recession or depression. Money for international cooperation, remittances of seasonal workers, prices of commodities, and demand in rich countries and therefore exports to them, all were at stake. Trade suffered a rapid downturn, as now stocks had become leaner due to just-in-time and globalization strategies within global chains, entailing continuous maritime and air transportation. When credit for SMEs and individuals became expensive and scarce, many firms rushed to shed stocks. Every private institution, including universities, with funds invested in the financial markets had large losses. Beyond the fall in real estate market prices, rippling global effects were being felt whereas there were no appropriate international institutions to handle the problem.

The consequences of this synchronic global crisis can be divided into conjunctural and structural. The liquidity trap in the financial sphere can be seen as a conjunctural consequence, as can the measures to solve it. Some enterprise and employment constraints may also be seen as conjunctural, provided there is rapid adaptation, strong safety nets and a healthy equity and/or asset basis to survive the downturn. In this case, opportunities arising from state-aided sectors and improving demand can be quickly taken up. For others, though, cash-flow constraints, abrupt fall in demand and the sudden halt within the global supply chains were too harsh a blow, even if companies and workers were efficient, skilled and promising. The extended and sudden loss of companies without any chance of restructuring could not fall within Schumpeter's concept of 'creative destruction'.[68]

Structural consequences may be seen in the rate of both public and private investment, due to both higher costs of borrowing new credit and the remaining or even increasing debt load. Both governments and companies try to reduce costs, including spending in labour training. Without state support in the medium to long term, many R&D efforts may be hindered, lowering the competitiveness of the countries hardest hit by the crisis. Further, labour mobility may be harmed if the fall in housing prices traps households, as the latter may either be unable to sell their property or have negative equity. Some firms are investing less in training when shifting towards precarious employment due to the fear of 'poaching', namely losing their trained workers to other competitors, in the case of fixed-term contracts.[69] Structural consequences include world-wide destruction of net wealth and the loss of socioeconomic cohesion, including a substantial number of entrepreneurs and workers taking their own lives.

Homes and pensions

Through a domino effect, US towns suffered from unemployment, credit card defaults and foreclosures. With the fall in property prices, almost half of the loans were affected by the fact that borrowers owed more than the underlying worth of the property. The US government earmarked $30 billion in aid from the TARP.[70] Germany and Japan were undergoing a similar deflationary situation. In early 2010, thousands of commercial properties, hotels and offices in the hands of a few investment funds of Goldman Sachs and Morgan Stanley were worth one third or less compared to the end of 2009.[71] And the situation remains fragile in the United States where, as loans mature between 2011 and 2014, 2,988 banks are exposed to losses of up to $300 billion in commercial property loans on office premises, shops and factories.[72]

In the UK, the Bank of England affirmed that bad debts from credit cards leapt from £812 million to £1.6 billion in the third quarter of 2009.[73] The hard-hit UK was not alone, though. The IMF, for its part, warned in November 2009 that a credit card crisis in Europe could take place because of families defaulting on their debts and anticipating that up to 7 per cent of Europe's consumer debt, which then totalled £1.49 trillion, could be written off.[74]

While property falls in value, the indebted owners must continue paying their contractual obligations. But what is the point of keeping a home that will never recover its original value? Particularly true of values at the peak of the bubble, these debtors have a debt that bears no relationship to the current and future value of the object. These same people read that bank executives get millions in bonuses after being saved with their money, public money. Some then choose to walk away, even to destroy their own construction and/or furnishing efforts. The consequences of such traumatic experiences and frustration are yet to be seen. For now, labour market weakness has made US households wary of taking on new debt. The Federal Reserve reported that total consumer credit declined by $1.73 billion in December 2009, in a string of eleven monthly declines, the longest since the Fed began keeping records in 1943.[75] The rate of price decline in the Shiller indexes implied that real house prices went down by more than 30 per cent between 2007 and the end of 2008: a loss of more than $7 trillion in housing bubble wealth (approximately $100,000 per homeowner). The lost wealth was almost equal to 50 per cent of GDP.[76] In 2010, Nevada was the worst hit with 48 per cent of mortgage borrowers in negative equity.[77] Between December 2007 and June 2010, the USA had a total of about 2.36 million properties repossessed by lenders through foreclosure, according to RealtyTrac data, together with 3.48 million default notices and 3.46 million scheduled foreclosure auctions. In the first quarter of 2010, banks repossessed nearly 258,000 homes, a 35 per cent increase year on year.[78]

In January 2009, a new US policy, the Home Affordable Modification Program, tried to modify home loans and hold back the shadow inventory of more than seven million loans at risk of foreclosure. However, only 442,000 borrowers had managed to secure permanent improvements by July 2010, in which case the old loans became new loans at preferable interest rates based on market value with a monthly payment taking only a third of the homeowner's monthly gross income.[79] The problem is that they are paying only interest instead of the debt principal, creating a potential debt balloon at the end of the 30-year period. Unfortunately, in 2010, equity lending was limited to homeowners whose properties were worth more than what they owed. Bank of America, the largest US lender, was holding $43 billion in loans in which debt exceeded the property's value.[80]

This crisis has taken its toll especially on owners, the poor and the baby-boom generation.[81] In his testimony of 25 February 2009 before the Senate Special Committee on Aging, Dean Baker explained that people between 45 and 54 had invested heavily in home ownership. These people were the ones losing the most with the crisis. And not only in equity, as US savings were down to nearly zero, and those engaged in the bubble did not save much. They included baby boomers retiring in the next few years. The collapse of both the stock market and housing prices, plus the weight of leverage on their outstanding debts, have cost the baby boomers in the United States dearly, not just in financial assets, but also in retirement benefits, pensions and access to health services. Many have to pay for homes not worth the debt. Dean Baker stated that they were forced to work later in life or had to cope with lower living standards.[82]

The impact of the crisis on households spread to other countries. France did not have the same problematic situation, either in terms of loss of household equity or of future pensions, because the idea to financialize the system was not in place when the crisis burst. However, French households have been strongly affected by the crisis, with many working families falling into poverty, while there is an increasing shortage of low-cost and decent housing. Gross available income per household decreased by 3.1 per cent in 2007 and 0.8 per cent in 2008, the worst decline since 1960.[83] On the other hand, the state expels families that cannot pay their rent to prevent the risk of 'restraining the housing supply' in an already strained market, even though there is a state fund to indemnify owners, to which local authorities can turn. But the fund has been cut by more than half from €78 million in 2005 to €31 million in 2008. At the end of winter emergency measures, families are sent on to the streets. In March 2010, over 60 French associations went to the streets in protest.[84]

Jobs and plants

According to the ILO, the crisis has already destroyed 20 million jobs across the world since October 2008, leading to the unprecedented global figure of 200 million unemployed people.[85]

Between December 2007 and December 2009, the US economy lost 8.4 million jobs. In January 2010, the number of 'discouraged job seekers' stood at 1.1 million, while 6.3 million people had been out of work for more than 27 weeks.[86] The Federal government's temporary hiring for the 2010 census pushed up payrolls, which took up half of those they had sacked a month earlier (40,000 out of 96,000 jobs). Firms employed the same labour for longer hours. However, manufacturing dropped 23,000 jobs and construction dropped 32,000 in December 2009. In early 2010, there were some signs of recovery, but labour was still stretched to the limit. The jobless rate held at 9.7 per cent in February 2010, down from the 26-year peak of 10.1 per cent in October 2009 and the economy expanded at a 5.9 per cent annual rate in the fourth quarter of 2009, the best in more than six years, according to the US Commerce Department.[87]

In the UK, up to 60,000 jobs were lost in the financial services sector in 2009, mostly in securities trading, building societies and life insurers. The CBI and PriceWaterhouseCoopers quarterly industry report echoed the IMF's concerns that the UK may go through a jobless recovery.[88] The forecast for the construction industry was not much better. The UK Construction Products Association (CPA) report published on 5 October 2009, affirmed that the construction output levels reached in 2007 would not be attained again before 2021 and warned that the UK construction sector would endure a slump in output of 15 per cent in 2009 and 2 per cent in 2010, and that only in 2011 would a slow recovery be possible. Declining house prices made the construction of new houses less attractive. As financial services and construction were the two major engines of UK economic growth, the over-dependence on these two sectors leaves the country in search of new engines for growth.[89] Jobs will most probably not come from a public sector in the red. In April 2010, for the first time, the extent of the envisaged public sector job cuts by the new UK government was exposed: £12 billion of savings, meaning the loss of between 20,000 and 40,000 jobs.[90] Neither could these jobs apparently come from manufacturing, a sector which has been falling at an annual rate of 3.7 per cent over the last few years, although it had been pointed out as a possible employment source.[91] Whatever was left of UK manufacturing suffered badly with the credit crunch and deflating prices. Jaguar, Land Rover and Honda, Visteon, the steel-maker Corus and Cadbury did not survive.

Germany, Sweden, Belgium, Ireland and France, among others, have all been affected by plant closures, causing waves of protests, sometimes very long, sometimes quite radical as in the 'bossnapping' by the head of Scapa Europe, Derek Sherwin, of five managers at a Hewlett-Packard subsidiary, or threats at a British-owned plant in Bellegarde-sur-Valserine in France. All of this put plant closures high on the political agenda and so helped workers negotiate better conditions and unemployment benefits, or even find a new owner. The converse is shown by a group of women who stayed quiet and ended up receiving only €1,500 in total. Nonetheless, in France, Sodimatex,

Poly Implant Prothèses, Sullair Siedoubs, Fonte ardennaise, Sin et Stes, Delphi, Surcouf, Gardy, Grass Valley, France Transfo, Interval, Lejaby, Essex, among others, were in open conflict, touching many regions and sectors such as automobiles and machine tools but also lingerie, cleaning services and retailing. Even URSSAF, the state administration in charge of taxes and benefits concerning work charges, was on strike. Some 2009 workers' struggles were continuing into 2010, for instance, Molex and Freescale.[92]

In Northern Ireland, in early 2009, workers took over the plants, or the roofs to be more precise, of the car-parts firm Visteon in Belfast, which had sacked 560 workers at three plants in Enfield, Basildon and Belfast with less than an hour's notice. Sacked workers at Prisme Packaging in Dundee also staged a lock-in. There was a seven-week-long occupation at the Waterford Crystal visitor centre in Kilbarry, where workers negotiated the maintenance of 110 full-time and 50 part-time jobs.

In 2010, Germany implemented work sharing and reduction of work time, keeping about two million workers in place, thus avoiding large scale riots. Only a few open conflicts were noticed, such as the protest on 8 April 2009 at Daimler's annual general meeting, where hundreds of workers demonstrated against pay cuts of up to 14 per cent for 73,000 white-collar staff and shorter hours.

The open question in continental Europe, where existing long-term employment endured well thanks to cuts in temporary jobs, flexible working conditions, tax cuts and subsidies, is the timing of the recovery. Permanent workers who have been sacked enjoy unemployment benefits. But as the crisis goes on, the continuation of such benefits depends on passing further legislation, otherwise the validity period of the benefits would expire, as they were meant to be granted on a temporary basis. In 2010, national and sectoral negotiations on salaries and working conditions were proving extremely taxing. In Belgium, the worst month ever in terms of enterprise bankruptcy was April 2010, with a total of 1,015 units. In the first four months of 2010, at least 3,470 companies disappeared, worse than in 2009, mainly in the catering, construction and retailing sectors.[93] The temporary permission to use fast-track dismissal was extended, leading to vast numbers of unemployed in 2009, stirring up a joint demonstration in December 2009 by Belgium's major trade unions.[94] Both the continuation of 'temporary' measures such as publicly subsidized jobs for TNCs like Caterpillar, and negotiations on new job cuts in 2010 were straining labour relations.[95]

In both the UK and continental Europe, workers like the 'Conti' have begun to travel to other plant closures in mutual support. Most of these actions are taken independently from national trade unions, although they are sometimes supported by local unions. Moreover, the crisis is leading to the creation of specific business groups' global trade unions. At Caterpillar, the world's largest manufacturer group of construction and mining equipment, a new trade union, made up of workers from seven countries (Germany, Belgium, Italy, France, Japan, the USA and the UK), was set up on 29 April 2010, as a member of the International Metalworkers' Federation.[96] Seventy representatives have exchanged first-hand information on employment and working plans, including suppliers and sub-contractors, on all sites throughout the world.

Workers who had been enticed into taking financial involvement in their enterprises were getting angry at managers' bonuses. On 14 April 2009, ground workers and mechanics at American Airlines demonstrated against executives' bonuses being paid while jobs in the company were being cut. Others were angry at discovering the loss of their pensions' value. In the UK, ex-RBS boss Sir Fred Goodwin's home was attacked over his benefits in March 2009, while in February, some UK bank workers protested outside parliament as four former top bankers were questioned over their role in the financial crisis.

Worsening working conditions have led to 35 suicides of employees at France Telecom in two years (2008 and 2009). France has now set up a monitoring agency for such cases, while other EU countries, such as Germany, do not count suicides linked to enterprises or working conditions.[97] Suicides are a sign of extreme distress in nihilistic contexts, linked to Durkheim's term 'anomie'. Although the ongoing crisis appears as a causal factor, workers' distress has been increasing due to trends within economic entities linked to the changing system of production and distribution (which we will examine in Chapter 3).

In Italy, in the region of Naples alone, and only in the retailing and services sectors, 20,000 enterprises closed down in 2009, announced Carlo Sangalli, president of Confcommercio.[98] Meanwhile, just in the northeastern region of Italy, there have been 18 suicides of entrepreneurs since the crisis began, according to the vice-president of Confindustria, Alberto Bombassei.[99]

In agriculture, after the commodities peak between 2006 and 2008, thousands of farmers were indebted when the crisis began. The fall in prices and demand put this sector under heavy stress. In France there were 800 suicides of farmers in 2009, according to the association of independent milk producers. Even if, according to other estimates, these figures were down by half, it still meant more than one per day.[100] Canadian farmers affirmed that they had reached their highest level of debt in history.[101]

A stronger wave of popular reaction began in 2009. In the USA, thousands of local government workers staged strikes to protest against pay cuts, blocking roads and bridges. In one case, the police even joined in.[102]

Towards the end of 2009, Western Europe began to see large unrest linked to structural reforms. In Rome, clashes took place on 12 December, the same week as in Greece and France, while Madrid saw a first open march by all trade unions. By May 2010, there had been five Greek general strikes, one with about 750,000 civil servants on 10 February at the announcement of the adjustment measures. Across Europe, protests have been taking place in the post, transport, and health services. Many measures, though, are not the direct consequence of the crisis: liberalization and privatization of European 'network industries' and services follow decisions taken at EU level in 2005. However, deeper public sector structural reforms are taking place, given the abrupt growth of public deficits after bank rescues, state aid and sectoral subsidies granted at the height of the crisis. States are falling under the IMF regulation, first in Eastern Europe and now in Greece. The EU has long been waiting to impose structural reform, but the timing of IMF policies can truly risk deflation instead of recovery.

As for China, the challenge was huge as its net exports contributed to one-third of GDP growth in 2007. The foreign trade sector employed more than 80 million people, of which 28 million worked in foreign-invested enterprises. Disruption in demand within the global chains of production and distribution has been fearsome: for example, from January to July 2008, more than half of China's toy exporters shut down – many owners simply ran away, locking factory gates instead of going through bureaucratic bankruptcy proceedings. There was evidence that at least 67,000 companies had closed. 'Stability Maintenance' offices were set up to catch the absconding bosses and to report on 'unstable' companies. Many cities set up alarm systems by mobilizing grassroots units to detect signs of bankruptcy. There was almost no social security for rural migrant workers. Provisions on mass layoff and collective dismissals were reorganized, so that firms looking to lay off more than 10 per cent of their workforce had to explain their intention to labour unions or to all their workers one month in advance. About 20 million Chinese rural migrant workers, or 15 per cent of the country's total migrant workforce, lost their jobs. Provincial authorities paid train transportation for migrant workers who returned home from cities or to help them start their own businesses by giving loans that could go over 200,000 yuan. There was an urgency to increase domestic consumption to counter the loss of foreign demand, as recession deepened.[103]

Trade and investment

On 24 February 2010, WTO Director General Pascal Lamy affirmed at a conference in Brussels that world trade had fallen by 12 per cent due to the crisis, the worst fall since 1945,[104] and worse than earlier WTO projections: in March 2009, the expected yearly fall in exports was 9 per cent. In addition, the WTO showed concern at the increase in WTO-approved trade remedies as well as with the coordination problems.[105] Such factors contribute to undermine investment in the real economy.

UNCTAD Secretary-General Supachai Panitchpakdi reported in 2009 that 'recent UNCTAD figures show global foreign direct investment (FDI) inflows down by 44 per cent and mergers and acquisitions by 76 per cent during the first quarter of 2009, as compared to the same period in 2008. In developing countries, inward FDI has declined by 39 per cent so far in 2009 and by more than 40 per cent in transition economies'. In 2008, global FDI had declined by 14 per cent.[106] The drop was so pronounced that it lent strength to the hypothesis that firms were using financial mechanisms to sustain trade. Decisions were taken too quickly before there was a drastic fall in consumption and business needed constant liquidity to keep rolling: uncertainty surely played a part. According to McKinsey, cross-border capital flows fell by 82 per cent in 2008, to $1.9 trillion. This was one of the most remarkable and almost immediate consequences of the Lehman Brothers bankruptcy.[107]

The final declaration of the G20 meeting in Pittsburgh on 25 September 2009 pledged to revive world trade and investment, reinstating the commitment made at their previous meeting in London: 'We welcome the swift implementation of the $250 billion trade finance initiative. We will keep markets open and free and reaffirm the commitments made in Washington and London: to refrain from raising barriers or imposing new barriers to investment or to trade in goods and services'.[108] As for the Doha Round, they pledged to 'seek progress on agriculture, non-agricultural market access, as well as services, rules, trade facilitation and all other remaining issues'.[109] Agriculture and services, trade facilitation and market access continue to be a contested terrain.

In May 2009, large firms expected the crisis to turn around by 2011.[110] Because trade and investment took time to normalize, governments came to the rescue of certain industries, such as the automobile industry and the US government began pumping cash into General Motors in December 2008. The GM finance arm GMAC, after being given the status of a 'bank' in 2009, obtained access to the $700 billion TARP created to strengthen the financial sector. In January 2010, the government took a controlling stake of 56 per cent in GMAC for $3.8bn, reaching a total of $16.3 billion.[111] GMAC is not only the lending arm to thousands of GM and Chrysler auto dealers but has been largely involved in the sub-prime and residential mortgage lending. GM also has an online consumer bank.

The retail car industry was also helped with the added goal of sustaining demand in Europe. Between early 2009 and mid-2010, old cars could be exchanged for new cars on very advantageous terms in many developed countries. However, as government subsidies were phased out, economic activity had not fully recovered.

All this does not help to ease credit constraints for the real economy, SMEs, rural areas, and households. In 2010, enterprises continued divesting while internal consumption went to cheaper imports. The growth at the end of 2009 may have been only a technical conjunctural factor of both de-stocking and government subsidies.[112]

In France, enterprise investment saw a fall of 7.7 per cent in 2009. Firms continued to shed employees and close sites. In terms of production, the 2009 decrease of 3.1 per cent was the worst in 60 years according to INSEE.[113] At the end of 2009, France was doing better than all the large Eurozone countries, including Germany, but data suggested that the crisis was still ongoing: GDP was falling, consumption was sustained by government subsidies, and international trade and stocks were declining.[114]

Now that both households and states are heavily indebted in many countries, trade and private investment are expected to take the lead in the recovery. But can they? Global chains of production and distribution, interconnected and interlinked, make the whole system highly sensitive to sudden changes and shocks. The brutal halt at the end of 2008 showed how fast the global system could react to events.

Large enterprises engaged in global competition through aggressive enlargement of the scale of business, acquisitions and internationalization take drastic decisions to leave national markets altogether or close dozens of hypermarkets with hundreds of job losses, such as Carrefour in Belgium and Portugal. Carrefour, a major global distribution company, had a fall of 74 per cent in net profits in 2009.[115] In Belgium, the company had been losing money for 10 years, but used the crisis to leave the market.

A working paper by the Bank of Italy on the crisis and the Italian system of production pointed to the north-west and central regions as being the worst hit, due to the fall in demand and problems with cash flow as the chain of payments was broken. More than half of the firms contained costs, more than 21 per cent reduced margins, 13.5 per cent tried market diversification and only 5.5 per cent tried to improve the product. Only the larger enterprises were thinking of delocalizing.[116] Italy's GDP contracted by 5.0 per cent in 2009, just like Germany,[117] in the worst fall since the start of the statistical series, before growing again in 2010.[118] Many enterprises squarely defaulted on their bonds – there were 265 firms that did not honour their debt obligations in 2009, compared to 105 defaults in 2008, the worst in the Standard & Poor's 29 years' data series: 193 in the USA, 36 in emergent countries and 19 in Europe.[119]

ECB Executive Committee member Lorenzo Bini Smaghi announced that the unsustainable growth in public debt and the deleveraging of banks would make it difficult for the global economy to be managed in the way that it had been in the past.[120] Enterprises first and foremost have to shed debt obligations. Deleveraging requires shedding patrimonial assets and the way this is done depends on how each firm's mother house perceives the future.

Less developed countries were not spared. As Joseph Stiglitz underlined:

> The current financial crisis, which began in the US, then spread to Europe, has now become global. Even emerging markets and less developed countries that managed their economy well, resisted the bad

lending practices, held high levels of foreign exchange reserves, did not purchase toxic mortgages, and did not allow their banks to engage in excessive risk taking through derivatives are likely to become embroiled and to suffer as a result.[121]

Mexico has probably been one of the worst hit, due to its export dependency on the USA, and deflationary measures such as increases in both VAT and income tax applied in 2010 with negative effect. Joseph Stiglitz called on Mexico to better support the recovery because the worst was still to come in 2011, when the economic stimulus to the private sector in the United States would end, if the system was not fixed by then.[122] In addition, the flows from workers' remittances from the United States to Mexico have been reversed, and it is now Mexicans that support their families in the neighbouring country: from Chiapas, there is more money going north than money coming in. On the other hand, the loss of economic activity has had grave effects on employment: Mexico lost about 750,000 jobs in 2009, suffering a contraction of 7.5 per cent.[123]

Traditional development cooperation may not be of help. The current crisis, as a catalytic force to change paths, has led to disengagement from aid. The cases of Denmark and the Netherlands[124] are emblematic because they were among the few developed countries that had carried out the commitment of 0.7 per cent GDP to fight poverty in the world, according to OECD figures.[125]

The World Bank and United Nations organizations have called attention to the plight of developing countries stemming from the crisis.[126] After the 2009 UN Conference on the global economic crisis, a participant organization noted the 'foreign exchange shortfall facing developing countries, which could range from up to $1 trillion (World Bank estimate) to $2 trillion (UNCTAD estimate). Besides falling exports and capital outflows, many countries are also facing increasing difficulties in obtaining fresh credit, all of which affect their foreign reserves position'.[127] There are calls for the allocation of $100 billion of Special Drawing Rights[128] to low income countries at no cost; a deferral of principal and interest payments with no additional cost as practised after the Asian Tsunami of 2004; the right to exercise temporary debt standstills and exchange controls; statutory protection in the form of a stay on litigation; the creation of a new international reserves system; and strengthening international surveillance of developed countries' policies. This fall-out of the crisis was however foreseen by the World Bank in mid-2008, given the incredible growth in the flow of private funds to developing countries, the control of which had been rejected by the latter during the Cancun trade summit of 2003.[129]

Curbing the crisis

Let us now take a look at the main types of measures that have been carried out to curb the crisis, as well as their impact and consequences.

State aid to banks: solvency and nationalization

At first, banks were helped on a case by case basis. In Stiglitz's words, it was tantamount to giving a blood transfusion to a patient suffering from a serious haemorrhage. It also meant one entity was saved and another was not. Everyone had to go it alone, helped by the highest possible level of liquidity. A freeze in financial flows ensued. The decision taken on 13 October 2008 to save *all* in the banking sector was, finally, a systemic common sense decision.[130,131]

Between the start of the crisis and early 2009, the USA gave massive aid to banks of approximately $210 billion, while Europe had a more modest intervention by country of between $4 billion and $49 billion. Meanwhile, banks wrote down about $800 billion and most had repaid governments by 2010. There was no common policy though: in Bear Stearns and AIG only common shareholders suffered, while the losses of Fannie Mae, Freddy Mac and Washington Mutual affected both common and preference shareholders.[132] With the closure of the latter bank, its host city Seattle suffered thousands of job losses and a brain drain, and has since had difficulty in retaining the status of financial centre.

The choice of which to save and which to let down, like Lehman Brothers, and the difference in treatment, like that of Northern Rock, recall Laurence Fontaine's analysis of Ancien Regime bankruptcy practices.[133] The UK suffered its first bank run with Northern Rock, nationalized it, and promised to resell it soon after. It was downsized drastically and its best customers were sent to other major banks, which the UK government also supported, first in secret and then openly. Lloyds' takeover of HBOS, although not supported by the government, was eased by the latter's change of rules. Northern Rock was split into a 'good' bank and a 'bad' bank in January 2010 but it has been weakened to such an extent that it may never get back on its own feet again. In early 2010, it had only 76 branches and it was too small to survive.[134] Northern Rock used to give credit at very low loan rates, and was looked down upon by the banking industry working with higher interest rates. From a building society, it became owned principally by pension funds but when the financial market froze, the UK government took a long time to become lender of last resort, while state guarantees of deposits were outdated.

Monetary injection and 'quantitative easing' followed first in the USA and the UK, later in the EU. It helped without solving the central problem, because the injection of currency had to capitalize banks to restore solvency in financial relations. It was no longer sufficient to have a loose monetary policy. A deflationary process impacting on the real economy needed urgent fiscal and active government policy, something that took place first in the UK and in France, and then in other OECD countries. A common policy in most developed countries promoted the trade of old cars for new ones, such as the US Automotive Stimulus bill called 'Cash for Clunkers' and the many national initiatives in the EU, which revived the car industry, as seen above. But, in the EU, state intervention was faced with the limitations of the Stability and Growth Pact, with its ceiling on budgetary deficits. Temporarily justified, financial markets used it later to push for reforms in European states.

State insurance on bank deposits undoubtedly eased fears, but it could not solve the central problem of frozen interbank circulation. After Lehman's collapse, Germany passed a financial market stabilization law, setting up a new institution, the SoFFin, with three goals: to guarantee newly issued debt securities and other liabilities; to recapitalize banks; and to assume risk positions. Another method of recapitalizing banks went through the Public-Private Partnership Investment Program, as announced by US Treasury Secretary Timothy Geithner in March 2009, involving government loans and guarantees to encourage private investors to exchange funds for the toxic bank assets, called 'legacy' in the programme.[135]

Did bank nationalization help? In many cases, 'technical nationalization' may be the more appropriate wording, as banks were allowed to keep the old management and shareholders. In the short run it did help, but did not solve the problem of 'toxic' financial products, unpaid bills and the unknown extent of liabilities. Nationalization transferred the problem to the public sphere. Sooner or later, in order to protect monetary stability, it became necessary to defend the national currency against various pressures. It is worth noting that, in reaction to the crisis in Iceland, the UK threatened to use its anti-terrorist law and to impose governmental control on capital flows, including on the exit side, had the 13 October plan not stopped the downward spiral. It justified it on the basis of decrees that ensured all deposits and the nationalization of banks.

In the USA, the state TARP recapitalized banks, guaranteed debt and absorbed toxic assets, in spite of being unable to value the latter, and not having representation inside the banks. The US authorities kept paying while the old managers remained in control. The justification for fearing nationalization was that a nationalized bank could lend to insolvent companies, which was exactly what the government was doing to save the banks. A new law allowing the government to deal with failed banks was approved only in 2010. Also in 2010, the US Securities and Exchange Commission took Goldman Sachs to court for civil fraud, reaching a $550 million settlement in August of the same year.[136] A public Senate hearing on the case took place in April 2010, but critics complain that the US government has punished unbridled contempt and outright fraud in a very limited manner.

Sweden was a good model for many: nationalized banks were split into a 'good' bank and a 'bad' bank, with a new management appointed by the government and, after a few years, sold to new private hands. The first country to follow the idea was Switzerland with UBS in 2008, where they agreed to a separate fund entity.[137] Then Germany followed suit with the creation of two 'bad' banks, one for private banks and the other for the regional banks. Later in 2009, when Ireland took a similar step with the National Asset Management Agency, Joseph Stiglitz and Nouriel Roubini criticized it publicly.[138]

On 7 October 2008, Iceland nationalized the internet bank Icesave together with its parent company Landsbanki, neither of which was registered as a bank in the UK nor were they regulated by the FSA, and thus consumers could not be protected within the UK.

Thousands were lured by higher interest rates to invest with Icesave, but lost everything. That was bad enough, but to make matters worse, Iceland found its debt growing overnight by benefits granted in some foreign countries to their citizens, without any previous agreement. In a rush, the UK and the Netherlands saddled Iceland with foreign debt amounting to an additional 40 per cent of Iceland's GDP, but failed to check whether the country was under a legal obligation to reimburse Dutch savers. Dutch Minister Wouter Bos, without any budget allocation or previous parliamentary consultation, affirmed that Iceland guaranteed €1.3 billion. The Dutch central bank covered its citizens' deposits beyond Iceland's 22,000 euro legal limits up to €100,000, just like other EU countries, although Iceland is not part of the EU.[139] This led to a dispute among countries, after Iceland's president rejected the deal to repay the debt to the UK and the Netherlands. The Dutch threatened an EU and IMF boycott. EU regulations stipulate that bilateral treaties apply in case of crisis, but the Netherlands had no such treaty with Iceland. And the Icesave problem did not represent a systemic threat to the Dutch which would have justified their taking such decisions as they did. Sweder van Wijnbergen from the University of Amsterdam, and former employee at the World Bank during the negotiations on the Mexican debt, pleaded for a restructuring similar to the Brady Plan in 1995. At the time, Mexico received a 40 per cent cut in debt after which there was an influx of capital and the economy restarted. The economy must grow again in order to pay anything. However, Mexico's debt was only 60 per cent of GDP and no one beyond that limit has ever repaid: Iceland is beyond the limit.

Stimulus packages

Many countries passed large stimulus packages which would have pleased Keynes. In December 2008, the European Council agreed on a package of €200 billion. But, compared to the USA and China, as a percentage of GDP, it was rather small and lacked coordination and information on what each country was to contribute and when.[140] The package allowed for discretionary national measures listed on a menu of support actions, both on the supply and demand side. It also allowed for the support of cash flow of businesses. Countries such as Poland, the Netherlands and the UK used one or two spending categories to deliver the stimulus, while Germany used them all.

China's two-year national stimulus package for $586 billion was mainly dedicated to infrastructure in eight areas: housing, rural infrastructure, water, electricity, transport, environment, technological innovation and rebuild-ing disaster areas (hit by the 12 May 2008 earthquake). The debt produced amounted to 3 per cent of its GDP and it had no buy-national approach, unlike the USA. Besides, China intensified its export policy,[141] investment policy including the tertiary sector and research,[142] bank restructuring and liberalized the use of the yuan by companies through pilot projects[143] that were making international inroads in August 2010.[144] China paid most attention to the needs of the real economy, the cohesion of the country and investment policy: finance policy had to adapt to such needs and not vice-versa. Of all countries, China was in the best position, as investment contin-ued to be high and the government had a low stock of debt. Some now say that China did not suffer much with the financial crisis; however, Chinese investors in Lehman Brothers and Bank of China's stakes in Morgan Stanley, Blackstone and Barclays suffered huge losses. China's main challenge in the crisis was how to deal both with the migrant workers that suddenly lost their jobs and the needs in the rural areas upon their return. The impact on the real economy was mentioned above. The other two challenges were how to sustain more equitable growth without encouraging inflation and how to build up a competitive financial system without losing control on invest-ment policy choices. Support measures to the rural areas included access to housing and credit, the restructuring of the Agricultural Bank of China, the most important modification to land use in rural areas, where there is no private ownership so far, and a rise in the procurement price for grain.[145] The standardization of the transfer of land use was also a response to the fact that there were few young workers left in the countryside, and to spur agricultural modernization without changing the land tenure system.

In the USA, the federal stimulus package fell short of plugging the pro-jected output gap,[146] as the ongoing cuts at state and local levels neutralized a much of it. At the end of 2009, German Chancellor Angela Merkel acknowl-edged that the crisis was continuing. Also in December 2009, Dubai World defaulted on its debt. Japan passed a second package of economic stimulus and China announced the intention of doing the same if need be.

State spending and solvency

We saw above the very large state aid and support packages provided to sus-tain national economies in developed countries. What about the solvency of these states after that? This point will remain a big debate in the years to come. The first case in the media was Iceland, yet the first ones to suffer were the municipalities, districts, states or provinces. In terms of nation states, Eastern Europe was followed by Western Europe.

Australia, Canada, Brazil, India and China displayed strong and rapid gov-ernmental reactions and a very good regulation of their banking systems. The governments of New Zealand and Australia regulated their money supply by decree for two and three years respectively. Latin America managed to sort it out even better, because the countries in the region had diversified their exports, in particular towards Asia. US debt will be further discussed in Chapter 2.

And the EU? On 13 October 2008, a part of the EU finally agreed to combined measures that should already have been in place, but implementation and later measures were uncoordinated. It was a sad demonstration of how a large liberalized market without a proper governing agreement lacks coherent policies and the legitimate authority to act urgently with expediency in the case of a crisis. Thus the euro has been weakened. The EU had to temporarily abandon the Maastricht approach of budgetary restriction. It put aside its restrictions to state aid, launched a vast investment programme in infrastructure, energy and in the social field, helped companies with fiscal measures to prevent unemployment. It also had to put together two enormous packages: to help Greece for €110 billion and to prevent attacks against the euro for €750 billion in May 2010. EU member states finally accepted that they had to give a more active role to the ECB, turned to the IMF for help to carry through structural reforms, and held their first meeting on joint economic governance at the end of May 2010. These actions caused a blow to the ideological consensus. But Europe had additional difficulties. Whereas Russia suspended its stock exchange for some time, the EU had difficulty because most stock exchanges no longer had the necessary autonomy to make quick decisions. Furthermore, the EU had a problem in defining and regulating capital and debt, equity and liability, as it depends on an externally controlled institution, the IAS Board, as we saw above. Another example is that of rating agencies, with the EU depending on extra-community organizations that can forbid a member to access its central bank, the ECB, for help.

Was state spending the solution? It helps initially, but as their debt and public deficits get troublesome, states enter a period of austerity and fiscal consolidation. Furthermore, growth after a sharp contraction depends on (a) whether the trend of growth path has shifted down permanently; (b) whether debt levels have risen to historical limits; and (c) whether there is international transmission of contraction or low growth impacting on the economy. An economy having contracted at least 3 per cent in one year falls into a lower growth rate. Therefore, the loss to an economy is the difference between the previous and the post-recession paths cumulated over subsequent years. Reinhart and Rogoff's analysis of 'debt intolerance' shows that when debt levels rise towards historical limits, indebted governments face difficult trade-offs concerning fiscal policy and the level and volatility of sovereign risk premia, depending on the composition of the debt itself (short versus long term and foreign versus domestic debt).[147] Europe is particularly vulnerable with its extraordinarily high levels of total external debt, debt issued abroad by both the governments and private entities.[148] International transmission now reaches the economy more rapidly through the global chains, liberalized flows and just-in-time inventories. In a highly interconnected global economy, a synchronous exit of governments from loose macroeconomic policies weakens world aggregate demand. In 2010, there was an inventories recovery but not a consumer recovery.[149]

So what about the US dollar as a saving currency after the crisis? China is calling for a new international currency to replace the US dollar. In 2010, the United Nations also called for a replacement to the dollar as reserve currency, while the IMF drafted a proposal for a new global currency called 'bancor'.[150] The crisis proved developing countries were right in accumulating currency reserves, although it might worsen the trend towards global imbalances. So, what allows the USA to maintain its influence on the financial system? The problem is like a Catch-22 situation: if China gets rid of its dollars and the dollar falls, its main market for export and source of growth will also be lost. The sensitive issue is being addressed by the US–China Strategic and Economic Dialogue, the first meeting of which took place on 27–28 July 2009. In turn, funds in euros are too limited to compete with North American government funds, because there is no EU Treasury, EU funds being issued by EU member states. The ECB has recently begun to buy member states bonds. But when it bought Eurozone government debt for over €300 million in mid-August 2010, there was disquiet that public debt issues in the EU were hampering trust.[151]

Governments face a public debt crisis

In 2010, pressures focused on state debt and deficits, with tensions in the debt markets that could also affect the performance of banks and credit availability to the real economy. Standard&Poors declassified the UK banking system from the category of least risky,[152] as the UK economy may lower the profile of its banking sector, due to the necessary deleveraging. As European banks provide 90 per cent of all finance to companies in Europe,[153] it was urgent to restore trust. Following the US example, stress tests on banks were performed in mid-2010 to calm down fears from possible state debt restructuring within the EU.

Greece was the first nation-state in Western Europe and within the Eurozone to fall under IMF and EU supervision. As seen above, other EU member states were already in that situation. The annual report of the Greek central bank acknowledged that the country's economy had fallen into a vicious circle, from which it could only come out through a drastic reduction of the deficit and debt. The budget deficit, forecast at 12.7 per cent of GDP in 2009, would hit 12.9 per cent, the bank said, estimating public debt at 115 per cent of annual output.[154] The ECB has limited powers. On the other hand, the Greek case was the ideal opportunity to tackle various issues at hand. Greece represents only a fraction of EU GDP and of the aggregate liabilities of European banks. It was a question of discipline.

But governments were facing tough electoral tests. In Germany, the most populated and industrialized German Land had elections on 9 May 2010, leading Chancellor Angela Merkel to repeatedly backtrack from every proposal.[155] The North Rhine–Westphalia election is a traditional marker for national German politics and with the crisis, the coalition in power was to lose. Merkel was waiting until 9 May to support Greece.[156] The ups and downs among Eurozone authorities on the bail-out measures led to worsening interest rates for Greece and further downgrading by rating agencies, plus huge capital outflows.[157]

The logical solution to the euro's difficulties was what Eurogroup Chairman Jean-Claude Juncker had proposed three years earlier,[158] that the ECB should be allowed to produce euro bonds with which each state could refinance itself, taking out the direct pressure on the euro that augments the interest rate with which individual states such as Greece must pay for refinancing their debt. Moreover, it would restrain speculative pressures. However, the euro bond solution was rejected on 9 May 2010.

In 2005, Charles Wyplosz had warned of the excessive rigidity of the Euro Stability Pact. Coupled with the excessive flexibility to lift the 3 per cent public deficit limit in case of economic difficulty, it was a 'recipe for disaster'. The Pact could not properly enforce fiscal discipline while it was opening a growing rift between small and large countries. In his opinion, the Pact should not have focused so much on annual budget deficits, claiming that dispossessing the parliaments of their right to set fiscal policy was 'lethal'.[159] Instead, it should have focused on debt stabilization. Public debt as a share of gross domestic product would not grow beyond certain limits, as enshrined in Poland's Constitution. In Wyplosz' view,[160] this was the valid definition of fiscal sustainability. We agree with his view for normal times, although Wyplosz did not foresee that a financial crisis could require a dramatic increase in the stock of public debt. Germany, having taken structural adjustment steps before the crisis, passed a law prohibiting the federal government from running a deficit of more than 0.35 per cent of GDP by 2016 and German Länder from any deficit after 2020.

However, fears of a global spillover from the EU hesitation have been haunting everybody.[161] Before 2 May 2010, when the EU and the IMF announced concrete measures to support Greece, after rejecting any debt restructuring that would lead to European banks underwriting part of the debt, the US fears were articulated by the Atlanta Federal Reserve Chairman.[162] As Europe undergoes cuts in spending, consumption and growth, US exports to the EU could suffer, affecting the US recovery. If the dollar gained value on the financial markets, US exports would suffer globally. Finally, if the Greek case ended in another blown-out crisis, investors could choose to exit the market of sovereign state debt altogether, which would definitely hurt the USA. We, therefore, observe that a global and closely relayed financial system carries a constant circular stream of events and consequences.

On the other hand, the euro lost some value although in reality it was good news. It was finally acceptable to say that an overvalued euro impacted on EU growth, and that a lower rate helped exports and recovery. Perhaps more than the euro, it was the relation between the 'debt' markets on the one hand, and banks and large companies on the other, that was the centre of attention.[163] The current crisis only magnified what was already at work and leading to a debt trap, which we will examine in Chapter 2.

Dutch research used Eurostat data for 12 Eurozone countries including Greece, showing a growing divergence among Eurozone countries in terms of inflation, annual GDP growth, productivity, unit labour costs, unemployment rates and debt position. For example, on the positive side there was Finland, whose national debt experienced a reduction to 39.7 per cent of GDP in 2009: in 1999, it had the smallest government debt with 45.5 per cent of GDP.[164] Such divergent paths endanger the common currency. This can be solved in basically three ways: first, harmonizing all Eurozone countries; second, accepting diverse treatment balanced by internal flows within the Eurozone; and third, risking the pressure from shadow finance through hedge funds and other financial entities. Several EU member states with larger public deficits become more vulnerable to speculation due to such growing divergence, while Europe's still prevailing consensus welcomes the shrinking or 'retreat of the state' in Susan Strange's words.[165] However, to curb speculation benefiting from the internal differences within the EU, or to manage such differences smoothly, states need to step in. The prevailing consensus (privatization, reduction of public employment, pay freeze, liberalization, tax exemptions to the wealthy) equally increases divergence in terms of inequality. If accompanied by poor growth in various member states, it may bring about xenophobic attacks as well as political and social polarization. In addition, Wilkinson and Pickett have shown that high social inequality and a higher degree of relative poverty lead to more health and social problems.[166]

Which strategies have been attempted to restart growth?

In the previous downturns, in the early 1990s and in 2001, US authorities had chosen the 'bubble' path to prevent deflation by promoting household consumption and connected industries, mainly construction and automobiles. As we shall see in Chapter 2, US authorities used to believe that there was no debt question at all, but now, when many countries must face their debts and save, they start thinking 'exports'. However, with chronic downturns, the prospects for export-led growth are not that bright. The global system has become more sensitive to factors stemming from the financial and communication technology spheres. The biggest problem remains the labour market: in 2009 the official figure for unemployment topped 10 per cent in the USA, although it descended somewhat after that.

Bosworth and Flaaen believe that:

the crisis is likely to come to represent a major regime change, greatly altering the future shape of the US and global economies. The era of self-regulation of financial institutions is over, and the role of monetary policy has been greatly altered. The binge of consumer spending also seems to have come to an end, as households focus on rebuilding their balance sheets. If the United States is to restore full employment, it must not only rebuild its financial industries but also rejuvenate its export industries and achieve a more balanced external position ... This raises two challenges for the rest of the global economy. First, it must develop new drivers of demand growth; countries will not be able to rely on growing exports into the US market, and they will need to emphasize the development of domestic and regional markets. Second, frustration with the effort to develop export markets in a time of slow global growth may push politicians toward a more protectionist policy stance.[167]

Another danger should also be pointed out: unilateralism in confronting perceived systemic risks, such as environmental or financial ones, access to natural resources such as oil etc., could result in the exclusion of traditional or possible allies, thereby causing tensions and uncertainty.

Therefore, where do we look for engines of growth that do generate wealth, in ways that do not entail easily reversible growth, repeated bubbles and wealth destruction across-the-board? We can thus far observe that the following paths are being attempted: technology and industrial policy, regionalization and deleveraging, investing in commodities and SMEs, and regulation to limit the worst excesses in lending, of which we give some examples below. However, they are not responses to boost aggregate demand, nor do they work out a balance between the needs for an export base with the growth of internal consumption.

Technology and industrial policy

A new trend is industrial policy related to the environment, green construction or the electrical automobile: industrial policy makes a big comeback from its taboo status. Yet, national strategies undertaken by all countries at the same time may not be efficient. Competition along global supply chains will be fierce. The need to come together and negotiate diverse positionings along regional chains while sharing the benefits will increasingly come to the fore. In addition, leasing, sharing and renting services are seen as a key part of the future. The access economy will easily succeed in largely populated cities but may not successfully connect the entire country without government support.

The counterpart to this bleak panorama generated by the crisis is the understanding of a crisis as an opportunity to change trajectory and in this case, slackening may be a blessing in disguise. The halt of part of 'previous technical progress' may not be all that bad, provided that 'new technical progress' starts taking place. The peak of the crisis has shown that the previous trajectory was unsustainable and should not be reproduced.

Regionalism and deleveraging

Another engine that many seem to focus on is the regional path. To restart the global financial engine, they promote both deleveraging by regionalizing units while separating investment from commercial banking, with the idea of creating strong regional institutions that are well coordinated with each other globally. Whenever possible, deleveraging tends to go to close allies. For example, the European Commission has asked the UK, due to its enormous state aid to banks, to sell off some of its businesses, brands and assets. The UK has chosen to extract the investment banking units out of Royal Bank of Scotland (RBS) and Lloyds, which are, in 2011, still under state control. Northern Rock, also under state ownership, would not be sold but used as consolidator for the future of investment banking by allowing, most probably, private equity to capture it.[168]

Banks are engaging in regionalization, with a focus on Asia. In the US, AIG, now 80 per cent owned by the state, constitutes a business group of around 200 firms in 130 countries. The *Wall Street Journal* estimated that during the last three months of 2008, AIG had lost 465,421 dollars per minute. AIG received 180 billion dollars in several aid packages and had to repay about 60 billion back to American citizens. In 2009, in exchange for the public money, AIG spun off foreign life insurance companies AIA and ALICO, and placed commercial insurance, foreign general insurance and private clients into a new (fully owned) company, Chartis. AIG also disposed of assets or subsidiaries, such as its car insurance to Swiss ZFS, and its headquarters in Tokyo to Nippon Life. The Federal Reserve took stakes in AIA and ALICO, in exchange for $25 billion in loans to the company. Giving up ALICO could repay a government debt of about $15 billion. Thus, AIG gave its Asian unit to MetLife. It helped that AIG's new CEO Robert Benmosche had worked at MetLife from 1998 to 2006.[169] MetLife also redefined its business in Asia, selling Metlife Taiwan to Waterland Financial, Taiwan's smallest financial holding firm.[170]

We also observe the idea of regional funds being used to confront speculative attacks gaining ground. The new EU regional fund echoes Asian and Latin American calls for regional funds after the 1997 financial crisis. To avoid IMF opposition, the EU €750 billion fund with regulatory oversight powers was set up with the participation of the IMF.

Investing in commodities and SMEs

Another path to generating wealth is investing in SMEs and commodities. Both can easily turn into political issues. In 2008, a US senate hearing substantiated that institutional investors' speculation was driving up food prices and making them volatile. In 2010, traders and investment banks as well as governments turned again to agricultural commodities to make rapid gains and/or to ensure national food supply. We would like, thus, to state here our gravest concern about the consequences that such speculation can bring about.[171] Due to lack of space, and since the book focuses mainly on internal dynamics of economic entities, we do not discuss commodities further. Concerning SMEs, the UK has recently approved the IFRS for SMEs, even though many institutions in Europe, including the European Parliament and the European associations representing enterprises, are against doing so, because of the very high, constant and changing costs in reporting on fair value over the short term: not the best thing to do during a downturn.

Also in the UK, a brand new vehicle has been invented to take part in SME equity, called the enterprise investment scheme (EIS). It is a high-risk investment vehicle for an expected high rate of return in three years' time, with large tax breaks for investors looking to diversify their portfolios beyond stocks and bonds. It pools money from investors to buy shares in privately owned companies, although some may be listed. Capital gains tax can be avoided or diminished and, most important, the liabilities can be off-the-balance sheet.[172] France is following this path to promote private equity into SMEs. If a bubble develops, and SMEs get indebted and destabilized, grave consequences may ensue as they provide a high proportion of employment.

Regulation to contain the worst excesses by banks and lenders

The efforts to curb speculative risky activities responsible for systemic risk are, in our opinion, part of the strategies in the quest for new paths for growth and wealth generation. For the time being, we see externally imposed measures on business and redefined roles for public regulators, but we are still waiting to see the acknowledgment of responsibility and proposals of new models stemming from the banking industry itself. The ongoing trend to rethink business models and supervision highlights the fact that developed countries have a diversity of business models and supervisory traditions. Apart from the idea of clearly separating investment from commercial banking, which could be tied at the top as a holding,[173] the idea of increasing capital ratios, which is necessary in the USA, remains highly contested in the EU because banks' business models and their importance for the economy are different.

The EU drafted a new regulation to control hedge funds and private equity investors, put to the vote at both the European Parliament and the Council of Ministers. The text, though, was suddenly taken out of the agenda of the EU Council of Ministers under pressure from the then Prime Minister Gordon Brown. The UK has 80 per cent of a total of 450 hedge funds active in Europe, with a combined £250 billion, most of them originally from the USA. The text received more than 1,000 proposed amendments, the work of 137 lobbyists. It foresees that non-European hedge funds should be allowed into the region *only* if they meet certain criteria: Europeans blame hedge funds for betting against the fall of the sub-prime market in the USA and against the euro. A touchy issue is whether to declare the 'equivalence' between the US and the EU financial systems, which would provide all US funds with a transatlantic passport to freely operate across Europe, effectively bypassing European regulation. In terms of supervision, the supervisors of central banks in EU member states control their banks very tightly. Those allowing banks to buy toxic assets were government agencies (Germany, Belgium, Switzerland) or independent agencies (the FSA in the UK). The exception was the Dutch central bank, which allowed its banks to go toxic.[174] Nevertheless, Rabobank, a cooperative bank, restrained itself, coming out stronger, as we will see in Chapter 4.

Most probably, measures on taxes, bonuses and benefits will neither avoid new bubbles nor save too large financial institutions next time. Better regulation of rating agencies, and a greater diversity and number of them, will probably emerge soon. The Chinese Dagong, rapidly gaining fame, is an example.

Models are in question and there is a growing tug of war between banks and private funding. The EU was striving towards greater transparency concerning the second model, while the USA was focusing more on banking. However, the Obama administration inserted derivatives trading in the package of financial reforms, and placed it under governmental oversight. The US financial bill deals with consumer protection through a new public agency; federal powers to seize and close down banks in trouble; and an early warning system through a new oversight national council; and it clarifies the jurisdiction of various regulators according to types of banks.

More importantly for the future is whether finance is 'out-banking'. Investment equity funds and securities analysts provide the following standard defences: the UK and US banks have lost 'allure'; global funds pretend to be a worthy replacement for national banking;[175] hedge funds are consolidating and restructuring',[176] positioning themselves to thrive;[177] business groups and large firms have turned to bilateral agreements to obtain private placements, replacing over-leveraged banks;[178] and direct investors, private equity and sovereign wealth funds may soon become key actors, while other funds may depend on computer-driven profits for their future. The evolution towards fast computer-driven capital flows has yet to be tested in its contribution to growth and national wealth. Security concerns, the importance of energy supply, the pro-cyclicality of the systems and the speed with which they can extract capital and dispose of assets may destabilize entire socioeconomic systems. Meanwhile, sovereign funds are multiplying. UK ex-Business Secretary Peter Mandelson proposed to follow the example of China, Norway, the Gulf principalities and France: the Labour government allocated £500 billion in the government's budget to set up a new public-sector backed financial institution. The UK idea diverged from that of other countries because Mandelson was thinking of attracting pension funds. Knowing that the state was in dire straits, he argued that most new investment would have to come from private investors. All these funds will, of course, be competing for capital, first and foremost with banks.[179]

Conclusion

The crisis flared up while a housing bubble was coming to an end in developed countries, in particular the USA. Subsequently, debt practices and extreme leverage within a highly interconnected and opaque financial industry and between the latter and the real economy led to a liquidity trap, a credit freeze and a major financial crisis. When the US government let Lehman Brothers collapse, the crisis turned global and into a worldwide real economy drama. Wealth was destroyed in many ways. Although states across the world engaged in important stimulus and fiscal measures, certainly helping to avert the worst and restart economic activity, uncertainty remains predominant three years on. The private sector continues to deleverage, consumption is low, credit is scarce, and developed countries are heavily indebted as a result of their active policies in support of banks and the real economy. These countries may face a long period of stagnation and rising inequality as austerity policy packages are implemented to restrain public deficits. Strategies to restart growth seem to tread the same path as before, and global and regional imbalances have not only not been diffused but may be strengthening.

Some initiatives have been extremely important, such as the public inquiries into the crisis. More recent ones, such as the proxy ballot allowing shareholders a real capacity to oppose and present alternatives to management, may force a rethinking of the increasingly risky vertical style of control that helps the capture and manipulation of information. The taboo of 'untouchable' derivatives has fallen apart. Derivatives start to get the transparency they deserve and platforms begin to provide pricing mechanisms instead of counter-party practice.[180] In April 2010, the US Senate Agriculture, Nutrition and Forestry Committee approved a derivatives regulation bill called 'The Wall Street Transparency and Accountability Act of 2010'. The taxation measures enacted in Germany in 2010 may limit speculative activity: levies on banks will reflect the risk their activities pose, and while the UK only plans to tax balance sheets, German annual levies will be based on both balance sheet liabilities and derivatives. Several governments such as those of the USA and Switzerland have, finally, set up institutions to monitor the degree of overall systemic risk, while the EU created a European Systemic Risk Board in December 2010. A comprehensive view is currently lacking, as it will take time to see whether these new organizations will have the necessary capabilities to effectively perform the task, given that many financial entities are multinational and/or have transnational activities.

In September 2010, Basel II was superseded by Basel III. The aim is to raise commercial banks' core tier-1 capital or tangible equity as well as to create counter-cyclical buffers, as proposed by the Bank for International Settlements.[181] Basel III should become effective by 2015. The requirement of holding a 7 per cent capital ratio was already attained in the USA in 2007 and applies only to commercial banking, not to the other key actors such as investment banks, hedge funds and structured investment vehicles. The Basel Committee on Banking Supervision is also considering a liquidity coverage ratio. Yet, according to the Economist Intelligence Unit, since US banks greatly multiplied their profits on leveraging between 1980 and 2005, there could be strong opposition.[182]

Nevertheless, from calls to reform the banks' activities, organization, incentives and size, proposals have turned to macro-supervision and states' indebtedness. It is obviously too early to assess the ongoing initiatives but they attract the attention for their partial scope and open-ended form. The US financial reform bill, for example, establishes many institutions with the task of working out frameworks and policies in the future. The Volcker rule, named after Paul Volcker (former Federal Reserve Chairman and current adviser to President Obama), originally banning banks from investing in hedge funds and private equity, was eased to allow lenders to invest up to 3 per cent of their capital in such funds, leaving a long period before the law comes into force.[183] The powers to wind down failed banks deal with national-only ones: Fanny Mae and Freddie Mac still await their restructuring. Only Germany has so far taken more drastic steps by banning particular activities related to derivatives.

On the other hand, instead of a political consensus, we observe that social and political polarization is on the rise in many developed countries affected by the crisis. There have been rifts concerning bank regulation such as in accounting and equity ratios. In 2010, bubble-building activity is rather constrained by a still frozen market in derivatives and a weak housing market in the USA, accompanied by strategies towards lower consumption, higher savings and cost reduction. The latter, unfortunately, also act as a deterrent to hiring new labour and making new investments. There is still no consensus on whether we may be facing inflation or deflation. In August 2010, a series of bad statistics in jobs and housing in the USA increased fears of a 'double-dip' recession.[184] Public debt is high on the agenda while other types of debt and leverage get waning attention. Austerity policies coupled with further privatization and state restructuring are up on Europe's political agenda, while in the USA, the debate heats up between pro-Keynesian calls for further stimulus support and those against further government spending.

Three years after it began, the crisis is not over. In 2010, the Bank for International Settlements talked of a financial industry in intensive care amidst daunting challenges for developed countries.[185] In parallel, the G20 summit in Canada told banks to hoard up to £130 billion in case of a new shock.[186]

In a highly interconnected global economy, sustainable wealth generation is hurt by rapid profit taking. This entails differentiating between long-term investment and financial frenzy, which in turn needs a larger and more equal base of consumers. Probably the most distinguished living Brazilian economist and thinker, Maria da Conceição Tavares, recently gave a magisterial address at the United Nations Economic Commission for Latin America and the Caribbean, ECLAC, in Chile on 'The Effects of the International Financial Crisis in Latin America and the Lessons from the Brazilian Case' to diplomats, academics and international organizations. In her words:

> The crisis has created a new international *disorder* in which the economic situation remains most unstable, with some bubbles that could go off and financial turbulences which emerge in different places ... consumption and government expenditure cannot continue to be the engines of growth in developed countries.[187]

She spoke of markets organized in an unsustainable capitalist 'canon law' tied to phantom credits and toxic derivatives and emphasized the need for two key policies: investing in infrastructure and implementing a universal social protection public system. Based on her thinking, in 2010, ECLAC published 'Time for equality; gaps to be closed, and paths to be opened'.[188]

So, is this the mother of all crises? We can say that, at least, it is the mother of all warnings. To delve deeper into the analysis of the crisis, let us now examine its causes from various standpoints and try to distinguish its underlying mechanisms.

2
Causes and Mechanisms: The Crisis as a Debt Trap

Introduction

Departing from the 'outer layer' of shocking events, let us now delve further into the underlying causes and mechanisms at the root of the crisis. The precise causes of the financial breakdown remain surprisingly controversial.[1] The very first reaction was one of astonishment at the appearance of an unexpected 'black swan'.[2] For others, it was the thing about to happen. Most explanations have dealt with household-mortgage defaults and shadow banking in their operations of the sub-prime market and their role in initiating the crisis.[3] What is certain is that too many loans were granted without considering the capability to pay back the debt thus created, and that it happened thanks to the inventive use of financial products that were believed to be secure. But behind these well-known events, debates rage about the main causes: were they monetary or institutional, the product of individual misbehaviour or systemically endogenous? Was the crisis due to a liquidity problem, a credit crunch or a debt trap?

Accordingly, reactions focus not only on macroeconomic issues but also on governance-related and supervisory ones, and at all levels, macro, meso and micro. So, what has the crisis been about? Individualistic, institutionalist and systemic hypotheses are analysed in the first section. As we shall see, each approach highlights some aspects of reality, without shedding enough light on the linkages between the micro and the macro, the financial and the real economy. To highlight such linkages we review, in the second part of the chapter, three mechanisms leading to and deploying the crisis, defining them as traps: a consumption trap, a liquidity trap and a debt trap.

Hypotheses concerning the causes of the crisis

The individualistic hypothesis

First and easiest is to blame it on individuals' behaviour. Hypotheses on individuals causing the crisis range from deviant behaviour to irrational panic and copycat actions. In reality, these hypotheses comprise two types of explanations: on the one hand, Robert Shiller's mass 'irrational behaviour'; on the other hand, stories about traders, individual outliers with Rambo-style behaviour bringing down long-standing world financial institutions such as Barings in 1995. We consider this set of hypotheses as being the first outer layer among the factors that may explain the origins of the crisis.

Robert Shiller helped demonstrate that the USA was living amidst specula-tive bubbles. In 2001, his stock prices and earnings data series from 1871 to 2000 showed that stock market prices had essentially been the same for a century up to 1982, when they began to head upwards uniformly and non-stop.[4] The spike took place from 1999 until the internet, technology and tele-coms crash in 2001. For Shiller, the bubble was a question of volatility caused by mass irrationality, connecting the spread of the internet and the new economic global media to mass psychology. He linked the bubble to a popu-lation left alone to face poverty, sickness and old age. The internet became widespread in 1997: US households with online accounts were expected to reach 9.7 million in 2003, up from 3.1 million in 1999.[5] Many of these were active investors from their own home computers. While monetary policies appeared restrictive for public action, they encouraged private capital 'cir-cuits' including the holding of individual shares in stock exchanges through the most basic home computer. Acting as a magnifier, loose fiscal policies for those with higher income ensured massive injection of funds in such circuits, while interest rates went down every time a financial shock appeared. This resulted in an added mass of available money in circulation without control, taxation or any other type of restriction: all the necessary conditions for large and repeated financial bubbles. In 1999, after evidence of stock price volatility due to blogging, the US Securities and Exchange Commission (SEC) made a 'Special Study: On-Line Brokerage: Keeping Apace of Cyberspace'.[6]

The 1982 pension reforms and the 401(k) plans shifted the shared respon-sibility for the elderly, conditions that included a shared interest in national growth, to the shoulders of individuals, creating the feeling that each per-son was responsible for his or her own welfare. Robert Shiller explains how people came to take decisions online as well as to invest disproportionately in stock markets or to flock around fashionable themes, risking their wealth in concentrated bets. He shows that people were not all able to articulate the received information, nor to put forward critical questions, nor to effect control over the process and outcomes. Shiller thus calls attention to a deep-seated and systemic change: computer-linked environments lead to synchronic global behaviour.

The early September 2001 crash, just before the 9-11 attacks, made 'inves-tors worried that, for the first time in a generation, all the world's major economies may be shrinking at once', while money managers like Jim Weiss saw better: 'We have low rates, lower taxes, lower energy prices and mort-gage refinances ... I just don't see the economy taking another leg down in

2002.[7] And so came the time for the mortgage and other assets bubbles. In 2002, Dean Baker commented on the existence of a housing bubble in the United States.[8] In 2001, Shiller had already stated that extremely high valuations were not driven by fundamentals: in the same period, US personal income and gross domestic product had risen less than 30 per cent, half of such increase being due to inflation.[9]

The second type of individualistic hypothesis concerns outliers, disturbances brought about by traders' misbehaviour. But on this occasion, the build-up was so massive that it could hardly be the work of a few individuals here and there. Jerome Kerviel, the trader who almost took down Société Générale was, in others analysts' trading experience, not only normal but totally rational. The incentive packages for traders and senior managers were a forceful motive since pursuing any other strategy would have been irrational in view of the gains. Moreover, all others in the same position were doing the same. The German stock market media star and writer, Dirk Müller, discharges traders from the responsibility of starting the bubble.[10] In his view, they were only rationally riding it! But he concedes that there are true 'rogues' like Kenneth Lay at Enron or Bernie Ebbers at WorldCom. When do they, in the view of other traders, turn into rogues? When, through levering up the firms' equity capital 30 or 40 to one in search of extra profits, their actions can bring down a whole economy.

Various accounts describe how certain behaviour was encouraged in the people appointed as traders, many of whom were not selected because of their knowledge or experience. They were given the post or sent abroad because they had flair, or were young and inexperienced, more indicative of a typical behaviour of Weber's patrimonialism[11] than of a rational modern bureaucracy.

In addition, systems mattered, connections, constant flows at ever increasing speed, and the standardization of financial products to be passed rapidly without having to delve into them separately. This technical rationality increases mimetic behaviour and discourages efforts to think it over, without the need for doubt. Internalized mimetic behaviour triggers a herding attitude. Moreover, the selected few keep to themselves in a closed circuit. In a closed world where people only meet their peers, there is limited capacity to deal with the unknown. On the other hand, a closed mentality helps to covet the object of work: money.

Hannah Arendt critically warned that where everybody is portrayed as guilty, no one is.[12] We must avoid this situation in order to understand. Not everybody bears the same responsibility: some may be more responsible than others, such as those having power to set standards, those holding information, overseers who opt to grant waivers instead of doing their supervisory job (as in the Enron case), or those ensuring that differing views are not listened to. Those taking systemic key decisions, be it in public office, in banks or other major institutions, should be responsible for their actions and be sanctioned if necessary. Some call themselves 'market makers' and it is true. Markets are built by human action, and there should be human accountability. Surely, the motives behind traders' behaviour include greed and 'hunger' for rapidly ascending social status, akin to Veblen's 'invidious' behaviour.[13] But this was institutionalized behaviour, honed by institutions that promoted it as the ideal.

The monetary hypothesis

The classic hypothesis is that financial crises are caused by monetary excess, in this crisis allocated to housing, leading to a boom followed by an inevitable bust. This excess may be explained in two main ways: (i) US monetary policy remained stimulative for too long after the 2002 recession; and (ii) excess savings outside the USA drove down global interest rates to levels that fuelled speculation, as Alan Greenspan claimed in his defence in April 2010 mentioning 'the complexity of the division of labour required of modern global economies', concluding that 'only adequate capital and collateral can resolve this dilemma. If capital is adequate, by definition, no debt will default and serial contagion will be thwarted'.[14]

Although this hypothesis explains part of the process that led to the crisis, it remains the most contested for three main reasons. First, lax monetary policy had been practised by Alan Greenspan for a long period before the early 2000s. Raines and Leathers[15] show how Greenspan's method was to sustain asset price increases above any other concern. Chairman of the Federal Reserve Board since August 1987, he shared with his predecessor Paul Volcker the ideal of the stock market as well as the perception that wages were the major threat to the stock market 'virtuous cycle'.[16] The time of supply-side policies had begun.

Moreover, US authorities sustained the stock-market cycle through policy agreements such as the one on housing through the National Partners in Home Ownership in 1994, signed by realtors, home builders, Fannie Mae, Freddie Mac, mortgage bankers and governmental authorities. According to Christopher Whalen, home construction firms had a two-million unit target to be built each year, and were only concerned about volume, nothing else.[17] Perhaps they never imagined what a drastic turn the policy would take once tied to traditional Wall Street style behaviour.

Second, lax monetary policy went hand in hand with a lack of regulation of unclear and untested financial innovations, mainly linked to debt and risk of default. In 1996, Alan Greenspan spoke as Chairman of the Federal Reserve to announce that the government role had changed: applying public regulation to the financial system was discarded.[18] In its place, the private sector should have its own systems to manage risk.

Third, the growth of foreign savings in US currency, which was one of the major consequences of the 1997–1998 financial crises in Asia, Russia and Brazil, was meant to be a protection against subsequent bubbles. But that is insufficient evidence for a global savings glut. Those savings continued to accumulate even after US interest rates began to rise in the mid-2000s, peaking after 2004.[19] In 2005, the IMF gave evidence of a savings shortage.[20] In 2009, ECB Chairman Trichet affirmed that industrialized economies were short of savings and international intermediation, namely banking, was called on to channel the excess of savings from abroad: economic activity in developed countries, consumption and investment, continued to be possible thanks to such savings.[21]

The US government encouraged easy credit to avoid deflation. The very first public statements on deflation were made in November 2002, in Ben Bernanke's address to the National Economists Club, 'Deflation: Making sure "it" doesn't happen here', and in December 2002 when Greenspan mentioned the word 'deflation' in his speech to the Economic Club of New York. Credit strongly picked up after the 2003 accounting scandals related to the government sponsored enterprises (GSEs) and the US Congress' review of such scandals. The US property market was considered to be an engine of growth and Bernanke affirmed that 'the banking system was healthy and well regulated and neither firms nor households had any particular debt problems'.[22]

But not all the credit/debt went into first-time ownership, leading to the idea that it was not so much a sub-prime craze as an overall drive to invest in bricks. A large part went to rental property.[23] Property investment for a population whose pensions depended on financial profits seemed a sound idea in a macro context of low inflation and low income growth. The bursting of the dotcom bubble shifted their financial flows onto housing. Finally, survivors of the 1929 Great Depression were few if any, and the memory of past pains, the consequent financial regulation and the more restrictive social conventions that had led to some stability were forgotten.[24]

As with the first set of hypotheses, the monetary factor is part of the explanation. However, it is neither the only nor the major one. If it were due only to monetary excess in the USA, the crisis should have happened earlier. Other factors and events taking place were piling up.

Problematic business models

The next major set of hypotheses is that the crisis was due to the business model itself. The blatant disregard of basic accounting and auditing principles was evident in the sub-prime sector. The failure of lenders and their auditors to perform a simple verification of borrowers' income and credit histories was a contributing cause to the crisis.

Institutionalist hypotheses come in various forms, focusing on issues of information asymmetry, wrong incentives and reputation control mechanisms. Nuances in the approach also depend on whether the systemic problem is basically sectoral or across the board. These carry differing views on the 'market'. Some view markets as constructions, institutions built with specific designs related to information, values, practices and regulation, which are essential to sustain their functioning. Others take markets as a given and do not reflect further upon them: for them, problems stem from deviant practices that should be restrained and punished. Earlier hypotheses on individual behaviour are seen here as dependent on a wider context. In addition, for some, there is also competition between business models.

A sector-only crisis may refer to banking, finance, sub-prime lending or accounting. For the Dutch CPB Netherlands Bureau for Economic Policy Analysis,[25] established by the late Nobel Prize winner Jan Tinbergen, the crisis is chiefly a banking problem. Self-governance based on reputation as a mechanism to prevent opportunistic behaviour cannot work well in the banking sector. Bank failure was therefore due to inadequate regulation and lack of an appropriate control mechanism, which only the nation-state could properly manage.

Van Denburgh and Harmelink focus on accounting. 'Basic bad debt accounting practices were likely not adeptly ... audited in the subprime lending sector'. In their analysis of the bankruptcy of New Century Financial Corp, the second largest originator of sub-primes, it was the whole sector that needed revision. In the case of New Century, the United States Bankruptcy Court for the District of Delaware received a commissioned report by Michael Missal, a court examiner. While the report contends that there were major auditing and accounting lapses, others have countered that the New Century business model was doomed to failure with the collapse of the US housing market.[26] In this case, there was a close connection between the firm and the consulting company KPMG: the New Century controller was a former KPMG manager, which gave way to pressures and tensions. KPMG did not have the authoritative capacity to impose itself in case of non-cooperation. Their solution was to have tougher accounting agencies instead of greater state involvement.

> Proper and effective self-regulation is an essential part of a smooth-functioning US economy. The risks of repeated failures by companies and accounting firms to provide effective controls over basic accounting issues have resulted, and will result, in greater government regulation (e.g., the Sarbanes Oxley Act) which over time will likely result in less effective controls than good old-fashioned rigorous accounting controls and auditing. [27]

For Roman Weil, accounting professor at the University of Chicago Booth School of Business,[28] it was the underlying and overlooked economics in real estate that brought down the firm. For any serious entrepreneur, it should have been incredible that with a lagging labour market after the 2001 recession and wages trailing behind inflation, housing loans could have such an amazing growth.

Another business model taking a trouncing was internet banking: one of the biggest flops ever. In addition to Iceland's Icesave, NetBank in the United States went bankrupt, after being one of the first internet-only banks, strongly fancied by Wall Street after its initial public offering in 1997. With weak earnings, mortgage losses made the business model unworkable.

ECB Chairman Jean-Claude Trichet focused on institutional changes to banks' traditional modus operandi in terms of values, practices and rewards that lessened trust. The main cause was compensation schemes based on volume. Trichet explicitly discharged financial innovation and securitization from being at fault: 'Over the past decades, our economies have greatly benefited from the effects of financial liberalization and financial innovation. For example, the securitization of assets has played a role in facilitating an efficient allocation of economic risks. It allowed the financial sector to offer credit'.[29] For Trichet, the crisis centred on the fact that the financial industry had made the creation and assumption of financial risk its core activity, and in the way it had decoupled financial positions from the real flows of goods and services. Loan managers' compensation schemes provided the wrong incentives as far as prudent behaviour was concerned, because these schemes were based on the volume of loans produced. Worse still, these sellers in the USA were independent from banks and did not hold the risk, reselling the loans as good merchandise. These were the so-called residential mortgaged backed securities (RMBS). As volume expanded, the loans were securitized by the banks, which made money on the fees by selling them, after mixing them with other assets as collaterized debt obligations (CDOs, see Chapter 1), to others who trusted them. In many continental European countries, however, banks are still the only institutions able to give credit loans: the system could not be more different.

Anna Katherine Barnett-Hart found out in 2009 that CDOs had been responsible for $542 billion in write-downs at financial institutions since the crisis began.[30] She provides evidence of the institutional patterns from the top originators, such as Merryll Lynch and Citigroup, in the heavy use of sub-primes with poor quality collateral in the CDOs' construction to the underwriting of CDOs with conscious engineering of credit ratings, through computer modelling with imprecise inputs. The latter was made possible by the working partnership between the rating agencies and the financial institutions. The Big Three rating agencies more than doubled their revenues between 2002 and 2007, from less than $3 billion to more than $6 billion per year, mostly thanks to ratings.[31]

The lack of cross-checks in the system were not only due to lack of government regulation. Those in charge of auditing went to work in some banks. Beyond the sharing of computer models, banks also took in agencies' workers, such as Shin Yukawa from Fitch, to work on Abacus.[32] The partnership allowed the fabrication of AAA-assets, for instance Abacus, sold by Goldman Sachs to the German bank IKB for $250 million and to the Royal Bank of

Scotland for $500 million. In between, partnerships included the active participation of investors such as John Paulson in meetings and decision making, including trips to Greece. Hedge funds used to receive 20 per cent profits on the mass of money invested and place it for a period of three to five years. Decisions on payments were kept within a close circle of top managers, who were the only ones to hold key information, while those working below only received segmented data. In this way, institutional failures reflect incentives that led to miscommunication.

The system was completed with the 'structured investment vehicles' or SIVs, some with CDOs only, portrayed as independent vehicles; shares or bonds were sold against them, thus putting them off-balance sheet. Managers of these financial institutions were paid on the deals and on the firm's stock options on the market, for which they needed to show constantly increasing gains.

The credit default swaps or CDSs invented in the 1990s, against which they could get indebted for more than 100 times their notional value, had no market value. The Bank of International Settlements estimated the total notional value of CDSs at more than $45 trillion in June 2007.[33] Banks at the origin of these practices internalized a specific type of relationship, the counter-party risk. Far from the concept of client saver or depositor, risk is taken by each counter-party on an independent basis: there is no entrustment as in traditional banking, where a depositor entrusts the deposit to a bank. Counter-parties do business together shouldered by the 'network' in front of a third party.

John Taylor's research shows that it was specifically counter-party fear that led to the liquidity trap and the crisis.[34] The April 2010 US Senate hearing on Goldman Sachs showed how the counter-party system was both at the heart of the financial industry and far apart from client–bank relationships. This is not a model of fiduciary trust or entrustment: institutional practices tend to differ from a client–bank relationship.

In 2006, even newspapers started to publish stories that house prices were beginning to fall and investment banks like Goldman Sachs began to 'go home' and resort to 'shorting'. In March 2007, foreseeing the application of the International Financial Reporting Standards (IFRS) in the USA that were to penalise any institution dealing with low-quality housing mortgages, the government sponsored enterprises (GSEs) closed down the worst lending practices. However, 'toxic' products were still sold everywhere. In August 2007, heavy re-pricing began. By mid-September 2008, apprehension turned into panic. When trust evaporated, the circular relationship between asset price appreciation, volume incentives, and excessive opacity in information became toxic.

A critical element was the mixture of old market practices such as stock markets with new practices over the counter, namely outside of the market. The US hearing on the Goldman Sachs case in 2010 showed that counter-party relations in the financial industry did not carry the same connotations of client–consumer relations of transparent information, fiduciary trust and market pricing. Counter-parties share the risk of their joint strategy, they go into it together, and the price they assign to the deal depends on their mutual positioning; moreover, they may have counter-positions on their own – the firm hub becomes 'market-like'. Access to the hub, the only one to enjoy information about all the connected elements, can allow for profitable 'informed' action. This may explain why analyses on institutionalization of markets in explaining the growth of derivatives and hedging need to go beyond the issue of information. The latter was indeed the most coveted possession, but in order to capture it, institutional building was first necessary through specific organizational models that could control flows. In 2010, the US SEC civil and penal claims against a Goldman Sachs' worker focused on internal access to key information that allowed particular interests to bet against other clients at Goldman Sachs. The latter has rejected the SEC claims.

More than the millions of deals, the key problem was to exchange and make the amounts of the deals circulate. The global and sudden loss of trust came about when, in the rush, there was no possibility to price assets in a consistent and transparent manner. Once calm returned, business continued as usual. One year after the fall of Lehman Brothers, the daily life of the City of London or Wall Street was just the same as before. The crisis had not brought any apparent change.

This set of hypotheses provides the most effective explanation as far as the origins of the crisis are concerned. They deal effectively with the supply side of institutionalized practices stemming from problematic business models: defective controls, capture of asymmetric information, values that lessened trust and special counter-party relationships instead of entrustment. Yet, they do not provide answers to major questions related to the crisis taking place amidst a historical tension between two major financial models – banking versus non-banking credit institutions,[35] nor do they point out that the crisis may be the consequence of a business model based on debt and leverage.[36] What about the demand side of these business models so decried now?

The systemic reproduction hypothesis

Many believe that the system is losing the capacity to reproduce itself, to remain on track. The crisis would be one of regulation in the sense of the French school of regulation that follows Boyer[37] and Chenais.[38] The fall of the financialized economic regime was due to debt practices going adrift, but the core of the crisis is double: one of both realization and accumulation.[39] After the crisis of Fordism, a financialized economic regime was built, where financial markets took the central role. Since the early 1980s, capital markets have regained their freedom through liberalization and deregulation, grown thanks to the massive inflows from the US pension system and the tax cuts to the wealthy, channelled transfer prices, off-shore placements, trust activity and currency hedging. From them all, the latter was probably the only unavoidable activity, necessary to international transactions once the system left behind the gold standard and centred on one national currency, the US dollar. In three decades, the system has accumulated a double crisis, a 'Keynesian crisis' due to poor aggregate demand, and lower profitability in productive investment since 2000. Leverage effects and capital markets came in to accrue financial profitability. In May 2010, developed countries were awash in debt: individuals, families, enterprises, and public institutions. And debt appears more central than capital. Only some may be in a comparatively better situation, among which are cooperatives, as we shall see from Chapter 4 onwards.

The present crisis, with its origins in one specific part of the world, is seen as one of the many crises that are caused by a regulatory model based on a certain ideological consensus that had already led to similar bubbles and crises in Russia, Asia and Argentina. Nouriel Roubini, while supporting the role of a renewed IMF, points out past mistakes.[40]

This set of hypotheses seems to be the most inclusive one. Solutions proposed by these authors appear more comprehensive and profound than those proposed in the case of previous hypotheses, as they comprise not only measures to restrain excesses but also a new framework for a different growth regime. However, these theories fail to explain two contradictions in terms of level and space. First, although the approach is global, its preferred path for solutions is at a lower level, the nation-state: the growth regime being proposed is designed in the framework of the nation-state, except when better regional coordination and solidarity is called for, as in the case of Europe. Pierre Dockès thinks that the crisis may only add some international regulatory instances to global financial capitalism, but does not imagine there will be deeper change.[41]

Second, the diagnosis is global but it does not see that the crisis is uneven: whereas the crisis has been particularly affecting developed countries, which are at the core of the financial system, other countries, which are also suffering the consequences, are, this time, not 'on their knees'. In turn, this macro approach takes for granted the economic organization of firms and households, failing to distinguish between those soaked in debt and those that continue to enjoy guarantees and are even reaping large benefits through acquisition of distressed assets and enterprises. How to apply systemic thinking about a crisis of regulation when only part of the system is put in doubt? We must thus continue to dig further down towards cognitive layers through practices, values and beliefs. We need to find out how a path is being built socially, institutionally and politically, in such a way that it ends up destroying more wealth than it generates.

The three traps

While taking stock of the hypotheses mentioned above, the analysis of the underlying mechanisms that paved the way towards the crisis may be grasped as traps: a consumption trap, a liquidity trap and a debt trap. Why a trap? A trap may be defined as an ambush aimed to lock in something, closing unexpectedly and perhaps even brutally. In the beginning, that 'something' was perhaps already in touch with the trap mechanism, even attracted to the trap by a pleasing feature placed in the trap itself. If we consider a trap in this light, we can suppose that the 'something' being trapped did not, most probably, expect to experience being caught like that. And even if the trapped one manages to break free, it may not happen without pain. Most important of all, if this 'something' is a living thing, it must grasp and grapple with the mechanism in order to break free, as so many institutions and people are attempting to do in the ongoing crisis. A trap thus comprises both a mechanism built by concrete things, institutions and behaviour, and a cognitive aspect, which pulls the victim into the trap while blurring its understanding of the impending danger.

The consumption trap

We mainly deal with individual and household consumers here. Consumption has a role of its own in the build-up to a bubble. The US case and the role of consumption in the bubble and the crisis are not unique. When demand turns to over-consumption, indebtedness is never far away. However, there is still a staunch belief that excess consumption demand for goods is ineffective when not backed by ready purchasing power. The crisis has exposed that consumption demand could and did continue to grow without any concomitant increase in purchasing power. A good example has been 'stated income' loans, namely access to money on the basis of a personal statement without records or proof. It is a constant in each crisis, but continues to be neglected by authorities, for example by not collecting data on household saving rates or indebtedness, or not comparing it at the international level.[42] This consumption trap may hurt families and individuals one by one but has macro-economic consequences. In the last decades, consumption was seen as a segmented, individualistic, ethnic and anthropological behaviour, generally disconnected from the 'important economy' of large firms or macro-economic factors such as investment and trade. Still today, attention and rescue packages focus on the interests of the 'important economy'.

Household debt was generally off the radar in the supply-side economic regime. Raines and Leathers (2008) track the record of US policy neglect:

> Neither Greenspan nor Bernanke considered household debt to be a causative factor of deflation. On the contrary, the record high debt of households in 2002–2003 was viewed as providing anti-deflationary support to aggregate demand and as evidence of the positive contributions of financial derivatives combined with an accommodative monetary policy.[43]

Although, in December 2002, Greenspan did acknowledge that deflation 'would convert the otherwise relatively manageable level of nominal debt held by households and businesses into a corrosive rising level of real debt and real debt service costs', the mortgage debt of homeowners and the total servicing costs faced by households relative to their income, or evidence that some corporate managers were beginning to venture out on the risk scale, were not a significant cause for concern for him.[44] Between 1997 and 2004, after the Asian, Russian and Brazilian crises, Greenspan talked of a 'deflation moment'. In 1999, he was anxious 'especially when positions are highly leveraged'.[45] In his speech of November 2002, Greenspan again dismissed the risk of debt, arguing that it had been efficiently allocated through extensive use of new highly complex financial derivatives, including credit default swaps (CDSs; see Chapter 1).[46] Meanwhile, in 2003, Bernanke claimed that 'fortunately, financial conditions in the United States today are sound, not fragile ... households have taken advantage of low interest rates to refinance their mortgages ... and using accumulated equity to pay off more expensive forms of consumer debt, such as credit card debt'.[47] In fact, Greenspan's deflation was connected to stock prices, not goods and services.[48] If debt was used to buy stocks or in short-sales or securities, it was fine.

The Levy Institute, using Fisher's and Minsky's hypotheses, reported that the private sector's debt position was unsustainable. It also showed that this debt system had developed strongly between 1992 and 2000, during which time economic growth was based on flows of net credit to 'an unprecedented rise in private expenditure relative to income'.[49] Greenspan in turn preferred to use Schumpeter's thesis of creative destruction through innovation, applied to financial derivatives, financial deregulation and globalization assuring future profits, a stream of investment and higher stock prices.[50] The general idea was that people's consumption in a global economy had little impact in terms of systemic stability and growth. The belief was that, in the case of a debt crisis in one part of the world, consumers could easily be found on the other side of the planet. With a globally interconnected planet and a globally shared downturn, this has come to an end.

Credit is good for development if connected to prior savings in the factors of production, including education and skills, thus providing a real capacity to repay the debt incurred. But credit is bad if it is manipulated and has nothing to do with real needs and aspirations of the local population. This bad credit diverts the allocation of investment and consumption very rapidly towards factors of production and sectors of the economy promoted by political and/or ideological stands, justified by short-term social, political and economic gains. The sectors collapsing most rapidly in this crisis have been those that received that type of bad credit, such as automobiles and real estate.

The loss of purchasing power by a significant part of a population, while the value system promotes debt-incurring behaviour with multiple incentives throughout the entire system (by way of the media, rating agencies, authorities and the word of mouth) tends to produce a consumption trap. The present crisis is partly the consequence of a structure that systematically encouraged consumption above saving, at all levels. When conditions surrounding easy money change, debtors usually face an unexpected and painful situation.

Once the trap closes in, it provokes the destruction of net wealth and the impoverishment of those who thought they were doing well. If the means of living are lost, work remains the main hope to sort out the situation, as in the pawning practices described by Laurence Fontaine or the debt bondage in M.L. Bush's account.[51] The return to harder credit times penalizes first owners and entrepreneurial innovation. At that moment, access to liquidity may make the difference to survival, and the fear of a liquidity trap, in Keynes' words, hoarding or shortage of money, flares up again. How do we arrive at such a situation? Evidence from the current crisis points at systemic endogenous mechanisms.

According to a McKinsey study:

> US consumers accounted for more than three-quarters of US GDP growth since 2000 and for more than one-third of global growth in private consumption since 1990. These trends were fuelled by a surge in household debt particularly after 2000, and a decline in the personal savings rate – to a low of −0.7 percent, in 2005. From 2000 to 2007, US household debt grew as much, relative to income, as it had during the previous 25 years ... from 85 percent in 1990, to 101 percent in 2000, to 139 percent in 2007.[52]

Personal debt was also allocated to non-productive uses, geared to social standing and perceived as socially 'protective'. In 2007, Alan Greenspan and James Kennedy confirmed their 2005 analysis: 'a considerable portion of the equity extracted through cash-out refinancings and home equity loans was used to repay non-mortgage debt, largely credit card loans. One interpretation is that much of the non-mortgage debt repaid with those funds was, in effect, bridge financing for personal consumption expenditure on home improvements and other goods such as automobiles or television sets.[53] Items purchased were not only essentials such as food, clothing and housing, but also communication, transport and leisure in increasing quantity and sophistication. Daily or ostentatious consumption was very often paid in three forms, by credit card debt, home mortgage and credit on home equity. The latter two forms were preferred during the boom because interest rates were not only lower than those of credit cards but were also deductible for tax purposes. Now that those two options are closed, credit cards are used as a type of emergency funding.

Governments have let large business interest groups advise them to a disproportionate extent and have provided passive or active promotion policies for the development of many of the agents that have led to the 2008 crisis, in particular the 'shadow-banking' actors.[54] The US model of 'disintermediation', with multiple and segmented loan providers coupled with services charging variable rates, led consumer defence organizations to criticize poor practices in terms of information and opaque charges. Authorities, however, have not prohibited those practices. Many consumers today have monthly charges including TV, mobile phones, car rentals, and others, which did not exist just a few years ago. Free credit cards are sent to households, without accompanying information, like a free gift. Moreover, the use of revolving credit to roll over existing debt, piling up high interest rates, can provide a temporary illusion of wealth, sometimes compensating for lower wages and increasingly precarious labour conditions. In March 2010, the French government recognized the problem and passed a new regulation on revolving credit. The recent US Credit Card Accountability, Responsibility and Disclosure Act has been another good step forward.

Many consumers resist, but others find these solicitations empowering. Consumption is perceived as a major means of social inclusion, of being accepted and treated kindly. In this sense, it has become a fundamental value in social well-being. There are, unfortunately, many ways in which people may be lured into over-consumption without being aware of the trap into which they are falling.

In the UK system of tax credit for households with claw-back clause, about 1.9 million families in 2003–4 received around £2.2 billion in over-payments. A couple of years later, they found out that they had to repay it to the government. In the end, both households and the state lost. The Public Accounts Committee affirmed that the way in which some of the money was recovered caused hardship to families, and that approximately £1 billion in debt from the first two years of the scheme was unlikely to be recovered.[55] With low income growth, falling savings rate and lack of liquidity, households were getting into debt in order to purchase necessities or assure other needs such as education. Consumption was seen as a vital engine of growth in the 1990s and 2000s, and now the state deficit lent support to calls for cuts in government spending in social services that in turn may hurt all citizens across-the-board, even those who used the tax credits wisely.

One major argument in support of easy credit for consumption is the fear of deflation. This may be justified in the case of a major crisis, like the present one. However, in order not to get into a crisis in the first place, several goals should be kept in mind: credit should be well allocated, resources should be well mobilized, systems should be sustainable in the long run, and prices of assets should remain within a certain control system that makes 'market makers' accountable and legally responsible. Nobody can presently affirm that the 'market' *per se* can achieve such goals.

Unbridled consumption and credit conditions were a major causative factor of the 1929 Great Depression, which Veblen, Galbraith and Mauss have written about. Marcel Mauss in his 1923–4 *Essay on the Gift* [56] shows how concerned he was about the grave problems caused by unrestrained consumption channelled through speculation, usury and changing credit conditions in the period preceding the 1929 crash. In his view, problems were not purely individual but systemic, because they concerned the very purpose of social exchange. [57]

Mauss's words sound very contemporary:

> First, we come back, and we must come back, to the mores of 'noble expense'. It is necessary that ... the rich return – freely and also necessarily – to consider themselves as a sort of treasurers of their fellow citizens. ... Then, there should be more concern for the individual, for life, health, education – which is also a profitable thing – for the family and the future of the latter. There is a need for more good faith, sensitivity, generosity in the contracts for hiring services, the rental of buildings, the sale of necessary foodstuffs. And we must find the means for limiting the fruits of speculation and usury ... However, it is necessary that the individual works. He should be forced to rely on himself rather than on the others. On the other hand, he must defend his interests, personally and as a group ... Social insurance, the concern for mutuality, cooperation, the professional group, all these legal persons that English law earmarks with the name of 'Friendly Societies' are more worthy than the simple personal security that the noble guaranteed to his lessee, better than the meagre living that comes from the daily wages assigned by the employer, and even better than the capitalist savings – which is based only on changing credit. [58]

Both Veblen and Mauss were highly concerned with changing credit conditions. The 1920s was the period in which innovations such as credit cards and payment instalments were adopted using Taylorism and standardization. Larger banks were welcomed by liberal governments because they provided large-scale means to ensure the circulation of payments, reducing the need for cash. The hope was that, just like today, there would be no more thesaurization or penury of money, which Keynes later defined as hoarding and was seen as a major factor in the extension and depth of earlier crises. Nearly a hundred years later, our society is again based on a culture of hyperconsumption that reaches the point of systemic indebtedness, whether by breeding compulsive or addictive behaviour, or by balancing acts of households to make ends meet.

An important debate deals with the hypothesis that the homogenization of consumption would create a common global culture. This common culture would connect people to each other through consumption of objects that can be spotted throughout the world. Consumption would ensure access to a global class and would help build the world citizen. Simon Langlois believes that, rather than homogenization, there is differentiation of cultures of consumption.[59] Zygmunt Bauman sees a process of social and cultural fragmentation in which consumption would be the enemy of the citizen.[60] This fragmentation would prevent individuals from intervening politically or coming together to express themselves in the public arena. In one way or another, the economy of objects appears embedded in an individualistic society in which identity and solidarity create a relationship expressed through the consumption of particular products.

A central intervening factor in modern consumption patterns has been urbanization, which has fractured the social domain where people used to know each other, where solidarity mechanisms were used in case of crisis or recession, when people could count on basic means for survival in case of shortage of cash and credit. Inclusion and exclusion also operate through consumption patterns. Austerity, re-usage, or keeping something for a long period of time, were out of favour until recently. By contrast, in earlier societies, the community would keep the object forever or would make it taboo in order to settle relations among its members. In addition, through the urbanization process, we pass from essential needs and usefulness to intangibles, the most striking example being food with a weakened or lost connection to the natural process of production as compared to rural culture. The urbanized space is the space of cash, even if the person is unemployed, marginal or poor. In any event, the person will be inserted into some mechanism ensuring the circulation of money, be it legal or illegal.

Since the Second World War, the pattern of consumption *par excellence* has been represented by the USA. Starting in the 1960s, studies analysed the linkages between needs and changes in the system of distribution, such as the influence of the opening of supermarkets. They focused attention on the 'democratization' of access and the key role of automobiles in accessing such places. Philippe Moati spoke of the adaptation challenge of business undertakings to the post-Fordist model of production and distribution to be able to respond to individuals. Urbanization, cash and changes in the system of distribution reinforced the trend towards repeated consumption of the same object, with its stream of waste, repair and recycling.[61]

This consumption pattern has led to an open-ended process. The fulfilment of social cohesion becomes an open question and new ways are sought through needs but also taboos, donations and stratification. Jean Baudrillard treated the question as enchantment, with its immediate loss and the need to constantly re-enchant products and places of consumption.[62] In the hiatus between the longing for recognition and the fragmented consumption, the sense of lacking cannot be satiated and the object of desire is posited in further consumption, in a powerful process of hypnosis.

Instead, the institutional approach by Thorstein Veblen on leisure consumption,[63] John Kenneth Galbraith[64] on the affluent society and Pierre Bourdieu on habits or 'habitus'[65] has highlighted practices that, in the long run, condition behaviour and create institutions: institutions in which consumers are central to the understanding of social classes and groups of interests in modern industrial societies – as well as post-industrial ones – following the growing degree of monetization of the economy. Bourdieu's 'habitus' corresponds to the disposition of individuals, which functions like 'structuring structures', something he will then rework through the concepts of economic and cultural capital to analyse classes and social groups in relation to social fields and lifestyles. In a period of high inequality, extravagant and ostentatious consumption exploits the social imagery to construct ideal models.

Critical analyses have been lagging behind. In France, for example, 'CREDOC's research on consumption avoids asking whether the consumer is tricked or manipulated – by advertising or by oligopolistic firms in particular – and avoids laying down that demand is being oriented from the outside in a deterministic manner'.[66] Macroeconomic analyses have been focusing on the social, but predominantly at the micro scale. Postmodernism seems to have prevailed in the analysis of consumption.

Few studies on consumption in the twentieth century attempted to connect the theoretical research on consumption on one side, to the global mode of production, distribution and finance, namely current capitalism, on the other. This is why, at the beginning of the twenty-first century, debates turn to Veblen. Moreover, some authors now treat consumer debt as addiction.[67] In addition, a disenchantment process is being expressed through groups of consumers demanding sanctions and traceability concerning the mode of production.[68]

In practice, how can the consumption trap be broken? First of all, households need to be able to reduce the debt burden without trimming consumption in the same proportion. A McKinsey report has proposed income growth of 2 per cent per year,[69] which would allow households to reduce their debt-to-income ratio and continue to consume healthily without falling into the debt trap. Second, if the income gap between rich and poor could be bridged to some extent, the overall system could create wealth faster across the board. McKinsey shows that without significant income growth, household deleveraging could seriously weaken consumption and the global economy for years to come. To do that, sectors that can employ massive numbers of people should be at the forefront of investment and productivity growth: McKinsey hints at health care and public bureaucracy. We agree with the argument concerning income growth, but McKinsey does not contrast the consumption trap to the debt trap (to be examined below). As the consumption trap extends, adding its contribution to a systemic debt trap, the need for the system to re-establish its balance may first require exports and the restraining of public spending, contrary to the idea of employing many in the public sector.

Second, solutions must be found in terms of demand. At first sight, we think that the USA and China are opposites, but is it so? Let's examine the linkages between the sub-primes and healthcare. The health insurance system in the United States was not providing until now universal access to healthcare, in particular to people with long-term illness or to the unemployed. This may be likened to the current health coverage system in China, which does not cover many citizens, especially in rural areas and the unemployed. Savings are enormous, largely because there is no generalized system of health or social protection.[70] In China's case, there have been genuine savings, whereas in the USA, people tend to invest in bricks, to own a house to rent out or to use it in exchange for health services, something that would be rare in Europe. In China, the little land that peasants have in rural areas, which includes the house, is used to obtain formal or informal credit[71] to pay for healthcare, education or to travel to work in the cities and coastal areas. Both countries are now trying to extend health coverage to the population as a whole. With a more balanced allocation of resources, aggregate demand and endogenous growth may be better assured. Another factor leading to the unbridled demand for credit is related to the precariousness of job conditions and contracts of both producers and workers, which takes place in the context of constant firm restructuring, as will be seen in Chapter 3. Many households then turn to credit as a sort of emergency 'bank' to sort out urgent short-term needs, although a heavier debt burden awaits them in the future.

Third, solutions must also come from the supply side. Some propose the idea of lenders' self-restraint. However, on the supply side of credit, it can hardly work under the current global competition for three main reasons. First, competition for enlarging business scales, coupled with stock market valuation and fair value accounting, shift the balance towards volume as well as standardization. Second, a vast number of segmented actors and the multiplication of intermediaries providing cheap and unchecked credit create downward pricing pressures to attract borrowers. Third, a merger or acquisition is always a threat. Who will dare put all the information on the table in a totally transparent manner? And who would shy away from credit volume when it could mean losing out to the competition?

If the state entrusts its functions to a self-regulated group of credit lenders, the group must be able to share information without being subject to the Damocles sword of acquisition by its group companions. If the job is badly done, the state should keep the power to break the contract of entrustment. In the end, the system of control must not be closed in itself; there must always be cross-checks and balances. The common good of trust is too crucial. Second, self-regulation covers only a specific policy area and it never assumes the role of last resort in political terms. All that is well then goes well, but in a major crisis, self-regulation is incapable of taking legitimate drastic measures. Global self-regulatory groups, such as the International

Accounting Standards Board (IASB), have not been able to provide timely and urgent solutions in the policy area of their concern and are not accountable to anyone. Political authorities then have to confront emergencies without necessarily having all the insider information.

As we have seen here, studies on consumption in the second part of the twentieth century did not grasp debt mechanisms and their linkages to the global political economy. Most studies focused on specific objects and places, within specific national borders, ethnic or age groups. Only occasionally, were studies on the same object of consumption compared, even though consumption is now global.

We have observed three debates that increase our understanding of how and why we could be facing a consumption trap: (a) whether consumption may lead to homogenization or not of habits and practices, and whether the latter are conducive to the building of institutions; (b) the link between consumption and the context of mass urbanization and identity building; and (c) the connection between consumption and the ongoing restructuring of the mode of production. Our civilization leads to a consumption trap for two main reasons: (i) because piling-up and constantly changing consumption trends respond to survival needs as well as to identity and social needs; and (ii) because consumption increasingly depends on credit, and thus on debt, with changing charges and burdens, submerged in a context of increasing inequality, boosting consumption needs in a vicious circle.

The liquidity trap

When we say 'liquidity trap', we think of Keynes. Yet, Keynes' liquidity trap in his *General Theory*, in which central bankers were unable to drive interest rates any lower because of people's determination to hold infinite amounts of cash, was merely a theoretical hypothesis.[72] But in 2008, it turned out to be as real as was the case of Japan in the 1990s.[73] Although the origins of the crisis and the bursting of the bubble came from elsewhere, a liquidity trap situation ensued, as interbank lending became paralysed. Capital moved into government bonds, enterprises and families began to curtail spending and save, and demand saw a free fall toward the end of 2008.

In his time, Keynes had to deal with the consequences of bank failure rather than stock-market failure, and the role of central banks with their interest rates. He focused on the problem of insufficient aggregate demand in a depressed economy, instead of inefficient supply (monopoly power or labour supply) to solve the question of why the Great Depression was long-lasting. Two types of effective demand failure were central to his theory: one due to increased savings, the other to lack of purchasing power of the unemployed. Keynes confronted the deadlock by proposing policies on investment, not on adjusting consumption. For him, recovery and regulation were distinct, the lasting solution relying on institutional structures and macro-authority regulation. Keynes' advice was not always expansionary.

In the middle of the 1919 inflationary investment boom fed by easy bank credit, Chancellor Austen Chamberlain requested his advice. Keynes replied that when capital goods and labour are fully employed, a sharp rise in interest rates to change businessmen's expectations and to discourage them from borrowing is necessary.[74]

A distinctive characteristic of the present crisis was the severe disruption of global markets, including the markets for asset-backed securities, commercial paper, and interbank lending. In developed countries, financial markets had continued to function without difficulty in previous crises. In 2008, various governments, after dealing with the first bank failures on a one-to-one basis, realized that general measures were necessary. Many have compared this crisis to the Great Depression, while US government policy makers implemented policies used since the 1980s when they saved Savings and Loans.[75]

Milton Friedman argued that the Great Depression of the 1930s was aggravated by the US Federal Reserve's failure to assist the credit markets.[76] The Fed did not repeat such a mistake: deposit insurance helped to avoid bank runs, while the Treasury temporarily guaranteed both the principal of investment funds and certain bank debts to ensure that banks would not lose access to borrowing markets. It lent to banks through 'quantitative easing' and arranged other lending facilities to introduce the risk premiums on privately issued debt. The US Congress authorized the Treasury to provide $700 billion to the financial system through the Troubled Assets Relief Program (TARP).[77] Around the world, government intervention avoided the policy errors of the 1930s, eased monetary policy, reduced short-term interest rates to nearly zero, and directly assisted the financial sector, followed by state aid to other sectors such as car manufacturers, as seen in Chapter 1.

Nouriel Roubini and Paul Krugman published analyses of the liquidity trap at the end of 2008. This trap affects the real value of nominal liabilities, and makes them rise as do real interest rates once the nominal interest rate is zero. Hoarding cash reinforces the trend and a deflationary spiral may take hold. Roubini worried about the consequences of indebtedness with falling prices. Investors were hoarding cash while the Fed funds rate was close to zero per cent and its policy of 'quantitative easing' had given the markets trillions of dollars of liquidity. In August 2010, Roubini affirmed that monetary policy was not working and that the liquidity trap was still very much present, arguing that the USA could not run a budget deficit of 15 to 20 per cent of GDP. He also remarked that US banks had $1 trillion of excess reserves that were not being used in credit and had profit rates of 0.25 per cent. He estimated a double-dip risk of 40 per cent.[78]

In 2008, Nobel Prize winner Paul Krugman investigated the woes of the global economy in *The Return of Depression Economics and the Crisis of 2008*,[79] using on the one hand the metaphor of a Washington-based 'baby-sitting co-op', and on the other hand the stream of previous crises that had flared up successively around the world. Krugman made an important contribution in explaining how an ideological consensus based on outdated theory, the so-called Washington consensus, had led to deflationary conditions by which repeated crises in the world had been engendered by deflationary policies implemented under the predominant consensus. For him, there was no 'black swan' in 2008.

Indeed, since the early 1980s, devastating financial and economic crises have taken place in Latin America, East Asia, Russia, Brazil and Turkey. In each case, bubbles and crises originated in debt, the worst being the Asian crisis of 1997 and Argentina's in 2001. In the former case, behind currency speculative attacks were large debts in the hands of national private banks. Argentina's problems originated in large firms' private debt, which was nationalized in 1982 by then Central Bank director Domingo Cavallo, when the country was in military conflict with the UK. At the end of the century, Cavallo, upon becoming economy minister, pegged the national currency to the dollar, which made the former highly over-valued. After the Asian crisis that in turn led Brazil to devalue, Argentina's pegging became totally unsustainable. Internal costs were extremely high and there was no external market to which to export, the last market being Brazil. Yet, devaluation and default came only after the population rejected the choice of dollarization of the national economy, through bringing down the government. Argentina, whose debt never ceased to grow although it repaid the original amount numerous times, returned to high growth after devaluation (while other key challenges remain unsolved, falling outside the scope of this book).

The 1980s and 1990s IMF interventions were inappropriate. By raising interest rates to very high levels, recessions were deeper and more painful with undue costs, both credit and liquidity were rare, leading to massive enterprise failure. Poor growth and further speculative attacks ensued, debt service grew more expensive than the initial credit, and countries looked to new credit/debt provision. As debts mounted exponentially, becoming impossible to repay, more loans were necessary to roll over the payment of interest rates. In Argentina's case, deflation was the chosen path, to such an extent that there was very little circulating national currency. Before the 2001 explosion, there were about 55 types of pseudo-currency in circulation, which could not be exchanged. Still, some currency did leave the country, because there was an immediate open-door policy, in contrast to Chile's control of such easy outflows. By 1998, these types of policies had brought the world to the brink of the first global deflationary downturn since the 1930s, a concern shared by Greenspan and Bernanke in their declarations at the turn of the century. This is when developing countries said 'enough', began exporting and accumulating currency reserves in view of future financial speculative attacks.

To explain the liquidity trap, Krugman's baby-sitting co-op idea is quite simple: 150 US congressional staff and their families get together to swap baby-sitting services with each other. Each member family gets a one-hour baby-sitting credit in the form of a printed coupon, which they have to refund when leaving the co-op. With the coupon system, each family can send their children to another family. Baby-sitters recover coupons from baby-sittees, and each couple tries to accumulate coupons for the future. But soon it appeared that there were too few coupons in circulation, as some worked and kept them because they felt no need to use them. As a result:

> [c]ouples who felt their reserves of coupons to be insufficient were anxious to baby-sit and reluctant to go out. But one couple's decision to go out was another's opportunity to baby-sit; so opportunities to baby-sit became hard to find, making couples even more reluctant to use their reserves except on special occasions, which made baby-sitting opportunities even scarcer.[80]

Thus, in Krugman's case, recession is inevitable: people accumulate coupons instead of using them. The governing board of the co-op therefore decides to oblige each couple to go out at least twice a month, but it does not work. It then decides to increase the supply of coupons, leading to a magical recovery.[81]

Eventually, however, things went bad again: during the summer months, most families wanted to go out in the evening (so there was a problem on the supply side), while in the winter, most families wanted to stay home and preferred to baby-sit and earn coupons (so there was a problem on the demand side). Faced with a structural lack of *available* coupons (in circulation) which the supply of new coupons could no longer fix, the governing board of the co-op decided to allow coupon borrowing, with interest rates adjusted to offer and demand. However:

> the seasonality [of the co-op's fluctuation of supply and demand for baby-sitting] was very strong indeed. Then, in the winter, even at a zero interest rate, there will be more couples seeking opportunities to baby-sit than there are couples going out, which means that baby-sitting opportunities will be hard to find, and that couples seeking to build up reserves for summer fun will be even less willing to use those points in the winter, meaning even fewer opportunities to baby-sit ... and the co-op will slide into a recession even at a zero interest rate.[82]

Of course, this is the perfect example of a closed system prone to implosion. Only one type of coupon is accepted. When hoarding takes place, solutions are heavy-handed through the allocation of a same number of coupons even though there are changing needs. Applied to today's economy, it is easy to grasp why, in case of fear, printing money and even lowering interest rates to zero do not help. Nothing helps except lowering the fear by confronting the real problem. In extreme cases, bartering deals may help, at least temporarily, which is not considered by Krugman. Or there could be a mechanism to rebalance the situation at the end of a period, let's say one year, which is the system used by cooperatives, to be discussed in later chapters of this book.

A word not mentioned in Krugman's 2008 book is debt. When a bubble is about to burst, everybody rushes to take away as much money as possible from the circuit, a growing risk in a period of free flows of capital and computerized technology. The 27 April 2010 US Senate hearing on Goldman Sachs' practices and their discussion on shorting and 'going home' between 2006 and 2007 is a good case in point.

But in a 1999 text, Krugman did explain the effect of large amounts of debt indexed in foreign currency loaded onto firms' balance sheets.[83] With devaluation, the new exchange rate leaves the firms bankrupt, leads to a credit crunch and reduces investment and output. This process also explains the lock-in effect in the preference for maintaining an over-valued pegging to an international currency at any cost: economic actors become too heavily indebted, which is normally in foreign currency, even if it means a loss of competitiveness, poor exports, increasing deficits, and unemployment due to labour costs in over-valued domestic money. This explanation can be used to explain the fears and anger in Central and Eastern Europe during the current crisis, as mentioned in Chapter 1. The case of Latvia was seen by economists as a test, drawing most of the attention.[84] This argument cannot apply to the US currency as long as it remains the international currency reserve, but the debt-deflation trap connected to the sub-primes is rather similar.

When banks are in a state of shock and must hold equity to save their reputation and net worth, loose monetary policy may help shore them up but will not restart loans and economic growth. The Bank for International Settlements was concerned, in December 2008, that near-zero interest rates could discourage banks from lending to other banks and that 'the scope and magnitude of the bank rescue packages also meant that significant risks had been transferred onto government balance sheets', to risk future defaults.[85]

Joseph Stiglitz's theoretical work links market economics with political economy, explaining the liquidity trap in a new light. Stiglitz explains why monetary policy may be invalidated in the present situation. What matters today is the availability of credit and the terms for obtaining it. Further, debt is resold to others, interlocking everybody and risking implosion within the system:

> In modern economies ... credit, not money, is required (and used) for most transactions, and most transactions are simply exchanges of assets, and therefore not directly related to GDP. The theory ... provides a new basis for a liquidity trap. It shifts emphasis from looking at the Fed Funds rate, or money supply, to variables of more direct relevance to economic activity, the level of credit, and the interest rates charged to firms (and it

explains the movement in the spread between that rate and the Federal Funds rate). We also analyzed the importance of credit inter-linkages. Many firms receive credit from other firms, at the same time that they provide credit to still others (violating Polonius' injunction 'neither a lender nor a borrower be' by being both.) ... a shock to one firm can be rapidly transmitted to others, in cascade with credit rationing (or the potential of credit rationing) ... not only does the firm's net worth (the market value of its assets) matter, but so does its asset structure.[86]

Indeed, nowadays, money is created in most cases when credit is granted by banks, and what we get in circulation is debt (credits emitted by banks). The Banque de France explains: 'The granting of credit by banks being at the very source of the mechanism of monetary creation, the follow up of the evolution of the distribution of the different types of banking credit naturally assumes a great importance in the definition of the orientation and conduct of monetary policy as well as in the evaluation of its effects'.[87] Moreover, all cash flows increasingly go through the financial institutions, wages included. In the event of a liquidity trap, the population at large is affected. In the case of rationing, chains of payments get stalled throughout the entire economy.

But the first, visionary, Nobel Prize winner in economics to call attention to the central role of credit in bringing about financial crises, including the Great Depression of the 1930s, was Maurice Allais.[88] For him, credit creates false rights by transformation: namely banks lending for the long term beyond the resources they can immediately dispose of. In this case, credit leads to speculation and in his view the only way to avert systemic risk entails more public regulation: to give the right of money creation back to the state, prohibit 'transformation' and banks from proprietary trading, etc. Allais also called attention to the fact that economic agents could engage in an exchange between two goods without having an idea of their value on the market. His idea was that consumption was now regulated by patrimonial phenomena based on currency.

Since such interlocked debts carry systemic risks, Skidelsky points out that taming risk with more transparency alone will not prevent future breakdowns. Following Keynes' distinction between risk and uncertainty, risk could be privately controlled but governments' role was to deal with uncertainty. 'Uncertain activities with large impacts should be controlled by the state in the public interest'.[89] In the USA, apart from reintroducing the Glass–Steagall Act to separate banking activities, there should be some restriction on international financial institutions, including higher equity ratios, a security fund, some taxation of international flows, and stricter control of home loans. We believe that the attribute of 'transnational' carries a certain importance, as not all banks operate at the transnational level. If most exchanges go through very large institutions with powerful managers, with prices set on a deal-by-deal basis, based on long-term relationships among counter-parties in close connection with those setting and changing the credit/debt worthiness, the perception of free markets made of individuals at arm-length is rather *dépassé*.

Acknowledgement of an endogenous crisis linked to credit/debt reconnects to earlier times, as seen in Laurence Fontaine's study of Ancien Regime practices, and in Fisher's and Veblen's analyses of the early twentieth century. Debt linkages meant work engagements, namely the means to maintain workers in their place, to take many others to other continents, or to ensure labour services in times of need. On the other hand, indebted persons used the linkages to ensure survival. Those in debt would, for example, work for the creditor, but by doing that, they would obtain food and lodging, namely some degree of safety. Fontaine analyses how credit practices differed according to the social and legal status of the debtor.[90] In the Ancien Regime, lowly institutionalized markets, such as today's CDSs or CDOs, showed that 'the ideal was to work in a network of mutual knowledge, the only thing capable of bringing the necessary information about partners and to give the best assurance against risk and uncertainty'.[91] Endogamy of the community is sought to protect the 'banking' system in its attachment to the credit network.

At the micro level, from the sixteenth century onwards, a new type of businessman ceased to take on moral considerations concerning debtors. In the eighteenth century, things really changed; even noble debtors were penalized. The Vatican and Rhenan nobility, in a more difficult position, resorted to decrees concerning land or works of art, subtracting them from lenders' claims. Reputation was linked, as William Stout wrote, to merchants' capacity to maintain debtors afloat, not to reduce them to bankruptcy.[92] This mix of foresight and order with flexibility and generosity carried the expectation of warding off market forces. Fontaine explains how bankruptcies were dealt with outside economic rationality, as enterprises did not face the same risks. The structure of the merchants' businesses was critical when some were chosen to survive or allowed to go under. In pre-industrial Europe, the logic of debt was plural: it allowed capturing land, controlling others' markets in labour and agriculture, and ensuring power over human beings. 'Debt is a bond of life and a knot of death'.[93] To be able to access cash enhanced the possibility of escaping destitution, debt bondage or servitude, which could explain why the idea of capital may have attracted the support of the lower classes.

At the macro level, we find quite a few similarities to the current crisis: 'the whole credit system functions as long as nobody really has the need to recover their claims. But it is enough that some of them claim payments, in a period where credit has multiplied, to set off financial panic'.[94] The geographical extension of the lack of money leaves ordinary merchants at a loss, as in France in 1760.[95] This encourages speculators, who do not have enough income to repay debts rapidly. They are then forced to sell assets or to borrow even more. But such a system only functions when the conjuncture goes upward. The solution to these crises is always to extend delays by transforming short-term into long-term debt, because interest rates lose all significance at times of money famine, since people cannot get money at any rate. At that precise moment, thesaurization, now called hoarding, and the preference for illiquidity by saving in precious metals would come in. The problem would then turn political: 'with trust and good commercial papers, a great part of trade is done without great need of money' wrote a merchant in 1758.[96]

Irving Fisher's analysis of nineteenth- and twentieth-century crises is of great value, not only because he identified the main role played by over-indebtedness followed by deflation, but also because he showed the continuous repetition of crises in capitalism.[97] Fisher described the chains of consequences following several nineteenth-century crashes in his 1933 book *Debt-Deflation Theory of Great Depressions* as the conjunction of excess debt and deflation. In the 1837, 1873 and 1893 crashes, debt was at the origin, deflation the consequence. Liquidation of assets, if concentrated, leads to the building of future leaders. The 1837 panic was followed by a five-year depression. First, there was a heavy demand for loans, and an increase in prices resulted in a bubble. After bursting, no bank wanted to pay in gold or silver coins. In the case of the 1873 panic, railroad companies had invented financial products with a fixed return. In 1871 investors doubted their value and as prices fell, these firms used short-term bank loans to keep expanding. The panic of 1873 reached the USA from the Vienna Stock Exchange crash in May, interest rates skyrocketed, and Jay Cooke and Company, the most important investment bank, defaulted on its debt in September. The stock market crashed, credit dried up, and a six-year depression with high unemployment ensued until 1879. In the process, those who were well capitalized concentrated cheap assets and established their reputation, Rockefeller and Carnegie among others. The 1893 crisis lasted for four years and was said to be due to over-investment, easy finance, speculation, and a run on currency (gold). Credit and liquidity were short, hoarding was rampant, thousands of enterprises and hundreds of banks went bankrupt. Fisher describes the path to the debt trap as one of easy money, speculation and an asset bubble stemming from new investment opportunities he called 'disturbances' creating oscillations, the standardized expectation of high returns in 'public sentiment' and 'the vogue of reckless promotions, taking advantage of the habituation of the public to great expectations' that can lead to fraud.

> Easy money is the great cause of over-borrowing. When an investor thinks he can make over 100 per cent per annum by borrowing at 6 per cent, he will be tempted to borrow, and to invest or speculate with the borrowed money. This was the prime cause leading to the over-indebtedness of 1929. Inventions and technological improvements (at the time) created wonderful investment opportunities, and so caused big debts.[98]

To deleverage, Fisher talks of liquidation of debts, causing falling prices and thus a heavier burden of the contracted debt that makes liquidation difficult. The way out is either bankruptcy or reflation through monetary and/or fiscal policies. Fisher saw disturbances as exogenous; neither innovation nor business cycles were an integral part of his explanation, and his views were not evolutionary or dynamic. He saw crises in eternal resumption. Such was the course of nature and nothing could be done about it.

When dealing with a protracted slump, Keynes followed a different path: the problem was endogenous, solutions entailed active intervention. The market *per se* would not lead to the best equilibrium, but rather maintain unemployment. Keynes was not optimistic about maintaining adequate demand in the long term. In the case of a lasting crisis, the state should sustain the economy through the level of investment, both aggregate demand and business confidence. He was in favour of public investment, not of debt-financed public works. Debt financing was an issue that Keynes avoided, but he thought it unfair that the private sector could get indebted without any negative connotations.[99] In order to prevent crises, he thought of commodity stabilization and buffer stocks, control of international capital movements, and a new international monetary system, which was only partly implemented at Bretton Woods.

With extensive international trade and capital flows, compared to the inter-war years, the relevance of Keynes' advice in today's world appears rather limited. However, Dirk Ehnts wrote:

> the General Theory could be interpreted as a model for the world economy. It becomes clear then, that too much money went into the production of investment goods. It is the faltering of demand which in the last months prompted investments to turn bad, and this is exactly what Keynes described in his General Theory ... In consequence, what is needed is (once again) a theory of capital. It should explain how savings are translated into investments in the banking or financial system, how in the process capital can be measured and how it is to be valued. This branch of economics has gone out of the mainstream, but should be brought back to light.[100]

However, this time it should be a theory of capital *and debt* that does not consider debt and the bursting of bubbles as something 'natural' and unavoidable. Debt practices have become an endogenous feature of a system being built by economic entities that have developed particular ways of organizing, institutionalized behaviour and practices, and are now taking active part in co-regulation with governments, as we will see in Chapter 3.

The debt trap

Although the arguments discussed in the first section concerning individualistic business models, monetarist and systemic accumulation hypotheses highlight diverse aspects and partly explain the crisis, the latter may be explained as a debt trap, considering that the other two traps mentioned above (consumption trap and liquidity trap) both flow into it. A debt trap is the consequence of systematic recourse to debt that thrives in contexts of increasing inequality and reduced government intervention. Opaque informal lending loads debt onto both private and public entities, and can build bubbles in asset prices just as in the eighteenth century. Recovery requires opening up the trap, for the debt must be dealt with. Choices are difficult, because debt interlinks the system; solutions are painful and losses extensive.

As we saw in Chapter 1, the background to debt is inequality. Before the crisis, the US and world growth had been sustained by a rising US house price bubble. Further explanation of indebtedness in consumption has been examined above. Depending on other factors, the consumption trap can worsen to such an extent that it may cause a systemic risk and turn into a debt trap. In 2006, George Irvin correctly described the US debt dangers lying ahead not only for the country itself but for the world at large:

> US net household debt is nearly $12 trillion and, since 2000, most of the increase consists of mortgages. Why is this dangerous? The problem is that when demand slackens and house prices eventually fall, consumers – starting with the most recent house buyers – find they hold assets worth less than the value of their debt; i.e. they hold 'negative equity'. When they can't repay their loans, the banks are saddled with 'non-performing' assets, and they in turn curtail lending (and in some cases go broke). As the Japanese experience of 1990 illustrated all too clearly, a burst property bubble can cripple an economy for years. The net indebtedness of consumers is merely part of the puzzle of US fragility. Household debt now far exceeds corporate savings, which means the private sector is in the red.[101]

The debt trap of home owners includes three major systemic issues: equity loss, the bearing on rental housing and socio-economic loss of cohesion. The three issues must be dealt with together but with varying approaches according to whether the various regions of a country have experienced a bubble or not. As housing bubbles are concentrated in some areas, the 'one policy fits all' can create real trouble. Both the USA and Spain had construction bubbles on the coasts. On the other hand, a debt trap takes hold when ownership costs 50 per cent more than the cost of renting something similar. In these cases, it may make no sense keeping people in their homes or subsidizing such housing. Home owners will tend to leave, default or turn the property into rental housing. Rental can help ease the trap of home owners, but not that of lending institutions, unless there is a specific policy and legislation to do it. Foreclosures also affect families that are evicted from rental accomodation, which further puts prices under strain. Indeed, as evictions are being carried out, demand increases, while supply of rentals diminishes due to the foreclosures. Policy must therefore include prevention of rental eviction by finding a middle ground. This helps social and territorial cohesion, as well as the timing of recovery.[102]

Beyond the issue of housing, which lay at the origin of the last bubble, the key question remains: why is debt so widely used now in the financial, productive and state spheres? There is still the need to rationally explain the function of debt in regulating systemic change. First of all, we have a world market and yet, as Susan Strange wrote, 'an important branch of social science seems blind to this kind of change... A better short answer, therefore, to the question: "Who, or what is responsible for change?" is three fold – technology, markets and politics'.[103] We would say that there has been a mix of technological, structural and value change and in such change, debt takes a key role in both the financial and the productive spheres.

In the financial sphere, globally interconnected computers have brought with them the proliferation of financial information and the standardization of products in such a way that, unless other internal information stemming from the real economy is given, they are not understandable. What is more, this technical evolution has transformed the source of profits and the financial industry itself and constrained the profit margins. Profits have ceased to come from old practices and now arise from ever more rapid computer standardized flows and new products, in particular debt. The French Centre d'Analyse Stratégique stated that 'the fall of profits from classical products since 2000 could explain the fact that investors sought their profits in risky alternative products'.[104]

In the productive sphere, deflationary tendencies have been at work not only due to policy packages, but also to the enormous growth of global supply at decreasing prices within an overall liberalization in trade of industrial goods and components. China's effective entry into the WTO in 2001 has increased the impact of such tendencies. Technical improvements in transportation, logistics and quality have made this over-supply readily available everywhere on the globe. Meanwhile, new capital goods and machinery last longer and are more productive, so replacement is effected at longer intervals and the output is larger, more constant and with fewer faults. Profit margins have diminished here as well, making it more difficult to finance new capital investment.

As far as firms are concerned, economic globalization over the last 25 years has entailed competition to enlarge business scales, and this has been done mainly through mergers and acquisitions, making use of debt mechanisms. This type of competition has taken place amidst a trend towards diminishing returns and aggregate demand. In fact, just like consumption without effective purchasing power, leveraged buy-outs of large enterprises can be done by individuals without putting a penny in them (e.g. the case of billionaire Bernard Tapie in France).[105] This may explain why the international system replacing the old international accounting, the IFRS, has not worked out a definition of equity, focusing instead on liabilities.[106] H. Kempf put it another way:

> For the first time in human history, speculation is the main source of revenue generation. The financial economy has amassed amounts 30 times higher than those exchanged within the real economy ... Now, the word 'investor' defines people or firms that play on the financial market and are nothing else than speculators.[107]

How much corporate debt was going around in Wall Street firms? An astronomic ratio of 32 to 1, according to Andrew Sorkin.[108]

And why did states use opaque debt practices, in the same way as private firms? First of all, states act upon political choices and debt is used to finance such choices. As long as debt goes into long-term productive investment, such as infrastructure and education, it can eventually be repaid, and there is nothing special about it. Yet, in the last decades, most states were ideologically constrained and under pressure from various international financial institutions and/or the so-called 'market'. Therefore, many states also used off-the-balance sheet 'vehicles' to park debt: nobody else knew except those engaged in the deal. This allowed better ratings, lowered pressure on deficits, provided leeway on public spending, and made it possible to join in a currency area such as the euro. Not only citizens, but also the financial and media industries, were happier. The problem arose when the 'vehicles' returned to the balance sheet, as in Greece.

Countries at the core of the crisis saw their debt reach maximum historic levels. On 25 August 2010, the US federal debt held by the public was $8,834,184 (principal in millions) while intra-governmental debt holdings were $4,516,439.[109] Although the figure seems colossal, its ratio to GDP is low compared to other developed countries. Debt burden comes from interest, currently at its lowest, and there is little speculation on the US dollar since it has the status of international reserve currency. However, investment prior to the crisis in the USA concentrated on a few sectors, such as the arms and defence industry, while that in domestic infrastructure, education and the overall competitiveness of the productive system, lagged behind. The crisis has suddenly inflated short-term borrowing and at some point interest rates will have to be raised. With low taxation and little national redistribution solidarity, many public services depended on local authorities and citizens' support. Now, the latter two are cash-strapped and debt-laden. The ideological consensus is breaking apart while there is no easy way out. In July 2010, the US Congressional Budget Office named gradually rising risks for the USA: 'crowding out' of investment as people's savings would go to purchase government debt; higher taxes; less leeway in fiscal policy and public spending; and a higher risk of a fiscal crisis.[110]

Before the crisis, the US consensus had a broad electoral base thanks to easy credit for part of the population together with cheap imports of inexpensive products from third-world countries where their own companies were located. The process exercised downward pressure on the income and working conditions of the lower income earners, limiting their purchasing power and leading them to use debt mechanisms in their individual consumption. The USA had a political Achilles' heel though, namely its trade deficit with third-world countries. China was so pressed to revalue its currency that it began to do so in July 2005 on the basis of a basket of currencies.[111] From that moment onwards, the US dollar went on a downward slope, whereas the euro was strongly revalued. In 2006 and 2007, the real estate and financial bubbles in China were dealt with by Chinese government decisions, including the restriction on investment and purchase of real state property by non-residents, with the exception of those having lived there for more than 12 months and with continuous activities in the country. When the rise of interest rates in the USA helped trigger the 'sub-prime' crisis, putting an end to the real estate bubble, the authorities did not pay much attention to the mounting consequences. A year later, some openly recognized that there was an issue, but thought it was merely a credit problem in housing.

Since the eighteenth century, when they abandoned the 100 per cent coverage of deposits, banks have been granting more credit than the capital they actually keep. To guarantee the printing of money, real economic activity must take place to repay the credit/debt, so that it returns to the banks and the system is sustainable. If it does not, banks park loans off balance-sheet, to keep lending. Since the 1970s, economic cycles have been linked to excessive levels of debt and the ensuing bursting of bubbles. Once economic actors are too indebted, they are obliged to stop spending. They either save more as in Asia since 1997, or they wind up existing activities in order to raise liquidity and wait until the next debt-leverage phase starts.

At that point, governments, in fear of deflation rather than inflation, undertake lax policies on credit, interest rates and liquidity. The new expansionist phase starts through enterprise leverage and household credit. Regarding business debt, Bernanke[112] lowered interest rates in the early 2000s partly to allow firms to restructure their debt by replacing long-term by short-term debt and reducing the ratio of current debt to assets.

Happy are those who manage to convert their private debt into a public one. Therefore, debt hits back, as in a revolving door, until claims are settled and real capital – not debt – starts making the real economy turn. When holders of debt are dispersed around the world with very diverse interests and agendas, settlements become more complex. Implicit and explicit liabilities and monetary debt lead to fiscal deficits, and investors seek safety.

Raines and Leathers studied the writings of Thorstein Veblen, Irving Fisher, Joseph A. Schumpeter and Hyman Minsky concerning deflation.[113] For them, Minsky was, unknowingly, the successor of Veblen's work.[114]

Fisher's 1933 explanation rests on the changing burden in nominal and real debt between prosperity and crises. While nominal debt leverage indicates there should be growth, the consequent deflation turns it into an unbearable burden of real debt that worsens the downward trend. Fisher's idea was that shocks were exogenous, rare and abnormal like a 'black swan'.

In contrast, Veblen, Schumpeter and Minsky thought that crises were endogenous and followed technological and financial innovation leading to institutional changes in both the real economy and the financial system. This view is particularly accurate in the case of the current crisis. Their differences lie in (a) the role of government policy, (b) the strategies of private business and financial actors and (c) the connection between deflation in the real economy versus deflation in the financial sector.

Hyman Minsky's financial instability hypothesis argues that firms issue debt to finance production in the expectation of future profits. During booms, the debt burdens of firms increase and therefore firms become highly leveraged with relatively lower and lower quality debt. The system becomes, in Minsky's language, 'financially fragile' and small shocks can lead to a massive one. The amount of successive bankruptcies reduces aggregate demand, leading to deflation and more bankruptcies. The debt–bankruptcy spiral had been previously argued by Keynes in 1931 and before that by Veblen.

Stiglitz explains that, in the previous periods,

> in debt contracts, typically not indexed for changes in prices, whenever prices fell below the level expected (or in variable interest rate contracts, when real interest rates rose above the level expected) there were transfers from debtors to creditors. In these circumstances, excessive downward price flexibility (not just price rigidities) could give rise to problems. These (and other) redistributive changes had large real effects, and could not be insured against because of imperfections in capital markets. Large shocks could lead to bankruptcy, and with bankruptcy (especially when it results in firm liquidation) there was a loss of organizational and informational capital ... If firms were credit rationed, then reductions in liquidity could have particularly marked effects. What is important is the availability of credit (and the terms at which it is available); this in turn is related to the certification of credit worthiness by banks and other institutions.[115]

In the case of household consumption, whereas prices decrease, the outstanding debt does not, and it may be better to let go of the item than to repay the debt incurred. This micro-economic situation, once it begins to multiply, can lead to a macro-economic deflationary process. For the creditor, mounting liabilities reflect a weak prospect that affects even the option of taking over the item in question. For an economic system as a whole, exponential structural debt constantly needs to increase liquidity to roll the debt over, carrying with it a growing systemic risk if the rolling over is halted.

The problem with the debt trap is that it potentially keeps trapping one 'victim' after another, like an open 'state of emergency', usually affecting first the smaller, the weaker and the peripheral. As mentioned above, credit is not bad *per se*, but its dark shadow is indebtedness. The latter is difficult to measure, since it depends on the conditions under which credit is contracted and how such conditions can be modified. Therefore, it is linked to the power relationship inscribed in the credit thus obtained. To prevent being trapped, information about changing conditions is vital but not sufficient. In hindsight, positioning to enjoy timely access to information flows and the articulation of the information are both necessary. It is therefore by improving timely access to information flows and by articulating such flows that changing credit conditions may be better dealt with.

In the end, the debt trap can be solved by political will, as in the recent pardon of African countries' debt. But what cannot be solved is what the debt trap leaves behind, namely the sheer destruction of wealth. It is similar to environmental damage: even if damage is halted and consequences are cleaned up, patience has to be employed until the system restores its balance. Or the system may become so unstable as to trigger great storms and disasters.

Debt has also played a key role in global labour relations and contributed to our current environmental concerns. In capitalism, debt has served two major goals complementing each other: 'to supply a sufficient amount of suitable labour'[116] and to lower wages compared to that which a free labour market would generate. In past periods, debt incurred to obtain credit was in great part the cause of servitude, besides slavery, serfdom and indenture. In debt bondage, labour was the source of collateral for credit. In eighteenth century Virginia, about three-quarters of whites arrived as bonded men, channelled first by the Virginia Company and then by English merchants. In the 1770s, 79 per cent of those arriving in this situation went to Virginia and Maryland.[117] Faced with the debt incurred by the Atlantic crossing, people accepted being sold into servitude or into bonded landless labour, in a parallel process to the slavery of black people. When their bondage was over, they either returned to Europe or were free to stay in the new country. Bush[118] thus believes that the US idea of personal freedom is related to modern servitude, including debt-regulated labour, and slavery. In addition, debt bondage thus laid the grounds not simply for consumerism but also for contempt for the resources of nature.[119, 120]

Conclusion

Although the explanations discussed in the first section do cover part of the causes that led to the crisis, we contend that the latter may be explained as a trap. After introducing the concept of a consumption trap closing around increasingly indebted individuals and households, and of a liquidity trap concerning monetary and credit circulation as a critical moment, we discuss the idea of a systemic debt trap as an endogenous trait of the current system. We thus see capital *and* debt as key elements of the system, and not only capital, echoing explanations by Veblen and Minsky.

A debt trap is the consequence of systematic recourse to debt that thrives in contexts of increasing inequality and reduced government intervention. Opaque informal lending loads debt onto both private and public entities. The consumption trap, appearing in the case of consumers and households, feeds into the build-up to the debt trap. Economic entities without appropriate internal mechanisms of checks and balances develop a preference for debt for various reasons, engaging in an unstable path. Finally, bubbles in asset prices may also emerge, increasingly speculative, just as in the eighteenth century.

Due to technological development and global free financial flows, opaque lending and the rolling back of the state, debt practices inflate and shorten. When an event halts the possibility of rolling over debt, the liquidity trap appears as the critical moment in which the debt trap closes in. The halting of credit and generalized fear transmits to the real economy, leading to contraction or depression. Recovery requires opening up the trap, as debt must be dealt with, and recourse to further debt avoided. Choices are difficult, because debt interlinks the system further; solutions are painful and complex; losses may be extensive. A debt trap will appear infrequently as long as real capital in all its forms is given preference over debt, equality is considered an investment to prevent structural indebtedness, and the long-term generation of wealth is distinguished from rapid growth and quick profit making.

This crisis is the most recent one in a long string of bubbles and debt crises. During the past decades, however, such crises were seen as events affecting only developing and emerging countries, from Asia to Russia, Turkey, Brazil and Argentina, to name a few. This time, however, both developed countries and the core of the global financial system were in the eye of the storm. The impact of the crisis spread across the globe but, as soon as the shock subsided, the management of its consequences has mainly been left to national and local governments, with a string of bailouts and structural adjustment policies such as in Latvia, Hungary and Greece, as well Ireland by the end of 2010, with more countries at risk of following suit. Debt must be dealt with, and to achieve this, a new political and social consensus must first emerge on how to break free from the debt trap: how much longer will we wait to make the difference, as Keynes did, between strategic investment in the real economy and finance policy, and between uncertainty and risk? How do we deal with inequality to avoid the consumption trap? How do we prevent and/or limit leverage that makes economic entities and our very future so vulnerable?

3
Shifting Control *versus* Ownership

Introduction

This chapter goes one layer deeper in explaining the build up to the crisis: indeed, we attempt here to demonstrate that a key link exists between the systemic debt trap (a macro issue) examined in Chapter 2 and the profound changes that have occurred over the last few decades in the pattern of control of economic entities (a micro/meso issue).

In the same way as, in Chapter 2, we discussed debt in relation to capital, this chapter deals with control in relation to ownership. We argue that, over the last decades, control in economic entities (banks, pension funds, TNCs etc.) has gradually been playing a more central role than ownership. Even though ownership, of course, remains important, its contours seem to be increasingly blurred. We also argue that the shift in control from stakeholders, including owners and producers, towards absentee control, has been facilitated by the simultaneous drives towards financialization and technification.

Well before the global financial crisis started, many scholars had discussed a new form of capitalism, either financialized or technified,[1] emerging amidst state deregulation and liberalization of exchanges. With financialization, the productive side and the generalized use of debt come to the fore. With technification, the major issue is rationality or rather the loss of it.

The first section of this chapter explains why, when discussing such macro issues as the debt trap, it is essential to examine the issue of how economic entities are organized. The global crisis prompts us to discuss the question of control in economic entities beyond public policy, co-regulation between private and public actors, and even self-regulation of entities seen as 'black boxes'.

The second section deals with the evolution of the concepts of control and ownership in conventional firms, and their reciprocal relationship, as well as the impact on them of financialization and technification, whereas control and ownership in cooperatives, defined as joint ownership and democratic control (a concept which should in no way be confused with centralized control), will be examined in Chapter 4.

In the third section, we observe how the shift in control takes place in relation to the basic roles linked to economic entities, namely the investor, the producer and the consumer, changing the building of the 'market', favouring debt practices and making the economic system increasingly unstable and vulnerable.

The relevance of discussing the organization of economic entities

What could be the relevance of discussing the organization of economic entities (firms, banks etc.) in connection with the debt trap if the latter is a systemic feature? Can behavioural and organizational patterns prevent a systemic debt trap? As we saw in the first section of Chapter 2, a number of authors do work at the level of firms in relation to the crisis, dealing with individual incentives and calling for a more ethical behaviour by bankers and traders. However, could such calls change a whole industry and prevent more crises? Micro-behaviour can certainly make a difference, but it can surely make a larger one if, across the board, new organizational patterns emerge, based on less predatory behaviour. Of course, in the event of a crisis, the more resilient economic entities can help by saving as much as possible from the wreckage. But a few individuals or enterprises cannot *per se* prevent a systemic debt trap.

In turn, the main arguments in favour of considering that the organization of economic entities could possibly be related to the debt trap and the crisis belong, in our view, to political economy considerations.

First, the sheer importance and impact of very large firms engaged in multiple activities across the globe bring about systemic risk to the economic system as a whole. Such systemic risk is now global because these economic entities have intertwined processes, products and activities in the financial sphere as well as in the real economy through globalized chains of production, distribution and finance, and, on top of that, have come to be connected among each other and through the now globalized stock-market system (as seen in Chapter 1). Confronted with such systemic risk, public authorities are not only the lenders of last resort but also the ultimate guarantors of social peace and, therefore, tend to do anything to sustain those firms, no matter what they do, while the average citizen foots most of the bill.

Second, many global actors (institutions, firms etc.) exert control from afar – as absentees – upon multiple economic entities. These entities under control tend to be marginal to the core interest of such global actors, sometimes temporary objects of interest. Yet, absentee controllers, in particular by capturing information, tend to heavily intervene in every detail of the economic entities under control, and to restrict their autonomy and rationality. When this happens in firms, they should more accurately be called 'quasi-firms'.[2] This practice, which is taking place on a wide scale across the world, focuses on rapid growth and profit-taking, and ends up hindering the long-term generation of wealth, which is key to the stability of the world economy.

Third, the distinction between private economic entities and public policy making has become obsolete: we should no longer think of public policy as totally separate from the world of firms. Over the last three decades, different types of large economic entity (both in the financial sphere and the 'real economy') have dramatically increased their level of influence over governments. The impact on US federal policy-making of 'shadow banking' actors prior to the crisis, recounted in Chapter 2 (the consumption trap), is just one example of this global phenomenon. But large economic entities are not only influential through conventional lobbying activities: in many cases, they are directly engaged in co-regulation with public authorities. Co-regulation has been integrated into a renewed concept of governance that steers away from the idea of public political authorities exercising hierarchical control over society. Studies of two parallel trends, globalization and regionalism (the European Union being an emblematic example of the latter), illustrate that the act of governing now includes private actors.

According to Renate Mayntz, the first trend in public–private co-regulation calls for 'a new mode of governing ... a more cooperative mode where state and non-state actors participate in mixed public/private networks'.[3] Today, the European Union explicitly promotes the participation of private economic actors under the concept of 'governance', which 'means rules, processes and behaviour that affect the way in which powers are exercised at European level'.[4] According to the EU White Paper on Governance, the latter is characterized by a 'multi-level' sphere that includes 'global governance' and 'economic and financial governance'. The White Paper uses the word 'actors' to refer to the key actors in each financial and economic sector, namely the very large firms: the 'actors' are called to build 'partnerships' on the basis of their 'skills and practical experience' in order to be more effectively involved in the 'shaping, application and enforcement of Community rules and programmes'. Several 'Regulatory Agencies' (some already established, others in the making) will work on the basis of the actors' 'sectoral know-how'.[5] Because of this power sharing, firms are now seen as political actors, as Sally Razeen observes.[6] A major question to ask is: can firms be partners in government in its broad sense and fulfil a co-regulatory role if they keep feeding on bubbles, traps and crises, after which they are saved by citizens' money?

The second trend in the study of governance is equally important. Schmitter[7] and Abbot and Snidal[8] link it to transnational standardization, aimed at the coordination of individual and social actions transnationally. In this case, economic entities acquire an increasingly central role because they obtain information that not even governments possess any more. The latter, therefore, welcome co-regulatory arrangements that cover specific policy issues and arenas, which may eventually decide policy agendas, goals and instruments.

The debate on the organization, rationality and long-term sustainability of economic entities should thus go beyond the issue of individual incentives and individual ethical behaviour, which is very important indeed, but on which we cannot place our only hope. Before returning to this discussion, we first need to distinguish what is control from what is ownership.

Ownership and control

The evolution of the concepts of ownership and control

For Thorstein Veblen, the origins of ownership resided in the social recognition of enforced control over a human being. In his view, women were the first object of personal property.[9] In this line of reasoning, control came first, turning into ownership through social recognition and, finally, into status. Laurence Fontaine also uses the example of women in the study of early modern economic practices to assert that, in order to be economically active, human beings need to exert enough control over their property and within family decision making.[10] The argument is that access to, and enjoyment of, property is not sufficient to exert control, while control is necessary to become an economic actor. In order to actively take part in the economy and the market, not only the know-how but also the 'power-to' and the support networks count, touching upon education, rights, social roles and social capital. Otherwise, it is not possible to enjoy legal responsibility or to take part in implicit and explicit contracts. When specific subjects are denigrated by being described as unable of effecting control, their rights to ownership are minimized.[11]

In nineteenth-century economic thought, in turn, ownership began to receive far more attention than control. Theories expected things to be owned for a lifetime and beyond, and the owner of the object had absolute power to decide on it. Even in the case of property disposal, ownership attracted more attention than control.

Joseph Stiglitz explains that:

> in traditional economic theories bankruptcy played little role, partly because control (who made decisions) did not matter, and so the change in control that was consequent to bankruptcy was of little moment, partly because with perfect information, there would be little reason for lenders to lend to someone, rather than extending funds through

equity (especially if there were significant probabilities of, and costs to, bankruptcy).[12]

Credit would have been impaired, 'without "clear owners" those in control would in general not have incentives to maximize the firm's value'.[13]

At the beginning of the twentieth century, Veblen proposed a critical analysis of control on firms. For him, shareholders of his time exercised control over listed companies, but financial control was not necessarily good. Veblen differed from Marx's idea of surplus extraction on behalf of vested interests to obtain a 'free income' and extravagant benefits in that he did not deal with labour value. He placed the emphasis on financial and consultancy vested interests and he talked of 'capitalism' as distinct from 'capital', with endogenous risks to capital development and wealth creation.

In Veblen's analysis, one of the main critical limits to the expansion or reproduction of capitalism was the risk of too great a level of exploitation of industry by business, namely financial concerns.[14] When this happens, too much of the surplus is distributed to activities such as takeovers, speculation, advertising, warfare and so on, and not enough going to activities that enhance productivity, productive investment, knowledge and skills. For Veblen, '[b]y this process of growth, such businesslike management of the industrial system has become incompatible with the current state of the industrial arts' and 'the continued management of industry for business purposes results in an industrial stalemate'.[15]

A century later, in 2010, a speech by Lord Mandelson was pure Veblen:

> [T]he result of intermediation and diversity has been to turn most shareholders into absentee or transient owners of companies ... This risks rewarding clever readers of the market more than industrial innovation, quality management, or entrepreneurial skill. On the face of it, it does not seem a model good at building companies with the patient but engaged ownership required for low carbon innovation or infrastructure investment or manufacturing on the back of new technologies in Britain.[16]

This disregard for the disposition of real assets recalls the concept of 'patrimonialism' (as distinct from 'patrimony') in Max Weber's work as a type of rule with many variants in which the powerful take discretionary, arbitrary and unexpected decisions, in a system coupled with liturgical elements.[17] Weber contrasted them to rational bureaucracy that cared for assets in the long term. We wonder whether this period could not be thought of as a sort of 'neo-global-patrimonialism'.

After observing the renewed interest in the concept of 'control' in the field of financial reporting (which aims to replace accounting), and the shift in the positioning of large companies striving to build a 'service streaming' economy, the issue of control has come back to centre stage at the beginning of the twenty-first century.

Financialization

In the middle of the twentieth century, as Alfred Chandler explains in *Scale and Scope*, managers rose in the hierarchical control of firms.[18] With the growth of the large international firm and its financing through the stock market, the separation between ownership and control became an issue again, although the belief in perfect information blurred the distinction.

Over the last decades, the ideological consensus tried to impose the idea that control was equal to ownership and the latter to the financial share, while top managers were turning into financial investors and owners: a state of affairs resembling Veblen's time. Everything else was ditched as 'fuzzy'. Yet we often find the opposite: for example, 'fuzzy' share-holding in some joint-ventures, where the venture is controlled by only one of the partners without taking on all the risks and legal responsibilities that come with ownership. The building of global chains and business groups has led to a very rapid turnover of ownership rights and many 'fuzzy' arrangements.[19]

In 2005, European Commissioner Charles McCreevy tried hard to impose on the whole EU the idea that 'economic democracy' meant one-share one-vote and that one financial share equalled one share of control:[20] therefore, the more shares, the more votes. Any attempt to place any type of limitation by the enterprise founders or the family owners was to be banned. The Commissioner failed because most firms and institutions in the EU staunchly opposed his project. The EU Economic and Social Committee expressed the opinion that 'the European company model in a market economy considers the company as a collective; regardless its statute, it remains a key factor in human society and a bond in our economic system'.[21] In such a model, power voting rights are not equal to financial shares, and enterprise rationality may therefore not be equal to financial rationality.

More recently, the differentiation between ownership and control has been addressed by the International Accounting Standards Board (IASB) and the Federal Accounting Standards Board (FASB) in the new International Financial Reporting Standards (IFRS), already discussed in Chapters 1 and 2. According to the recent debate in both the IASB and the FASB, it is said that: 'some users misinterpret the term control and use it in the same sense as that used for purposes of consolidation accounting. The term [control] should focus on whether the entity has some rights or privileged access to the economic resource'.[22] Therefore, a 'controlling' entity has access to, or privilege over, an economic resource, while ownership is related to the net assets: 'under the basic ownership approach, an instrument would be classified as equity if it (...) entitles the holder to a share of the entity's net assets'.[23]

In our current system, owners may or may not be those in control of the venture and of its resources. As seen in the previous section, and as Veblen explained in 'Absentee Ownership',[24] financial and other vested interests could control the firm to the peril of the latter, by which the firm's owner loses out to the investor under the form of debt in a highly leveraged manner.[25] We will come back to the investor function below.

Technification

Technification accrues the impact of financialization through standardization, mathematical modelling and financial decimalization. It facilitates both the movement of financial flows and control by financial absentee investors. The technification of finance intertwined with the real economy adds paradoxical questions concerning rationality. In the end, it increases the risk of systemic implosion due to interlinkages as well as nihilistic attitudes from human beings.

Neither technology nor science is responsible for our traps and crises. Technology that serves social, craft and artistic needs has brought great advancement. Greek philosophers like Plato and Aristotle used the word *Techne* for technical solutions to survival needs, always subordinated to life and social priorities. In the East, technology means engaging in the world with technical means to improve effectiveness, but always subordinated to a socio-political understanding of the situation and context, similar to the Ancient Greeks. Chinese philosophy and Taoism see the world in constantly changing movement. *Wu wei* (無爲) and *wu nian* (無念) respectively refer to 'not on purpose' (or rather 'not forcefully') and 'no thought' (or rather 'not dominated by thought'). This is an approach to an immanent system that takes things as they are, but without having in mind a teleological deployment of destiny.[26]

Since the seventeenth century, in the West, technology has taken over the Greek concept to currently signify techno-science. The problem appears when social linkages are over-determined by the prevalent use of technology. Our age is especially prone to this: on the one hand, we believe that technology is there to make our life secure, such as machines in the nineteenth century. Recently, this belief has been compounded with the 'zero-risk' angst, which rejects instability and the unexpected. On the other hand, globalization has brought with it a process of standardization of parts and components, processes and communication, with the idea of facilitating global trade and simplifying regulation. Between standardization and 'zero-risk', technology has an impact today that goes well beyond the means and arts of production. It is a key driver of our modern culture and civilization.

Many thinkers have warned us that technology potentially entails the risk of losing sense, leading to tyranny and even totalitarianism, among them Husserl, Habermas and Heidegger.[27] Others have argued against the loss of responsibility in a system organized like a machine, which may result in extreme dehumanized behaviour.

The current approach to technology comes from another Western tradition.[28] In the West, the episteme of an eternal and transcendental being facilitates this approach to technification: as the necessary and progressive manifestation of a programmed determination over life. Technification of decision making can adapt to continuing change because it functions on the basis of hypotheses. On such a basis, machines can automatically relay orders to the 'market', to which humans should constantly keep adapting. In turn, human beings feel that they are losing control.

Psychologist and philosopher Umberto Galimberti explains how human capabilities of perception and imagination are paralysed by both the magnitude of technical performance and 'the infinite fragmentation of working processes ... in which, after a certain number of passages ... we find out that we are no longer capable of following the thread, with the consequent obliteration of the sense of whatever we may be doing'.[29] The more gigantic the effects, the more interlinked with other structures, the less capable we are of perceiving the processes, the effects and the scope and condition of which we are part. In such a gap, humans tend to react with an inadequate sense of responsibility or the lack of it. How can traders, bankers and absentee investors become aware of risks if technification may render them incapable of it? Furthermore, the system can be halted or implode with almost complete instantaneity. Any small human mistake is now automatically relayed by computers directly connected to financial trading platforms. An originally small mistake can lead to a systemic breakdown, as occurred in May 2010 in Wall Street. Recent technology applied to the financial sphere leaves no time to think twice or doubt; the activity of high-frequency trading computers is hardly perceptible.

In Chapter 2, we mentioned that financial decimalization had led to higher risk taking. First, when profits ceased to come from old practices, they were transferred to ever more rapid computer standardized flows. Moreover, purely abstract data facilitate the total capture of the original information. How can the large majority of people be aware of the risks involved? In *Irrational Exuberance*, Robert Shiller talks of computer use that leads to risk-taking strategies.[30] Just before the crisis exploded, not even global financial institutions, so proud of their computer technology, were able to keep track of what their workers – traders – were doing. Financial innovation called 'securitization' and aimed at lowering risk, was not that secure after all.

Recently, Nobel Prize winners in physics and chemistry have attempted to initiate a new understanding in economics. Benoit Mandelbrot and Richard Hudson have discussed the current crisis following chaos and fractals theory.[31] For them, as for Minsky, stability tends to be temporary.

Keynes worried about the use of mathematical modelling and over complex language. Skidelsky claims that Keynes 'would have been utterly opposed to financial innovation beyond the bounds of ordinary understanding, and therefore control'.[32] Keynes' belief in uncertainty and Minsky's financial instability hypothesis are calling us back to real life. We thus need to rethink what could function as effective checks and balances or 'opposition' in Susan Strange's words.[33]

Control *versus* ownership in key economic functions

The investor function

Adair Turner, who was appointed Chairman of the UK Financial Services Authority in 2008, has talked of an industry serving needs: 'A global market economy remains the best means of delivering global prosperity: it requires a global banking system focused on serving the needs of businesses and households, not in taking risks for quick return'.[34]

However, the biggest shift in the role of finance in the last 20 years has done the opposite, during the passage from passive to 'active investor' that has gradually built powerful world actors: investment funds and sovereign wealth funds. The passive financial shareholder has turned into an active controller while the active agent or manager has turned into an owner.

A shareholder economy is supposed to be an economy in which the shareholders are the owners and controllers of the enterprise. Until the 1980s, financial shareholders were predominantly concerned with the expected financial dividends delivered by enterprises in which they held shares, forgetting their role as controllers. As a consequence, managers tended to have a *de facto* predominant power over the organization and strategy of economic entities even if they did not hold shares, resulting in an increasing gap between ownership (in the hands of the traditional shareholders) and control (in the hands of the managers).[35]

The development of global supply chains, together with the use of debt mechanisms, has altered this order. On the one hand, financial interests have gained more control, whereas the managers retain power but increasingly hold shares, thus becoming owners. Middle-level management has been particularly reduced in restructurings following mergers and acquisitions. This affects the internal flow of information and work organization within firms: trust diminishes; communication keeps changing the message; negotiations with other stakeholders become difficult; arrangements are only temporarily effective.

Tensions arise between the rationality of financial interests in short-term returns, external to the firm, and the long-term development of the firm. Compromises need to be made and debt weighs the balance in favour of creditors and their changing conditions. Absentee global shareholders bring with them borrowed money that leaves the firm indebted and under external control, and loaded with costly charges related to consultancy, services and restructuring. If the short-term benefits do not follow, they can easily divest and reinvest elsewhere. Whenever these increasingly absentee owners and controllers do not shoulder entrepreneurial risk as owners in the real economy, they may hardly be considered as stakeholders.

Meanwhile, the real stakeholders of the enterprise (producers, workers, suppliers, clients), namely those having a stake in the enterprise as a productive unit, sharing the risk if the enterprise goes through a crisis, defaults or is liquidated, lose bargaining influence. The external controllers instead can maintain benefits, if they believe they should do so, by allocating production parts or processes to other units in other regions of the world. Enterprises become like replaceable chips. Global experts and advisers coordinate the process: they identify, target and/or store units (in a pool under surveillance, e.g. equity funds, etc.) to insert them later wherever it may seem beneficial.

Debt provides benefits to investors as a disciplinary tool to control managers and as a tax shield.[36] The first reason is that, under financial pressure, enterprise managers will pursue shareholder value more aggressively. The penalty for not doing it well is not necessarily the withholding of rewards for the firm managers. Benefits to management do not normally appear in the standard recommendations of business associations. The penalty would rather be a takeover by new financial 'owners'. A private equity guide shows that the project is presented to managers as a major way to turn into owners of the enterprise themselves.[37] The agent would have a key interest in the firm's share value above all. Concerning the preference for debt as a tax shield, recent studies show that 'empirical results confirm a robust and significant positive impact of tax-rate differences within multinational groups on the use of internal debt, supporting the view that internal debt is used to shift taxable profits to low-tax countries'.[38]

Thus the key to acquisition and the firm's Damocles sword is debt leverage, leaving the firm in a net of debt interlinkages. Joseph Stiglitz, in his analysis, emphasized 'the supply side effects of shocks, the interrelationships between supply and demand side effects, and the importance of *finance* in propagating fluctuations', and recognized that 'the problems that we saw with the models that we were taught was not only that they seemed wrong, but that they left a host of phenomena and institutions unexplained … Why did equities, which provided far better risk diversification than debt, play such a limited role in financing new investment[?]'[39]

In the case of private equity, taxation is a major issue, as Watt and Galgóczi point out, as the 'national taxation systems seem to privilege the private equity business model in a discriminatory way in a number of areas. The private equity model is clearly tailored to reducing the tax liability of its portfolio companies. Interest payments on bank loans are tax deductible (privileging debt over equity) in almost all jurisdictions'.[40]

The shift began with the pension funds as key new actors in finance. Michael Useem studied this evolution, and showed how US pension funds, both local public and private enterprises such as that of General Motors, were chronically underfunded.[41] Their pools, as in Krugman's depiction of the baby-sitting co-op (see Chapter 2), were too small and dependent on few big donors. They were unsustainable in the long run. Instead of enlarging the base to make them open, sustainable and fluid, the choice was to extract profits from abroad. Several strategies comprised taking part in the huge wave of privatizations worldwide, starting in Latin America and ensuring that liberalization allowed their financial flows to be automatic. In addition, in 1992, the US government requested American investors in pension funds to behave exactly in the same fashion as at home, namely as 'active investors' calling for them to control any enterprise in which they placed money, in order to restructure and extract as much profit as possible. According to Useem, they knew that by doing so they would soon be requesting the standardization of all enterprises in the world. Consequently, to allow for evaluation across the board, automatic and easily understandable in their native language, the US government had already begun to work on the International Accounting Standards within NAFTA with Mexico and Canada in the early 1990s.[42] By the mid-1990s, they were well aware that the position of the USA in the world was sustained primarily by world foreign assets, and that they had to work out a way of evaluating them.

The debt crisis in the developing countries, following the bubble of easy credit in the 1970s that burst with the then Federal Reserve Chairman Paul Volcker's decision to raise interest rates, forced these countries to open up their economies and their enterprises to foreign acquisition. His successor, Alan Greenspan, in turn, provided massive liquidity, following the October 1987 stock market crisis and the early 1990s recession, when banks were dealing with losses in real estate and foreign loans. As of 1992, accounting standards activity and pension funds 'active' investment in foreign assets gradually built an alliance. This alliance, articulated through the stock market, believed that the world could follow Greenspan's leadership in a steady upward 'fair value'. US monetary policy therefore adjusted to these needs, without simply reflating the economy through consumption. In addition, innovation in information technology contributed to the idea of phasing out money, and banks turned depositors and owners into standardized contractual service users.

Just as with any other actor in the financial sector, banks took an active part in the globalization process before the crisis, engaged in concentration, mergers and acquisitions, enlarging their own business scales. Those not engaged in the trend were soon acquired by others. According to *American Decades*, during the period:

> [f]inancial analysts attributed the record profits generated to these massive consolidations ... In 1997 the income of the banking industry was $59.2 billion, an increase of 13 percent ($51.5 billion) over 1996. According to statistics compiled by the Federal Deposit Insurance Corporation (FDIC), 599 bank mergers took place in 1997 alone, reducing the number of banks in the United States from nearly 14,000 to 9,143. Consolidation

sent bank stocks soaring. From their low point in 1990, bank stocks rose nearly twice as fast as average stocks, which themselves increased in value at a rate nearly twice as fast as the historical standard.[43]

The big battle was to reach the largest possible scale in order to take part in foreign asset acquisitions on behalf of pension funds. The banks worried more than anything else about offering all the necessary services to all those engaged in such funds. In this sense, the US Senate hearing on Goldman Sachs on 27 April 2010 was revealing. The banks' relationship with large institutional investors turned into their core interest. This relationship was one of counter-party, of equals in specific initiatives where both had a joint interest. Counter-party action and being a market maker became important, not client relations. On the other hand, as foreign asset acquisitions multiplied while the financial world remained volatile, banks knew that active investors would need hedging.

The banking system was geared to be functional. Even commercial banks had to adapt to the pressure of citizens and small investors that compared banks looking for financial returns. According, again, to *American Decades*:

> Mergers were part of a complex, ongoing revolution that by the 1990s had already begun to transform banking, finance, and investment. At the centre of this revolution was a conflict between what bankers call 'consolidation' and 'disintermediation', the latter meaning the removal of intermediaries, for example banks, from financial transactions. The advocates of 'disintermediation', such as computer-software giants Microsoft and Intuit, believe that the future belongs to companies that can master new technology and give customers and investors almost total control over their finances',[44]

which means bypassing banks. At this stage, making banks more ethically accountable or breaking them down may not prevent future bubbles or debt traps, although it might restrain some of the risks. Even if banks disappear, other institutions are in place to take control of real-economy enterprises.

However, in order to avoid instability and let the real economy grow, pension funds may have, after all, to be embedded again in the real economy, probably region-wise, in as open and broad a manner as possible. This goes against the predominant predicament that covering the whole population is too costly and that privatization is necessary to find the missing revenue through both financial markets and equity participation in assets and enterprises abroad. Still caught up in this predicament, pension funds in 2010 sought more powers to check on managers through the proxy ballot option. A good question is what would happen if large Chinese pension funds, with money from hundreds of millions of people, began to come to the USA as active investors to restructure US enterprises and quickly sell them on to another Chinese fund, requesting accounting information in Chinese? And what would happen if developed economies began closing their companies and organizations to foreign pension funds' equity participation and control? We can assume there would a rethinking of the whole business model based on the active investor.

Some measures are being considered to calm down speculators looking for short-term gains from financial products. Financial instruments and investment abroad would have to be declared and may be taxed in the future. In February 2010, the FASB and IASB agreed on the future income declaration. Instead of net income, the financial declaration should state a 'comprehensive income' reflecting future gains and losses, thus not yet realized, including expected ones on securities or derivatives, pension costs, foreign investments and currency hedges. In addition, the financial declaration will have to provide one amount for the aggregate income tax effects on the comprehensive income.[45]

In the UK, Lord Mandelson, in his speech of 1 March 2010, explained that:

> [t]he debate that is happening within business on business models, especially the reliance on debt over equity, needs to be part of a wider reassertion of the values of the long term, of organic growth and value creation over the temptations of excessive leverage and the fast buck. One of the big problems behind the credit crunch was a sort of financial abstraction. People and companies bought and sold financial assets with little regard to the real assets they represented. At the centre of financial markets is the tension between the need for long term investment in a real asset, and the desire for short term gain from a financial asset. Should the prerogatives of the latter trump those of the former? What kind of economy will we end up with if they do? We have to address these questions.[46]

As we have seen here, the active investor has taken on a role that has shifted the borders between ownership and control, by which asserting control over the entire enterprise has also led to the latter's standardization, not so much to improve the firm's efficiency as to ensure easier valuation and financial information, and thus flexibility and replaceability within global chains. Yet, many do not regard financial holders as owners, as they are not aligned with the long-term interest of the business, taking a temporary financial stake. We shall now discuss real-economy stakeholders, such as entrepreneurs and workers, and how notions of control and ownership may be shifting for them as well.

The producer function

Much of the critique has been addressed to the financial sector in general, and bankers and traders in particular. Yet the growing demand for debt instruments has not only been in the interest of the financial sector but a systemic feature of the current mode of production. This missing link is a key factor in the shifting boundaries between ownership and control in the sphere of production. The producer function seems to be changing for both owners and workers in the real economy. The treatment of workers as service units and firms as replaceable chips in global supply chains are two symptoms of this phenomenon. The issue of control and ownership in relation to the function of producer is discussed below in relation to *presentee* owners in the real economy that may include workers (through employee shareholding schemes), as well as workers in the traditional sense who own nothing of the firm.

Presentee owners

One of the main arguments in favour of the financialization of the firm is the pressure exerted on management to cut down wages and raise productivity. But it is public knowledge now that many mergers have failed to create long-term value. Another view is that firms otherwise have to rely more heavily on retained earnings.[47] In 2008, Robin Blackburn explained the crisis as the result of the evolution towards financialization in which debt was a central element.[48] Capital markets are key enablers of the use of debt, with the expectation that firms are capable of controlling risk. The issue of risk, in particular the aversion to unrewarded risk, justifies financial hedging and speculation. At the level of the firm, risk aversion has led to excessive debt. And the use of debt without limits and transparency can make the system sink as in a 'black hole'.

We are used to thinking only of nation-states and banks as being in need of rolling over debts to continue functioning. Yet, firms are nowadays doing the same. Take, for example, the French case: gross indebtedness of all enterprises to the financial sector rose from 111 per cent in 2004 to 121 per cent in 2008, the worst ratio since 1991. Between 1991 and 1998, enterprises deleveraged to 100 per cent. Between 1998 and 2001, around the time of the internet bubble, they got into a debt frenzy again and did not deleverage. In 2008, their financing needs took 7 per cent of their added value. Indebtedness went partly to new investments that could give them new income to repay debt, but a large part also went to the distribution of dividends, bonuses and other rewards. To equal the amount of investment and gains, while increasing dividends and bonuses, enterprises must look for further borrowing. At the height of the global crisis, firms were cut off from the amounts they needed, and forced to deleverage by shedding anything they could, from labour to unproductive or costly plants.[49]

Why would firms prefer to use debt mechanisms and not equity financing? The first argument is that managers hold key information and tend to know whether their shares are overpriced or not. If they are, they would be unlikely to issue new equity shares, because that would signal lower future returns.[50] In this sense, the application of the pro-cyclical fair-value system in an upward trend would enhance the use of debt instead of equity. Moreover, only when debt obligations are not available would enterprise managers turn to issuing shares because the latter may dilute their control, and more so in the case of the entry of 'active investors'. On the other hand, during a crisis, banks find the opportunity to convert debt into equity, extending their influence in the real economy. In Italy, for example, between 2008 and 2010, the conversion of debt to equity and the subscription to capital increases or the purchase of equity packages by banks multiplied, even if the creditors were reluctant: the amount converted by banks into equity was approximately 2 billion euro, as compared to the 46 billion euros of debt restructured since the start of the crisis.[51]

'Control' as a systemic element on which the use of debt and leverage has an impact was proposed by Ruigrok and Van Tulder as early as 1995.[52] Using a political economy approach, they analysed the competition among industrial groups and chains. The concept of control, in their terms, is an ideal type referring to an 'entire set of desired bargaining relations', not only within a firm but also across firms linked in chains.

The IASB's separation of control, in terms of resources and ownership of assets, explained above, seems to echo Ruigrok and Van Tulder's earlier analysis of sets of 'bargaining relations', which determine both privileged access and impact on economic resources in the process of international restructuring, as well as on the management of those resources to produce goods and services. International political economy and institutional theory can improve our understanding, since the search for the internationalization of stock and capital provisions, followed by standardization, corresponds to the needs of firms in the real economy that are leading globalization. Ruigrok and Van Tulder discuss five control dilemmas in capitalism: control over the labour process, over supply, over distribution and consumption, over (production) technologies, and over finance. These dilemmas are resolved differently and various types of control may be in rivalry with each other. When one becomes predominant, it may do so for a temporary period. For example, 'the Toyotist logic of outsourcing and vertical de-integration is also applied to the financial sphere. Toyotist firms generally own only a minority of their operating capital. Under Toyotism, debt-equity relations of 80 per cent are not exceptional. These debts are usually shared by several banks'.[53]

When we go to the macro level in terms of market building, characterized by competition for business scales within globalization, we can observe that the building of global chains of production and distribution has been leading to structural control instead of direct control, thus blurring the issues of ownership and control.

Control from within becomes even more vital due to the lack of clear public regulation. In 1997, at the very end of his book *Globalization: Critical Reflections*, James Mittelman affirmed that globalization:

> is about challenges that emerge from the loss of control over economic and technological flows that circumvent the globe and easily escape

regulatory frameworks. There is not only a reconstitution of the role and purpose of the state but also, to varied degrees and in different forms, a revitalisation of the independent organs of civil society.[54]

Let us take a recent case of automobile platforms and the recall of apparently defective parts by various automobile firms, among them Toyota. Its innovative hybrid car uses a brake, which is a component shared with other automakers through standardized platform plants such as the one in the Czech Republic. The construction of the car as an end product is today made up of various standardized components or parts coming from diverse sources. The trend is towards more rapid change and invention concerning the outward appearance of the product, while the inner parts are standardized and circulate freely worldwide without much public control. Such world platforms produce specific parts and assemble them, but the brand name of the various car makers is still used for publicity and services, to retain profits globally. The problem is not the fact that there are too many owners of the joint platform, but that control mechanisms from within should be running in real time. There is neither public global control nor previous requirement of significant testing in real world conditions before putting the product on the world market (testing cold, wind or temperature change) while the risk (the part not previously tested) is circulated globally by many automakers. A small event can therefore trigger panic throughout the sector and society. In effect, car makers have adopted the principle of testing on the run, namely, by users. If things do not go well – for example, if there are accidents in which people suffer damage – cars will be recalled to undergo a check. When the recall is global, there may be a political storm. Who has the authority to control and regulate world platforms that are standardized and used jointly by many automakers from different countries? If the global firm's reputation is stained and the costs deemed too high because they are global, the firm may be saved by the national government where the firm is perceived as a national champion, adding to state deficits.[55]

The building of global supply chains is appearing in the service sector as well. From mobile phones to internet access, a chain can allow for a multitude of services. Where Nokia and Ericsson previously had an advantage, the US firms Google and Apple (with their software) have teamed up with China's Huawei and ZTE (with their cheap hardware) to provide internet access to services either for business or for young users by using iPhones and Blackberrys in the West, and cheap smartphones in Asia.[56] In China, cheap mobile phones are sometimes given out free of charge. The service chain is what matters and the information flowing through it.

In Sanchez Bajo (2001), industrial business strategies were analysed to grasp their various linkages across the national and regional levels into globalization. The research found that the building of regional and global chains in production and distribution was taking place by sector, and then snowballing up and downstream, causing firms in control of the raw materials, inputs, knowledge and services to team up. Specialization, which others may call focus on the core business, was being built transnationally to enlarge business scales. Such strategy included the separation of existing activities and plants before linking them up in global chains. Specific activities and departments were linked up with similar or closely related ones at the regional and world level, before listing them on stock markets. Functional to the financial markets, it heightened visibility and tracking. This strategy was thought to bring growth in terms of value for the financial shareholder. Consequently, responding to short-term pressures to produce high returns, firms were kept under constant restructuring. The strategy found its limits in the global crisis and, since we are now in a circular and closed global system, the crisis has hit highly specialized activities particularly hard, even if they are global.

As debt-financing grew, control within supply chains was increasingly exercised through decisions and supervision relating to financial profits, global brand reputation and access streaming. Large firms adapted their strategies. The example of General Motors, mentioned in Chapter 1, shows that one of its main activities was financial: through lending, leasing, franchising, not only to dealers selling the GM brands but also to citizens through sub-prime housing and residential mortgages. This is not the traditional idea of a car maker. An example in the consumer retailing sector is Carrefour in Belgium, receiving state aid,[57] but closing 21 of its own units across the country and sacking 1,672 employees. Simultaneously, it franchised 483 units making up 42 per cent of turnover of the group in Belgium.[58] The expected profit is financial but the risk for franchisees is very high and if financial results are not good enough, they may face termination of the contract. They may also be surprised by the franchisor selling the territory to investment funds, as was Carrefour's intention with CVC Capital Partners in 2008.[59]

With these changes, what is the main remaining element of a firm? If production is left to others through subcontracting, if labour supply and management is subcontracted, if R&D is left to start-ups that can be bought if the innovation is marketable, if data processing can be outsourced, what is left? Potentially, branding and advertising through long-term contracts, connecting with Rifkin's idea of the Age of Access (see the section on the consumer function below).

Workers who own nothing in the firm

And what is the place of workers in the new system? It is no secret that workers have lost bargaining power in the process, and that trade unions are now restructuring, with a big merger having taken place in 2006 among the two biggest global unions. Furthermore, the function of the worker-producer has changed, considered now as a service unit, which should automatically adapt to circumstances that keep changing. A 2010 report by top French managers explains what is dysfunctional in the workplace, leading to workers' suicides. Hierarchy within each plant has been de-structured and a host of 'experts' and changing managers come and go. Proximity managers have become simple transmission belts without margin for decision making and workers have difficulty in identifying their superior. Changes arrive from outside, all of a sudden, sometimes even brutally: for example, Philips sent two letters over a weekend to workers on one site in France, one telling them to stop working and the second one asking them to accept immediate placement in Eastern Europe for around 550 euro per month, far below any salary and living costs in France. This goes well beyond the fear of unemployment.[60]

The report goes on to say:

> The increased frequency of reorganizations, restructuring and changes in the enterprise perimeter, which impact on all or part of the organization and sometimes brutally change the conditions in which the employees exercise their activity... the use, and sometimes misuse, of new technologies, which 'cannibalize' human relations: they weaken the boundary between privacy and professional life, depersonalize the working relationship in favour of virtual exchange and accelerate the relation with the time at work, introducing a confusion between what is urgent and what is important... the development of new forms of Taylorism in the tertiary [service] sector. Characterized by the standardization and fragmentation of tasks and relationships, they can lead to the loss of sense at work.

Simultaneously, workers are requested to take initiatives placing them in a situation of 'paradoxical injunction', because they are unable to address anything.

The report then shows that the whole internal organization is destabilized. Management has been discredited. Financial performance decides the value scale: 'The increasing weight of [standardized] procedures in labour relations, the insufficient association of proximity managers with the decisions or even the development of the matrix organizations, contribute to destabilizing this vital link in the organization'.[61]

In Belgium, Carrefour had been losing money since 2000, when they bought Belgian GB supermarkets and expanded into hypermarkets. Constant management changes did not help and trade unions were at a loss in terms of adaptation and restructuring.[62] The French report submitted to the Prime Minister also called to attention that '[c]ompanies must make sure that they do not transfer psychosocial risks onto their suppliers'.

Suppliers, assembly platforms, workers, management, in fact, the entire organization in the sphere of production, are apparently losing direction. Although we continue to hear a repetitive narrative praising entrepreneurship and jobs, with values based on a traditional market system, the function of producer, even in the case of owners of enterprises in the real economy, is undergoing a shift as producers are trying to adapt to a rationality which is sometimes guessed at, many times unknown, and mostly in flux.

The consumer function

The individual consumer

In capitalism, the economic function of the consumer is necessary for the comparability and replaceability of goods and services. This leads to market competition, exchange and risk according to supply and demand. Recent trends in streaming services and routine access have brought about changes in such functions. The trend towards long-term routine access does not comply with market exchange, in which there is comparability and replace-ability. Moreover, routine access needs credit around the clock, such as an open account to be used according to changing needs and wants. By giving access on the basis of open credit in consumption, the diversity of credit sources is breaking away from traditional banking. To report on secured profit, services are being built as constant streaming flows, enshrined in long-term contracts. They are no longer understood as an exchange but as a system of instant access. Asset ownership goes to those in effective control of the service.

Jeremy Rifkin believes that the core of the system based on private owner-ship may be giving way to another one characterized by business controlling access to services and the ensuing 'commodification' of the usage of the ser-vice, or of the users' experience.[63] This trend departs from the old idea of usage and user in the real economy, as in the use of resources in the 'commons'.[64] In addition, according to this trend, individual choice ends in ascription. Whereas choice implies the freedom to not only choose once but also change your mind, ascription does not. A person ascribed a given segment or profile will be offered a range of choices depending on the category of ascription. But can the user-consumer's subjectivity be taken as a constant attribute? On the one side, life is change. On the other, future individual needs and tastes can-not be foreseen with precision. Finally, renting, leasing and franchising suggest types of investment perceived more as a burden or a liability than an asset. Risk is then externalized.

Maurice Allais's general equilibrium model with random risks comprised two types of sector: a differentiated one with decreasing returns to scale and a non-differentiated one with increasing returns to scale.[65] Service-streaming based on long-term contracts belongs to Allais' second type of sector, as it minimizes costs, sells at marginal cost and strives to keep the property based on intangibles. As returns to scale increase, a single firm is more efficient than several. For Allais, the optimum in the second type of sector was attained by public state property. However, this type of sector is now mostly in private hands. Given the global competition among large firms in such a sector, a main goal is to keep the streaming of services for as long as possible. However, individuals cannot measure with certainty their future needs or the satisfaction which they will draw from needs in the future.[66] Discussion in the industry focuses on output, volume, standardization and the speed with which products are sold. Nevertheless, future users' aggregate demand cannot be measured exactly, either in relation to future needs or solvency and therefore to any possible accumulating risk through global systemic interdependence. This aspect, and the fact that long-term contracts of future incoming service streams need open credit accounts, will pose new challenges.

It is no mean feat to turn consumers, who used to exchange products or money for a product on a hands-off basis, into long term 'loyal' clients through long-term legal contracts that provide recurring access. In the latter, only one long-term transaction is involved. In the supplier's interest, this method diminishes transaction costs and ensures a stream of steady income, which becomes vital as a financial asset. But the 'loyal' client may get into a relationship in which the information he or she obtains is incomplete and changing.

In capitalist markets, buyers and sellers exchange ownership, but in a 'stream economy' consumers may not dispose of the item, not even in the case of the termination of the legal contract. The electronic e-reader is an example. Readers may think they acquire a book when they pay for it and download it into their e-reader, but the company selling the latter may erase the text from all e-readers if there is a court suit. This does not necessarily mean that the other forms of exchange are going to disappear, but it is an increasing trend. The evolution co-exists with barter and traditional exchange of property, while vying to lead market 'making'. The more the system is based on long-term loyal subscriptions for a credited open stream of services, the more access will turn into a legal duty for the user-client. Examples are everywhere, from the gym to telecoms and to photocopying machines that are leased to organizations.

Rifkin argues that the new access economy provides peace of mind and convenience for users, but does not discuss the issue of debt. If consumers behave as in the past and do not realize that they are having access on credit, they may possibly over-consume, abstain from saving and diminish their ecological concerns. It could make it easier for them to fall into the consumption trap, which we discussed in Chapter 2.

The case of private finance of public projects in the access economy

The evolution towards an access economy could perhaps be seen in a more positive light if the high public structural indebtedness did not come into the picture. The projects carried out as 'public private partnerships' (PPPs) and 'private finance initiatives' (PFIs) are a good case for discussion.

Since the public sector is supposed to control the project, it has to account for the debt incurred by the project as its own. And this in turn may lead to

higher fees for citizens in order to access the service. The extent of this unfortu-
nate outcome has been due, as the IMF said, to the objective of circumventing
fiscal constraints in the first place.[67] As with Greece's CDOs and other off-the-
sheet debt instruments, many 'public investment' projects are actually a debt
practice with routine access paid by the population as users and/or citizens.
The PPPs and PFIs, as in UK and French hospitals and roads, are defined by
long-term contracts of up to 30 years that include all aspects of the project,
from design to construction, maintenance to management, and the provision
of the service. Since the 1990s, they have to be financed by private concerns
and paid by the state or the local public authority as if it was a rent. The 'rent'
covers the expected profit and can come either from users of, for example, a
hospital, or directly from the state. If the 'rent' cannot be paid, the hospital
may be closed down or be used for something else while the state gets indebted
to the private investors. There is a common type of PPP that is a joint venture
between the public authority and the private companies. The analysis by
David Hall of PPPs is unfavourable: results are reportedly not positive and debt
now appears on the states' balance sheet. He further explains that:

> In the UK the total value was nearly £60 billion (€75 billion) by the end
> of 2007. The value of all PPPs in the rest of Europe had risen to a total of
> €31.6 billion by the end of 2006. In EU countries as a whole, transport
> infrastructure accounts for 82 per cent by value of all completed, current
> and projected PPPs; in the United Kingdom (UK) over half of all the proj-
> ects are in health, education and local government.[68]

State debt linked to PPPs used not to appear on the balance sheet because
the projects did not appear as investment or government borrowing.[69]
The EU encouraged their use in order to lower the public deficit figures.
However, the international financial reporting standards (IFRS), which were
changed in 2004 recommend that asset ownership in service concessions
should be decided on the basis of who exerts effective control, and not of
risk transfer, which should force governments to treat PPPs as public debts.[70]
The recognition of asset ownership on the basis of effective control goes
against EU statistical decisions which, also in 2004, had established the PPPs
to be non-government assets and off balance sheet because the private interest shouldered both the construction risk and the supply-and-demand risk.
   To sum up with regard to the consumer function: on the one hand,
ownership of physical property may be given up through routine access
while, on the other, control is being used to determine asset ownership.
Consumption has come to be viewed as the end of global chains of production and distribution, something that should be functioning all year
round, incessantly and just-in-time. Therefore, the shifting borders between
ownership and control may not only change the economic function of the
consumer but may also impact on the very notion of market.

Conclusion

The crisis has shown the centrality of debt linking both the financial and the real economy. Debt is functional to a series of objectives: as a disciplining tool; to avoid taxes; to develop global chains; to solve the chronic under-funding of pension funds; to redesign the entire set of bargaining relations; and to avoid ownership risks and obligations. In addressing not only the financial sphere but also the real economy, this chapter links the concept of debt trap to economic entities at the micro/meso level.

Financialization and technification have facilitated a shift in the control of economic entities, in conjunction with debt and leverage. Control is as important as ownership but distinct from it. In a capitalism that is both financialized and technified, the two tend to disconnect not only in the financial sphere but also in the real economy. In order to deactivate the debt trap, we need to establish limits through checks and balances in economic entities, with a necessary matching control. Indeed, control has to be reconsidered as coming not only from outside, but first and foremost from within.

When the global financial-economic crisis fades away, many dreams, certainties and beliefs will have been shaken. The consensus that prevailed during the last 30 years has been broken. The extreme generalized indebtedness which we are witnessing today is to a large extent the manifestation of something deeper. There is a shift from the central role of ownership in the earlier phases of capitalism towards a system using control to obtain benefits without carrying the risk of ownership. On the one hand, there is a change in the type and scale of control and, on the other, a loss of control by the real economy stakeholders. This process has encouraged further indebtedness.

An economy branded as ideal was in fact loaded with debt, accompanied by a loss of control in economic entities, making the latter highly vulnerable to any critical event, building up systemic risks and endangering general wealth. In brief, the 'debt trap' has been one of the major mechanisms in the crisis; and although the arguments advanced in this book are not the only ones to reconsider for our future, the issue of control from within through checks and balances needs to be seriously considered in order to limit future traps, bubbles and crises.

4
Cooperatives: Importance, Resilience and Rationality

Introduction

Chapter 3 highlighted the shifting boundaries between ownership and control. We saw that such a shift was closely connected to the debt trap seen in Chapter 2, which we identified as being one of the main mechanisms having led to the global crisis, and that it was causing an increasing loss of control by the real stakeholders in economic entities, hindering economic sustainability and, in the long run, wealth creation. Where can solutions come from?

In the present fading of old certainties and the quest for new ideas, theoretical insights re-emphasizing control by the real stakeholders and the priority of the common good over the systematic predominance of financial short-term profit are obtaining due recognition.[1] In this debate, cooperatives, which offer the advantage of being an existing type of economic organization, and not purely a theoretical alternative model, may be worth looking at. Their experience and internal control mechanisms could prove to be of importance beyond their own bounds, as they could make a good case for debate, practice and policy. However, we should first make sure if, and to what extent, they are both a sufficiently important economic actor in the world and a sufficiently differentiated model of economic organization on the ground, in particular in terms of their control mechanisms and their specific regard towards capital and debt.

Cooperatives assert that they have a different redistribution system and are geared towards members' needs. They herald a moral value system, with such declared values as democracy, equality, equity, solidarity, honesty and social responsibility. They lay a strong emphasis on education and training, and claim to be concerned with the community. Are these only noble ideals, or do cooperatives act as full-fledged enterprises while practising such values? Are they true to their claims in the first place? Is there anything flawed in the way they act on the market?

More widely, can the model of joint control and democratic checks and balances which cooperatives claim to practise be useful in tackling the increasing lack of control by stakeholders which feeds the debt trap, as we saw in Chapter 3? Can cooperatives *truly* be the promoters of a 'stakeholder economy' as opposed to a 'shareholder economy', one which can work for the common good and the creation of shared wealth? These questions must indeed be addressed.

We attempt to respond to them in this and the following chapters. But, in order to do so, we cannot overlook some of the most important critiques that have been formulated against cooperatives in the recent past. Therefore, in the first section, we briefly review some of these critiques, without arguing whether they are correct or not, as this is something that we will gradually find out through the general data and the concrete examples that we will see throughout the rest of this book.

We then attempt to gauge the importance of cooperatives in the world: are they, globally, an important economic actor? How many are their members–owners? What is their impact on employment?

In the following section, we look at the response of cooperatives to the ongoing global crisis. Have they maintained their activities and their jobs better than other enterprises? Have they even developed?

We move on to delve into the underlying rationality of cooperatives: what is their main *raison d'être*? What are their common standards and how were they elaborated? How do they organize internally? What do they want to achieve? What is their system of capital accumulation and profit distribution? Do they avoid falling into the debt trap? We also briefly mention the common points and differences between cooperatives and mutual aid societies (not to be confused with 'mutual funds').

The final section places the evolution of cooperatives' standards in a political economy perspective, linking up on the one hand internal debates and international organizations' definitions, and on the other the wider context of world economic restructuring.

Critiques of cooperatives

Ideas and theories that are critical about cooperatives have been expressed by a number of scholars and have inevitably had some bearing on public opinion, especially over the last few years.

One theoretical strand maintains that cooperatives are responses to niche markets and market failure. It considers that many cooperatives are born out of a struggle by small producers or consumers against cartels and monopolies, and maintain their *raison d'être* until the market failures are overcome. When the market and competition become effective, this *raison d'être* allegedly disappears. Daniel Côté illustrates this theory by using the example of ULN (Union Laitière Normande), a French milk cooperative group that was born as part of a struggle by local farmers against cartels and ended up in demutualization 45 years later, when the original cartel conditions had changed completely.[2] The theory appears to suggest that large cooperatives in highly competitive markets are either non-existent or exceptional: we will check whether this is correct or not.

Since cooperatives are supposedly born to overcome market failures, they would tend to have a merely transitional role, and be bound to disappear in a modern economy – 'only in the special case of chronic market failure would an infinite life be predicted', according to Laurence Harte.[3] Thus, whereas no enterprise in the world pretends to be destined to eternal life, cooperatives supposedly have a shorter lifetime than conventional businesses. In the following sections and chapters, we will try to gauge the actual longevity of cooperatives.

When they do manage to survive under complete market conditions, cooperatives are allegedly not adapted to the needs of the modern economy. According to Harte, this is because they are more prone to financial risk.[4] On the contrary, for Henry Hansmann, employee-owned enterprises are particularly risk-averse, in that 'workers, lacking the ability to diversify risk by taking jobs in a number of different firms simultaneously, are in a worse position than investors to bear the risks of fluctuating residual earnings'.[5] We will eventually try to see whether cooperative businesses are more or less risky than others, and whether cooperative members are more or less prone to take risks than other types of business owner.

Another issue is the cost of decision making. Hansmann considers that cooperatives are characterized by a very high cost of collective decision making,[6] as underlined by the new institutionalist school and, in particular, by Oliver Williamson, who heralds the beneficial impact of vertical and hierarchical decision making in centralized management upon decentralized and participatory management, which he brands as 'communal'.[7] Robert Schediwy applies this theory to the German cooperative banks: he maintains that the sharp increase of competition and the tendency of competitors to merge makes the traditional three-tiered cooperative system (with banking structures at the local, regional and national level) of the German Raiffeisen cooperative banking group increasingly obsolete and irrelevant.[8] In Chapters 7 and 8, we will examine concrete cases of complex decision-making processes in cooperative groups such as Raiffeisen, and see whether this practice should be seen as a cost or, rather, as an investment.

If they do happen to become big, according to Hansmann, cooperatives tend to turn into something barely distinguishable from ordinary public limited companies (PLCs), until 'the enterprise has essentially assumed the character of an investor-owned firm'.[9] According to Serge Koulitchisky and René Mauget, in order to adapt, cooperatives allegedly evolve towards hybridized forms of management between elected decision makers and managerial decision makers. This is because, according to these authors, the demands of modern-style management and the challenges of globalization are obliging many cooperatives and cooperative groups to hire managers with appropriate technical skills and expertise, which, in turn, allegedly reinforces a tendency towards increasing concentration of power into the hands of a reduced managing techno-structure that leads the cooperative with a 'heavy hand' and a techno-language that the ordinary members can no longer understand.[10] Chaves and Monzón argue that this phenomenon, in turn, tends to create an ever deeper gap in terms of enterprise culture and endangers the active democratic participation of members within the system, making them more prone to opt for demutualization and the adoption of capitalistic legal forms and vertical governance.[11] In the empirical cases and general considerations throughout the remainder of this book, we will check whether this evolution towards less democracy and more technocracy in cooperatives is inevitable and whether it is actually taking place.

The Kerry dairy cooperatives in Ireland have been mentioned as a classical example of a *gradual* (but seemingly inevitable) demutualization process due to the inability of the cooperative form to adapt to modern economic realities because of its higher transaction costs. The control power of the members, through the elected Board, gradually decreased in favour of management. No surplus was distributed to members, who lost interest in the cooperative and, in turn, wanted to enjoy a market value for their shares and additional capital for the growth of their farms. Part of the cooperatives were then acquired and turned into PLCs. One cooperative has been maintained but exercises all its activities through a company in which it has a 55 per cent controlling interest. In the other PLCs, surviving milk cooperatives are now minority members. The author studying the case, Harte, considers this phenomenon as being an inevitable evolution of the Irish milk industry. The demutualization process, according to the author, was bound to take place, and should in fact have taken place sooner had the cooperative form of organization not inhibited the needed change for some time.[12]

Cooperatives are also criticized for being artificially promoted through specific tax, legal and policy advantages.[13] According to Harte again:

> the efficiency of cooperatives is not proven by their survival and development over so many years, as cooperatives in most countries have been favoured by government policies (and sometimes have been used as instruments of government policy) through tax breaks and other direct and indirect supports.[14]

This critique was relayed by the European Commission in 2008, when Competition Commissioner Nelly Kroes dealt with a set of complaints filed against Italian consumer and credit cooperatives for the specific tax regimes related to cooperative surpluses earmarked for indivisible reserves. Kroes expressed the opinion that large cooperatives had very probably lost their cooperative character and advocated the need to develop a 'pure mutual cooperative model', thereby indirectly questioning the Italian cooperative legislation and going beyond the European Commission's mandate.[15] In the next sections and chapters, we will verify whether cooperatives generate specific social goods and financial reserves with specific property regimes, which would then justify corresponding compensatory policies and tax regulation.

It should be noted that most of the above theories on cooperatives were formulated between the second half of the 1990s and September 2008, namely the formal beginning of the crisis. This period was characterized by a highly self-confident and upbeat approach to the mainstream economic and entrepreneurial stock-market model (in spite of significant failures such as Barings or Enron, which were decoded as being the exception that confirmed the rule, constant rescue packages and debt made public to save private 'too big to fail' enterprises in so many countries, and the string of subsidies and tax breaks granted to TNCs). Many scholars were, during that period, under intense pressure to comply with this dominant stream of ideas. Nowadays, it is not only these specific theories on cooperatives that are put in doubt, but the whole frame of mind that until recently conditioned research on the economy and economic entities.

Since these theories are part of a wider frame of mind which is being questioned, we will not refute them, but put them to the test. Through the discussion on the role of cooperatives in the world (next sections) and the empirical cases (Chapters 5, 6, 7 and 8), we hope to gradually 'falsify' them, namely to check whether they correspond to reality or not. Meanwhile, let us keep them in mind.

The economic and social importance of cooperatives in the world

Economic importance

Table 4.1 provides an indication of the contribution of cooperatives to the GDP of the ten biggest economies of the world (most of which are at the centre of the global crisis) in 2008, which in turn constituted 73 per cent of world GDP that year. We observe that the aggregate turnover of cooperatives in these countries is around 10 per cent lower than the GDP of Italy, and makes up just under 5 per cent of the aggregate GDP of this group of countries.

A number of considerations should be made about these data. First of all, the estimate is conservative, since, in part of these countries, not all cooperatives have been accounted for (in particular cooperative banks). In addition, the count does not include mutuals (in the sense of 'mutual aid societies', rather than 'mutual funds') which, at least according to the international understanding of the term, are very close to cooperatives, as we will explain below.

Second, these conservative estimates only concern the aggregate turnover which cooperatives produce *directly*, and do not include the sales generated by producers who belong to cooperatives in order to benefit from key

common inputs, such as independent bakers, butchers, mechanics, shop-
keepers and other types of self-employed people, nor the sales generated by
the millions of small businesses which contract productive loans with local
credit cooperatives and cooperative banks. Nor do they take into account
the uphill, downhill and sideline businesses which the activities carried out
by cooperatives generate.

We will return to the economic contributions of cooperatives that cannot
be retrieved from GDP ratios at the end of this section. For the moment, let
us limit ourselves to examining the *direct* share of the cooperative economy
in some key sectors.

In banking, the 7,708 US credit unions had, in 2009, over $899 billion in
assets and held 6 per cent of the market share of financial institutions' assets.[16]
The cooperative banks of the EU have total assets worth $7,768 billion and, in
2008, held 18 per cent of EU market shares in deposits and 16 per cent in EU
credit.[17] At the national level, the corresponding percentages are, for example,
19 per cent and 16 per cent for Germany, 34 per cent and 32 per cent for

Table 4.1   Aggregate turnover of cooperatives in G10 countries and their share of
nominal GDP

Country	GDP (2008) in million US$	Coop aggregate turnover in million US$	Coop percentage of GDP
United States	14,256,275	652,903	4.7
Japan	5,068,059	184,104	3.2
Germany	3,352,742	244,098	7.3
China	4,908,982	221,065	4.5
United Kingdom	2,183,607	56,568	2.1
France	2,675,951	207,166	7.7
Italy	2,118,264	157,285	7.4
Spain	1,442,704	90,050	6.2
Canada	1,336,427	39,216	3.4
Brazil	1,574,039	48,200	2.3
Total G10	38,917,050	1,900,654	4.9

Sources: The country GDPs are the nominal 2008 GDP figures provided by the World Bank,
see http://siteresources.worldbank.org/DATASTATISTICS/Resources/GDP_PPP.pdf. The sources
for the national cooperative aggregate turnovers are: for the US, Research on the Economic
Impact of Cooperatives by the University of Wisconsin's Center for Cooperatives, 2009, avail-
able on http://reic.uwcc.wisc.edu; for Japan, communication from Yoshiko Yamada, Japan
Worker Cooperative Union based on the figures published by the Japanese Joint Committee of
Cooperatives (JJC) (2009); for Germany, see www.dgrv.de; for China, communication All China
Supply and Marketing Cooperative Federation and all China Handicraft Industry Cooperative
Federation; for the UK, Cooperative UK's Cooperative Review 2009 available on http://www.coop-
eratives-uk.coop/live/images/cme_resources/Public/CoopReview/2009/Review09.pdf; for France,
Chiffres Clé 2008 des organisations cooperatives adherents au GNC, Groupement National de la
Coopération.; for Italy, see Legacoop: Imprese, occupazione e valore aggiunto, 2009; for Spain, see
www.cepes.es; for Canada, communication from the Canadian Worker Cooperative Federation
based on CCA and CCCM figures; for Brazil, communication by OCB.

Finland, 37 per cent and 32 per cent for Austria, 42 per cent and 46 per cent for France, and 43 per cent and 30 per cent for the Netherlands.[18]

In insurance, the global market share of cooperatives and mutuals (a type of economic organization which, as mentioned above, is very similar to cooperatives, as we will examine later) in 2007 and 2008 was 24 per cent. In other words, cooperatives and mutuals cover almost one-quarter of the global insurance market.[19]

In agriculture, cooperatives in the EU as a whole have a share of over 50 per cent in the supply of agricultural products and of over 60 per cent in the collection, processing and marketing of agricultural products.[20] Cooperatives account for 83 per cent of Dutch agricultural production.[21] Finnish cooperatives are responsible for 74 per cent of the meat products and 96 per cent of dairy products.[22] Swedish cooperatives are responsible for 60 per cent of the national forestry market. This is not a EU-only phenomenon: 30 per cent of farmers' products in the USA are marketed through cooperatives.[23] In Brazil, cooperatives produce 40 per cent of the agricultural GDP.[24] In New Zealand, they are responsible for 95 per cent of the dairy market, 70 per cent of the meat market, 50 per cent of the farm supply market and 70 per cent of the fertilizer market.[25] In Japan, they make up 95 per cent of all rice production and 90 per cent of the fishing trade.[26] In India, they account for 46.2 per cent of the production of sugar and 26.5 per cent of the production of fertilizers.[27]

In retail and distribution, consumer cooperatives' share of national retail markets is 55 per cent in Singapore,[28] 43 per cent in Finland, 38 per cent in Denmark, 24 per cent in Norway, 21 per cent in Sweden, 17 per cent in Italy and 14 per cent in Hungary.[29] Japan's consumer cooperatives report a total of 5.9 per cent of the food market share.[30] And 25 per cent of all retailers in France are grouped in cooperatives,[31] whereas in New Zealand, cooperatives make up 62 per cent of the grocery market.[32]

In housing, cooperatives make up 8 per cent of Austria's total housing stock, 10 per cent of Germany's total renting stock and 15 per cent of Norway's housing market (40 per cent in Oslo).[33] In the health-related sectors, cooperatives account for 21 per cent of the Spanish health market,[34] and in Belgium, the market share of cooperative pharmacies is 19.5 per cent.[35] In Italy, cooperatives are the first private supplier of social services.

The above data do not pretend to be exhaustive. They are only examples aimed at making it clear that cooperatives are a substantial economic actor in general and in several key sectors in particular, using the most conventional measurement system (market shares). In addition, these market shares have been maintained, and many instances have increased, since the advent of full-fledged global competition. Although the development of cooperatives throughout the various sectors is uneven in different countries (for a number of historical reasons that exceed the scope of this book), the school of thought mentioned above, according to which cooperatives develop mainly in quasi markets and cannot fully expand under full market conditions (not to mention under a globalized economy), simply does not resist the analysis of available data. The other main critique mentioned above, that most of those that grow large lose their cooperative nature, can only be fully addressed by understanding the underlying economic rationality of cooperatives, which we will examine later in this chapter, and how this rationality translates into practice, which we will verify through the four empirical cases in the following chapters (Natividad, Ceralep, Desjardins and Mondragon).

Social and employment importance

The aggregate number of cooperative members in the world who are part of the system of federations that are directly or indirectly members of the International Cooperative Alliance is above 906 million.[36] A number of national cooperative organizations and experts, however, point out that there is bound to be a substantial amount of double counting in this overall figure. But, even if all cooperative members in the world were members of two cooperatives, their actual number would be as high as 450 million. However, it is common knowledge that the majority of cooperative members are members of only one cooperative, and that members of more than two cooperatives are unusual. Therefore, even if we take double counting into account, and if we hypothesize that half of cooperative members are members of one co-op and half are members of two co-ops, the actual number of persons in the world who are members of one or more cooperatives should be higher than 650 million: around one tenth of the world population,[37] or around 15 per cent of the world adult population. Although the individual experience and awareness of being a co-op member varies greatly from one situation to another, it remains the case that, through the cooperative system, hundreds of millions of ordinary people in the world are co-owners of hundreds of thousands of cooperative enterprises, a social and economic phenomenon that cannot be overlooked.

Figures may be more consistent sector-wise, because it is more difficult for there to be double counting. For example, cooperative banks in the EU have 50.5 million members-owners (10 per cent of the EU population, and up to 17 per cent among the six founding nations of the EU), whereas the US credit unions have 91 million members (30 per cent of the US population).

Employment-wise, cooperatives are also an important actor. They *directly* employ 4.7 million persons in the EU,[38] 4.58 million in China,[39] 2.14 million in the USA,[40] 1.2 million in India,[41] 285 155 in Russia,[42] 171 000 in Brazil[43] and 150 000 in Canada.[44]

But cooperatives are even more important in terms of *indirect* employment or self-employed activities which depend on transactions with a cooperative: for example, 15.4 million self-employed persons in the case of India.[45] In Germany, 'approximately 60 per cent of all craftsmen, 75 per cent of all retail traders, 90 per cent of all bakers and butchers and over 65 per cent of all self employed tax advisors are members of a cooperative'.[46] The figure also includes the hundreds of millions of farmers and fishermen around the world who are members of an agricultural or fishery cooperative. For example, almost all German farmers, gardeners and winegrowers are members of a cooperative.[47]

Another key social contribution is that cooperatives are a substantial contributor to housing and other services of general interest. In the European Union, they provide housing to an estimated 28 million citizens.[48] In Italy, the over 7,000 social cooperatives constitute the first provider of social services with 3.3 million users, and of work integration of disadvantaged citizens with over 30,000 disadvantaged workers.[49]

Economic and social contribution that cannot be measured by conventional methods

The quantified contributions of cooperatives to the economy and society, mentioned above, are measured through traditional measurement tools such as GDP, market shares and employment numbers and ratios. Although, as we can see, cooperatives can claim substantial figures according to these measurement tools, the latter cannot fully reflect the specific contribution of cooperatives to the economy and to society. Indeed, none of these measurement tools can calculate the longevity of cooperatives, or their capacity to innovate or to adapt to change, or their capillarity in the locality, or their capacity to share the produced wealth instead of concentrating it in reduced islands of prosperity, or the sustainability of jobs, which contribute to their expansion.

A number of national case studies have shown that cooperatives tend to have a longer life than other types of enterprise, and thus a higher level of entrepreneurial sustainability. In Canada, for example, a governmental survey found that the rate of survival of cooperatives after three years was 75 per cent, whereas it was only 48 per cent for all enterprises put together, and that, after ten years, 44 per cent of cooperatives were still in operation, whereas the ratio was only 20 per cent for all enterprises.[50]

The longevity of cooperatives also appears in research conducted by the ICA about the world's top 300 cooperatives and mutuals (or groups of cooperatives or mutuals). Apart from their strong economic importance (in 2006, they had an aggregate turnover of $1.1 billion and total assets worth $9.5 billion), the longevity of these cooperative or mutual enterprises or groups is striking: as many as 25 of them were established in the nineteenth century, 67 during the first half of the twentieth century, and 38 between 1950 and 1980, the trend being that the oldest ones are also the largest and strongest entrepreneurially.[51]

In the same vein, IMF experts have recognized that the stability of cooperative banks was even stronger than that of commercial ones. A 2007 IMF study concluded that:

> cooperative banks in advanced economies and emerging markets have higher z-scores than commercial banks and (to a smaller extent) savings banks, suggesting that cooperative banks are more stable. (...). We suggest

that this observed lower variability of returns (...) may be caused by the fact that cooperative banks in normal times pass on most of their returns to customers, but are able to recoup that surplus in weaker periods. To some extent, this result can also reflect the mutual support mechanisms that many cooperative banks have created.

The authors add that the:

high presence of cooperative banks appears to weaken commercial banks, in particular those commercial banks that are already weak ... This empirical result can be explained by the fact that a higher cooperative bank presence means less space for weak commercial banks in the retail market and their greater reliance on less stable revenue sources such as corporate banking or investment banking.[52]

Referring to this document, Ghislain Paradis from the Desjardins banking cooperative group commented at a UN 2009 panel on cooperatives and the crisis that: 'Put in other words, cooperative banks collaborate not only to stabilize the market, but also to "purify" it and to force corporate and investment bankers to improve their risk management'.[53] This important economic function, of course, does not appear in GDP ratios.

Another feature which cannot be deduced from GDP ratios shown in Table 4.1 is the capillarity of the cooperative presence. As we will see in Chapter 7, the Desjardins banking group is the only banking institution providing financial services to local people and local businesses in as many as 600 Quebec municipalities. Similarly, there are over 20,000 outlets of cooperative banks in France,[54] and if you travel through French villages, you will find out that, very often, the only local bank is a cooperative bank, the only insurance company is a mutual one, and the only grocer is part of the 'Super U' grocers' cooperative network. In the USA, rural electric cooperatives, which distribute 10 per cent of all kilowatt hours sold in the country, operate 42 per cent of the electric distribution lines, covering three quarters of the US land mass and providing service to 42 million rural people (12 per cent of the total US population), as well as to 18 million businesses, homes, schools, churches, farms, irrigation systems, and other establishments in the countryside.[55]

In addition, as will be shown in the following chapters, it should be underlined that jobs in cooperatives tend to be more stable and last longer than those in other enterprises, because, as we saw above, cooperatives tend to have a higher longevity and because, being based on local members, they normally do not delocalize.

In 2009, Joseph Stiglitz, advised by Amartya Sen, chaired a commission which drafted a manifesto explaining why and how GDP should be supplemented as the *de facto* measure of progress, while other dimensions such as material living standards, work, education, health, political voice, among others, should be taken into consideration.[56] Such new measurement tools would certainly better value the contribution of cooperatives to shared wealth. We will return to this argument in Chapter 9.

The resilience of cooperatives to the crisis

Since the crisis began, cooperatives have displayed a comparative strength in terms of resilience, in spite of the considerable difficulties that the economic situation has inevitably caused to their activities, as emerges from a number of reports from various cooperative sectors.

Since September 2008, most cooperative banks, generally small local banking structures grouped in horizontal *ensembles* (such as the Desjardins group in Canada), have continued to serve chiefly local users. In the USA, loans by credit unions increased by 6.68 per cent in volume between 2007 and 2008, whereas those granted by the 8,300 US traditional banks decreased by 0.39 per cent over the same period.[57] The growth of credit union loans continued to rise in 2009, though at a lower pace (1.2 per cent) but the growth of their productive loans reached 11 per cent that year, against a fall of 15 per cent for conventional banks. At the same time, in 2009, the growth rate of US credit unions' total savings and assets reached their highest figure since 2005, with respectively 10.3 per cent and 8.9 per cent.[58] Their capital adequacy ratio in 2009 was 9.9 per cent (more or less the same figure since 1994), which 'well exceeds the 7 per cent ratio needed to be classified in the highest category of "well capitalized"'.[59]

In the EU (where, as we saw, cooperative banks represent 19 per cent of all bank deposits and 16 per cent of all bank loans), no cooperative bank has failed, whereas several public and commercial banks have.[60] They continue to have an average market share in SME financing of around 29 per cent.[61] Whereas French Crédit Agricole's central bank experienced huge financial losses in 2008 for having traded derivatives through its commercial subsidiaries (after which, in keeping with the cooperative democratic control pattern which we will examine in the next section the leadership of the group was dismissed by its constituent cooperatives),[62] its own autonomous local banks, like those of all large cooperative banking groups in France, Germany and the Netherlands, have been largely unaffected by the financial storm.[63]

The European Association of Cooperative Banks explains that:

> Satisfactory solvency ratios (the overall tier-1 ratio of European cooperative banks on 31 December 2007 was 8.6 per cent) mean that European cooperative banks are not being forced to resort to the recapitalization plans introduced by government authorities. In the few instances in which cooperative banks have resorted to these facilities, they have done so with the intention of sustaining a rate of growth in their lending

tailored to a severely degraded and risky environment, such as in Austria or in France with subsidiaries.[64]

In France, the Crédit Mutuel – CIC group (Crédit Mutuel is a cooperative banking group and CIC is a controlled subsidiary; the whole group is France's fourth banking institution and second for retail banking) had an 11.8 per cent tier-one capital ratio in 2009 (against 9.8 per cent, in 2008 and 9.3 per cent in 2007). In spite of the slump in demand, the group increased its credit by €8.6 billion to reach €304.2 billion (plus 2.9 per cent) in 2009 and gained 0.6 per cent in the national credit market share, reaching 17.5 per cent. In addition, Crédit Mutuel is the first French banking institution to have repaid (in October 2009) the aid provided by the state (€1.2 billion out of €20 billion as part of a support package provided to the French banks as a whole), including principal and interest.[65]

In Germany, where cooperative banks provide 19 per cent of bank deposits and 16 per cent of bank loans:

the issuance of credit to enterprises by cooperative banks increased by 2.1 per cent in the first half of 2009, while the large banks (minus 2.4 per cent), the landesbanken [commercial banks] (minus 1.4 per cent) and regional banks [public banks] (minus 4 per cent) reduced their credit award. The cooperative banks deliver such an important contribution that a general credit clamp has not occurred in Germany ... Admittedly, cooperative banks have undergone problems with value adjustments and reductions in the cases of Lehman Brothers and the Icelandic banks. However, the cooperative banks as a whole have been less affected than most private banks and regional banks. As a consequence, the cooperative financial system is the only one of the three pillars of the German banking sector that has not relied on state reinforcement measures.[66]

The Dutch cooperative bank Rabobank has maintained its dominant national market share in savings during the crisis, in spite of a slight downward trend (40 per cent in 2009 against 41 per cent in 2007), and consolidated its market shares of loans to SMEs (41 per cent in 2009 against 38 per cent in 2007) and in mortgages (30 per cent in 2009 against 28 per cent in 2007).[67] In January 2010, the Dutch government invited them, as a success story, to a public hearing on the crisis.[68]

By contrast, a series of ex-member-based British Building Societies (akin to cooperatives) that had earlier been *de-mutualized* (namely converted into conventional banking entities) against small windfalls distributed to members (e.g. Abbey National distributed £130 to each ex-member) distinguished themselves for being at the very heart of the banking crisis in the UK, and did not survive (Northern Rock, Abbey National and Halifax being the three biggest casualties). According to Alan Cole, Director of the

UK Building Society Association, branch closure in the remaining building societies amounted to a reduction of 2.8 per cent, against 4.0 per cent in conventional banks between 2000 and 2003, the main hypothesized reason being that 'public companies [namely those listed on the stock exchange] are under more pressure to make cost savings as they are driven by the necessity of producing value for shareholders. Such pressures ... led to banks closing not merely branches that were losing money, but also branches that were profitable, *but just not profitable enough*'.[69] Cole adds that, on average, 'management expenses plus dividend payments are 30–35 per cent higher than management expenses alone in the converted institutions,[70] thereby weakening their entrepreneurial sustainability.

Consumer cooperatives in Europe have been substantially affected as has, indeed, the whole distribution sector, especially hypermarkets. Nevertheless, the percentage of sales of the coop brands has increased, as well as the number of members of this type of cooperative.[71] The Italian Coop enjoyed a 0.9 per cent increase in sales in 2009 as compared to 2008, with a rise of 1.1 per cent in the number of employees and 3.5 per cent in the number of members, whereas, over the same period, Carrefour saw its sales decrease by 24 per cent and was partially or completely withdrawing from a number of countries, laying off many workers,[72] as we saw in Chapter 3.

The resilience of housing cooperatives to the crisis has been stronger in the case of rental housing cooperatives (namely cooperatives where members pay rent), whereas ownership housing cooperatives (namely those where members own their houses) have suffered more because of the shortage of mortgage loans and the fall in asset values, which have affected the whole housing market (see Chapter 1).[73] A central problem for both types of housing cooperative is the availability of credit, and solutions are being put in place or currently being discussed. For example, 40 out of the 2,000 German housing cooperatives have established saving institutions of their own.[74]

Industrial and service cooperatives have been unequally affected, depending on the economic sector, but, even in those most affected, they have generally managed to resist better than other enterprises by resorting to special measures decided by their worker-members, such as the non-distribution of annual surpluses, reduction or, in extreme cases, even temporary suspension of wages. Almost all national responses to two successive world surveys in 2009 and 2010 conducted by CICOPA, the global organization of industrial and service cooperatives, indicate that the economic situation of the enterprises had generally worsened within one year (although this depends on the sectors: for example, social services are even undergoing a phase of expansion; innovative practices by cooperatives in some sectors have been successful, such as some Spanish construction sector cooperatives having converted to solar energy).[75]

However, the level of indebtedness of industrial and service cooperatives is reported to be lower than that of traditional enterprises of the same size and in the same sectors. As for enterprise mortality, it has remained minimal and has also been more modest than in other types of enterprise; most of the cooperatives that have closed down already had problems before the crisis, the latter providing the *coup de grâce*. Those with the strongest level of reserves and those that are best integrated in cooperative groups (such as Mondragon, which we will examine in Chapter 8) are resisting best.

Employment-wise, the situation in industrial and service cooperatives in Europe has indeed worsened, but the percentage of job losses is, again, lower than in other types of enterprise in the same sectors. For example in Spain, job reduction in industry between 2008 and 2009 was 6.4 per cent in cooperatives, against 11.9 per cent in other types of enterprises. In parts of the world other than Europe, job losses in industrial and services cooperatives are reported to be less important or nil. It should also be noted that successful transfers of businesses in crisis to the employees under the cooperative form, with net job salvation, are intensifying under the crisis, in particular in Southern Europe and South America.[76] In Chapter 6, we will examine one case of this kind in some detail.

The above data, though incomplete, are largely sufficient to demonstrate the relative resilience of cooperatives to the global financial and economic crisis. In order to understand why it is happening, we now need to analyse the rationality of cooperatives: what are these enterprises for? Whose interests do they serve? What do they want to achieve? How do they function?

Understanding the essence of the cooperative rationality

The underlying rationality of cooperatives remains largely misunderstood. However, if the cooperative mode of economic organization is to be seriously considered as one which can contribute to solving the debt trap (Chapter 2) and the issue of control in economic entities (Chapter 3), its underlying economic rationality should first be properly analysed and comprehended.

The international cooperative standards

In spite of regional and typological variations, all cooperatives in the world that are part of the organized system of representation linked to the International Cooperative Alliance (by far the largest part of them) refer to a single and explicitly worded set of world standards that defines their underlying value system, their socioeconomic objectives, their internal modalities of ownership and control, and their surplus distribution mechanisms, all of which distinguish them from those of conventional businesses. Therefore, if any common rationality and organizational pattern is to be found in cooperatives at the global level, it should be sought through these standards.

Defining a cooperative has been a unique historical process. It started as early as 1844, when members of a consumer cooperative in the Manchester suburb of Rochdale spelt out five organizational principles defining the functioning of a cooperative business.[77] These original cooperative standards have remained basically unaltered to this day, even though they have undergone several amendments. It should be emphasized that they have been defined, updated and disseminated (first across Europe, but very rapidly within the Americas, Asia and Africa) through democratic procedures, with debates and general assembly decisions. Although Rochdale is conventionally upheld as the first cooperative experience, probably because of its written principles or standards, we have historical evidence of cooperatives that were established earlier, e.g. in France and in the USA.[78] In turn, Rochdale signals the beginning of the cooperatives' standardizing process.

The cooperative standards initiated at Rochdale have gradually been translated into national laws regulating the functioning of cooperatives, as well as their supervision and sanctions enacted against non-compliance with the model, in the vast majority of countries in the world, China being among the latest with its first national cooperative law (Law on Farmer's Professional Cooperatives, 2006). This huge body of national laws has contributed to clarifying the cooperatives' rationality and organization, although some weak and incoherent provisions still remain.

The most recent version of the international cooperative standards was approved at the 1995 Congress of the International Cooperative Alliance (ICA) in Manchester, through a text called the *Statement on the Cooperative Identity* which had previously been debated in depth within the ICA member organizations. Seven years later, the contents of this cooperative identity statement were enshrined in full in Recommendation 193/2002 of the International Labour Organisation (ILO) with the unanimous approval (barring one abstention) of all 105 governments that were formally present, as well as national trade union confederations and employer organizations from all over the world, thereby transforming a cooperative internal and private standard into an international public norm.

ILO Recommendation 193/2002 on the Promotion of Cooperatives superseded the previous ILO Recommendation 127 of 1966, which was limited to developing countries. The universal character of the new ILO recommendation was ushered in by a resolution voted one year earlier by the General Assembly of the United Nations, called 'Cooperatives in Social Development' (UN Resolution 56/114). In 2004, two years after the approval of ILO Recommendation 193, the European Commission published its Communication 'on the Promotion of Cooperative Societies in Europe', the first-ever EU policy text exclusively dedicated to cooperatives, also explicitly recognizing the international cooperative standards.

Through the whole drafting process of ILO Recommendation 193, the international cooperative standards, earlier defined by cooperatives themselves, were to be tested during the international debates among states, trade unions and business representatives which took place under the ILO coordination between 2000 and 2002. Extensive preparatory work included an in-depth survey conducted by the ILO in 2000 with member governments, trade unions and employer organizations (the three ILO constituencies) as well as with cooperative organizations across the world.

At the 2001 and 2002 sessions of the International Labour Conference, two intense rounds of negotiation of two weeks each between the three ILO constituencies as well as cooperative representatives[79] took place. Indeed, a small group of cooperative representatives (around 10)[80] were accredited in either of the three ILO groups (governments, trade unions and employers) and could thus take part in the discussions of the drafting commission and hold specific meetings with various groups of representatives in between formal meetings. Among many contrasting opinions, which were expressed and dealt with throughout the discussion, these cooperative representatives had to explain in detail the underlying rationality of the cooperative standards. They had to provide examples and facts, in order to convince all other parties that these standards should be inserted in full in the Recommendation and in this, they were successful.[81]

The fact that governments, trade unions and employers from all over the world agreed in a final consensus to incorporate the ICA 'Statement on the Cooperative Identity' in full in the Recommendation shows that the underlying rationality of the cooperative type of economic organization had gradually become clear to them.[82] Let us now examine this rationality in the light of the international cooperative standards.

The first layer in understanding the cooperative rationality: the international definition

According to the international definition approved internally within the ICA and inter-governmentally within the ILO,[83] a cooperative is an 'association of persons' carrying out certain types of activities 'through a[n] (...) enterprise'. The word *through* indicates that the 'enterprise' character of the cooperative, although full-fledged, is subordinated to its character of 'association of persons'. This latter expression is in contrast with associations of capital, which conventional enterprises, based on the remuneration of capital, can be considered to be. Being an association of persons entails that the decision-making system is also based on persons and not on capital, and that, therefore, such persons are considered as equals in the internal business decision-making process, just in the same way as they are equal in the UN Universal Declaration of Human Rights or in the constitutions of virtually all countries of the world. Therefore, in a cooperative, the 'association of persons' develops its activities through an enterprise that is 'jointly owned and democratically controlled' (in its entrepreneurial processes and activities). Although they can delegate day-to-day management onto one or several appointed professionals, such persons ultimately take decisions jointly and jointly control the enterprise.

It is interesting to note that, whereas, in Chapter 3, we had observed an increasing dissociation in the globalized economy between ownership and control among key stakeholders (investors, producers, consumers), the cooperative definition, in turn, clearly affirms that cooperatives are characterized by a conjunction of ownership and control by the persons involved in the 'association of persons', leaving no room for external control. The concrete examples that we will analyse in the following chapters will show that the complete blending, in cooperatives, of associative and entrepreneurial characters and of ownership and control is not only possible, but can even be a source of long-term entrepreneurial development.

Broadly speaking, the double nature (entrepreneurial and associative) of the cooperative economic organization tends to make some international actors (e.g. some international development banks and multilateral institutions) as well as some national entrepreneurs and trade union bodies uncomfortable at the conceptual or theoretical level. There is difficulty in accepting that the two natures are not mutually exclusive, not even partly. But, with the crisis, the recognition of limitations in economic theory will probably operate paradigmatic changes, hopefully allowing for the due recognition of this double nature.

In order to go one decisive step forward in our understanding of the cooperative rationality, we need to examine the remaining part of the definition. The cooperative, it says, aims to enable the persons who own it jointly and control it democratically to 'meet their common economic, social and cultural needs and aspirations'. Indeed, 'Meet[ing the](...) common economic, social and cultural needs and aspirations' of persons is *the* key element in the economic rationality of cooperatives. In the case of cooperatives, the needs and aspirations that are common to many people, be these needs and aspirations of an economic, social or cultural nature, are met through an economic entity (an enterprise). Indeed, a cooperative is meant to solve needs and aspirations of persons *by means of entrepreneurial activity in the private sphere*. Otherwise, other types of institutions, such as clubs, associations and NGOs among others, can be established.

What types of persons could thus be motivated to come together to '*meet their common economic, social and cultural needs and aspirations*' in an enterprise-type structure? Key typologies of such individuals are, for example:

- Bank account-holders (private individuals, farmers, small entrepreneurs, owners of SMEs etc.) who want to save, obtain credit or get insured with a high level of guarantee and with the best possible services at the fairest possible cost, ensuring the permanence of financial services in their locality (particularly if it is rural and remote), as in the case of the Desjardins group which we will examine in Chapter 7.

- Users of essential distribution systems such as water, electricity and telephone who want to guarantee access to such goods and some level of price control over them, in particular in rural and remote areas.
- Consumers who want to ensure the permanence of a commercial outlet in their town or village, and/or the price and quality of the goods they consume.
- Workers and people in search of a job who want to establish or reinforce stable employment in competitive industrial or service enterprises, or who want to save their jobs when the enterprise risks closing down (as we will see in Ceralep in Chapter 6).
- Farmers who transform their agricultural produce in common, carry out joint purchases of inputs, or share access to machinery.
- Fishermen who sell their fish together, or share and distribute quotas and fishing areas (as we will see in the Natividad Island cooperative in Chapter 5).
- Craftsmen, such as bakers, mechanics or masons, small traders, or self-employed professions such as doctors, architects or lawyers, who want to mutualize a series of common services.
- People seeking housing at a reasonable cost and in a controlled environment.
- Persons who want to carry out cultural or sport activities (e.g. cultural centres, music bands, folklore troupes, festivals, football teams, etc.) in an economically sustainable way while keeping control over them.
- Local communities of citizens who want to ensure basic general interest services (e.g. health, education, social services, transports, etc.) that are not (or no longer) managed by the public authorities, and who want to maintain adequate control over the quality, affordability, geographical accessibility and long-term sustainability of these services.

Looking at the various typologies of persons mentioned above, one fundamentally finds all major basic *stakeholders* that are found in society. Cooperatives therefore systematically develop a 'stakeholder economy', by which these stakeholders give themselves the possibility to 'meet their common economic, social and cultural needs and aspiration' either because it is the only way they can possibly do so, or because the cooperative allows them to do it under better conditions of price, quality, accessibility and long-term economic sustainability than they could get on their own or through economic organizations that they would not control and which would have another type of rationality. It can thus be easily understood that *joint ownership and democratic control* exerted by the stakeholders over the enterprise is fundamental in order to guarantee the maintenance of such conditions. As we can see, cooperative members, like cooperative enterprises, are characterized by a double nature: both stakeholders and owners–controllers.

The second layer in understanding the cooperative rationality: the operational principles

The second layer in understanding the rationality of cooperatives is the analysis of the seven operational principles which condition their functioning and define (a) the relation of the enterprise with its surrounding environment; (b) the internal organization of the enterprise; and (c) the system of financial accumulation and distribution.

The relation with the surrounding environment

As a first consideration, the cooperative is defined as being an autonomous and independent enterprise (fourth cooperative principle, 'autonomy and independence').[84] Considering a cooperative as a para-public type of business is often the result of confusion between the concepts of 'public' and 'common'. In spite of their 'joint' characteristics (joint control, joint ownership, joint stakeholder approach etc.), cooperatives are full-fledged private enterprises enjoying complete autonomy and independence from the state or any other third party. They develop what one could call a 'common-private' economy ('common' in the sense of 'common good' mentioned at the beginning of this chapter, as opposed to 'individual'), where there can be partnerships, but in no case confusion, with the public sector. The empirical cases presented in the following chapters will make it easier to grasp this (apparently contradictory) 'common-private' character.

Another characteristic is that cooperatives do not limit themselves to satisfy the needs and aspirations of a closed group of citizens, but, instead, are meant to be open to all the persons who share the same needs and aspirations as those served by the cooperative (first cooperative principle, 'voluntary and open membership'), which depends on the typology of stakeholders which it has the mission to serve.[85]

This openness towards the outside world, however, is conditioned by concrete limitations, such as the geographical area served by the cooperative, the pace of its entrepreneurial development, or the necessary skills required for a new job in a cooperative among workers. Economic development being crucial for this openness to be really effective, the cooperative's pace of openness must be controlled if it is to fulfil its mission. This is something that we will see in the case of the Mondragon cooperative group (Chapter 8): only through gradual economic development geared towards the long term can new workplaces be created, and then new worker-members be admitted. In the Natividad island Divers' and Fishermen's Cooperative (which we will examine in the next chapter), the slowness in admitting new members is linked to the policy of conservation of natural resources, and therefore, ultimately, to the long-term viability of the business as well. In some cases, this conjunctural contradiction between economic development and the pace of openness of cooperatives can lead to painful decisions, such as the one not to admit all workers in cases of business transfers to the employees, as we will see in the case of Ceralep (Chapter 6).

A wider interpretation of the first cooperative principle could nip the business transfer project in the bud, thereby destroying the very purpose of the cooperative being established, and all the potential jobs along with it.

As a logical consequence of being both open to the surrounding community and oriented towards the satisfaction of needs and aspirations of important categories of stakeholders active in the locality (as we saw in the cooperative definition above), cooperatives are inherently linked to the development of the surrounding community, even when they are not directly and explicitly involved in community development (seventh cooperative principle, 'concern for community').[86] Accordingly, cooperatives 'work for the sustainable development of their communities': at the same time, the private character of cooperatives is reaffirmed, as their contribution to the community must be carried out 'through policies approved by their members'. From the small Natividad cooperative in Mexico (Chapter 5) to the large Mondragon group in Spain (Chapter 8), we will see how decisions having a local or regional impact are taken by the cooperative members through democratic procedures.

The cooperative standards also contain a principle (the sixth one, 'cooperation among cooperatives') referring to a wider 'cooperative movement' to which individual cooperatives belong and contribute,[87] namely an open and dynamic community of human beings, with a mission towards socioeconomic development, in line with resolution 56/114 of the UN General Assembly, '[r]ecognizing that cooperatives in their various forms promote the fullest participation in the economic and social development of all people'.[88] Cooperatives in many parts of the world have displayed a strong capacity to develop mutualized and democratically controlled business support institutions and horizontal groups among themselves, allowing them to become mainstream economic actors in the globalized economy. The examples of Desjardin and Mondragon are particularly developed models of cooperative groups, as we will see, but they are by no means the only ones: we find very important cooperative groups in other countries, including the vast majority of the G20.[89] In the case of Ceralep, we will see how a number of cooperative actors (a regional federation, a bank, three non-banking financial institutions) mobilize themselves to save an artificially liquidated SME and turn it again into a viable business; similar examples from the UK, Italy, Spain, Brazil, Argentina, Canada or China, among others, could also be documented. In terms of representation of interests, the cooperative system has managed to gradually put in place federative systems, with national, continental, and sectoral structures with one global umbrella organization, the International Cooperative Alliance.

The fact that cooperatives declare support for each other as stipulated in this sixth cooperative principle does not mean that they will automatically help each other *directly* in the same sector or among sectors, for example cooperative banks financing industrial cooperatives. Some cooperative banks such as Crédit Coopératif (one of the banks of the French Banques Populaires group), or the Caisses d'Economie (a fraction of the 481 credit cooperatives of the Desjardin group – see Chapter 7), or the Mondragon group's Caja Laboral bank (see Chapter 8) have indeed been playing the role of development banks for cooperatives or for a wider stakeholder-based economy, as per their founding mission. In turn, most cooperative banks are not based on such founding mission, but, in turn, are dedicated to the development needs of millions of farmers, small craftsmen and SMEs, the regional economy needs or the consumer needs of millions of citizens who co-own them: there is no reason why they should change their founding mission. In the same vein, there is no reason why housing cooperatives should be obliged to cater for the housing needs of the workers of worker cooperatives, unless, of course, they both share the same need and agree to it. In turn, indirect support to the wider cooperative system is a common practice among cooperatives, including very large ones, through federation fees, contribution to development funds, sharing of know-how, etc. Cooperatives act in this fashion to help develop the cooperative system, not to gain market shares nor acquire or control start-ups, restructured enterprises or other types of economic entities.

The internal functioning of the enterprise

The cooperative standards specify that the democratic control by members which we saw in the cooperative definition above must be implemented not through a one-share-one-vote system but through strict one-*person*-one-vote procedures (second cooperative principle, 'democratic member control').[90] Here, the cooperative emerges as a citizen-based enterprise, as part of the *politeia*. The cooperative is controlled by local long-term stakeholders who change neither identity nor socioeconomic stakes overnight (producers, workers, inhabitants, account-holders, borrowers etc.), rather than by managers working in the interest of external shareholders whose behaviour is dictated by the highest possible return on investment. They, therefore, tend to opt for more long-term enterprise strategies, based on the stability of the enterprise within its locality, on sustainable jobs and sustainable operations. They aim to create wealth, and thus must remain profitable together with a long-term strategy (thence they are not likely to fall into the debt trap!).

Democratic member control, if properly carried out, makes it far more difficult than in conventional enterprises for an external person or entity to control the firm, and impossible through acquisition, unless the enterprise has first been 'de-cooperativized', or, in other words, once the members have legally and definitively renounced their democratic control and joint ownership rights over the enterprise. Only then may the activity and equipment be sold.

On the other hand, democratic control by members is not simply limited to formal procedures in general assemblies. In other words, it is not only an Athenian, 'agora' type democracy, but also a 'republican' democracy: like the separation of powers in a modern state, cooperatives are characterized by checks and balances exercised by various internal instances. While checks and balances are fundamental in a single cooperative, this is even more so in complex cooperative *ensembles*, as we will see in the cases of Desjardins and Mondragon. These complex spaces of negotiation and elaboration of strategies make it possible to jointly adapt to the unknown and the unexpected.

In a separate but related principle (the fifth one, 'information, training and education'), the cooperative standards underline the importance of both information and training.[91] Information is fundamental for whoever needs to control and manage a business, independently from whether there is an external 'controller' as in global chains (Chapter 3) or joint internal 'controllers' as in cooperatives. A whole body of literature has focused on the problem of information asymmetries in enterprises.[92] However, information is not sufficient in itself. If cooperative members are only provided with information, without enough training on how to deal with it, they will most probably not be able to process and articulate it, and, in that case, they will not be able to use it in order to exercise their control over the enterprise. The more complex a cooperative system in which ordinary members are joint 'controllers' is, the more difficult it is to process and articulate such information without appropriate training.

On the other hand, members of a cooperative have, as we saw, ordinary economic or social roles such as farmers, fishermen, consumers etc., and they are not all holders of an MBA. Nevertheless, they do have to take 'hard' entrepreneurial decisions as joint 'controllers', owners and managers of the enterprise. Therefore, the only way in which 'democratic member control' can be ensured effectively in stakeholder-based enterprises such as cooperatives is to invest strongly in training and education, not only for board members and higher executives, but for ordinary members as well.

However, education and training are not only instrumental to implementing democratic member control: they are also at the very core of the cooperative rationality. A cooperative is a type of enterprise by which ordinary citizens have a unique chance to become fully trained in shouldering entrepreneurial responsibilities and in being involved in economic democracy. For example, tens of thousands of ordinary citizens who are board members of the Desjardins local credit cooperatives undergo systematic training, as we will see in Chapter 7.

Cooperative education, though, is not only about enterprise management. Desjardins, as we will see, also organizes wide-ranging educational programmes on how to manage a family budget: as a financial movement for a whole region, it is a core part of the group's mission to enable ordinary citizens to better manage their own finances. Similarly, we find participative educational activities launched by consumer cooperatives, such as 'consumer circles' in Argentina, where topics such as 'food and health', 'prevention of illnesses', or 'protection of the environment' are discussed,[93] a 'coop school' in Italy for training on 'awareness in consumption',[94] etc. These examples are about educating people to fully shoulder their responsibilities as specific stakeholders (consumers, fishermen, etc.), but also, more generally, as fully aware and responsible citizens, and not only as joint owners–controllers of a business.

The system of financial accumulation and distribution: the third cooperative principle

The third cooperative principle, 'member economic participation'[95] is the most relevant one to the topic of this book, and derives from the other six. It contains four parts which we will now analyse separately.

1 Contribution in, and remuneration of, capital

'Members contribute equitably to, and democratically control, the capital of their cooperative'.[96] Members subscribe certain amounts of share capital. Depending on the different cooperative sectors or regimes, the amount subscribed can be symbolic or substantial, equal among all members or different (but in all cases, as mentioned above, the 'one person one vote' principle will be maintained). In some cases, such as in the Mondragon group, the worker–members invest an amount equal to one year's wages in cooperative shares. In addition, in order to 'democratically control' the share capital, members must hold in their own hands the totality, or at least the overwhelming majority, of the latter.[97] Barring a few borderline and rather isolated exceptions, the cooperatives are therefore not listed on the stock exchange and cannot be in the hands of private equity investors either (unless they are first 'de-mutualized'). Even in the case of national provisions allowing for minority shares to be in the hands of external investors, such provisions can be implemented only if the cooperative's general assembly approves it, and always up to a fixed threshold, generally not more than around 30 per cent. The internal shares in the hands of cooperative members cannot be traded with the outside world nor can they be traded among members themselves. The redemption and thus release of cooperative shares do not take place as commercial transactions, and thus need the approval of the cooperative decision-making bodies. This ensures that cooperatives respond to the economic and social needs which they aim to satisfy, and avoids the establishment of vertical power.

'Members usually receive limited compensation, if any, on capital subscribed as a condition of membership'.[98] This provision is aimed at preventing the capital subscribed from devaluating, rather than to enable members to obtain an income from it. Generally speaking, the rate of interest provided is similar to, or slightly higher than, the rate paid on an ordinary deposit account in a bank. In any case, it can never constitute a financial motivation.

2   *Surpluses returned to members*

'Members allocate surpluses for ... benefiting members in proportion to their transactions with the cooperative'.[99] Part of the surpluses is normally redistributed to members. However, this type of redistribution has nothing to do with shareholders' dividends, since, as we saw above, only marginal remuneration of the members' capital invested in the enterprise is allowed in a cooperative. Surplus redistribution in a cooperative is, in fact, a year-end adjustment of the average *price of the transactions* (unlike ordinary transactions carried out between buyers and sellers or between job-providers and workers) carried out between the cooperative and its members during the year.

In order to explain the reason for this price adjustment, one needs to understand that the price of any given transaction between the cooperative and its members is, in essence, an advance payment on the definitive price. Indeed, since the cooperative members are its co-owners and not ordinary clients, the 'correct price' of the transaction with members can only be known once the annual accounts have been closed and when the annual surplus has been calculated. This price adjustment can be on the purchasing price (in the case of a cooperative among individual producers), on the selling price (in the case of a cooperative among users), or on the price of labour remuneration (in the case of a cooperative among workers). Indeed, before this price adjustment, the transactions with the producers, consumers or workers are only advance payments on the final price.

3   *Reserves*

'At least part of [the] capital [of the cooperative] is usually the common property of the cooperative ... Members allocate surpluses for ... developing their cooperative, possibly by setting up reserves, part of which at least would be indivisible'.[100] The systematic and long-term constitution of reserves in cooperatives is an important protection against the debt trap. We will see in later chapters the importance that the constitution of common reserves including at the group level has played in Desjardins and Mondragon's economic development and resilience to successive crises covering decades. They have the same importance in all cooperatives in the world, of different sizes and scopes of activities, and this for two main reasons.

First, as we saw above, the share capital of cooperatives is made up of members' shares, and cooperatives as such have no access to ordinary financial markets. Some, like Mondragon's Eroski distribution chain, do issue bonds without voting rights. A number of non-banking financial institutions belonging to the cooperative system exercise a lever effect on banks, and some of them issue non-voting 'participative certificates' (assimilated to own funds), as we will see in Ceralep's case (Chapter 6). But these financial instruments can hardly compensate for the concrete financial limitation which many cooperatives are faced with in terms of share capital. Reserves are therefore essential. In many cooperatives, having experienced a steady expansion over decades, reserves are often ten times as high as the amount in share capital, or more.

The second reason is that if cooperatives aim to have a long-term economic life, they need to protect themselves as much as they can from market volatility, and times of crisis invariably show they are correct, considering their long-term objectives. Cooperative reserves are generally invested in the long-term development of the enterprise, but can also be used as collateral or common guarantee systems when it is necessary to negotiate urgent loans with the banks, as has often been the case during the ongoing crisis. In cooperative banks, the fact that a high percentage of capital is constituted by reserves rather than share capital tends to substantially raise its quality and rating, as we saw earlier in this chapter and will further discuss in Chapter 7.

This third cooperative principle, as we saw above, also mentions the possibility that part of the reserves 'would be indivisible'. Indivisible reserves are assets that can never be redistributed to members even in case of winding up of the cooperative. They have so far been more widely used in countries with Roman law traditions than Anglo-Saxon ones. Countries such as France, Italy, Spain, Portugal or Argentina make such reserves mandatory. Interestingly, though, the UK, which previously made indivisible reserves only an option, recently passed a 'Community Interest Companies' law (under which cooperatives or other types of business can be registered) in which an 'asset lock' is mandatory.[101] This tendency is spreading, as can be seen in recent legislation trends in different parts of the world.

Under an indivisible reserve regime, if the enterprise is closed down, its reserves (if there are any after payment of any outstanding debt) are transferred to a federation, a cooperative development fund or a similar institution promoting cooperatives. Therefore, indivisible reserves make the 'common-private' nature of cooperative ownership even clearer. They establish a specific property regime in no way comparable to individual private ownership. For this reason, they are generally submitted to a different tax system than divisible reserves in traditional enterprises (and this 'falsifies' the last critique in the first section).

In addition, indivisible reserves are a powerful deterrent against fraud as well as de-mutualization and external take-over attempts. Indeed, the external acquirer needs to convince cooperative members to renounce their democratic control power through a general assembly decision. Even when the enterprise has been de-mutualized and acquired, the acquirer can never claim possession over such reserves.

Indivisible reserves provide us with another fundamental clue in the under-lying rationality of cooperatives, which are seen as belonging not only to their present members, but also to their past and future ones. This is logical, because if a cooperative is indeed a 'common-private' economic entity, its membership should indeed be seen in a time perspective, across generations.

4   *Funds for the development of the cooperative system*
'Members allocate surpluses for … supporting other activities approved by the membership'.[102] In a number of countries, part of the surplus is ear-marked for funds which are not to be used by the cooperative itself, but for the development of the cooperative system at the national level. This financial mechanism is one possible way to carry out cooperation among cooperatives (a concept enshrined in the cooperative standards, as we saw above). For example, the Spanish cooperative legislation, in the wake of the Mondragon experience, earmarks different percentages of surplus (depend-ing on the region of the country) for an education and promotion fund. In Italy, a national law obliges all cooperatives with positive results to trans-fer 3 per cent of their surpluses to cooperative solidarity funds aimed at promoting cooperative entrepreneurial projects (start-ups, transformation, development, etc.), therefore generating thousands of jobs and hundreds of economic activities, including in the field of social services.

Cooperative values
Last but not least, the international cooperative standards include a set of simple and easily understandable values which almost every business would probably claim to adhere to: 'self-help, self-responsibility, democracy, equal-ity, equity and solidarity; as well as ethical values of honesty, openness, social responsibility and caring for others'.[103] The major distinctive feature, though, is that, in the case of cooperatives, these values are not justifying ones but underlying ones, in the sense that they must be translated into concrete organizational and financial provisions: indeed, they are at the very basis of the cooperative definition and the cooperative operational principles that we saw above. We do not maintain, of course, that they cannot be upheld by other types of business as well, but that, in the case of cooperatives, they should be underlying values (so long, of course, as cooperatives follow the model). Therefore, cooperatives have a fundamental contribution to share in terms of underlying economic values, and in terms of mechanisms to implement these values in practice.

The present crisis, precisely, is offering an open forum for many people (scholars, opinion leaders, ordinary people) to reflect on values. To some extent, it is also a crisis of values. What, in the end, does the economy aim to achieve? What values should be promoted? To what extent must human beings master the economic system on the basis of underlying values or, in turn, let the economic system be fully dominated by values such as greed, inequality, unfairness, egoism, individualism, dishonesty, shadiness, irresponsibility towards fellow human beings and our common environment? Which founding economic values do we want to bequeath to our children?

Mutuals, a very similar type of economic organization

A terminological confusion should be dispelled at the outset: a 'mutual' (also called 'mutual aid society' or 'friendly society') is a completely different concept from a 'mutual fund'. According to the *Oxford Dictionary of Finance and Banking*, a mutual fund is 'the US name for a unit trust', which is 'a trust formed ... to manage a portfolio of stock-exchange securities, in which small investors can buy units. This gives the small investor access to a diversified portfolio of securities, chosen and managed by professional fund managers, who seek either high capital gains or high yields'.[104] We saw an example of such 'mutual funds' in Chapter 1 with Washington Mutual or Wamu. This type of economic entity has absolutely nothing to do with cooperatives.

In turn, according to the same dictionary, a mutual is 'a company that has no issued stocks or shares and is owned by its members or depositors. Most UK building societies and some insurance companies have this structure'.

According to the UK's 'mutuals manifesto', jointly published by the UK Building Societies Association, Co-operatives UK, the UK Employee-ownership Association, and the UK Association of Financial Mutuals, mutuals encompass a wider reality than cooperatives, while including the latter: they 'take many forms and operate in a wide range of business and social environments'. But their common denominator is that they 'are organizations that are owned by, and run for the benefit of, their current and future members'; they are 'membership based organizations' which share 'a common heritage and ethos – to serve their members and work in the wider interests of society'.[105]

The generally agreed international understanding of a mutual, which is enshrined in many national laws, is not as broad as the one existing in the UK, but remains very close to that of a cooperative. According to the Association of Mutual Insurers and Insurance Cooperatives in Europe (AMICE), a mutual, like a cooperative, 'is collectively owned by its members' and is characterized by the 'congruence of ownership/control'; 'every member of the mutual has an equal vote in members' meetings'. The main difference with cooperatives is that 'mutuals are not established through the provision of capital by their members', although, like cooperatives, they 'have the possibility to re-distribute profits to membership, e.g. via refunds and rebates'.[106] In other words, mutuals explicitly differ only on one of the four provisions included in the third cooperative principle described above. They do not explicitly have the fourth principle (autonomy and independence), the fifth (information, training and education) or the sixth (cooperation among cooperatives), but they generally behave in a similar way to cooperatives under these aspects as well. However, mutuals do not possess such clearly codified international standards as cooperatives have, even though their model of economic organization is very comparable, to the extent that, from a number of standpoints, they could be examined together with cooperatives.

Most mutuals are active in the insurance sector, either general insurance (life, risks, etc.) or health insurance, and, in this sector, they have generally become more important than cooperatives.

A political economy approach to cooperatives

The evolution of cooperatives as we know them today is linked to two socioeconomic factors that have intensified in Europe since the nineteenth century, and then gradually extended to other parts of the world: (i) the transformation of traditional socioeconomic structures and (ii) two successive waves of economic globalization.[107]

The partial or complete *transformation* of *traditional structures* (corporations, extended families, clans, etc.) through which the socioeconomic needs mentioned in the previous section were channelled, brought about new forms of solidarity and economic association between persons. With the Industrial Revolution, the social protection mechanisms, which had earlier prevailed, broke apart, as Karl Polanyi described in *The Great Transformation,* strongly encouraging the requirement for labour flexibility to direct migratory flows towards the new workplaces.[108]

In nineteenth-century Europe, debates on cooperatives were related to the transformation of industrial society. A book, published in 1839, discovered at Heudicourt Castle in Normandy mentions cooperatives in relation to poverty and the need to find responses to the marginalization of the working classes that could endanger the social and political order. This nineteenth-century debate is having some resonance at the beginning of the twenty-first century. Likewise, today, authorities speak of the struggle against marginalization and for social inclusion while being concerned with the long-term unemployed and immigrants, thinking of cooperatives as a key actor to deal with such concerns. However, while authorities tend to see cooperatives only as a means to ensure social peace, cooperative members also see their economic future through the building of strong economic entities.

The second factor in the evolution of cooperatives is constituted by two successive *waves of economic globalization* which the world has experienced. In the wave which took place in the nineteenth century, increasing competition and enlarging business scales pushed ordinary people to share their common knowledge, information and resources to better satisfy their needs when confronted by an increasing level of economic concentration. Indeed, the cooperative system makes it possible for ordinary citizens to reach economies of scale which can, in certain cases, be significant. In the most recent wave of economic globalization, dating from the beginning of the 1990s, cooperatives regained dynamism in various sectors such as industry, services, banking, insurance, etc., with many requests for support and exchanges originating from developing countries.

Following the Great Depression in 1929 until the 1970s (except for the Nazi–Fascist period and centrally planned communist regimes), many nation-states implemented social welfare policies that either channelled the added value of cooperatives or let the latter act as a factor of social cohesion. Except for some 'developmentalist' regimes in developing countries, they did this while preserving their autonomy. Since the 1980s, nation-states have retreated amidst structural reforms and the construction of a global market of services in phase with economic globalization. Questioning cooperatives has become fashionable, including their characteristics in terms of socioeconomic organization and embeddedness in the local economy.

Cooperatives have been under pressure to dismantle and become companies listed on the stock exchange, such as the ex-UK building societies mentioned above. With economic globalization, the trend towards standardization and the building of global chains have heightened such pressures.

It is in this overall context that the above-mentioned ILO Recommendation 193 initiative took place. Thanks, partly, to the mobilization among the representative organizations of the cooperative movement, Recommendation 193 finally incorporated the cooperative standards elaborated earlier by the cooperative movement itself, thereby recognizing the latter as an entrepreneurial actor with its own characteristics and standards, distinct from other types of enterprise. In addition, the Recommendation calls for the responsibility of nation-states in promoting cooperatives through a regulatory framework complying with the cooperative standards. But the ILO text is not exclusively the result of the mobilization of the cooperative movement. Indeed, with each financial and economic crisis (as seen under the 'liquidity trap' in Chapter 2), the stock market and the financialization of the economy both come under the spotlight, and other paths tend to be explored and promoted.

Against all odds, the pressures to deprecate the cooperatives' distinctive type of economic organization may have led to an improbable outcome: a slow mainstreaming process may be under way. The international recognition of the legitimate and identifiable existence of this type of economic organization across the world now includes developed countries as well, and not only developing countries as before. We may thus be slowly witnessing a new thinking about economic entities in general.

Let us now turn to a few empirical cases of cooperatives and see what has happened to them over the last few years amidst the global financial crisis.

5
Natividad Island Divers' and Fishermen's Cooperative, Mexico: Managing Natural Resources to Generate Wealth

Introduction

We begin our series of empirical cases with a small Mexican fishing cooperative, located close to the border with the USA. This example provides a link between the cooperative system and environmental issues. Natividad is a tiny and arid island, six by two kilometres, off Baja California's coast in Mexico. Barely 400 people (80 families) live there. Life on the island depends entirely upon the Natividad Divers' and Fishermen's Cooperative, which exploits the maritime areas according to a concession contract with the government. The divers spend four to five hours every day under the water, linked to an oxygen tube and assisted by colleagues on a small boat above them. They mainly gather abalones, a very rare and expensive shellfish, and they earn a lot of money: a diver can earn up to US$10,000 a month.

The cooperative has an administrative office on the mainland, in the port city of Ensenada, from where it ships its products abroad under the brand name 'Island Pacific', in particular to Asia, where abalones are considered a delicacy.

The evolution of the cooperative

Life has not always been rosy in the Divers' and Fishermen's Cooperative. Established as early as 1942 (the second oldest fishery cooperative of Baja California), it evolved in a slow and humble way, as current president Esteban Fraire explains: 'the main historical landmarks of the cooperative have been when we bought our first boat to transport goods, when we built our packaging plant, our power-generation station, and our desalinization station'.[1] Over the past 25 years, the cooperative has been through several crises. In the 1980s, the El Niño stream warmed up the waters and reduced stocks. Then, the reserves were over-exploited through the fault of the cooperative itself and illegal fishing by people from outside. But, by the end of the 1980s, the cooperative had managed to overcome these difficulties and has, since then, been able to control predatory practices and the rush for short-term growth. It engaged in a more scientific and environmental approach, and, among other measures, appointed a biologist.

Martin, the ex-president of the cooperative, explains how they changed the fishing practice of the company:

> During the crisis, we took the decision to close a specific [maritime] zone. We did it in order to see the results. Then, at the general assembly, we decided to close it off for four years. This helped us a lot. In one season, this measure generated enough money for us to install our tinning and conditioning factory. The result was beyond expectations. We had fore-seen that, with this measure, the abalones would reproduce, but we never thought we would draw such high benefits from it.

The success was so obvious that the cooperative attracted the interest of the scientific community. Clément Dumont, a researcher on maritime resource management at the oceanic institute of Stanford University, regularly carries out research on the island, working in close contact with the cooperative's biologist, Antonio. He comments: 'The advantage of having a biologist [in the cooperative] is that he can create a link with the scientific community while maintaining a very close relation with the fishermen, and to make the fishermen understand the scientific data, which is often a big problem for us [scientists]'.[2]

A few years ago, Antonio submitted to the general assembly of the coop-erative the idea of investing in maritime reserves in order to ensure the future population of abalones, sea cucumbers and sea snails. The idea was approved by the cooperative members. The closure of this maritime space caused an immediate reduction of income of $300,000 per year for the cooperative. The members made this decision because they had the neces-sary information at hand to take joint decisions, with the help of research-ers from Stanford University and other academic institutions, and therefore understood why they were taking such measures and which long-term advantages they would draw from them.

Dumont comments: 'it is fantastic to have such a relation with the fisher-men, they will not ask you questions such as "do you think it will work?". They know it will, and they will test it by themselves. In turn, what they are concerned about is whether people from the outside are not going to fish in their waters', namely in the protected maritime zones which they have been formally entrusted since the 1990s according to a concession system with the government.[3]

Indeed, at the end of the 1990s, the cooperative endured the effects of heavy illegal fishing by fishermen from the outside, within the maritime zones under its own management. But the cooperative took the matter into its own hands, initially, without any government aid. A fisherman comments:

> Now, there are almost no pirates left, they dare not come, because they know that two of our boats continuously patrol the coasts. Two boats go around the island all the time, including during the night. When a boat tries to oppose resistance and continues fishing [in the areas that must be kept off limits to maintain the eco-system], we intercept it. We break the ship so that it does not escape. The whole region is full of pirates. Sometimes they use weapons and we can get killed'.[4]

Fortunately, the government has recently come to support these endogenous surveillance efforts by providing land units to control the seashore.

Internal organization, impact of the crisis and partnerships

Not all workers are cooperative members. The cooperative has 82 worker-members and 56 workers who are not members and who thus cannot vote in general assemblies. The latter can only replace worker-members on a job, and work on lower added-value products, such as algae sold to the pharmaceutical industry. One of them, Toxi, always gets up earlier than the members, hoping to have the opportunity to replace a member on a job. 'I am sacrificing a few years of my life, in order to hit the jackpot in the end. I try to reach the next step, which is to become a member'.[5]

At the beginning of the 1980s, there were 120 members. But because of over-exploitation and reduction of stocks and income, they decided to admit no new members for several years. Non-members try to work as well as they can, hoping that they will be admitted one day. 'You need to have discipline, work a lot and be responsible',[6] says Toxi, who must wait until a member retires in order to become a member. He is on the top of the list but he will have to wait for another year at least: the general assembly has just decided not to take in any new members for the time being, in spite of the retirement of an old member, Servando, a diver for 24 years.

Servando, 48, is retiring because his body can no longer allow him to dive. The cooperative asked him to retire after 23 years and he accepted. At the general assembly, Servando, applauded by his colleagues, starts his speech with a sob: 'I am discovering that I am a sentimental guy. It's hard for me to hide my pain. But I would like to say good-bye to all of you. I would like to thank the cooperative. I will always remember I was part of such a nice and good company, which preserves the values of the group and teaches good things. It has been a school, a school of life. It has been the best one'. Then Servando bursts into tears and goes back to his seat, among the noisy applause of his fellow members.[7]

Cooperative members who live on the island with their families have a number of advantages, such as free water and electricity. However, life is austere: there are no bars, people work six days a week, and the only common hobby is the baseball match on Sunday.

The pensioners live on the mainland in the city of Enseñada and the cooperative takes full care of them: the poorer ones are completely taken care of in a special home, whereas the divers get a $300,000 bonus, with which they can open businesses in the city. Several times every month the ex-members meet in seaside restaurants.

The global crisis did not spare the cooperative, as described by president Esteban Fraire: 'The crisis was particularly hard in 2009. We reduced our functioning costs and even the members had to sacrifice part of their income. But fortunately it is already behind us now'.[8] Even during the crisis, the cooperative managed to have a turnover of $4 million in 2009, a satisfactory figure for a small fishing SME of 138 workers in Mexico.

Cooperative members look at the future with some optimism. The government is now paying more attention to the cooperative, in particular through its regulatory entities, Inapesca and Conapesca, and is providing support for some of its projects, such as the modernization of the packaging factory according to EU norms and a laboratory for abalone semen. The fishing concessions will have to be renegotiated in 2012 but members are confident that they will be renewed. Esteban Fraire considers that 'this gives us the necessary legal security to do long-term planning for the fishing areas and the development of the cooperative'.[9]

The relationship with Stanford University is ongoing. Other institutions, COBI, a Mexican environmental NGO, and Reef Check, a US-based NGO working throughout the world on the environmental protection of seashores, share with Stanford the responsibility of monitoring the natural reserves. New research agreements have been signed with CICESE (Enseñada Scientific Research and Higher Education Centre) and UABC (Autonomous University of Baja California).

Managing natural resources

Work organization on the island is very strict. The divers' and fishermen's day starts at 7 am. Inspectors who are cooperative members distribute different roadmaps and very precise fishing quotas to each team. Discipline can be seen at all stages of the fishing process: when distribution is carried out in the morning, when each team's catch is controlled in the afternoon, everything is weighed and calculated exactly. Before each season, the cooperative evaluates its stocks, and does so in a very precise fashion, thanks to a unique segmentation of its fishing area, with a strict mapping of the existing resources and a rotating fishing system. In this way, the teams know what they have in each block and what they should catch in each of them.

This practice is reportedly close to innovative concepts within the scientific community, where points of view on the management of natural resources have evolved. In the past, the sea used to be considered as a single uniform basin; therefore, it was thought that biological resources could be measured over very large areas. The new trend is to work on smaller scales and at various depths.[10] The Divers' and Fishermen's Cooperative of Natividad Island has become a model to convince sceptics. COBI, one of the scientific partners of the cooperative, testifies that the cooperative 'has a model management of its fishing resources, and, in its assembly, defines policies that are far more precautionary than those diagnosed by the fisheries authorities'.[11]

This story strengthens the argument of economics Nobel prize winner Elinor Ostrom in *Governing the Commons*,[12] according to which natural resources are bound to be depleted if left under the sole management of businesses exclusively motivated by the short-term maximization of profit. Instead, they need to be managed under the joint control of the local inhabitants who have a stake in the maintenance of these resources.

It is also in line with the work of Riccardo Petrella on the management of water resources. In *The Water Manifesto: Arguments for a World Water Contract*, Petrella argues that:

> It is important to destatize water: that is, to free it from the bureaucratic-centralist logic of state power by affirming the value of state citizenship. Destatization of water does not, however, mean privatization in the form of a transfer of ownership and control to private corporations. A cooperative type of enterprise delegated to run a public service (one that really does operate on the basis of cooperative principles) is neither the state nor a private capitalist company.[13]

In fact, as discussed in Chapter 4, cooperatives are 'common-private' businesses able to establish strong partnerships with the public authorities without being dominated by them.

Conclusion: combining long-term environmental, economic and social interests

Hypothesizing that cooperatives tend to get stuck in quasi-markets, as some scholars maintain (see Chapter 4), then the Natividad island cooperative does not comply with the model. This business not only operates on the international market, but has also managed to go up in the value chain by canning its products and to do R&D on resource management in cooperation with a first-class US university and other research institutions.

This cooperative example shows us how proper democratic control and management can ensure the preservation of the local environment, while also providing members–stakeholders with above-average incomes plus a whole array of social advantages. Indeed, Natividad is not only an environmental experience, but also an economic one. In fact, the cooperative members' motivation is not environmental. For them, the strict management of the natural resources is just common sense, a way to ensure the long-term sustainability of their economy and of their economic activity, which is both environmentally and economically sustainable, provided, of course, that one agrees to give priority to long-term economic sustainability over short-term gains.

On the other hand, the self-discipline that the cooperative imposes on itself is made possible because members share all the information, on the basis of which they can then debate and take joint decisions, including hard ones. These decisions thus contain a high level of legitimacy, which is even higher due to the successful results of such commonly enforced discipline.

In spite of the first cooperative principle, 'voluntary and open membership', which we saw in Chapter 4, the key policy of conservation of natural resources justifies the slowness in admitting new members. Indeed, such slow pace of admission is linked to the long-term viability of the business and, ultimately, to the very interest of the candidates for membership, future members and the local community as a whole.

As the protection of the natural resources maintains and develops the general wealth of the local community, the cooperative avoids falling into the debt trap, a danger that could loom large if these natural resources were exhausted. In addition, since the cooperative has built a high-level social protection system, the joint interest of the cooperative and the individual interests of its members converge, which helps prevent the members themselves from falling into the debt trap as individuals.

Cooperative president Esteban Fraire summarizes the members' vision in the following words:

> it is through the cooperative that we make our living. Normally, each member works in the cooperative for more than 21 years. Although the income we get is high, we think that it is even more important to have certainty about our future. Thus, on many occasions, we have to renounce part of our income as fishermen for the development of the cooperative.

6
Ceralep Société Nouvelle, France: David and Goliath in the Global Economy

Introduction

In Chapter 3, we examined the use of debt by absentee investors in order to control enterprises via global chains. We also saw the workers at a loss while management and enterprises seemingly began to follow irrational strategies. The Ceralep story is a typical example of this kind of trend, until the workers reversed the destiny of the business.[1]

Ceralep is a French SME producing ceramics insulators, established in 1921, acquired by a US equity fund in 2001, liquidated at the initiative of the latter in 2004, and then transformed into a cooperative by its own employees with the help of a network of local and national cooperative institutions. After the change of management, business picked up quickly, and the enterprise is now in full expansion, hiring new employees, with a solid client portfolio, a substantial ratio of exports, and new business prospects in Asia.

Saint-Vallier is a small township of 4,122 inhabitants, located on the banks of the Rhône river, about 70 kilometres south of Lyon. It is the centre of a district of around 15,000 inhabitants with a high density of SMEs. The district is characterized by a long worker tradition and a strong industrial culture. Until the 1960s, many factories had been producing ceramics products (tiles, houseware, etc.), but they were gradually closed owing to technological changes. At the same time, Saint-Vallier is embedded in an agricultural environment based on grapes and fruit trees. Many families have members who work in factories and others who are farmers. Unemployment is high (officially around 10 per cent) and has been increasing with the crisis. The first to suffer are short-term workers. Poverty is increasing too, with more and more people attending the 'banque alimentaire' ('food bank', a food distribution system) and the local 'resto du coeur' (a chain of French canteens for the poor).

In the first half of this chapter, we recount this surprising story: how this SME was acquired by a series of owners, how the crisis blew up, how the various parties involved (the workers, the bankers, the support institutions, the local community leaders) experienced it, and how the company switched from a net loss situation to one of profitability and expansion in less than a year. We then move on to the actors of the drama telling us which tentative lessons they have drawn from this story.

Evolution of Ceralep up to 2003

Ceralep was first established in 1921 as 'Electroporcelaine' by the Merlin Gerin company (now Schneider Electric) and since the beginning, it has developed an expertise in electrical insulators. In 1973 it was renamed Ceralep after a merger between a subsidiary of Merlin Gerin and another important French producer of technical ceramics. Since then, it has remained the only company in France producing very large ceramics insulators.

In the 1980s, the French group Alstom (specializing in nuclear plants, later acquired by Areva) purchased a 40 per cent participation in the company's share capital. In 1989, Ceralep was purchased by the Swiss firm Laufen, which in turn sold it to Austrian company Ceram, in 1993.

After the company was taken into foreign hands, its workers began to perceive changes in their relation with management, but they still felt that they were dealing with professional industrialists. Trade union leader Driss Kharchouf recalls:

> after the Swiss purchased Ceralep, they often came to copy our know-how. Once, they invited us to Switzerland and we saw that they were making some of the pieces which, according to what they had told us before, the market did not need. Then, we were bought by the Austrians. For some time the relationship was fair, but they gradually took away our know-how as well. But at least they were not financiers. They were a family business. They did many things for Ceralep, we should recognize that.

During all that time, Ceralep had maintained and developed commercial relations with a series of substantial and stable clients including nuclear giant Areva, French railway company SNCF, French electricity company EDF, and many other important clients abroad such as Pirelli. In spite of a wave of 56 lay-offs in 2000 because of technical modernization, the company was considered as a highly viable business.

In 2001, the US ceramics firm PPC Insulators acquired the insulator section of Ceralep's Austrian mother house Ceram. PPC insulators, in turn, had been purchased in 1998 by Riverside Equity Fund, itself participated in by a series of US pension funds. The control relationship is shown in Figure 6.1.

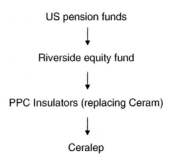

US pension funds

↓

Riverside equity fund

↓

PPC Insulators (replacing Ceram)

↓

Ceralep

Figure 6.1   Ceralep control relationship

According to its website, Riverside's 'unwavering focus on the smaller end of the middle market has led to a proven buy-and-build strategy that maximizes potential for portfolio companies while creating wealth for sellers, partners and intermediaries' (but not for the acquired enterprises themselves). Riverside 'exit[s] investments after achieving shared goals for growth and value'.[2]

After the purchase of Austrian Ceram by US PPC Insulators, the Ceralep staff noted a significant shift in their relation with management: 'Their attitude changed completely. First, they fired our director, who told us: there is a big danger for you, I give you ten more years' life at most', recalls Driss Kharchouf. All the other interviewed witnesses made similar statements. According to Driss Kharchouf:

> What was very strange, was that each time we asked for a pay rise, they granted it without hesitation. At the same time, production fell very low, we had nothing to do. We understood that something awkward was about to happen. Most of the executives were no longer here: our marketing director was promoted director of the three European factories of the group: France, Austria and Slovakia. He moved to Vienna and we almost never saw him around. Once, in 2002, he came back and we kept him in his office until he spoke, and he confessed that Ceralep was going to be closed. So we knew what they had in mind.

Indeed, in 2002, Ceralep had a deficit. PPC Insulators was not investing in the business, and was systematically transferring know-how and more profitable production goods to other plants of the group. Emmanuel Mottin, a technician working in the conception and design unit remembers: 'The investments were at the minimum level, nothing more. I saw no project to improve the workplaces, no focus on development'.[3]

The climate between management and the workers worsened rapidly, and the pressure became unsustainable to some employees: one of them even took his own life. Luc Garnier, from the technical and marketing service, committed suicide in the plant and left a letter, in which he explicitly stated that he had been put under pressure.[4]

During that period, the workers prevented several attempts to remove big pieces of machinery by physically blocking the trucks at the gate of the factory. Karine Iglicki from the regional union of worker cooperatives (URSCOP Rhône-Alpes, which later advised the company for several months) comments:

> What is important is that the workers grasped the situation, and tried to prevent the group from getting all this transfer of competences, and then from stopping production, which was their intention. The group in the end had to file a petition for bankruptcy because the blockage carried out by the workers gave them no other alternative if they wanted to close down the business, and this is what eventually made the worker buy-out possible. Indeed, otherwise, the company would have been emptied of its technology and machinery, and there would have been nothing left to buy out.

The petition for bankruptcy

Then, in September 2003, suddenly, PPC Insulators filed a petition for bankruptcy and Ceralep was put under the administration of a trustee for six months. PPC Insulators alleged structural problems, including too high production costs, lowering markets, and strong competition.[5] Technician Emmanuel Mottin recalls: 'I did not expect it. I came back from my holiday. It was a shock. I never suspected it would reach that point but, with hindsight, it is obvious that they were trying to take away our technology and our client list. At the same time, I observed that the ratio of low added value products had reached 80 per cent. They had probably planned the bankruptcy since the beginning of 2003'.[6]

The workers immediately wrote an open letter to the district attorney, the trustee and the prefect of the Drôme département, calling for an enquiry, arguing that 'this scandalous practice demonstrates that management and our shareholders are really aiming to break up the enterprise and condemn the 150 workers, as well as the economic and social fabric of the Saint-Vallier district'.[7]

In November 2003 over 50 workers were laid off, leaving the company with a staff of 93 employees. However, the company continued production under the administration of the trustee. The works council started to study with a chartered accountant a worker buy-out project in which, they hoped, the company would be handed over to them for the symbolic amount of one euro.

In January 2004 they presented their project to the local commercial court and then awaited the ruling. Meanwhile, works council deputy secretary Robert Nicaise contacted the regional union of worker cooperatives URSCOP

Rhône-Alpes, and Karine Iglicki, who was a business advisor there, had a first series of meetings with the workers. She recalls:

> I went there and explained the cooperative statute and the type of business plan that was needed, and the workers said: 'that's very good but we have another project with the chartered accountant. Your project sounds more interesting, but we don't have the money'. The project designed by the chartered accountant did not comprise a real business plan. The workers thought there would be no financial problems, and that they could get by with a few orders coming from clients. I told them 'ok, you'll survive for a while, but after six months you're dead'. That was on a Wednesday, and the court ruling was planned for the following Friday. Our lawyer told me: 'The court will most probably say no'. Indeed, on Friday, the court decided to wind up the company. In the evening, after hearing the news, a woman from the works council called me in tears and asked me: what are we going to do now?

From liquidation to the establishment of the cooperative

Karine Iglicki goes on:

> At that point, things were getting more complex, but it was not hopeless. We could still propose a worker buy-out project to the judge. So Michel [Rohart, director of URSCOP Rhône-Alpes] and myself arrived from Lyon on the following Monday morning. The company was locked and guarded, and the workers had no access to the site, they were burning tyres in front of the factory, they were all depressed, some were crying.
>
> We explained the situation. We said: 'It's a mess, ok, but now how do we sort it all out?' We told them that they needed to draft and present to the judge a whole buy-out project with a sound business plan within three weeks, otherwise the clients would go away for good. But we had no access to the factory to get the necessary information to build the business plan, and, as we later found out, there were no documents left inside anyway.
>
> We had to work very quickly and build something credible. We knew it could fail, but we had to minimize the risks. It was really acrobatic. Only one of the executives, the marketing director, had remained, all the others had left. Nobody in the staff had any overall vision of the business. But there was a lot of good will. So we started working. We interviewed them to reconstruct the history, mixing them in small groups from different departments. The marketing director managed to reconstruct the client list. We began collecting the information: for example, the cost of raw material, the time to produce a piece, etc. We thus built an estimated profit and loss account, which was checked by the marketing director, and it looked coherent.

The business plan showed clearly that the project could not take on board all 93 workers, but only 52. Therefore, over 40 workers would have to be left aside. Fortunately, there were around 35 workers who preferred to receive their lay-off indemnity and immediately expressed their intention not to get involved in this new venture. At the same time, it was necessary to check every position and make sure that there was one competent person for each workplace remaining. At the end, only two or three of the workers who wanted to be in the cooperative had to be left out.[8]

Bernard Valla, from the Rossignol business consulting firm which regularly assists URSCOP Rhône-Alpes in business transfer cases, also played an important role in the drafting of the business plan. According to his explanation, the business plan took into account three elements: first, the cost of acquiring the assets; fortunately, the offer could be kept low, because any offer would be more advantageous than the only remaining alternative, namely winding up the enterprise for good and selling the assets piece by piece; second, the financing of the first emergency investments, without which the company could not be sufficiently competitive; and third, the need for working capital, which was the most important. For an estimated turnover of €4 million, the working capital required was €900,000.

Bernard Valla considers that 'raising those funds was possible because the project was obvious, it was easy to explain, and it was easy to make people understand that it could work. This was the last enterprise of this kind in the country, with a few big clients like EDF, Areva, SNCF, and a technical know-how that was unique in France and probably in Europe'.[9]

However, Bernard Valla also adds: 'Apart from being coherent, it was equally essential for the project to have a person to carry it out'. Karine Iglicki confirms:

> A leader was necessary. [Works council president] Robert Nicaise was the obvious choice, but for him it was not so obvious in the beginning. Having been the main opponent to management from his works council position, he was now asked to become the manager. After a few days, he understood that if he did not do it, the project would fail anyway. So he decided to throw himself into it. But, then, the whole environment (the court, the chamber of commerce, the banks...) considered that he was not credible as a manager.[10]

This is when a retired high-level TNC executive from Saint-Vallier, Dominique Artaud, came into the picture. Artaud had successively been human resources director at Olivetti, general director of Coca Cola France, CEO of Steelcase Strafor Europe (an office furniture company), CEO of a cash-in-transit company, Brinks for France and North Africa. In his childhood, he had been Robert Nicaise's schoolmate. When, after decades, they re-met over the Ceralep case, Artaud immediately threw himself into the project, on a voluntary basis.

Dominique Artaud explains this first stage: 'There was a clear lack of competence, only one executive had remained. So I proposed my competence to Robert. But I have to underline that the help we got from URSCOP Rhône-Alpes was critical. Those cooperative people are of a rare competence, including financial, I wish I had met people like them during my business career'.

Community mobilization and fund raising

In order to raise the €1.5 million that were necessary to launch the project, €100,000 in share capital were first needed. According to Karine Iglicki:

> We met with the workers with a megaphone in front of the factory, and explained them that they had to find €100,000 within one or two days. They went home, looked at their savings, spoke with their families. We installed a small ballot box in a public hall lent by the municipality, where the employees could write small notes with the amount of share capital which each of them could invest. The collected sum was only €50,000. Thus, another €50,000 were needed.

Robert Nicaise then had the idea to collect money in the local community, and the workers agreed with it. They printed leaflets and started collecting money at the local market, at people's homes, and mainly on the A7 national road where Ceralep is located. As recalled by Driss Kharchouf:

> Those who gave us money were ordinary people, workers from other factories, passers-by, even a small child broke his piggy bank and gave us three euros. When I speak of it now, I still have gooseflesh. We collected between 5 and 50 euros per person. The supermarket across the road gave us 1,000 euros. They wanted Ceralep to remain alive, because there was a rumour that another supermarket would be built on our site. On top of that, they gave us food every day, so we could make lunch for all the workers in front of the factory gate for a few weeks. We also fed the guards who were keeping the gate. They discreetly allowed a handful of us to make shifts in the factory around the clock in order to maintain the machinery. Even the police were on our side. Once, the gendarmerie captain came and we shared sausages and coffee with him.

Within barely ten days, 802 donors had pledged the aggregate sum of €50,000.

Saint-Vallier mayor Jacques Cheval remembers: 'You could hear people talking about Ceralep in town all the time. We felt a strong outburst of solidarity. We saw the consequences of this economy in which financial capital is more important than labour, in which pension funds fix unrealistic profit targets. People were aware. They could see beyond St Vallier'. The local and regional media abundantly relayed this popular mobilization. Many newspaper articles were published, radio and television stations often came and made headline news.

However, after collecting the €100,000 needed in share capital, another €1.4 million were needed to raise the €1.5 million required by the business plan before going to the judge.

The first institution that intervened was Socoden, a French solidarity fund established in 1965, directly under the French worker cooperative confederation CGSCOP, with the aim of supporting the creation and development of worker cooperatives and help them overcome economic crises. Socoden is capitalized by one per thousand of the turnover of the worker cooperatives affiliated to CGSCOP all over France (presently over 1,900 enterprises). Its decision-making structure makes it possible to unblock funds within a few days. In the entrepreneurial projects in which it takes part, Socoden normally provides a matching contribution of one to one to the enterprise's own funds. In this case, since the workers had managed to raise €100,000, Socoden also pledged €100,000 as a loan to the project.

The second institution to be mobilized was ESFIN-IDES, a company in which CGSCOP and other French social economy institutions participated, and capitalized mainly through non-voting participative certificates. ESFIN-IDES provided €100,000 in long-term capital considered as equity, thus generating a lever effect when negotiating with the banks. SPOT, another financial institution under CGSCOP, provided an additional €50,000 in participative certificates.

The next financial actor that was solicited was, as is often the case in France in this kind of project, the Crédit Coopératif, a cooperative bank. Gaetan de Chanterac was in charge of the Crédit Coopératif branch in the neighbouring town of Valence at that time. He recalls:

Before I joined Crédit Coopératif, I worked for a commercial bank which is now part of the HSBC group. The great strength of Crédit Coopératif, as I could eventually observe, is to combine a strictly financial analysis with a sectoral one, and this is done with the help of partners who are professional organizations from the sector, with a deep knowledge of that sector. As a banker I am, by definition, a generalist. In order to understand a project, I must understand professional elements about it, and the persons who are carrying it out. Institutions like URSCOP Rhône-Alpes know both the sector and the people, and complete the information which we have already gathered. This working pattern is the great strength of Crédit Coopératif.

If I had been a conventional banker, I would certainly not even have considered Ceralep. But we went there because other actors were involved, including URSCOP Rhône-Alpes, the workers of the company, and the local population itself. We started being interested in the dossier because it was proposed by people. It was a model case.

However, after I visited the factory and held a first meeting with representatives of the workers, I thought it would be impossible. I was really frightened: the task looked pharaonic. But then, I thought about it carefully. One fundamental element was that URSCOP Rhône-Alpes understood that this team of employees with no experience in management had to be strongly backed, and they mobilized a series of experts to work on the project. The second big strong point in favour of the project was the product itself. Ceralep was a world leader in large-size pieces in ceramic. And there was also a leader with determined people following him. So, you had one top world product, strong leadership, people with an iron will, and a supporting team with a group of experts. All the ingredients for success were there.[11]

Karine Iglicki recalls:

Meanwhile, all the main local public authorities, such as the département, the municipality, the local association of municipalities, supported the project, and provided substantial help, including financial, as they were the ones who initially purchased the fixed assets. In turn, none of the institutions of entrepreneurs, such as the local chamber of commerce, supported the project, and this even included an association of business leaders specializing in business transfer.[12]

Banker Gaetan de Chanterac adds that 'most business people felt very reluctant. They wanted to put a spoke in the wheel, because there was an unthinkable message for them: a trade union delegate would now become the boss of a business of 50 people'.

The workers finally secured the €1.5 million funding which they needed, and presented the buy-out project to the judge, barely a few weeks after liquidation had been announced. In France, this type of decision is made by only one commercial court judge and not by a panel of judges, as had happened one month earlier with the liquidation. In addition, judges of French trade courts are business leaders, not professional judges. The judge in charge of the case hesitated several days, backing down several times with a series of objections, which URSCOP Rhône-Alpes managed each time to counter. Finally, being short of arguments, the judge authorized the cooperative project.[13]

The Ceralep Société Nouvelle cooperative

After the decision was made, everybody rolled up their sleeves. It took another two weeks to establish the cooperative as a legal entity and start production. Driss Kharchouf recalls:

> When we got the green light to start producing again, we all spontane-ously became our own bosses. Robert [Nicaise] went to check, but he found out that everything was ok. It's incredible, isn't it? An enterprise moves under the control of the workers and things change completely. Now we work for us. Now if I detect the smallest flaw on a piece I am working on, I improve it until it is perfect. Before, I did not care that much. We workers spontaneously began taking decisions like staying an extra half an hour to finish a job, or to come on Saturday morning when there was a big order.

Another worker, Jean Marie Pellegrini, adds:

> Yes, we were working without a boss for the first time. It was just trusting each other. It was good to be involved, and we did all we could to make it work. But believing in it was not easy either, in the beginning. In the orga-nization of the factory, now, people are more integrated, they feel more responsible to make things work. We don't need to wait until someone comes and tells us what to do, we know what we have to do. I always try to make an eleventh piece whereas before I used to make ten, not one more.

On the expenditure side, the company no longer had to shoulder the high wages and representation costs of the previous management. The previous director earned €8,000 per month, while Robert Nicaise kept his salary at €2,400, only twice the lowest wage, and refusing successive Board decisions to raise it.[14]

But spontaneous self-management was not the key to everything, far from it. Karine Iglicki describes the intense advisory and follow up work done by URSCOP Rhône-Alpes during the first few months:

> The new elected CEO, Robert Nicaise, was very talented but he was inex-perienced. We came to Ceralep at least half a day every two weeks, and we had constant telephone conversations between meetings. I was not alone, the whole URSCOP Rhône-Alpes was involved, other specialists in training, financial matters, strategy etc. regularly came from Lyon. The new chartered accountant helped with management tools. Dominique Artaud's contribution was also invaluable: he worked half time for six months without asking a penny. Another thing is that we had to train the whole Board, we had to explain to them what were the important

decisions they had to make. Besides, we also systematically trained all 52 workers, through 2–3 day training cycles in small groups.

However, producing, training, reorganizing, and managing were not the only issues at stake. Regaining the previous clients was an essential element to make the business sustainable. But it was an uphill struggle: no sooner had the cooperative resumed production, PPC Insulators opened a commercial office 10 kilometres away from Saint-Vallier (employing an ex-cadre from the commercial department of Ceralep), and sent letters to all clients advising them that Ceralep had no right to use their logo, thus trying to undermine the company's commercial credibility.[15]

Ceralep patiently convinced its clients. Robert Nicaise explains that 'the two persons in charge of marketing went to meet each of our 130 clients. At the beginning, the clients were a bit afraid. But in 2004, SNCF homologated our products and started sending orders. In 2005, the biggest among our regular clients, Areva, came back'.[16]

Robert Nicaise further describes the clients' initial hesitations: 'We mainly received orders for full body products, which are easier to produce and thus less profitable [than the empty-bodied ones]. Our clients probably wanted to test us before they entrusted to us the production of more complex products'.[17]

Meanwhile, technician Emmanuel Mottin 'had to learn how to talk with clients. In the beginning, I often called my previous boss to ask him for advice. Now I know how to reassure the clients'.

In 2005, the new management could make a first assessment of their first few months of production. They had managed to survive, although production and turnover were below the fixed target.

The figures in Table 6.1 give us the following indications:

- Although still below the volume of the early 2000s, production and turnover grew steadily between 2004 and 2008. The slight fall in 2009 is moderate considering the ongoing economic crisis.
- The percentage of exports has remained high during the whole period.
- Apart from a slight fall in 2009, labour productivity has been improving. Even in 2009, labour productivity is markedly higher than in the 2000–2 period.
- While labour has been better utilized, there has been net and steady employment growth since 2004, with an employment increase of 17 per cent in 2009 as compared to 2004.
- Apart from 2008, there has been a steady reduction of waste since 2003.
- The moderate but stable annual profits (2007 being exceptionally good) contrast strikingly with the consecutive deficits between 2000 and 2002.
- While financial reserves were depleted between 2000 and 2003, they have gradually been rebuilt since 2006. If the company continues to grow at

Table 6.1 Yearly comparison of production figures for Ceralep

Year	Production (T)	Turnover (million €)	Export (%)	Added value (million €)	Labour productivity	Waste (%)	Employment (persons)	Profit (million €)	Reserves (million €)	Share capital (million €)
2000	3248	16.07	n.a.	9.10	80.5	18.20	207	−4.12	1.00	2.86
2001	2481	14.18	n.a.	8.11	84.4	17.90	168	−4.01	0	2.86
2002	2331	14.03	n.a.	8.82	84.5	21.80	166	−1.24	0.04	2.86
2003	n.a.	n.a.	n.a.	n.a.	0.0	20.20	93	n.a.	n.a.	n.a.
2004						17.80	52			
2005	941	4.89	49	3.03	90.7	20.10	54	0.12	0	0.29
2006	1165	4.92	55	1.97	91.1	17.00	54	0.11	0.05	0.36
2007	1117	5.78	35	2.69	103.3	15.20	56	0.64	0.09	0.41
2008	1208	6.15	41	2.65	104.2	22.30	59	0.16	0.38	0.51
2009	1014	5.90	36	2.79	96.2	14.00	60	0.19	0.44	0.54

Note: The figures under 2005 are for 2004 and 2005. Since production only started late in 2004, the first accounts of the new cooperative included both years.

Source: Data provided by Ceralep.

the same pace, the original €1 million in reserves of 2000 will be recovered within a few years. In addition, the present reserves are of a totally different nature, since, as per the French cooperative law, they are indivisible, which means that there is an asset lock and that no external acquirer can ever get hold of them (see Chapter 4).

- The share capital is also increasing steadily. As of now, though, its growth will probably become slower. As we saw in Chapter 4, capitalization in cooperatives is carried out through common financial reserves rather than through share capital.

In addition, while gradually building reserves and capital, Ceralep has been able to contract loans and repay them. In the initial financial structure, there was only €250,000 in capital (€100,000 in share capital proper and €150,000 in quasi-own funds in the form of participative certificates) against €1.25 million in liabilities (including factoring). In spite of having contracted further loans in 2007 (for an investment project) and in 2010 (to replace the initial factoring part of the debt) for a total of €1.05 million, it only had €814,000 in outstanding debt owed to external entities in mid 2010 (plus €226,000 in debt owed to its own worker–owners under the form of a wage savings scheme), against €867,000 in capital plus reserves (plus the initial €150,000 in participative certificates).[18] As we can see, the debt/capital ratio has considerably improved in only six years under the cooperative form (from 6 to 1 in 2004 to around 1 to 1 in 2010), especially considering the critical situation in which the company was when it became a cooperative. In view of the stability of the annual turnover even during the crisis, Ceralep should have no difficulty in repaying its outstanding debt and contracting new loans for future investment projects or cash flow needs, while increasing its assets (capital plus reserves).

Main lessons from the Ceralep experience, as viewed by the participants

Absentee investors *versus* real economy producers

Dominique Artaud, the ex-TNC executive who helped Ceralep transform itself into a cooperative, explains his sentiment towards equity funds and pension funds:

> I have a natural aversion against those funds, they are invisible people, you never meet them, but they are there and they only want profitability. I have seen that many times in my professional life. The interests of such funds and those of productive enterprises are not compatible: nowadays, in an enterprise, if you have a regular 5 per cent profit after taxes, it is a very good performance. But those funds want 15 per cent. By doing so,

the only thing they do is to dry up the wealth of the business. The managers of those funds believe that by delocalizing to low-wage countries and resorting to business-to-business relations for suppliers, they will get the money they want. In the end, from a business point of view, they are totally incompetent.

Gaetan de Chanterac, Ceralep's banker, considers that:

We have seen the limit of those funds that set themselves very high remuneration targets. I really don't understand how equity funds can enter an enterprise, because an enterprise has a societal role, with human beings that evolve in it. An entrepreneurial project cannot take place in five years, which is the average investment cycle of equity funds. How can there be a common enterprise vision between an entrepreneur and an equity fund? Wealth is something that can only be created over time.

How Ceralep was transformed into a cooperative

First of all, the Ceralep experience shows to what extent local community support was important. As Karine Iglicki comments, 'the main characteristic of this experience is mobilization. The local people really mobilized themselves. In addition, the mobilization remained in place for some time'.

Second, in contrast to absentee investors, the involvement of real actors taking entrepreneurial responsibilities was fundamental. Dominique Artaud considers that 'the process of having people in the enterprise with *real* roles, real shouldering of responsibilities is fundamental in gains of productivity and quality. It is for this reason that I think that the worker cooperative experience should be much wider'.

Third, the experiment began to succeed when the stakeholders elaborated a vision of their enterprise and a sound project. External business adviser Bernard Valla thinks that:

in this particular project, the main characteristic was that it was so obvious. When you explain the Ceralep case, you can do it in simple words. It is a real fairy tale, but a clever one. In a period where we regularly see employees opposed to employers, banks to firms, here you find people who are able to understand the reality of their business, change roles, and ask themselves how to continue creating wealth, and who, in the end, conclude that they can do it by themselves, thinking 'we are not more stupid than others, we can be good entrepreneurs, we have a vision of our enterprise'. So, we observe a complete reversal of the situation: those who were expected to bring about a sound project and create value did not do it, whereas those who did it were the workers. They made it, and now, with their business performance, they can raise the envy of many American pension funds.

Fourth, there was a group of iron-willed persons to initiate the project. Banker Gaetan de Chanterac sees Ceralep as 'a lesson for everybody: an enterprise is a group of persons, and if they are determined, their project has good chances of success. The cooperative concept of having the workers themselves invest in the enterprise is extremely modern, it is in the mood of the times, and it is in everybody's interest to develop this type of approach'.

On the cooperative model

Dominique Artaud, who sits on Ceralep's Board in the name of the local Association of Friends of Ceralep, and who previously sat on boards of various TNCs, considers that 'there is a big difference between this board and those of classical enterprises, where minutes are written in advance. This is really meaningful, workers can bring something. People bring in new ideas'.

Robert Nicaise considers that:

In Ceralep we moved from a pyramidal type of management to a horizontal one. Before, the group used to give orders to management, who forwarded them to executives who transmitted them to their team. Now, after each Board meeting, there is a meeting with all the workers, where the CEO uses simple words, explaining whether things are going well or whether we should all make an effort, and not hiding anything. All this happens naturally, because each one of us is a member of the company.

The president of the General Council of the Drôme Département, Alain Genthon, for his part, believes that 'cooperatives are real laboratories of human relations, embedded in market realities, but also with internal negotiations, and this is unique in our very brutal world. This capacity of people to self-manage themselves jointly and at the same time be active in the market is great, especially in this era of internationalization of labour'.

Bernard Valla, the business consultant who advises different types of businesses, thinks that:

the cooperative model of capital accumulation is a big advantage, and it shows in periods of crisis. The most fragile businesses now are the indebted ones, those who thought that their results would be as regular as the taxes they paid. It did not happen like that, and many are bogged down in indebtedness. It is much better to have cash at home than debts with your banker, because when things don't work, it is more risky to ask your banker who might be in a bad mood and send you away. Furthermore, I meet businesses with a 4 per cent profit margin, but who pay 3 per cent in bank costs: whom do they work for in the end, for themselves or for the bank?

Conclusion

We have seen the case of a company whose rationality was distorted by continuously changing absentee investors, who became controllers at distance and dealt with the firm as a replaceable chip in a global supply chain, a living example of the shift towards financial control at distance discussed in Chapter 3. This rationality brought the firm to failure. After the cause of failure was removed, the company has been doing well. Furthermore, as a cooperative among workers, additional elements of business efficiency can be appraised in the statistics shown in Table 6.1. The workers–entrepreneurs have improved their well-being, the company has begun to build solid cooperative reserves, assets are strong and equity is healthy. The financial balance has been restored and unproductive costs have been reduced. The firm is still repaying loans, but it is able to repay them in full, and is not suffering the debt trap.

Transparency and circulation of information have improved as governance is more horizontal, allowing the Board members to take timely decisions. Minutes are not vertically imposed in advance onto the shareholders, who are now the worker–members of the cooperative.

Control has been transferred from controllers at distance to *presentee* stakeholders who shoulder the risks. Three active institutional investors from the cooperative system do contribute to the capital of the company, but they do so based on a long-term perspective and as a development tool, and are not loading the company with structural debt nor demanding impossible returns while cutting down the means of production and commercialization, as the previous investors had been doing. In addition, their contribution is part of a coordinated support environment which is internal to the cooperative system itself, providing training and follow-up.

7

The Desjardins Cooperative Group: A Financial Movement for Québec's Development

Introduction

With this empirical case, we will see the linkages between, on the one hand, finance and consumption indebtedness, which we examined in Chapters 2 and 3, and embeddedness in the real economy on the other.

Desjardins is ranked the first financial institution in Canada's Québec province, and the sixth in Canada. With assets worth US $155.5 billion, it is one of the main financial and economic players of the world's ninth economy. Its tier-one capital ratio for 2009 was 15.85 per cent, 83.7 per cent of which was made up of its own reserves (namely non-remunerated capital), and rose to 16.13 per cent for the first quarter of 2010. Desjardins is also the only financial institution in Canada to have set up its own safety fund, with a net value of US $620 million in 2009. Its resilience to the global crisis is striking: in 2009, *Global Finance Magazine* published that Desjardins ranked 26th of the top 50 most secure financial institutions in the world from an analysis of the 500 largest financial institutions.[1]

Desjardins' shares of the Québec financial market are: 44.2 per cent in savings, 45.3 per cent in agricultural loans, 39.6 per cent in mortgage loans, 27.3 per cent in commercial and industrial loans and 23.4 per cent in personal loans. Except for agriculture (where there has been a slight decrease), these market shares increased in 2009 compared to 2008.[2]

Desjardins is also the largest private employer in Québec with 39,000 employees and amongst the top 20 most important employers in Canada, with a total of 42,000 employees across the country.

In spite of all these economic, financial and entrepreneurial strengths, Desjardins does not seek to maximize the return on investment to shareholders, but to ensure the financial service satisfaction of its 5.8 million owners–members, including 5.4 million individuals (a 70 per cent penetration rate in Québec, the total population of the province being 7.8 million) and 400,000 enterprises (a 44 per cent penetration rate). Its geographical coverage is also very dense, with a presence in 58 per cent of all municipalities of Québec. In 600 small towns and villages, including in 11 Inuit villages of the province's great north, it is the only banking institution to be found. Its over US $1 billion surpluses are partly earmarked for reserves and partly distributed among its members, while over US $70 million are devolved to the community in a number of initiatives such as educational or development projects, including an international cooperative education centre and an international development institution helping credit cooperatives in developing countries through technical support and investment funds for micro-credit.

And yet, Desjardins is *not* a single banking institution, but a horizontally led cooperative group constituting 481 autonomous local financial cooperatives called *caisses*, the equivalent of the credit unions in Anglophone Canada and in the USA, who jointly own and control it.

In the following pages, we review the historical evolution of the group over its 110 years of existence. In order to better understand how such a huge cooperative complex made up of millions of members–owners can function, we lay particular emphasis on the institutional functioning and on the various institutional reforms which the group has engineered throughout its history, seeking each time to respond to concrete challenges that could endanger its service offer to its member base, which constitutes its core mission.

Desjardins' first steps

From the time when the French settlers arrived in the early seventeenth century until the mid-nineteenth century, Québec's economy was based on mercantilism, first under the French and then the British. Barely six decades after the British took over in 1760, British merchants displaced French Canadian fur-trade merchants, and established financial institutions of their own. The French Canadians were then largely excluded from the conventional financial circuits.

At the root of Desjardins' creation were the financial needs of small farmers, small producers, and wage-earners, who were often prey to the avidity of usurers.[3] Claude Béland, Desjardins' president between 1989 and 2000, explains that 'then, most of the economy in Québec was in the hands of anglophone Canadians, whereas the Québec people and the French Canadians [around 80 per cent of the province's total population] had generally no access to banking services'.[4]

At the beginning of the Desjardins group's history in 1900, its founder, Alphonse Desjardins, wrote that time would be the best ally of the movement he had launched.[5] History seems to have confirmed his vision. The early pioneers opted for a very slow pace of development, and even more so because, since the beginning, they have chosen to give each cooperative member only limited liability, thereby obliging the system to stick to a very rigorous financial management style. Up to the 1990s, the qualifying shares and the common reserves, built up through accumulated surpluses year after year, constituted the capital guaranteeing deposits in case of repayment default. The *caisses* developed a strong level of autonomy, both in terms of management and finance, evolving on a totally self-financed basis. Many years were needed for the *caisses* to accumulate the necessary capital to enable them to engineer their own development.[6]

The first *caisse* was founded in 1900 in the city of Lévis, near to Québec city, with around 130 founding members. Eleven months later, the members already numbered 721. The success of the Lévis *caisse* and, beyond, of the whole Desjardins project, owes much to the contribution of Dorimène Desjardins, Alphonse Desjardins' wife. Pierre Poulin, the main historian of the Desjardins movement, explains:

> sharing the cooperative ideal of her husband and with a gift for management and accountancy – Alphonse Desjardins called her his 'finance minister' – she got very rapidly involved in the daily business of the Lévis people's *caisse*, founded on 6 December 1900. A careful manager who listened to members whom she often welcomed into the family home, she displayed a high level of prudence at a time when the institution enjoyed no legal recognition whatsoever. Her concrete commitment and her constant championing of the development of the Desjardins *caisses* would turn Dorimène Desjardins into an acknowledged and influential interlocutor with the *caisses* leaders after the passing away of Alphonse Desjardins. ... On the very day of her death [in 1932], a Québec city newspaper wrote that her death was 'a great loss for French Canada, because she certainly was one of the most informed women about the economic question seen from the social point of view', adding that 'we should recognize that, without her, the Desjardins people's *caisses* would most probably not exist'.[7]

The dissemination of the model from the Lévis *caisse*, however, required appropriate provincial legislation, which was approved in 1906. The project received logistical support from the clergy and church structures, because it was perceived as being in line with the new social doctrine of the Catholic Church. The *caisses* began to multiply. Claude Béland recounts: 'Many of the *caisses* were located in church basements. It was largely a hidden phenomenon: the people were afraid to say too loudly that they were members of a *caisse*. Eventually, the *caisses* managed to leave the basements of the churches, and the movement continued in the open'.[8] The model grew slowly but surely: in 1920, at the death of Alphonse Desjardins, there were already 140 *caisses* with 31,000 members.

This was also a time of dissemination of the model across North America. The Desjardins model directly inspired what was going to become the credit union movement in the USA (today composed of 7,708 credit unions, with

91 million members, and total assets worth US $899 billion).[9] Desjardins even received an invitation by US president Howard Taft in 1912, and directly contributed to the first US draft laws on credit unions and to the establishment of nine US credit unions, the first to be established in the USA.

In 1921, the Desjardins *caisse* network faced an economic crisis for the first time, as European countries dramatically reduced their imports of Canadian farm products, leading to a big drop in agricultural prices. Alphonse Desjardins had imagined that the *caisses* would be linked to a federation and a central *caisse*, but he did not live to see it, as the *caisses*, at that time, were jealous of their independence. However, the need for a coordinated system was being increasingly felt: the very survival of the system was at stake.

In 1920, the *caisses* began to regroup at the regional level, through second-level cooperatives called 'regional unions' with harmonized rules among themselves, and a supervisory and auditing role. In 1925, 65 per cent of the Desjardins *caisses* were already grouped under regional unions. A law making the annual inspection of the *caisses* by regional unions compulsory was passed in 1925. This law, which had been requested by Desjardins' elected leaders themselves, would substantially reinforce the role of the regional unions.[10]

The Great Depression: an opportunity for the Desjardins network to grow

The Desjardins network of *caisses* then faced a much tougher challenge: the 1929 Great Depression, which struck Canada as forcefully as the USA. The inspection by the regional unions, initiated shortly beforehand, was not yet functioning properly, and no common safety fund had been put in place. Between 1930 and 1933, 37 *caisses* had to stop their activities, and another 20 had to suspend them temporarily. In the same time span, the aggregate assets of the system decreased by 25 per cent. However, the *caisses* managed to reimburse all their members' savings and recovered most of the loans, including in kind (even under the form of maple syrup).[11]

In 1932, the Desjardins system finally established a central federation for the whole Québec territory, which received an annual subsidy of 20,000 Canadian dollars from the Québec provincial government, aimed at coordinating the inspection of the *caisses*.[12] Consequently, only 31 years after its establishment, the Desjardins system received its first regular subsidy, as a compensation against the implementation of a fundamental auditing task.[13] In the beginning, the federation only received very light powers from the regional unions. Nonetheless, this step was a decisive one, as it made it possible to raise the financial safety of the whole network.[14] More importantly perhaps, 1932 marks the beginning of Desjardins as an integrated cooperative group, able to tackle more effectively, and on a wider scale, the effects of the Great Depression.

After the first destructive impact, the Great Depression paradoxically proved to be a source of development for the *caisses*, now under the coordination of the new federation. Poverty and joblessness generated a sense of solidarity across Québec society. Thirty-three *caisses* were established every year, on average, between 1933 and 1936, and 61 between 1937 and 1942. The total number of *caisses* rose from 189 in 1932 to 944 in 1945. The number of members multiplied eightfold between 1933 and 1944, from 36,000 to 304,000. The credit cooperative model then spread to other Canadian provinces. At the same time, a number of educational institutions launched cooperative training programmes. In the wake of the *caisses*, Québec also experienced a strong development of other types of cooperative, such as in agriculture, fisheries, forestry, distribution.[15]

Along with its expansion, the group was accumulating increasingly strong financial reserves, enabling the *caisses* to establish joint subsidiaries, first of all within the insurance sector, with the establishment in 1944 of Société d'Assurance des Caisses Populaires (SACP, today General Insurance Group), a general insurance subsidiary which signed 7,000 contracts within eight months. In 1948, Assurance Vie Desjardins (AVD), a wealth and life insurance subsidiary known today as Desjardins Financial Security was established: by 1961, it had grown to be the fourteenth life insurer in Québec.[16] AVD financed sociological research and an educational TV programme on family budget management called 'Make both ends meet', followed by around one million people. Other financial subsidiaries were established later in the fields of trust, investment funds, commercial and industrial credit, venture capital, securities and asset management. The system therefore covered most financial sectors.

Whereas this type of subsidiary became common among Canadian banks when financial globalization fully reached Canada in the early 1990s, Desjardins was a pioneer in this field as early as the 1940s. Furthermore, the Desjardins subsidiaries followed another type of logic from conventional financial institutions, as they were created as financial levers aimed at addressing the needs of the *caisses* and of their members and at contributing to the economic development of Québec. However, as they gradually made up an increasing percentage of the system's total assets (up to 15 per cent in 1971), the subsidiaries began to increase their influence on the rest of the group. This favoured the rise of a new technocracy and of new marginal decision-making centres within the group, and so prompted the latter to gradually redesign its coordination structures, as we will see later.

The post-war period, the 1960s and 1970s: the debate on consumption patterns

After the Second World War, a profound change in consumption patterns, which we examined under the 'consumption trap' section in Chapter 2, raised the issue of family indebtedness in Québec as well. New financial agents appeared, proposing interest rates that could be as high as 24 per cent, whereas the conventional rates were 6 per cent,[17] and low-income families tended to get strongly indebted. At first, the Desjardins system, which was exclusively designed to deliver productive loans, remained rigid on the issue of consumer credit. It provided loans only for long-lasting consumer goods that could also be seen as having a productive function, such as houses (mortgage loans then made up 40 per cent of the Desjardins system's assets), but not loans to buy such items as cars, fridges or washing machines, which it then regarded as luxury goods. This triggered a debate in Québec and within the Desjardins membership at large: should the *caisses* provide loans for consumer goods? On the one hand, there was a danger of distorting the original purpose of the system. On the other, Desjardins' inflexibility on this issue contributed to promoting unscrupulous financial agents who applied very high interest rates, and even eased the resurgence of usury in the Québec society. Desjardins thus found itself faced with the dilemma of possibly acting against its own mission. The group then commissioned an in-depth sociological research from Québec's Laval University, which confirmed the exponential increase in indebtedness among Québec families, but also the fact that consumption credit and indebtedness had become part and parcel of new living patterns. The group first engineered a prudent easing of its lending policy, and approved a formal, but measured, change of policy at the 1963 Desjardins *caisses* congress.[18] In addition, in order to fight against indebtedness, the group also launched a campaign of economic education to which it dedicated important resources.

In the 1960s, the Desjardins system attained maturity, as most Québec localities had their own *caisses*. The system comprised 1,227 *caisses*, 1.2 million members, and 1 billion Canadian dollars in aggregate assets.[19] On top of opening itself to consumer credit, the group enlarged its service offer thanks to the acquisition of subsidiaries in the fields of insurance, fiduciary activities and investment funds.

But it is in the 1970s that the most spectacular phase of the expansion of the Desjardins group took place. From 1 billion in the early 1960s, the assets of the system grew to 11.5 billion Canadian dollars in 1979, and this in spite of the oil shock in 1973. Desjardins' growth rate in those years oscillated between 19 and 23 per cent, twice as much as any other Canadian banking institution. The group further increased the range of its services through the establishment of an investment and industrial credit society, allowing it to offer risk capital and participate actively in the development of enterprises (not as an active absentee investor of the type we saw in Chapter 3, but as a financial service institution belonging to, and controlled by, its members, including entrepreneurial members).

In the 1970s, the debate on the credit lines resumed. Although consumption credit had become available during the 1960s, its progress had been particularly slow, growing from 8.8 per cent in 1961 to 19.3 per cent in 1971 (against 45 per cent for conventional banks). Discussion groups among *caisse* members were then organized throughout Québec to identify and formulate their expectations about savings, credit and the involvement of *caisses* in Québec's society. Some members expressed staunch criticism of Desjardins' conservative credit policy, even accusing the group of paternalism and lack of discretion, and requesting credit cards, which had recently appeared in Québec, to be integrated into the system. They argued that the *caisses* should not encourage members to invest in shares or bonds, but should at least provide information on these products to their members, and should be more involved in consumption education.[20]

Meanwhile, inter-bank competition increased. Through new banking regulation in the 1970s, the Canadian conventional banks increased their share of the credit and savings market, competing with the Desjardins *caisses* on their own ground. The *caisses* were, therefore, obliged to raise their level of credit and diminish their level of savings in the same proportion: through the 1970s, the loans rose from 52 per cent to 72 per cent of total assets, whereas liquidities shrank from 44 per cent to 25 per cent. As a consequence, the *caisses* had to make an increasing effort to rationalize management, and from there, a profound shift towards more professional staff and management methods emerged.[21]

The 1960s and 1970s were also marked by an important reinforcement of the support institutions of the group. Regional unions developed a whole array of services to the local *caisses*, in administration, education and training, technical analysis, staff management, and financial services (cashier, compensation, credit, loans, investment, etc.). The central federation also saw its powers and responsibilities reinforced, following a growing need for more coordination, training and harmonization of accounting and computing tools, with a project to develop a national computer network. New departments were being established, such as research, information and publicity. In those two decades, the staff of the central federation increased eightfold (from around 100 to over 800). New Board committees were established in the fields of education, inspection and labour relations. The federation made a new training programme available to the regional unions to train their own staff, the elected leaders and the ordinary members of the *caisses*. In 1963, Desjardins established a residential training centre for adults, the Desjardins Cooperative Institute. Hundreds of elected officers and general managers underwent training in that centre, as well as interns coming from among the Northern Inuit minority and from African and Asian countries.[22]

The federation also played a decisive harmonizing role in the field of the new ITC, with the signing, in 1970, of a contract with IBM for the computerization of the whole system, thereby granting Desjardins a few years' advance on its banking competitors. Indeed, the group was a partner in the design of a computer system allowing the computerization of all the operations of the *caisses'* general books by linking them to a central computer: Desjardins was the first financial institution in the world to have carried out this technological leap forward. A derived product of this innovation made it possible for any member to carry out financial operations from any of the *caisses* of the group: Desjardins was, again, the first financial institution in the world to have proposed such a service to its clients.

The 1980s and 1990s: the North American free trade agreement and globalization

A powerful economic crisis hit Québec in 1981–2, the worse since the Great Depression. Interest rates reached historical records, and a recession ensued, with a slump in loans by individuals, a decrease in production (6.5 per cent in 1982) and long-term investments by companies, a rise in bankruptcies and a worsening of the job market (with a 13.8 per cent unemployment rate). Families came back to saving more and consuming less.[23] Canadian banks were affected: some merged, and two went bankrupt. The Québec economy recovered rapidly, but public and private indebtedness prompted the government to decrease its role as a promoter of economic development in favour of private enterprise.

In spite of the crisis – and, at the same time, because it was stimulated by it – the expansion of Desjardins went on unabated in the 1980s. The system reaped the fruits of its conservative (and previously criticized) liquidity policy. It established a new safety fund (out of the merger of two smaller safety funds created after the Second World War) which made critical interventions in as many as 200 local *caisses*.[24] Meanwhile, the group integrated or reintegrated a number of *caisses* and small federations that were shaped on the Desjardins model but had left the network, such as a small federation in the Montreal region, or had never been part of it, such as the *caisses d'économie* based on specific professions, crafts, work environment or ethnic groups.[25] Desjardins' share of Québec's agricultural and industrial-commercial credit market increased, reaching 53.8 per cent and 23.3 per cent respectively in 1991 (a 30 per cent and 300 per cent increase respectively, compared to one decade earlier).[26] Desjardins was beginning to be a banking institution for the development of SMEs.

Another decisive event that would considerably reinforce Desjardins as a business group took place in 1981: the establishment of CCD, the Desjardins Central *caisse* or bank, by which the group now became a *de facto* part of the Canadian banking system, even though it continued to be regulated by provincial legislation. The main functions of this entity are to represent the Desjardins group to the Canadian Payments Association and the Bank of Canada, to respond to the liquidity needs of the local *caisses* and the other institutions of the group, and to act on their behalf in the international market. It rapidly established a vast network of relations with banking institutions around the world, most of them being cooperative banks or credit union networks as well (e.g. in the USA, France and Germany).

At the same time, Desjardins needed to adapt to a rapidly evolving financial environment. Following the general trend in North America, pension funds were capitalizing and looking for new investment opportunities across the world (as we saw in Chapter 3), while enterprises were increasingly issuing shares and bonds, a trend which was encouraged by the Canadian government's tax policy. Competition with other financial institutions became more acute and a trend towards financial market 'shopping' emerged in society, gaining Desjardins members as well. This obliged the group to adapt its financial product offer, so as not to lose its members.

Claude Béland, who was Desjardins' president throughout the 1990s, observes that:

> Globalization caused a complete shift in values. Till the 1990s, there was more concern towards social considerations and towards social wealth created in Québec. When the 1990s came, monolithic thinking, global village and individualism took the lead, and our big clients who, in the past, were satisfied with the same returns on capital as the small ones started requesting higher returns. Cooperative members being the owners of the *caisses*, we had to adapt to what they requested.[27]

The group's service improved decisively in the 1980s and 1990s, with automatic counters (1981), credit cards (1982), and debit cards (1989). Two further innovations were the sale of general insurance products within the *caisses* and the establishment of a subsidiary for asset management. Services abroad also developed thanks to the establishment of the Desjardins Bank in Florida and various international agreements concluded by the group. The virtual cashier was inaugurated in 1996 with the launch of the Desjardins. com website and internet banking.

Meanwhile, the general erosion of the capital ratios and liquidities of banks, initiated in the 1970s as we saw above, continued to affect the Desjardins group as well, although to a lesser extent. The research department of the federation engaged in foresight studies, and saw an increasing trend towards fixed-term saving, with a consequent increase of the interest on deposits paid by the *caisses*, and consequent risk of insolvency. The need for more and better coordination in terms of image, financial equilibrium and synergy between the *caisses* and the subsidiaries, while maintaining a decentralized system, was increasingly pointed out. A pressure towards higher efficiency and cost reduction of the whole system and more professional staff was mounting.[28]

The growth of the Desjardins group slowed down in the 1990s. With the signing of the USA–Canada free-trade agreement in 1989, the Canadian financial system became far more open to global competition, with the attraction of new financial products such as investment funds with much higher yields on investment. Moreover a new recession occurred in Canada, similar to the one of the early 1980s, with rising unemployment, bankruptcy and a real estate crisis.[29]

The effect of this recession was deeply felt in the Desjardins group, while its expansion capacity began to be limited, with its membership now reaching 5 million members, namely most of the adult population of Québec. On the one hand, Desjardins remained by far the most embedded financial institution in Québec's society, with an undisputed pre-eminence in savings deposits (41.7 per cent against 36.5 per cent for the other big six Canadian general banks put together) and housing mortgage market (37.7 per cent against 30.7 for the other big six). However, those activities were precisely the ones most affected by the recession of 1990, while in new sectors and products such as non-fixed assets brokerage, Desjardins was lagging far behind the other banks. This strongly limited the development capacity of the *caisses*. In addition, the transaction costs needed to generate income were substantially higher than for other banks, with US \$0.75 for US \$1, against US \$0.63 for other Canadian banking institutions.

In order to solve this situation, the *caisses* started to dedicate a higher percentage of their surpluses to reserves, and so attained a higher capital ratio than that prescribed by the international standards. As we saw in Chapter 4, the cooperative system foresees that a substantial part of the surpluses are earmarked to reserves; moreover, in the case of Québec (as in many countries or regions across the world), those reserves are indivisible, even in the case of winding up (see again Chapter 4). In addition, the group proceeded to carry out a series of mergers between its subsidiaries, in particular in the insurance business. On the other hand, facing huge levels of mergers and acquisitions among its competitors, the Desjardins federation acquired a large part of the assets of 'La Laurentienne', an important financial group, thereby jumping from the sixth to the fourth Canadian banking institution. In a parallel development, the Desjardins safety fund, which had been restructured in 1980, increased its capital twelvefold in a decade, attaining 0.5 per cent of total assets in 1990. The fund, which proved to be a critical tool in such a decentralized financial system, probably contributed substantially to raising the credit rating of the Desjardins loans and the credibility of the group with its members and on the financial markets.[30]

Nevertheless, capitalization remained a problem within the group, particularly within its subsidiaries. In the 1980s, the federation had authorized its subsidiary CID to issue shares on the market and established four new portfolio companies. In 1989, the capital ratio was 4.07 per cent against 3.8 per cent one year before. In 1990, the group created another capitalization instrument, namely permanent shares, which, at the time, represented a substantial fiscal advantage.[31] In 1994, Desjardins' subsidiary Capital Desjardins launched the Desjardins capitalization bond on the global financial markets, and in 1995 issued US $200 million in debentures with institutional investors. These were non-voting bonds and, therefore, complied with the cooperative nature of the Desjardins group, which, as with cooperatives in general, does not grant voting power to capital (see Chapter 4). The capitalization ratio reached 11.13 per cent in 1995, well above international standards and slightly higher than in other Canadian banking institutions.[32]

New service offers were being put in place, in particular towards commercial and industrial credit, where the *caisses* were still lagging behind, in spite of a substantial increase in this field in the 1980s, as we saw above. Alain Brideault, president of the Canadian Worker Cooperative Federation, recalls that 'Till then, Desjardins had not really managed to enter the enterprise market, because the individual *caisses* did not have the capacity to do it. For example, they lost the market of the forestry cooperatives, because they would have needed a much bigger service capacity'.[33]

Although the *caisses* increased their share of the industrial credit market in the 1990s, this market itself was decreasing. The *caisses* built alliances among themselves and, as of 1998, established a series of Enterprise Financial Centres (CFE) providing services to business. Desjardins president Béland recalls: 'I was deeply involved in establishing the CFE. It was impossible for each of the 1,000-odd *caisses* to have the necessary expertise. Instead, if they regrouped in business centres, they could gradually build up expertise and help entrepreneurs through a professional follow-up and in real partnership with them'.[34] In August 2001, there were 64 centres across Québec, employing 1,400 people. Still in the field of offering services to business, other important steps forward were made thanks to the specialized services provided by the central *caisse* and by the subsidiaries, among which were Desjardins Capital de Risque. In addition, the establishment of Capital Régional et Coopératif Desjardins and the dissemination of regional investment funds made it possible for the group to play a more active role in regional development.

The subsidiaries Crédit Industriel Desjardins and Fiducie Desjardins, integrated in the portfolio company Trustco Desjardins, suffered substantially from the recession of the early 1990s. Desjardins then bought back the minority shares of those two companies in order to shift them entirely under its control. Cooperation between Fiducie Desjardins and the *caisses* gradually expanded, as the *Revue Desjardins* (Desjardins' journal), quoted by Poulin and Tremblay, commented:

> Sometimes perceived as a competitor of the *caisses* in the past, Fiducie now offers them a way to keep within the Movement savings which otherwise would go to the banks and 'trusts'. In order to face competition, the Desjardins funds are a powerful weapon: within two years, they have increased their market share by 65 per cent, thus placing the Movement as number five on the Québec market.[35]

Indeed, while the *caisses* of the group were expert in traditional savings, the ordinary Québecois saver increasingly resorted to investment funds (called in North America mutual funds, not to be confused with mutuals or mutual aid societies, which we examined in Chapter 4), and the Desjardins member therefore tended to use the services of the Desjardin subsidiaries that specialized in such instruments. The *caisses* tried to fight against this tendency through conventional tools, such as fixed-term deposits. As expressed by Poulin and Tremblay, the Desjardins leadership asked itself: 'Is resisting possible? Is it appropriate? If we adopt the point of view of the member, we can think that he wants to have access to the whole array of products that are available on the market at a reasonable cost. From this point of view, market trends are quite clear: people increasingly invest their savings in mutual funds and in non-fixed assets'.[36] This new challenge required a much closer type of coordination among the various components of the group.

Desjardins then launched an innovative product called 'savings deposit with equity return on capital', with a guarantee on the principal and a variable return indexed on stock exchange indexes. This new product was extended rapidly to the whole group in 1997. In an interview, the designer of the product, Clément Roberge, explained that this extension had made it possible to sell 800 million Canadian dollars' worth of this product, whereas only 40 million Canadian dollars could have been sold if it had remained the exclusivity of one institution of the group. In order to attain its full potential, however, this dynamic required that all components of the group involved in the financial chain created, including the leading institutions, acted fully according to a network behaviour.[37]

The internal debate on the group's restructuring in the 1990s

In the following paragraphs, we will examine how the group initiated a profound restructuring process, thereby producing a substantial level of organizational innovation in order to face the future. This was done through a large democratic debate within the group.

The strong development of the Desjardins group, with the regional unions and the central federation as central players, together with the need to maintain the democratic nature of the group, raised the problem of redefining the sharing of responsibilities between both types of entities, as well as the other institutions of the group. The debate on the competences had been launched as far back as 1974,[38] but this central governance issue grew in importance in the 1980s and became even more pressing in the 1990s with the strong increase in banking competition and the need to reduce transaction costs. Over the years, a number of reports had been commissioned, committees had been established, resolutions had been discussed and approved by congresses and boards. But a strong resistance to further integration could be perceived on the part of the regional unions and the *caisses*.

Indeed, the whole system had been built on the basis of the highest possible autonomy at the grassroots level, and higher integration of the group needed to be carried out while maintaining the autonomy of the local structures and their democratic control over the group as a whole, which belonged to them. In addition, apart from the debate between centralization and decentralization, another key issue had to be introduced in the equation, namely the level of flexibility required under financial globalization, so that the system could continue to develop while maintaining its cooperative identity.[39] In keeping with the cooperative mode of organization, this could only be negotiated democratically.

The debate on the sharing of competences between the different levels of the group was re-opened in 1989 under the new presidency of Claude Béland. Between 1989 and 1992, three successive committees tried – but failed – to put forward concrete institutional reforms. An in-depth consultation of the boards of the regional federations (as the regional unions were now renamed) was then launched and, all through 1992, the latter held meetings with their affiliated *caisses*. This time, a broad and in-depth debate across the whole group had started.

On the basis of this initial feedback from the grassroots, the leadership of the central federation tried to imagine an ideal structure projected towards the year 2000 and proposed 'a complete and in-depth questioning of the group's organizational structure with a document called *Vision for the year 2000*, stating that "the present structure of the Desjardins Movement is no longer in a position to ensure an optimal support to the cooperatives at an adequate cost"'.[40] However, the debate on structural change was not seen as an end in itself but one geared towards the future strategic needs of the *caisses* and the reinforcement of their cooperative nature. A conference on the sharing of responsibilities in 1992 led to contrasting positions, in particular concerning the powers of the central federation. However, a consensus was reached on a list of '46 powers' to be granted to the latter.[41] The governance structure of the central federation was changed, with a distinction between the elected board and a committee of regional general managers. In spite of this, no consensus could be reached on other issues. But, at least, the fact that the issue of structural change had been addressed would later facilitate the debate: this is what Desjardins' then president Claude Béland called the 'pedagogy of change'.

Meanwhile, other initiatives also favoured cooperation on restructuring within the framework of the movement, such as an initiative in favour of technological and electronic re-engineering of the whole system.[42] The committee in charge of this initiative found out that substantial costs could be avoided by eliminating repetitive actions with no added value. A huge effort in re-training was then offered to the staff across the group.

The issue of how to optimize the grassroots structures was back on the agenda. In 1998, a handful of pioneering regional federations attempted to rationalize their regional constituency, by defining local 'micro-markets' and proposing mergers between local *caisses*. A number of mergers were carried out, after being approved by general assemblies of the merging entities. At the same time, the *caisses* increasingly requested that the productivity of the subsidiaries of the group also be optimized.

All those reforms put back on the agenda the far more delicate issue of reforming the general structure of the group. The debate, again, was based on the analysis of costs and how to reduce them. A working document called 'the role of tomorrow's federation' estimated that the productivity ratio of the Desjardin group was around 77 per cent, against 62 per cent for its banking competitors. In order to bridge this gap, 400 million Canadian dollars had to be saved, 250 million of which were supposed to come from the re-engineering project. Another 150 million in cost reduction had to be found in the second (regional federations) and third (central federation) levels of the group.

The stage was thus set for the launching of yet another reform committee called 'Committee on the operational functioning of the costs of the second and third level and of the integration of subsidiaries in Desjardins', with total independence in the formulation of proposals and composed exclusively of elected officers and general managers of grassroots *caisses*, not of institutions of the second or third level (who might have had a vested interest in avoiding radical change at those levels), and nominated in their capacity of private individuals, and not as representatives of their respective institutions.[43]

A first issue to be dealt with was the one of representation. The voting power of the regional federations within the general assembly of the central federation was then mathematically designed on the cooperative principle of 'one person one vote', considering each regional union as a (legal) person for all effects and purposes. The international cooperative movement, through a congress of the International Cooperative Alliance held in Vienna in 1966, had legitimized another interpretation of this principle for higher-level entities, namely a form of representation which was proportional to the number of physical members in the grassroots entities. From this standpoint, the voting power of the regional unions was unbalanced, with different sizes of grassroots member populations.

In 1997, a number of Canadian banks proceeded to mergers, and the finance ministry of the Québec province even suggested that the Desjardins group should merge with another bank. This kind of project gives the measure of the growth ambitions of the large Canadian chartered banks at that time. With the increase in banking scales, the productivity (cost/profit ratio) gap between the conventional banks and Desjardins continued to be wide, although the latter's situation was improving steadily, not least thanks to an acceleration of the mergers among the local *caisses*, prompting the leadership to foresee a reduction in the number of *caisses* from 1,275 down to around 800 in a few years' time.[44]

As they were, therefore, doing their part of the job, the grassroots *caisses* raised their pressure on the support institutions of the group for them to reduce their own costs. The question of the size of the super-structure, made up of one central federation, 10 regional ones plus a federation of 108 profession-based *caisses d'économie*, which had joined the group 20 years before and had always remained a distinctive constituency, was becoming increasingly acute. The committee recommended lesser costs but also more integration: the central Board's decisions should become binding, and the superstructure should be highly simplified. The idea to completely eliminate the second (intermediate) level made up of the regional federations was discussed for the first time, at least in terms of operational structure (while maintaining a three-tiered structure for decision making). Meanwhile, the president of the new Desjardin central *caisse* warned against the dangers of a decrease in the credit rating by the rating agencies.[45]

In 1997, a declaration calling for a Congress of the group was upheld by 79 *caisses*. Between the end of 1998 and the beginning of 1999, the number of formal and informal meetings on restructuring intensified greatly. The idea of having only one coordinating body supporting the *caisses* emerged more and more clearly.

Nevertheless, strong resistance to this project was mounting from some quarters, and not least from the *caisses d'économie*, which feared that the disappearance of their atypical federation (the only second-level structure which covered all Québec and was not based on a specific territory) would threaten their specificity. Although in a minority, the *caisses d'économie* could not be brushed aside so easily, with their 260,000 members active in around 700 educational, health, research, culture and manufacturing institutions. The press began to take sides, and the main Québec trade union CSN openly supported the *caisses d'économie*'s point of view, arguing that the planned restructuring would cause many job losses.

Finally, a consensus emerged between the two sides on the central Board in January 1999, concerning the establishment of a single federation (thus eliminating the second level) which would even have reinforced powers as compared to the whole set of 12 second- and third-level structures of the group.[46]

The Desjardins XVII Congress in March 1999 provided the opportunity to discuss the Board's proposed consensus among thousands of delegates converging from grassroots *caisses*. Before the congress, the delegates received a 75-page background paper focusing not only on the restructuring proposals, but also on the big changes occurring in the Canadian financial sector. As far as costs were concerned, the document provided a break up of the

12.3 per cent productivity gap between Desjardins and the conventional Canadian banks:

- 2.7 per cent were due to the cooperative nature of the group (e.g., general assemblies, congresses, etc.), and could not be further compressed. In addition, it could be argued that the cooperative model brought other advantages in terms of long-term business sustainability.
- 3.3 per cent were due to the capillary presence of the network, including in rural and suburban areas where no other banks had branches, which is an intrinsic part of the group's mission, and could thus not be compressed either.
- Another 6 per cent could be compressed through cost rationalization.

Seventy-six per cent of the 2,825 delegates expressed their approval of delegating more powers from the *caisses* to the higher levels and of making the decisions of the latter mandatory (although half of them with reservations), and 75 per cent were in favour of establishing a single federation. At the same time, most delegates were of the opinion that the grassroots *caisses* should always be consulted on the broad orientation and mission of the group.[47]

The restructuring process then moved to a new phase, with the nomination of a new committee for the revision of structures, comprising ten elected *caisse* officers (among whom were six presidents) and five *caisse* general managers, and with the technical support of Ernst and Young. Two restructuring scenarios were studied: a single federation with 16 regional offices, or the maintenance of the second level but with a reduced number of structures. In comparing the two scenarios, the committee diagnosed that the first was clearly advantageous, not only in terms of cost reduction (75 million Canadian dollars saved against 44 million for the second scenario), but also in terms of democratic functioning and clarity in the division of competences. Except for the delegate from the *caisses d'économie*, all other members of the committee gave their preference to the first scenario. One of the big problems with the restructuring was the prospect of job losses: up to 900 jobs could be lost, even if the figure could be partly offset by staff retiring. An agenda of one-and-a-half years to implement the changes (against the five years initially envisaged) was proposed. The central Board approved the committee's decisions, but with continued opposition from the *caisses d'économie*.[48]

Over the following days, 14,000 elected officers of the *caisses* and federations received a copy of the report and were invited to comment on it. The committee members travelled to the various federations to explain the report. A large video-conference was organized. The central federation received 600 questions and recommendations from the local leaders, concerning the respective powers, the division of territories, the governance system, etc. All questions were analysed and responded to.

Meanwhile, opposition to the proposed restructuring gained support from part of Québec society, headed by the CSN trade union. The federation of the *caisses d'économie*, although part of Desjardins, joined this public opposition as well, while a handful of *caisses d'économie* began to rally to the restructuring project.

On 4 December 1999, the 11 federations held simultaneous general assemblies. A two-thirds majority of both the grassroots *caisses* and of the federations was needed for any decision to be valid: 81 per cent of the territorial *caisses* spread across the general assemblies approved the decision, whereas 95 per cent of the *caisses d'économie* rejected them.

Between 2000 and the global crisis: Desjardins' big transformation

An extraordinary general assembly of the central federation was held on 19 February 2000, confirming the decision made in the individual federations. The *caisses d'économie* first expressed their opposition, but, a few months later, finally agreed to re-join the group.

At the extraordinary general assembly, Alban D'Amours was elected president out of seven candidates, replacing Claude Béland, and had the daunting task of implementing the approved restructuring provisions, while maintaining the group as fully operational with no interruption. Alban D'Amours compared this task to 'making two big 747 [aircraft] land one above the other, obliging them to land on the track at the same time as if nothing special was happening, and making sure that everybody arrived safe and sound, while, at the same time, being ready to take off in a new aircraft in order to pursue their journey'.[49]

In particular, a new financial enterprise of 3,800 staff had to be established out of 12 existing ones, within a period of 18 months, and laying off as few people as possible. In addition, the new operational regions had to be redefined on the basis of micro-markets. A high level of coordination was developed between coordinators specifically entrusted to deal with eleven distinct aspects of the restructuring process, and the whole restructuring plan was implemented within the prescribed times. All job profiles were redefined, and a process of new nominations was put in place, taking into consideration both seniority and the maximum correspondence between the previous, and new, job profiles: by so doing, up to 83 per cent of the job nominations could be successfully processed. The job losses, which were feared would affect 900 people, resulted in only 225 net lay-offs out of the 3,800 staff members, considering that a number of people were reaching retirement age. The way in which the reform was implemented was well received in the media and society, and lay-offs had, in the end, been far more modest than the trade unions had anticipated.

Meanwhile, the constituent assembly of the new federation was held on 1 July 2001. Shortly afterwards, Alban D'Amours emphasized that huge investments would have to be made very rapidly in market and technological development in order to develop activities with higher added values. In his words, 'we must have a very clear vision of how to utilize the surpluses ... while maintaining our presence everywhere in the territory, ensuring a response to the small needs as well as the large ones, thus implementing our mission in full. This is how we are different from the banks and from our competitors'.[50]

As historian Pierre Poulin observes, Desjardins during this period:

> evolved in a renewed framework which was better adapted to the challenges raised by the adaptation to the changing needs of members and clients as well as to competition. The *caisses* experienced a real metamorphosis. They dedicated a great deal of energy and resources to the reconfiguration of their network (merger between *caisses* and relocation of service centres), the development of their advisory services and the improvement of their automatized and on-line services. Thanks to a law which came into force in 1999, they were in a position to establish an integrated service offer to members, with a whole array of financial products and services offered by the [group's common] subsidiaries and, thence, to re-define themselves as cooperatives of financial services.[51]

As far as the reconfiguration of the *caisses* network was concerned, Alban D'Amours' presidency had to face the tricky problem of inter-*caisses* mergers. On the one hand, the latter were necessary in some circumstances, but these years also saw a strong trend towards mergers, influenced by the big string of mergers and acquisitions across the world. The danger with an excess in mergers was that the *caisses* might have lost their capillarity and their close contact with the population. Alban D'Amours explains:

> We created regional networks between the *caisses*, which we called 'grassroots interest communities', aimed to evaluate the relevance of the mergers between *caisses*. This made it possible to proceed to mergers, but in a moderate and democratic way, and thus to maintain a strong level of local embeddedness of the *caisses*.[52]

A landmark of Alban D'Amours' presidency was Desjardins' XVIII Congress in March 2003 under the theme of 'Cooperative Renewal'. A large consultation was held, not only with members, but also the public at large: around 40,000 people took part, either through surveys or through their participation in seminars organized by the *caisses*. The group generated a concrete action plan to reaffirm and reinforce its distinctive cooperative features. Indeed, the conclusions of the Congress made it possible to reaffirm and, at the same time, update the objectives of the *caisses*, and to provide a renewed impetus to the practices that are part of the cooperative rationality (which we examined in Chapter 4). The endeavour was to provide access to high quality and tailored financial services to all members of the *caisses*, independently from the extent of their needs, providing them with concrete financial advantages together with a service characterized by respect and consideration to the client. They also consisted in contributing to local development and to the development of the cooperative system.

Strategic planning is another important step forward of this period. As Alban D'Amours explains:

> the establishment of the new Federation made it possible to move towards a unified strategic direction for the whole movement. Desjardins, as an integrated financial group with a cooperative nature, based its strategies on the *caisse* as a centre of financial expertise, the mergers between the *caisses* guided both by market and geographical considerations, the redeployment of distribution networks, the quality of services, proximity and accessibility, the mastering of technologies, sustainable development and the Desjardins brand. The strategic objective that inspired all these initiatives was the reinforcement of the service logic against a profit logic confined to the short term.[53]

The in-depth institutional transformation which was implemented under the presidency of Alban D'Amours brought about a number of decisive improvements. First, this period counts among one of the best in the whole Desjardins history in terms of financial performance. The renewed organizational efficiency brought about substantial cost reductions. The group's capitalization became one of the highest among the Canadian financial institutions. Almost 45 per cent of net surpluses were returned to the members and the community.

Another important step forward of this period took place in the field of business development based on the provision of services aimed at meeting members' needs and contributing to local development and, with implementation indicators based on members' and clients' satisfaction, developing independently from the type or scale of their needs. As part of the services provided by the group, this period saw an improvement of education, namely cooperative, economic and financial education to members.[54] Several measures were adopted to reinforce Desjardins' positioning as manager of its members' financial assets. The service offer to enterprises continued to develop thanks to the CFE (enterprise financial centres, see above), the central *caisse* and Desjardins Risk Capital, as well as Desjardins Regional and Cooperative Capital and newly established regional investment funds. The *caisses* reinforced their presence in the city of Montreal through new service centres (West Island Financial Center, Carrefour Desjardins, Centre d'Affaires Moyennes Entreprises Desjardins). The expansion of the group's business also rested on the expansion of its activities in the USA (Desjardins central *caisse* US Branch) and in Canada, in particular with the inclusion of the Ontario People's *Caisses* Federation within the group, after several years of partnership. Similarly, the insurance subsidiaries widely contributed to the prestige of Desjardins' brand name in other Canadian provinces.

Alban D'Amours explains that:

> the success of this huge transformation initiated under the leadership of Claude Béland was largely the consequence of a new type of governance where democracy, both representative and participative, had come to fully play its role. Such governance, designed to ensure that the *caisses* could maintain the level of creativity which they wanted to possess within the framework of a coherent and solidarity-based network, made it possible to obtain the expected results of this huge project in terms of political equilibrium, organizational efficiency and reduction in functioning costs. The group's governance experienced a profound transformation in how the importance of the role of elected officers was reaffirmed, how the key role of the general directors was recognized, how the influence capacity of the *caisses* was reinforced, and how the distribution networks were more efficiently integrated. The renewal of the democratic basis has allowed for new mechanisms in terms of networking, survey and consultation. The councils of *caisses* representatives, which are the centre of the political equilibrium of the movement, and the assembly of representatives have become instances whose responsibilities are on the one hand to deepen the embeddedness of the *caisses* in their territories and, on the other hand, to exercise a power of orientation on the main strategies of the movement. The establishment of a new Desjardins Cooperative Institute focusing on the Desjardins' 'know how to be' and know how in terms of governance, managing a cooperative, and innovation has provided a distinctive meaning to the development of the competences that were needed in order to carry out the changes initiated by the elected officers, employees and managers.[55]

To sum up, the first years of the new millennium allowed the Desjardins group to substantially strengthen itself through its distinctive business model, allowing a community of millions of citizens to converge towards common objectives in terms of economic and social development, and to brace itself to face the global crisis that was now looming on the horizon.

The global crisis and the future

Alban D'Amours, who was Desjardins' president when the crisis began to flare up in 2007, explains that, by then:

> [Thirty-six] billion dollars' worth of asset-backed commercial papers had been issued in Canada by non-banking institutions. In August 2007,

when the markets stopped functioning, Desjardins decided to re-purchase the asset-backed commercial papers which its members and clients had acquired and put them on its own balance sheet. We thereby managed to mutualize the losses anticipated by our members and clients and build a critical mass in the ownership of these bonds as an investor. This gave us the necessary influence in the subsequent negotiation aimed to allow these bonds to be converted into long term ones, and to securitize a large share of the value of these bonds.

Alban D'Amours also underlines that 'nowhere on the planet have investors been able to do what the Canadian financial institutions then managed to achieve, and this occurred in part thanks to Desjardins' leadership role'.[56]

The process was not easy, though. Indeed, as the group explained in a press release:

in the absence of an active market for this type of financial product and in compliance with the Canadian accounting standards, Desjardins had to proceed to an evaluation of the fair value of its portfolio of asset-backed commercial paper on 31 December 2008. Thus, for the fourth quarter of 2008, the cumulated devaluation rose from 30 per cent on 30 September to 41 per cent on 31 December.[57]

The negative impact on the 2008 balance sheet of Desjardin was tangible, but not dramatic. The group's total income in 2008 was US $8.3 billion, a 13.4 per cent decrease as compared to 2007.[58] Nevertheless, the core business of the *caisses* remained highly sustainable, with only 0.4 per cent of bad loans.

The asset-backed commercial papers, converted into long-term bonds, eventually regained part of their original value, as seen above. The group thus fully regained its usual economic figures in 2009, with a surplus of US $1,065 million (against US $77 million in 2008).

The September 2008 financial slump, *per se*, did not fundamentally affect the group. It took place just a few months after the election of the new president, Monique Leroux. Desjardins' work plan set in 2008 included five main points, namely: the group's strategic development and growth; collaboration, participation and connection with the network; the changing role of the federation and the group structure; the optimization of the group's performance; and mobilizing all the human capital, culture and values of Desjardins. At the Desjardins Congress in November 2009, five key strategic orientations were widely debated among the 1,700 delegates, namely: cooperation and involvement; member/client experience; growth and innovation; profitability and financial stability; and leadership and mobilization.[59] These orientations were then formally approved at the March 2010 general assembly. It is still unclear how this new reform will be carried out, as, at the time of completing this book (end of 2010), it is still in the early stages.

The subsidiaries are now being incorporated in four business sectors, and each of the four common areas (finance, human resources, technology, risk management) are being put under the authority of one key leader of the group.

A new overhaul of the organizational and human resource structure is being put in place with a view to reduce the number of hierarchical levels, in order to be closer to the clients and to the *caisses*, and to attain more cohesion. In each of three years, 300 jobs, namely 900 in all, will have to be terminated.[60] Although it is hoped that part of these job losses will be offset by retirements, it is likely to be one of the biggest job reductions in Desjardins' job-preserving history.

The group is also trying to focus more strongly on its service offer to enterprises. André Chapleau, Desjardins' general director for relations with the media, explains:

> Through the ongoing restructuring process, we have grouped under one single business sector all activities and services linked to enterprises, such as the subsidiary for risk capital, institutional loans, 50 CFE offices, etc., which previously tended to act as 'silos', and sometimes people did not really know which entity to contact. The new structure attempts to abolish this fragmentation. So we have one directorate for all services to enterprises, linked to the entities I've just mentioned. We will see the results of this restructuring over the next few months and years. But we can already observe that our market share of the Québec enterprise market has increased by 1.3 per cent, from 26 per cent to 27.3 per cent, which is quite a lot in such a competitive market. The CFE are our entry points to the enterprises. We want to work more with enterprises because each enterprise has a number of positive effects on its environment, employment, local services, suppliers, accountancy, etc. Thus, by helping businesses we also support the community. We presently have agreements with over 500,000 enterprises. The main evolution now is that we are beginning to move from assisting small enterprises to medium ones, and we already have a few large enterprises among our clients.[61]

Concerning the new focus on performance and productivity, president Monique Leroux insists that these are 'notions that are not incompatible with a cooperative. The only difference is that, here, we put them at the service of the mission, not of profitability. We do not have to pay stock options to leaders or dividends to shareholders'. The performance of the system must be geared towards 'maintaining a sufficient and reassuring profitability level, in order to ensure the long-term sustainability of the movement'.[62]

Conclusion

As we saw throughout this brief historical account, the Desjardins group first managed to democratize and decentralize financial services, making them accessible to all strata of the population and spreading them across the Québec local communities. In the first half of the twentieth century, it took a large part in the modernization of agriculture. After the Second World War, it enlarged its mission by providing mortgage loans which helped many families own their homes. It enabled several generations of Québecois to act collectively to develop their local and regional economy. Hundreds of thousands of Québecois learnt the basics of savings through their school *caisses*. Today, 6,258 presidents and board members of local *caisses*, generally ordinary citizens, have learnt how a bank works and have responsibilities in overseeing it.[63] Tens of thousands of stable jobs have been created, making Desjardins the largest employer in Québec and one of the main employers in Canada. The group is developing an integrated offer to businesses, with half a million business clients. The system has always managed to strike a fine balance between financial constraints and social concerns, and between the members' long-term financial security and their short-term aspirations.[64] By so doing, the system works in the opposite direction of the consumption trap and the debt trap which we examined in Chapter 2. Indeed, it does not build up systemic risk: it supports long-term socioeconomic development, and fosters equality and trust.

The structuring of the *caisses* into a horizontal group has unleashed a huge economic and social potential: instead of remaining isolated structures, as they were in the beginning and could have remained, the Desjardins local credit cooperatives or *caisses* have managed to create one of the largest financial groups in North America, while maintaining their capillary presence and remaining totally dedicated to servicing local citizens and local businesses. The trend towards an excessive level of mergers has been controlled. The danger that the subsidiaries could increase their influence, in particular in terms of technocratic management, has also been averted, by a number of successive governance reforms in which the level of joint control over those subsidiaries has increased.

By extending the cooperative bottom-up logic from the local *caisses* to a system as large as Canada's Québec Province (almost 8 million inhabitants), Desjardins has been a key promoter of a 'meso-economy', having on the one hand been, for over a century, one of the main actors in the development of local communities in Québec, and, on the other, having played a key role in the financial stability of Canada. This became particularly visible during the crisis, contributing to Canada distinguishing itself as being one of the most stable banking systems in the world.

Against the theories that argue that democratic management is an expensive cost (as we saw in Chapter 4), the Desjardins experience suggests that its democratic procedures are partly a cost indeed, but for an irreplaceable social function (such as the capillarity in remote municipalities, and the fact that it is the only banking institution in Québec which is open to the poor), while they are mainly an investment over the long term, because they legitimize decisions and provide stability to the institutions, and because the level and sophistication of the debates makes it more likely that all points of view will be taken into consideration, thus leading to the most sustainable decision.

In addition, against the information asymmetries that many stakeholders suffer, such as clients of big financial institutions where depositors' entrustment is being superseded by opaque and segmented counter-party arrangements (as seen in Chapter 3), Desjardins not only nurtures the notion of a movement of owners-clients to which it is dedicated, but provides the latter with information on the business group, discussion papers to help them make up their mind in decision making, and training to help them manage their local cooperatives.

The history of Desjardins also demonstrates that successive crises (the Great Depression, several crises in the 1980s and 1990s, and the ongoing global crisis), instead of threatening the existence of the group, have in fact reinforced it and provided it with the opportunity to carry out institutional innovation and improve its core mission of servicing its members.

Finally, it should be fully recognized that the Desjardins experience, including in its most recent developments, is neither old-fashioned nor redundant in terms of policy making. It shows us that the study of economic entities as actors is useful in order to rethink policies that promote accountability and visibility. It is a living example of the fact that an economic entity is no 'black box': rationality and ethics do make a difference, provided they are allowed to find their way in the organization through the institutionalization of routines, checks and balances, and strategic priorities.

8
The Mondragon Cooperative Group: Local Development with a Global Vision

Introduction

In this chapter, we share our recent fieldwork focusing on how the Mondragon group has been coping with the ongoing global crisis. The group had previously experienced a series of economic crises, in particular in the early 1980s and, to a lesser extent, in the early 1990s. We therefore compare the mechanisms and strategies used now and in earlier periods.[1]

We hope that the reader will grasp the extent of the complexity of Mondragon's institutional system, its checks and balances, and its solidarity mechanisms, which make the whole cooperative group resilient, efficient and innovative. We will see that the structure of the group makes it difficult for the three traps (consumption trap, liquidity trap and debt trap) analysed in Chapter 2 to take hold. We will also observe how general wealth and capital have been built, and how the 'joint ownership and democratic control' of the international cooperative definition, seen in Chapter 4, can be applied to a modern industrial group.

Mondragon is a horizontally integrated group of over 110 cooperative enterprises, involved in various industrial, service, financial, distribution, educational and research activities, in the Basque autonomous region (Euskadi) in Northern Spain and mainly centred around the small town of Mondragon (Arrasate in the Basque language).

The first industrial cooperative enterprise of the Mondragon group was established in 1956 with 24 workers lacking capital. Fifty-four years later, this fledgling SME has given way to a huge corporate conglomerate, producing white goods, machine tools, computer parts, furniture and home fixtures, office fittings, construction materials, transformers, car components, moulds for cast iron, cooling systems, medical equipment, foodstuffs and other manufactured goods. It is also involved in a series of service activities such as engineering, urbanism, catering, and legal services, doing research in various industrial sectors and in nano-technologies, and comprising a large national supermarket chain, a bank and a university.

The figures speak for themselves. With assets worth €33 billion, €14.78 billion in sales in 2009, it is the first corporate group of the Basque region and the seventh in Spain. With globalization, Mondragon has become an increasingly internationalized group, with 73 plants in 18 other countries and regions in Europe, Latin America, Asia and Africa, plus corporate offices in another five.

At the same time, the Mondragon group has been and remains a key actor in local, regional and national development. With its 85,000 workers (more than twice as many as a decade ago), it is the largest employer in the Basque region and the fourth largest in Spain, just behind the main telephone company, the post office system, and the biggest national department store chain. Over the years, it has developed most aspects of the local economy (industry, agriculture, services, credit, investment, education, culture, research, social protection, etc.) under the cooperative form of enterprise, with a long-term strategy.

Mondragon is a small town within a valley in the Cantabric mountain chain of Northern Spain. The centre of the cooperative group is located within the same valley, which has a total length of around 40 kilometres, and with a current population of around 100,000 inhabitants. This is the area of major concentration of cooperatives, but the zone where the cooperatives of the group can be found includes the whole Basque Autonomous Region (2 million inhabitants), and extends to neighbouring Navarra.[2]

The Basques have a long tradition of democracy. During the Middle Ages, the municipal councils were elected by all the male citizens. Nevertheless, in the seventeenth century, the Spanish authorities prohibited this practice and granted the right to vote only to the wealthiest families. The Basque Country has throughout its history developed a number of economic activities based on collective structures, such as the sporadic practice of neighbourhood work in agriculture, fishermen guilds, and the organized exploitation of communal land. A mainly pastoral region for centuries, the Basque Country also has a long tradition of manufacturing industries, mainly foundries and shipyards, that were also organized in guilds.

In the following pages, we review the historical evolution of the group, distinguishing four separate periods: the creation and early development of the cooperative network (1943–79); the economic crisis of the early 1980s and the subsequent entry of Spain into the EU and the Single Market (1980–91); the period of consolidation and internationalization under the Mondragon Corporation (1991–2008); and, finally, the ongoing global crisis (2008–10). In the conclusion, we then attempt to draw the main lessons we can learn from the Mondragon experience.

The first stage: education and research, self-finance and entrepreneurial development (1943–79)

The very first steps

In the middle of the twentieth century, Mondragon was a small township of 8,000 inhabitants. Although there was one large industrial enterprise, a foundry called Union Cerrajera, Mondragon's geographical situation (in a valley) did not make it particularly propitious for industrial development. It did not even have a secondary school.

Jose Maria Arizmendiarrieta, the inspirer of the Mondragon cooperative group, arrived in Mondragon in 1941 as a 26-year old parish priest, two years after the end of the Spanish civil war. Since the beginning, he displayed a keen interest in the social problems of the region.

In 1943, Arizmendiarrieta founded the Mondragon Escuela Politecnica (later known in Basque as Eskola Politeknikoa), a vocational school for youths between the ages of 14 and 17. The school could be launched thanks to the positive response of 15 per cent of the adult population of Mondragon, who provided the initial funding and constituted an association. Arizmendiarrieta had regular meetings with his pupils and ex-pupils on a number of social issues, including ways to reform the property system within industrial companies. The first batch of pupils left the school, and some were appointed as foremen by the local Unión Cerrajera industry, while pursuing studies in industrial expertise at a Spanish university in the region, without physically attending the classes.

In 1955, as part of an expansion programme, Unión Cerrajera began selling shares. Five of the ex-pupils of the Eskola Politeknikoa proposed that shares be sold to the workers of the enterprise and, therefore, be allowed to take part in the management of the latter: but the company refused. They then decided to create their own enterprise with the envisioned joint-control characteristics which they had discussed at length in their regular meetings with Arizmendiarrieta.

However, it was extremely difficult in Spain at that time for ordinary workers to obtain a licence enabling them to create a new enterprise. The opportunity was found when a factory in a town nearby went bankrupt: they could buy the licence and start producing. The licence was for mechanical and electric products for domestic use. The five ex-pupils purchased the factory licence with the financial help of other Mondragon inhabitants who were interested in the project and called it Ulgor, after their initials. One year later, in 1956, the five founders moved the enterprise to Mondragon itself and ran it as a cooperative, together with another 19 workers.

After Ulgor's foundation in 1956, three other cooperatives were established along the same lines by other pioneers from Arizmendiarrieta's vocational school: Arrasate was created in 1958 with a production line of machine tools, some of which were sold to Ulgor; Copreci, founded in 1963, specialized in spare parts for domestic and industrial cookers, and for years sold almost all its production to Ulgor; Ederlan, also founded in 1963, was a foundry.

Basic characteristics of a Mondragon cooperative

The statutes of Ulgor, which were laid down in 1959, served as a matrix for all the cooperatives that were eventually organized (see Figure 8.1).

As in any cooperative, the supreme power rests with the General Assembly which meets at least once a year, but can be called at any time by the Governing Council of the cooperative, or by a percentage of its members (which has varied according to the period).

The Governing Council is the highest organ of management and representation of the cooperative. The members of the Governing Council are elected for a period of four years, and do not receive any financial compensation for their task. The Governing Council nominates the manager and the managing team for a period of four years, and can nominate it for another four years after an in-depth analysis. The manager has a voice but no vote in the Governing Council. All the major decisions concerning the staff must be taken by the Governing Council, under the manager's proposals.

The Auditors' Council provides an internal auditing system on the financial operations and on the previously defined financial procedures. Its three members are elected by the General Assembly.

The Direction Council assembles the manager and the heads of the various departments. Its task is to make proposals (strategic plans, work plans, etc.) to the Governing Council and to determine how executive decisions taken by the Governing Council will be implemented.

The Social Council is responsible for such issues as social security, remuneration systems, labour hygiene and welfare projects. In any such matters, the Governing Council must first consult the Social Council. The members of the Social Council are elected by the General Assembly for a two-year period, and half of its members are renewed each year. Re-election is not encouraged: the intention is that as many members as possible should become members of this Council at least once in their life.

The annual surplus of the cooperative are divided as follows:

- A minimum of 10 per cent for educational, cultural and welfare activities; later, this 10 per cent will be dedicated to a common fund for the whole group, plus 3 per cent for a solidarity fund.
- A certain percentage for the enterprise's reserve fund (35 to 52 per cent in the 1960s, only 10 to 29 per cent in the 1970s, more than 50 per cent in the 1980s, and around 45 per cent nowadays). This fund is indivisible (indivisible reserves are discussed in Chapter 4): therefore even in case of closure, these assets cannot be distributed to the members–owners nor cashed in by an acquirer, but are allocated to another cooperative structure. It must be underlined that the reserve fund provides an index of the

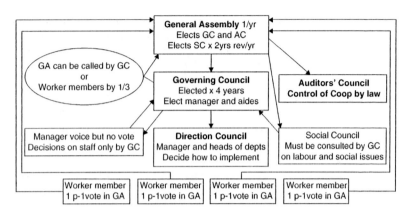

Figure 8.1   Basic structure of a Mondragon cooperative

level of socialization of the enterprise, making investments and future-oriented vision and strategy possible.
- The remaining part (around 45 percent today) called 'cooperative returns', is distributed among the members proportionally to their working hours and to their index of compensation. Whereas the surpluses returned to members are a basic cooperative institution (see Chapter 4), a characteristic of Mondragon is that they are actually paid to members only a few years after they leave or when they retire, and are therefore capitalized for years or decades. The founders of Mondragon have always maintained that this policy of very strong capital accumulation, which has been applied to all cooperatives of the group, is certainly one of the main factors behind the impressive expansion of Mondragon in the 1960s and 1970s.

Another characteristic of Mondragon is the high level of individual members' contribution in share capital, which is the equivalent of around one year's wages. The remuneration of the share capital, as in most cooperatives (see Chapter 4), is a fixed interest rate which is slightly higher than the remuneration for a long-term deposit account, and is meant to compensate for inflation. In addition, if a member leaves a cooperative to go and work in a factory which is in direct competition with the cooperative he/she is leaving, up to 20 per cent of his/her share capital can be kept by the cooperative as penalty.

The birth and development of the group's support institutions

It would be impossible to understand the evolution of the Mondragon group by only studying its individual enterprises and without analysing the role played by its various second-degree institutions, which have been developed since the early phase of the Mondragon experience, to which the cooperatives have democratically delegated strong competences in the fields of loans and investment, consultancy, sectoral coordination, insurance, education and training, research and development, etc.

At the root of the Mondragon experience: the educational institutions

The educational component of the Mondragon cooperative group is the oldest. As we saw above, the founding of the Eskola Politeknikoa goes as far back as 1943, 13 years earlier than the establishment of the first industrial cooperative. As soon as the first cooperatives were created, the Eskola Politeknikoa began interacting with them. In 1965, it was itself converted into a cooperative.

In 1966, Alecoop, a students' cooperative, was launched within the Eskola Politeknikoa. With spiralling teaching expenses, this cooperative was seen by the Mondragon founders as the best alternative to a dramatic increase in school fees, which would have discriminated against children from poor families. Alecoop was meant to give half-work/half-study opportunities to the pupils of the school, integrating its activities within the surrounding cooperatives by producing industrial products under contract. The member-pupils attended classes for five hours and worked another four hours a day in the Alecoop workshop and in the cooperatives of the group, in production or in technical jobs, which would facilitate their integration in the cooperatives after their studies. Therefore, the cooperative had two daily shifts, and the school offered two equivalent programmes each day.

When they first designed Alecoop's internal structure, the Mondragon cooperative leaders tried to strike a fine balance between their desire to let the pupils take part in the decision-making process of the cooperative on the one hand, and the need to preserve the economic strength of the enterprise on the other. In order to do so, a fine three-tiered decision-making structure involving teachers, students and other cooperatives of the group was worked out.

Arizmendiarrieta and his followers believed that the pupils of the Eskola Politeknikoa needed to be members of a producers' cooperative as early as possible. Indeed, Alecoop provided the pupils with the unique opportunity to directly experience cooperative life. Ex-Alecoop members from the 1960s and 1970s later became the second-generation leaders of Mondragon. Alecoop still exists today and thrives within the group.

In the 1960s, new educational cooperative structures were established, mainly in technology, management and languages, some of them being university-level institutions. Among them, the school of business administration, ETEO, would become an important institution in the 1990s by being a founding component of the Mondragon University (see below).

Caja Laboral, the group's bank

Among the support entities of the group, the one which played the most concrete role in the creation and early development of the Mondragon cooperatives is certainly Caja Laboral, the group's bank.

Caja Laboral was established in 1959 (three years after the establishment of the first cooperative, Ulgor) as a credit cooperative by the first four industrial cooperatives (Ulgor, Copreci, Arrasate, Ederlan), plus a consumers' cooperative, which had been established in the meantime. It was originally designed as a development bank, focusing exclusively on the development of cooperatives in the Spanish Basque Country, with a specific focus on the creation of long-term employment.[3]

Caja Laboral's governance structure is an attempt to balance the interests of its member cooperatives and of its worker-members. Each of the two interest groups has a percentage of votes at the General Assembly, and its Governing Council comprises eight persons elected by the cooperatives and four by the worker-members.

Moreover, for the first 28 years of its existence (1959–87), Caja Laboral was not only a bank, but served as the *de facto* head unit of the whole group: for the 100 or so cooperatives that were created over that period, the membership of the group took place when they initiated financial participation in the bank and signed a 'contract of association' with it.

Caja Laboral established within itself a powerful 'Enterprise Division', which, until the late 1980s, promoted the creation of the subsequent cooperatives and institutions of the group, provided managerial and technical consultancy to all cooperatives, and even intervened in case of economic crisis.

The bank's defaulting rate has been extremely low over its history. Up to the early 1980s, it suffered only one failure in establishing a cooperative (in the fishing industry), losing its 24 per cent share of this venture's start-up investment.[4] It has never been in the red.[5]

Caja Laboral's financial resources at the time of its creation were extremely scarce, but capitalization proceeded thanks to the bank's member cooperatives' contributions: they deposited enough share capital and reserves to ensure Caja Laboral's solvency; they cancelled all financial and economic operations with other banks; for the first 14 years, they deposited their welfare reserve funds into the bank; and for the first 20 years, they guaranteed all the bank's financial operations through 25 per cent of their share capital.

At the same time, Caja Laboral launched a policy of individual savings, and became a highly successful savings bank open to the public, with attractive interest rates and premiums.

This policy of attracting both enterprise and individual capital was so effective that the bank soon enjoyed a surplus of financial resources. In 1966, the member cooperatives were still financially stronger than Caja Laboral, with the latter's resources only reaching 26 per cent of the aggregate financial assets of the group; within only four years, the ratio had risen to 70 per cent.[6]

Lagun Aro, Mondragon's social protection system

Caja Laboral established within itself, in 1959, a health and social welfare insurance system, called Lagun Aro. The objective was to help the worker-members of the first Mondragon cooperatives, and their families, solve their welfare problems (health and safety, assistance, social security). At that time, worker-members of cooperatives were not covered by the State Social Security system and were thus unprotected.

In 1973, Lagun Aro was transformed into a distinct higher-level coopera-tive, by spinning it off from Caja Laboral. Its role would become predominant in the 1980s, as we will see in the next section.

District-based groupings among cooperatives

In 1966, the first Mondragon industrial cooperative Ulgor attracted around itself the other three (Copreci, Arrasate and Erdelan), with Arizmendiarrieta's discreet encouragement, into something they first called an 'industrial com-plex' and eventually a 'district-based grouping', called ULARCO. One of the Ulgor founders, Alfonso Gorroñogoitia, then wrote: 'The objective that we are pursuing is to establish a technically harmonious "industrial complex", which would not only deal with the production of consumer goods, but also equipment goods and components of various types'.[7]

ULARCO's role was to coordinate the business strategy and the annual plans of its constituent cooperatives, set up common administrative systems, launch new activities and new enterprises (including by spin-off), establish common research and distribution services, manage new production licences, engage in common training programmes and common human resource poli-cies, etc. ULARCO also inaugurated mechanisms of common financial redistri-bution and financial solidarity, which, in turn, helped finance other common cooperative institutions. The inner structure of the district-based grouping was similar to that of the grassroots cooperative enterprises. The General Assembly of ULARCO was made up of the constituent cooperatives, with a number of delegates per cooperative which was proportional to the number of their respective physical worker-members. It elected a General Council, with a definite number of members (usually two) from each of the constitu-ent cooperatives. The General Council nominated a General Directorate. The latter's role was planning and coordination, as well as the recommendation of annual and long-term plans and the coordination of commercial policies. The General Directorate was also responsible for administrative matters such as the purchase of processing licences and the relationship with external organizations. It also provided legal and accountancy services to the member cooperatives and coordinated the short- or long-term transfer of members from one cooperative of the grouping to another. The grouping also had a central Social Council, made up of delegates from the social councils of each constituent cooperative. The central Social Council had to be consulted on any important decision within the cooperative grouping.

ULARCO actually served as a matrix for other similar 'district-based group-ings' and, 25 years later, for the Mondragon corporation itself. Another of the Ulgor founders, José Maria Ormaetxea, explains that the establishment of ULARCO was not an easy and spontaneous process: 'We had to do it among cooperatives and cooperative members who had a very staunch con-cept of the sovereignty of their enterprises'.[8] Nevertheless:

> one has to take into account that, between cooperatives, sovereignty is not acquired by contributing capital to each other, which is the usual practice to obtain control in conventional joint-stock companies. Therefore, only deeds, ideals, and a latent but permanent ethical com-mitment to solve any possible conflictive situation or any simple tech-nical problem, were the basis for the evolution towards a prosperous industrial fabric.[9]

R&D

In 1966, one of the teachers of the Eskola Politeknikoa began doing indus-trial research and made several trips to France and other countries to visit industrial research institutes. In 1968, the Eskola established within itself a working group made up of teachers who were partly freed from their teach-ing tasks so as to dedicate themselves to research.

The creation of this team had a double objective. On the one hand, research was to become an input in the improvement of teaching. On the other, the school aimed to find practical applications in the industrial coop-eratives with which it had already established initial collaborative contacts, laying the basis for future cooperation.[10]

At the beginning of the 1970s, Spain's technological panorama was limited. Years of isolation had left a heavy legacy on the capacity for technological development. It was common to purchase licenses and patents, many foreign models were also copied, which generated technological dependence. Some companies had departments where they developed their own products, but they were limited and there was no time left for technological research. Nor was there a habit of outsourcing such activities. Research was confined to universities and did not service industry.

In 1972, the school established an automation laboratory which signed research contracts with several Mondragon cooperatives. In a 1973 document titled 'Towards Research' laying the bases for the new centre's operations, José María Ormaetxea, then general director of Caja Laboral (one of the main promoters of the project) made a detailed analysis of the structural and financial needs of the centre, defining even the geographical location and the partners that would be needed for its future evolution.[11] Several industrial cooperatives supported the project. Finally, in 1974, a distinctive industrial R&D cooperative, Ikerlan, was established.

During the same period, Ikerlan's core team visited private laboratories and public R&D centres in Spain and across Europe. Soon after those visits, a report detailed the equipment that the cooperative would need to launch its activities.

The way in which Ikerlan's governance structure was designed reflects, again, Mondragon's concern to see all stakeholders hold a substantial share of democratic control over the enterprise: it was decided from the beginning that the staff of the cooperative would hold a 40 per cent voting power in the General Assembly, the industrial cooperatives 30 per cent, and the support institutions such as Caja Laboral and the Eskola Politeknikoa the remaining 30 per cent.

How the bank was involved in the creation and early development of the cooperatives

Caja Laboral was the main entity involved in the creation and early development of the cooperatives during this first phase of Mondragon's history. Any intervention in creating or consolidating cooperative enterprises was then done primarily through its Enterprise Division.

Prior to all interventions, the Enterprise Division established with the beneficiary cooperative a 'contract of association', spelling out the cooperative's main guiding principles, including an emphasis on job creation.[12] According to the contract, the cooperative first provided an initial contribution to the capital of Caja Laboral, and had to commit itself to matching all projects requiring a bank loan with a substantial level of co-financing from its own resources. Caja Laboral could audit the accounts of the cooperative every four years. In addition, a number of features regulating the associated cooperatives were stipulated, such as the maximum gap between higher and lower wages, the percentages of surplus redistribution, and the provision that all workers had to become members after a testing period.

The prevalent type of intervention by Caja Laboral was incubation. Feasibility studies were made to define new enterprise sectors. Then, a core group of local persons was identified to launch the project. As many as 45 out of the 99 cooperatives that were members of the Mondragon group in 1990 had been launched in this fashion.[13]

Another key enterprise creation method was to establish a new cooperative by spin-off from an existing one, under the joint guidance of the bank and of the district-based grouping to which this cooperative belonged. Persons from a cooperative belonging to a district-based grouping who proposed creating another cooperative would present a project to the General Directorate of the grouping, and not directly to Caja Laboral. For two years, the project proponents would then rotate among the various services of their own cooperative in order to gain the necessary experience to set up the new one. They would also be given half of their working time to concentrate on planning their project. They would try to involve two or three persons from outside the cooperative, for example friends, as candidates to start the new cooperative with them. These persons would be admitted temporarily into the cooperative where the proponents were still working, and under the same working conditions as the proponents. At the end of this period, the directorate of the cooperative grouping would make its own feasibility study. If the latter was positive, the cooperative grouping would either help finance the project, or would guarantee loans provided by Caja Laboral, or both. The two to three years' wages provided to the founding members in the beginning were a separate loan granted by the district-based grouping to the new cooperative. Around ten producers' cooperatives were established according to this model.[14]

After the cooperatives had been established, Caja Laboral continued to play a critical role in assisting them in their development stage, through loans for their expansion projects, promoting job creation whenever this was possible.[15]

Caja Laboral also began working on restructuring operations. Five conventional private businesses were transformed into cooperatives in the 1960s and 1970s. In 1969, Caja Laboral became involved in another restructuring operation by helping nine very small and poorly performing local consumer cooperatives to merge with each other. This merger would have an enormous impact on the Mondragon group's destiny two decades later, as it gave birth to the EROSKI consumer cooperative, today one of the strongest enterprises of the whole group, and its largest single employer. Mondragon was thereby entering a totally new sector, distribution, in which isolated cooperatives lacked innovation capacity, and were even condemned to disappear, as became clear later.[16] Since its foundation, EROSKI has had a distinctive governance structure, whereby power is equally distributed between the cooperative's two types of members, namely the consumers and the workers. Indeed, each of these two groups has 50 per cent voting rights at the general assembly and on the Governing Council.

In all its operations, Caja Laboral endeavoured to create as many jobs as possible, always according to a strict entrepreneurial rationality. Thomas and Logan found that production in Mondragon's cooperatives could be even more capital-intensive than in conventional enterprises. 'In 1976, for mechanical and engineering industries, the cost of creating a new workplace averaged 2.5 million pesetas in the Mondragon cooperatives, against 1.5 million pesetas in conventional enterprises of the region'. In an average conventional enterprise, 'investments continue but capital-intensity is relatively low, and many jobs are lost due to company failures. The cooperatives adopt a higher capital-intensity and simultaneously expand the number of workplaces. This is only possible, of course, if capital-intensity is closely guarded'.[17] Individual cooperative members were unable to pool in such huge financial resources on their own. In 1975, the founding members of a typical Mondragon cooperative covered about 20 per cent of its start-up capital, government low-interest loans provided another 20 per cent, and the remaining 60 per cent came from Caja Laboral. Five years later, due to increases in job creation costs, employees' contribution had shrunk to 10 per cent.[18] Even then, considering the high capital-intensity involved, the individual employees' contribution to the cost of creating their own jobs (10 per cent) was quite substantial, and the creation of such capital-intensive jobs was made possible only because of the bank's high matching contribution.

The second stage: economic crisis, entry into the EU, globalization (1980–91)

In the early 1980s, the Basque region of Spain experienced one of the worst economic crises in its history. The unemployment index rose to 25 per cent of the active population and even surpassed 50 per cent for youth unemployment. The crisis was almost immediately followed by Spain's entry into the EU in 1986, and, simultaneously, by the advent of full-fledged economic globalization. These three successive challenges (the crisis, the EU and globalization) obliged the Mondragon group to undergo profound changes.

Javier Salaberria, then legal director at Fagor Electrodomesticos (as Ulgor had then been renamed), explains:

> In the 1970s we did not foresee what a crisis would look like. We had the feeling that we would grow without end. The Spanish market was totally protected. Exports were very few. With the crisis in the 1980s, we learnt many things and we found the response to many problems. And when we entered the EU, we lost protectionism. Each cooperative alone would never have found the resources to face the situation.[19]

The crisis of the early 1980s

The reform of the social protection system

In the early 1980s, the Lagun Aro social protection system was reformed. New norms in support of employment were approved, giving absolute priority to maintaining the right to work for unemployed worker-members instead of allocating a financial subsidy (unemployment benefit) as the social security system normally does. This became a very original feature of the Mondragon system, which gave the preference to employment over any other solution, in pursuance of the cooperative principles applied to worker-members.

The system included temporary placement in other cooperatives, unemployment benefit for persons who had no possibility to find another job (but such subsidy could not be granted for more than twelve months over a two-year period), partial unemployment, early retirement schemes (once a worker had reached 58 years of age) and occupational retraining.

Financial support was given for a one-year period to cooperatives where either 10 per cent of the workforce or 40 members were redundant. The aid was designed as a cyclical support which had to be fully or partly repaid over a five-year period. To this end, 20 per cent of the net surplus accumulated over five calendar years by the beneficiary cooperatives had to be devoted to the reimbursement.

Javier Salaberria recalls:

> At that time, as we had a self-employed status, we had no unemployment benefit. With the Lagun Aro system, all cooperatives were obliged to accept people from other cooperatives if they also wanted to obtain social coverage themselves in bad times. Subsidized unemployment was really a solution of last resort. The members had contributed financially to Lagun Aro for years, so when they became unemployed they could get unemployment benefit from Lagun Aro.[20]

Interventions to save cooperatives in times of crisis

The Contract of Association between Caja Laboral and the individual cooperatives (see previous section) provided Caja Laboral's Enterprise Division with considerable powers of intervention in case of recession. This clause became particularly important during the crisis of the early 1980s.

The Enterprise Division worked in close coordination with Lagun Aro. As a first step, the Enterprise Division drafted a feasibility study. In general, the study concluded that the cooperative could be saved, but only at the cost of drastic measures, such as changes in the production line or in the marketing structure, wage cuts, compulsory new share capital to be contributed by members or, in extreme cases, staff reduction or, when everything else had failed, the liquidation of the cooperative.

Most intervention cases succeeded: out of 34 interventions performed by the Enterprise Division in 1983 (the worse year of the economic crisis), only two small cooperatives had to be liquidated, and virtually all jobs were saved thanks to the redeployment system.

The following example of enterprise salvation, the case of Zubiola, shows how far Caja Laboral was able to go to save an associated cooperative, with the help of Lagun Aro.

Zubiola, a cooperative producing machine-tools for wooden furniture, was established in 1966 out of a transformation from a conventional business, and became a Caja Laboral associated cooperative and a member of Lagun Aro in 1970. With Caja Laboral's financial and managerial assistance, Zubiola managed to conquer 70 per cent of the Spanish market for its type of product. Its workforce grew from 15 in the beginning to 144 at its peak in 1979.

However, when the crisis arrived, profits suddenly dwindled because the client enterprises failed to repay their debts in time. Zubiola's management did not immediately realize the gravity of the situation, and contracted loans with Caja Laboral to compensate for the debtors' defaulting. Then, as things went from bad to worse, an emergency diagnosis by Caja Laboral was requested. It indicated that the main problem was over-production. This meant that 50 out of the 126 worker-members of the cooperative had to be laid off.

In 1983, 23 of these 50 surplus employees could be permanently rede-ployed in other cooperatives of the group. Only temporary relocation could be arranged for the remaining 27, six of whom then volunteered to establish a new cooperative of their own. Caja Laboral requested each remaining member of Zubiola to provide the equivalent of €3,000 in share capital (the money was lent by Caja Laboral as individual loans to be repaid within five years through a 20 per cent reduction of their normal wages), and drafted a drastic restructuring plan.

However, the restructuring plan was in the doldrums within a few months, when some key leaders of Zubiola, who were supposed to implement it, decided to leave the cooperative to work in the conventional private sector. The URKIDE district-based grouping, which Zubiola belonged to, then proposed a new plan by which the production sections of Zubiola and of another cooperative of the grouping would be merged, and Zubiola's remaining surplus employees would be relocated to the newly merged cooperative. After lengthy negotiations, this was finally agreed. The Enterprise Division asked Zubiola to draft a new business plan, and approved a substantial new loan, while writing off part of the cooperative's debt. It was only in 1986 that Zubiola began recovering from the crisis: in all, the intervention process by the Enterprise Division had lasted five years. All jobs were maintained.[21] Twelve years later, in 1998, an important investment was made to increase Zubiola's production capacity.[22] Today, it is a lively cooperative enterprise in the Basque Country, even though it has left the Mondragon group.

The cost of enterprise salvation during this period was co-financed by Caja Laboral and the cooperatives themselves. The interest rates on loans for cooperatives in recession was 14 per cent in case of a 'warning level' from the Enterprise Division, 8 per cent for 'medium risk' diagnoses, and down to 0 per cent only for 'high risk' ones. Forty per cent of the Enterprise Division's consultancy costs were shouldered by Caja Laboral itself, and 60 per cent by the beneficiary cooperatives, thus reflecting, again, an important cost-sharing level.[23]

Considering the number of necessary interventions that were performed, Caja Laboral president Ormaetxea estimated that around half, if not more, of the Mondragon cooperatives which existed at that time would probably not have survived without such a strong 'interventionist' policy by Caja Laboral, which, in turn, was matched by reciprocal control by the coopera-tives over the bank.[24] But this was a winning strategy, as not implementing it would in fact have been far more costly, as confirmed by Javier Salaberria, then one of the directors of the FAGOR district-based grouping:

> Salvaging cooperatives in crisis was a huge economic effort for Caja Laboral and the Mondragon group as a whole. Without the group, many cooperatives would not exist today. On the other hand, the cost of *not* doing it would have been enormously higher than the cost of the whole restructuring. Furthermore, the crisis made it possible for the group to accelerate its reform process: modernizing products was possible only through sectoral specialization and technology. The internationalization drive could only be carried out through the group.[25]

Surplus distribution ratios and wage calculation defined by a district-based grouping to adapt to the crisis

As a reaction to the 1980s crisis, the FAGOR district-based grouping changed the basic distribution formula so that a minimum contribution of 50 per cent of net surplus was allocated to the grouping's own reserve fund, up from the earlier 20 per cent. It is interesting to review the democratic process which led to this decision.

The new plan was sent to FAGOR's Central Permanent Commission (CPC), composed of representatives of the Social Councils of all member cooperatives of FAGOR, in order to explain the management's proposal to the workers, and eliciting their responses. Under the management's plan, wages would still be adjusted annually in line with the cost of living, but they would also be connected to the cooperatives' economic performance. The plan also suggested reducing the wages to finance the economic restructuring of the member cooperatives.

An extensive consultation process followed. The CPC responded to the Board's proposal with a detailed critical report. The CPC sent representatives to explain the proposal and obtain responses. Discussions lasted several weeks.

During this period, cooperative members organized interest groups that included the participation of the trade unions and other independent parties. In all, four alternative proposals to that of FAGOR's Governing Council were developed: one by the Social Council of the Copreci cooperative; one by a group connected to a trade union; a third by a faction connected with Basque political groups and other unions.

A final proposal was formulated by members calling for no change in the current system. The CPC polled all FAGOR members on possible options. Among the 68 per cent who responded, 90 per cent supported the principle of changing the calculation of wages. One faction won a majority in the advisory vote of the Social Councils, while the Governing Council's proposal came in a close second.

The FAGOR Governing Council then adapted its own proposal. In a final and binding vote, FAGOR's General Assembly was asked to choose between a modified Governing Council proposal or no change at all. The Governing Council's proposal received a two-thirds majority vote required. The entire process took four months.[26]

Entry into the EU and the beginning of the Mondragon group's restructuring

In 1986, Spain entered the European Union and, soon afterwards, the European single market was established. This meant that Mondragon now had to compete directly with the largest corporations in the world, both inside and outside Spain. In 1980, the Spanish import tariffs averaged 35 per cent, whereas in 1991 they had dwindled to 5 per cent. Multinationals were buying up key Spanish industries at a breathtaking rate and were themselves engaged in a frenzy of mergers and acquisitions all over Europe. In 1990, the number two and number three Spanish firms in domestic appliance manufacturing (one of Mondragon's key activities) were purchased by foreign corporations (by Sweden's Electrolux and Germany's Bosch-Siemens respectively). FAGOR remained the only Spanish group producing domestic appliances. The huge efforts employed by FAGOR during the crisis a few years earlier in terms of cost reduction, the fight against unemployment, education and R&D had indeed paid off. Witnesses from that time are adamant that FAGOR would otherwise not have survived.[27]

At the same time, the opening up of Europe to continent-wide flows of capital and corporate concentration was occurring as a second economic slowdown struck Spain only a few years after the severe recession of the early 1980s. Spanish economic annual growth rates were above 4 per cent in 1987, 1988 and 1989, but dropped to 2.5 per cent in 1990 and to less than 2 per cent in 1991. There had been no job expansion in the industrial cooperatives of the group since the mid 1980s. The Mondragon leaders understood that the group's restructuring process had to be intensified.[28]

Discussions on restructuring within the group had in fact started as far back as 1982, in the middle of the economic crisis, around three complementary pillars: (i) the need for Caja Laboral to evolve from being the main development engine and coordinator of the group towards being a more conventional cooperative bank; (ii) the establishment of a new institutional system replacing Caja Laboral for the coordination and development of the whole group; and (iii) the restructuring of the district-based groupings into sectoral ones.

Owing to Mondragon's expansion, Caja Laboral had grown to such an extent that its function as a bank was in danger if it continued to perform non-banking functions as well.[29] 'Concretely, between 1964 and 1982, within 16 years, the sales [of the Mondragon group] had grown 38 times; but, during the same period, the resources of Caja Laboral – without counting those of Lagun Aro – had increased 127 times', wrote Jose Maria Ormaetxea, then president of the bank.[30] Moreover, the Spanish banking regulations were increasingly incompatible with Caja Laboral's non-banking tasks. Javier Salaberria comments: 'Caja Laboral could not remain the head, because, as a financial entity, it was not economically correct for it to maintain that role, apart from the fact that the Bank of Spain no longer allowed it to play it. So the Mondragon group had to build a new head unit for management and strategy, as an alternative to Caja Laboral'.[31]

In 1982, Ormaetxea published a paper from within Caja Laboral, named 'Reflections regarding change concerning the Mondragon experience' where he proposed the creation of a Cooperative Congress and a Council of Groups, which would 'support the constitution of sectoral cooperative agreements'. The paper also argued that the 'sectoral links' to be promoted were needed in order to develop the industrial technology in the Mondragon cooperatives. In addition, the document proposed the extension of Caja Laboral's financial activities towards clients outside the cooperative movement, and the establishment of an Inter-Cooperative Solidarity Fund (FISO).[32]

In 1983, Caja Laboral drafted a second paper called 'Bases for an industrial policy', stating that 'sectoral groupings are the appropriate channels to potentiate [the industrial sector's] technological capacity', and proposing a first sectoral classification of the 108 industrial cooperatives which were then associated with the bank. The document also tried to re-define the identity of the whole Mondragon group towards a more entrepreneurial and sector-based approach.

In 1984, Ormaetxea organized a debate around a third Caja Laboral paper called 'District-based groupings versus sectoral groupings', arguing that the Mondragon group would no longer benefit from economies of scales with the district-based grouping system. FAGOR and the other groupings at first did not agree.

At the same time, the statutes for a 350-member Mondragon cooperative congress were drafted. Each cooperative had at least one representative in the Congress. To limit the total number of delegates attending, larger cooperatives did not have representation in direct proportion to their size. The congress was to meet at least once every two years and was designed as the major long-term policy body of the group, defining the statutes and the bye-laws of the cooperatives, the group's position on social issues, and all relations with the national and foreign governments. Proposals had to be presented in written form and be seconded to be debated with their pros and cons, while resolutions that passed the vote were to be published in a Congress book and distributed publicly. A whole section of the rules dealt with the basic cooperative organization, ensuring a certain common ground allowing, eventually, for common policies such as those on social security and pensions to be implemented. The Congress had to elect a General Council. A Council of Groups, made up of managers of the 12 district-based groupings plus those of EROSKI, Lagun Aro, Ikerlan, and the president of the Congress was also foreseen, focusing on maintaining a unified industrial policy for all enterprises, and coordinating finance, investment, promotion, and R&D strategies, meeting at least once every three months.

In October 1987, the first meeting of the Cooperative Congress took place. Alfonso Gorroñogoitia was elected Chair of its General Council and Jose Maria Ormaetxea became Chair of the Council of Cooperative Groups. The fact that Gorroñogoitia and Ormaetxea, two of the founders of the first Mondragon cooperative 21 years earlier, founders of Caja Laboral and of the FAGOR grouping, were still in positions of leadership of the new Mondragon group's governance structures illustrates the continuity of leadership. But at the same time, the fact that they both had divergent opinions concerning the need to reform the district-based groupings into sectoral ones, leading to a wide-ranging debate within the Mondragon group, is a measure of the democratic culture which had developed within it.

The 1987 Congress did not solve the issue of the district-based groupings. But a number of structural changes did take place. First, as of that moment, all the bank's non-strictly banking functions were gradually transferred to other second-degree institutions of the group, leaving Caja Laboral with a strictly banking role.[33] Part of the staff of Caja Laboral's Enterprise Division (around 150 people) went to work in the new central coordinating unit which was then being established and another part to two new cooperatives, LKS Engineering and LKS Consulting. Second, it was decided to establish the Inter-Cooperative Solidarity Fund FISO (with 10 per cent of the surpluses of each cooperative and 20 per cent of those of Caja Laboral).

Meanwhile the sectoral debate continued. In 1988, the Council of Groups organized a three-day workshop with 70 cooperative directors, called 'The Mondragon Cooperative Group and the European Community'. The conclusions of the workshop explicitly advocated a sectoral approach, with research centres for each sector, and more delegation of entrepreneurial power from the cooperatives to the groupings.

In 1989, Ormaetxea drafted a 73-page paper called 'From a sociological experiment towards an entrepreneurial group', stating that 'in order to attain the objectives corresponding to the mission that has been entrusted to it, the Cooperative Group shall act from a competitive perspective, generating and coordinating human and financial resources'.[34] In addition:

> it shall be endowed with entrepreneurial support and welfare coverage services, generate economies of scale, promote innovation and research, create employment under the cooperative regime, and arbitrate the necessary means to attain corporate leadership in the European Single Market in sectors that are defined as being of priority interest by the bodies of the Group.[35]

The document, again, proposed 'entrepreneurial adjustments' based on sectoral groupings, defining 12 economic sectors. It was approved unanimously at the Cooperative Congress in 1989.

Two more years were needed to draft the 'basic norms on the organization of the sectoral groupings', according to which 'all the adhering cooperatives ... shall have to belong to the relevant Sectoral Grouping'.[36]

The third stage: the development of the Mondragon corporation (1991–2008)

Finally, at the third meeting of the Mondragon Congress in December 1991, the decision was made to restructure Mondragon into a full-fledged corporation – Mondragon Cooperative Corporation – and to convert the district-based groupings into sectoral ones. The debate had lasted nine years.

Implementing the restructuring process

The new arrangement did not imply any reversal of the previous horizontal, bottom-up system based on democratic control. Indeed, each institution within the group continued to hold its own General Assembly and Governing Council meetings. At the second Cooperative Congress in December 1991, where the whole new structure was approved, each cooperative had delegates and had had the opportunity to discuss these changes in advance internally. Javier Salaberria recalls: 'We did it by means of a "pact", as a community which changes its rules by common agreement, through freely agreed democratic procedures'.[37]

Implementing it was not easy. Javier Salaberria explains how FAGOR underwent this transformation:

> FAGOR was the typical district-based grouping, made up of eight well-integrated cooperatives, working on financial and human resources, labour standards, statutes, recruitment policy, etc. After the congress, we examined how FAGOR could transform itself from a district-based grouping into a sectoral grouping. During the transition there was a lot of overlapping. For example at some point, we had three different general directors, depending on which sectoral grouping we belonged to. This process also entailed large transfers of personnel: for example, I was in the legal advisory office of the FAGOR grouping, which merged with the legal advisory office of Caja Laboral to become LKS Consulting. So I left FAGOR to join LKS Consulting.[38]

The sectoral groupings, in turn, were grouped into wider divisions, which numbered nine in 1995, including six in industrial sectors, one in the financial sector and one in distribution and food.[39] In 2005, the system was further reformed through a merger between the sectoral grouping and the division levels, leaving the latter as the sole intermediary level between the 110 individual cooperatives of the group and the Corporation level.

The restructuring, again, avoided much higher costs: 'It was a very important change, but it would have been much more costly not to do it, if we had maintained the previous system, in which cooperatives were more isolated sectorally', Salaberria affirms.[40]

The change brought about by the establishment of the Mondragon Cooperative Corporation (MCC) reflects the particularly lively and flexible institutional dynamic within the group, but also the latter's adaptability to the new challenges of globalization: with a growing presence on the international scene, and within an increasingly competitive world economic environment where mergers and acquisitions had become routine, the group needed to be even more finely coordinated than ever before.

Expansion and internationalization

Among its various functions, the Mondragon Corporation became the coordination hub for the group's expansion and international activity. The internationalization of the group was indeed one of the main driving forces for its establishment, and has also been one of its main achievements. Under the Corporation, international services, representation offices abroad and overseas plants multiplied rapidly.[41] A strategy of production and marketing centres closer to the group's customers was seen as a must for its expansion.

The new policy allowed Mondragon cooperatives to continue to expand under the globalized economy. In 1993, the Corporation made a first visit to China and soon established a permanent office in Beijing. In 1994, Mondragon was chosen by General Motors as the corporation of the year in Europe for its 'quality-service-price'. The cooperative Irizar successfully presented and produced a new bus model, the 'Century', and had to adapt it to the British driving system. The construction sector cooperatives Orona and Urssa built some of the buildings of the Seville Universal Exhibition and some of the facilities of the Barcelona Olympics. In 1995, Urssa built the metallic structure of the Guggenheim museum in Bilbao and won the tender for the 'Metro' in the same city. FAGOR's positive market image was decisive for its selection as official supplier for the Seville Universal Exhibition. The air transport of a 50-ton production line of refrigerator doors for General Electric in the USA tested the logistical capacity of Fagor Arrasate in 1994.[42] These are only a few significant examples.

New financial mechanisms

Caja Laboral now invests largely outside the cooperative system, and its new investment division focuses on investments outside the Basque community. Its financial reserves have become so high that the Mondragon cooperatives only manage to absorb a fraction of its lending capacity: from 64 per cent in 1964, such capacity went down to 36 per cent in 1980, 10 per cent in 1993, 6 per cent in 1996, and only 3 per cent in 2009.[43]

However, lending to the cooperatives of the group remains very substantial in absolute terms.

The cooperatives have reorganized the management of their financial needs under the new Corporation. Apart from credit from Caja Laboral, they have established agreements with all the main Spanish banks. They also lend to each other and use common guarantee systems.

Each year, all cooperatives hand over 10 per cent of their surplus, and Caja Laboral 20 per cent, to Mondragon-Investments, a body managed at the Corporation level. The funds come back to the cooperatives to finance their projects, e.g. internationalization, development, new cooperatives. It is led by a Governing Council that approves the investments, and nominates a commission that analyses each proposal before submitting it to the Governing Council of the Corporation.

Financial solidarity mechanisms between the cooperatives exist at two levels. At the central level, when cooperatives have a surplus, 3 per cent of the latter (on top of the 10 per cent mentioned above) goes to an inter-cooperative compensation fund; cooperatives with a deficit can request a coverage of up to 50 per cent of the deficit from this fund. At the level of the divisions, cooperatives put in common between 15 per cent and 40 per cent of their profits according to their choice, which is then redistributed across the cooperatives of the division according to the wage levels.[44]

Evolution in the distribution sector

One of the main features of this third period is the strong expansion of the consumer cooperative EROSKI. The Mondragon group decided to dramatically expand EROSKI's presence in non-Basque markets. A $249 million investment programme was approved in 1990 (the largest ever, and a 36 per cent increase over the previous year), more than 40 per cent being for the expansion of EROSKI. As a result, EROSKI's overall sales increased sixfold between 1990 and 2000. Outside the Iberian Peninsula, the cooperative took a majority interest in Altis, a joint venture with the Adour Pyrenees Consumer Cooperative to manage commercial establishments in the south of France. Within Spain too, EROSKI acquired several supermarket chains, such as Caprabo.[45]

As a result of this rapid expansion, EROSKI has become by far the largest employer within the Mondragon group, with 46,000 workers, namely around 50 per cent of all jobs in the group. But only 9,000 are members, while an additional 5,000 are potential members. Most workers work in controlled subsidiaries.

Since the mid-1990s, EROSKI has tried to gradually change this vertical matrix structure. In 1995–7, it established three entities having the Spanish statute of 'civil societies', namely a type of company, with a few thousand workers being members, and covering about 500 to 600 retail establishments. Through these three societies, workers have been able to lay the basis for future cooperatives, through workers' participation in the ownership, results and management of these societies.

EROSKI president Dacosta explains:

> We started with a document, we refined the proposals for one year, and we then had two more years of debate. We then created the three civil societies, one for sporting facilities, one for hypermarkets and one for supermarkets, each with its own Governing Council, General Assembly, and Social Council, as in Mondragon cooperatives. Once a year, each of these civil societies first convenes preparatory assemblies at the regional level because their worker-members are all over Spain. In these regional assemblies we [EROSKI] do not participate at all. Then they all come together in a national General Assembly, in which we [EROSKI] do participate. In the Governing Council of the three civil societies, the representation quota is 50 per cent for the workers and 50 per cent for EROSKI.
>
> Three years ago we went one step further with two referendums (one in the three societies and one in EROSKI) on the statutes of these future cooperatives, in which all voted favourably. There is now a statute, after a two-year debate and the referendums on the statute. The statute was finally approved on 17 January 2009. It was planned that after five years we should become a cooperative group. However, the crisis has postponed the calendar of implementation, due to uncertainty, and because workers may retract due to fears of investing when consumption falls sharply, or, worse, they might think we want to load the crisis onto their shoulders. So we decided to wait until the crisis is over. Then we plan to continue in a similar fashion with our remaining 30,000 workers, if they agree of course. It takes time because it is fundamental to first build a common culture. We are not sure whether all this process has a cost. We think that the balance will be favourable and even that there may be costs in not doing it.[46]

For the foreseeable future, EROSKI is planning to limit this process to its Spanish establishments, thinking that it is still too complicated to replicate it across the border in France. However, the successful cooperativization of those EROSKI subsidiaries may prove to be a fundamental precedent for the group's industrial cooperatives, many of which have subsidiaries around the world, while some are already trying to put in place institutions of participative democracy in them.

Exploring new activities: social services

A new activity of residences for elderly people was launched just before the crisis began, generated from within the Corporation. Javier Sotil, the new Corporation vice president in charge of innovation and new sectors comments:

> At the moment, we have 10 residences, 800 people are being looked after, and we have 450 worker-members working in them. In some cases, we are

co-owners, while in others we are only the managers of public sector residences. In the Basque region, the needs are enormous, so it is a key challenge. We have proved we can do it better than others and at lower costs, about 30 to 40 per cent lower. On the one hand, the public sector sometimes cares less about how the expenditure is really done. On the other hand, the capitalistic private sector will do anything to cut down costs at the expense of the old pensioners and their families, sometimes causing them to live in terrible conditions. As for the foundation-type charities, they don't do it badly, but they always go to the government to ask for money, threatening that otherwise they would have to close, so they are creating difficulties for the government. In our case, we provide transparent information to the workers, we redistribute the profits. The promoting entity is the LKS consultancy cooperative, and another cooperative manages the residential services, some of which are now being converted into cooperatives.[47]

Education and academic research

The educational area of the Corporation comprises educational cooperatives and associated institutes and training programmes in the region. Mondragon's educational system has become very comprehensive. The Mondragon group now counts six various educational institutions, and actively supports the system of *Ikastolas*, namely Basque language primary and secondary schools.

But the most striking innovation is the creation of Mondragon Unibertsitatea (Mondragon University) in 1997, out of a merger of the Eskola Politeknikoa (engineering), ETEO (business studies), and Huhezi (education and humanistic sciences). Mondragon University presently has around 4,000 students and offers 22 different degree courses. Postgraduate courses include 15 Masters and 8 university specialization courses.[48]

The university's fundamental mission is the development of all-round quality education, which also incorporates technical-scientific knowledge, the necessary skills for professional life as well as the values derived from the cooperative experience. It also attempts to respond to the challenges set out by the evolution of knowledge and the permanent transformation of the business world and the social environment in general.

According to the Business School of Mondragon University, research tasks must be oriented both towards business innovation and academic training, bringing about new knowledge, tools, theories and methods, and be based on business praxis. Research at the Business School now focuses on the development of sociological studies, models, tools, theories and methods to support the efficient operation and the transformation of organizations, both at the social-human level and at the technical-business level.[49]

Within the university, the Lanki Research Institute focuses on the cooperative type of organization. Its mission is to conduct research into cooperative reality and self-management from a range of disciplines, and on such basis to offer food for thought and training services to the cooperatives and other entities.

Another educational institution of Mondragon, distinct from the university, is the Otalora training centre, which was established in 1984 by Caja Laboral, and has developed strongly since the early 1990s. Its mission is to focus on cooperative education and, more widely, on entrepreneurial education in the Mondragon cooperatives, in particular for those in leadership positions. It produces teaching materials and organizes training courses tailored to the different educational and professional levels of the cooperative members, and in particular the members of the Governing Councils and Social Councils of the cooperatives. It strives to reinforce cooperative awareness among cooperative leaders and ordinary members, and to arouse such awareness in new members. Courses are organized upon request by the various cooperatives of the group. It was recently decided that Otalora should provide training to all cooperative members, and not only the leaders, through two-day courses.

Otalora also opens its doors to other cooperative people and organizations at home and abroad. For example, in 1992 and 1993, a delegation of Chinese cooperative leaders attended training at Otalora. In 1998, cooperative leaders from central-eastern Europe took part in a similar activity. Many groups from Latin America have been trained there. According to its director Mikel Lezamiz, only in the long term will it be possible to evaluate the results of such exchanges.[50]

R&D

Since the 1990s, technology has become key for competitive businesses in a globalized economy and in an increasingly small world. Today Ikerlan (which, as we saw above, was established in the 1960s) is a technological research centre with strong experience in comprehensive product development, collaborating with companies to improve their innovation skills by offering creative and effective solutions that combine the most suitable technologies and methodologies for each concrete situation. Ikerlan became vital when Mondragon was already an important industrial cluster and when Spain opened up to Europe. Under globalization, its role has become even more strategic for the group.

A few examples of Ikerlan R&D projects include: reality simulator for training in the safe use of construction machinery; automatic varnish thickness inspection; home automation network for integrating brown and white goods; automating transport for container terminals in sea ports with expansion problems; electronic units to control the experiment on separating proteins in microgravity.

But Ikerlan is not the only R&D centre in Mondragon. Following the sectoral restructuring of the group, several new technological centres have been established since the late 1980s. Mondragon's R&D centres now number 12, in areas such as automation, nano-technologies, engines, machine-tools, forming and assembly technology, welding and electronics.

The fourth stage: managing the crisis (2008–10)

Impact of the crisis on Mondragon

It became apparent in our interviews with several Mondragon leaders in March 2010 that this global crisis is perceived as the harshest which Mondragon has ever known, even harder than the big crisis of the early 1980s, which we examined above. After 15 years of particularly successful business activities, they gradually sensed in 2007 that a crisis was approaching. EROSKI then observed a substantial drop in consumption. The industrial cooperatives strongly felt the crisis coming in early 2008, already bracing themselves for an incoming new phase of worker redeployment from one cooperative to another within the group (which had not occurred since the early 1990s). The problem was even greater in the automobile sector, which makes up 20 per cent of Mondragon's sales, and in which 30 per cent of cooperatives were in difficulty.[51]

In 2008, the aggregate surplus of the group plunged to €71 million, compared with €792 million in 2007.[52] In 2009, profits dwindled even further to €61 million, a further 14.2 per cent fall in profits compared to 2008.[53] 'Of course, this is not brilliant for our group, but if you compare this with the big majority of enterprises which are in the red or have even had to close, this is not such a bad result after all', comments Mikel Lezamiz.[54]

The group has been suffering more in some of its sectors in which its main market, Spain, has been particularly affected, such as construction and household goods. Exports to Europe fell similarly to sales in Spain, and in 2009 total sales fell by 11.9 per cent. According to Jose Maria Garate, 'Automobiles were badly hit, with enormous stocks of completed cars, so enterprises stopped passing orders and production was paralysed, orders then fell by 50 per cent. There was a recovery in 2009 thanks to public aid in several countries in Europe, but after this temporary measure the situation appears very uncertain'.[55]

Caja Laboral did not incur losses. 'But in 2008 we had a big fright. In the end, the Caja's profits in 2008 were a bare €100 million. It had to make up for the loss of some Lehman Brothers assets. It had invested in Lehman Brothers, which then was highly recommended and had the highest rating, and we had trust in the rating agencies', Mikel Lezamiz admits. The bank's 2009 profits were even lower, with €56 million (in spite of a rise of 0.2 per cent in loans and of 4.5 per cent in individual savings, following the overall increase of market shares by cooperative banks under the crisis which we analysed in Chapter 4).[56] Lezamiz adds: 'We have had the same kind of scare with Lagun Aro, where profits have been very modest too, but at least we have always avoided having losses'.[57] The economic figures of Lagun Aro were even lower in 2009, but again, like Caja Laboral, Lagun Aro has not run into any deficit so far.[58]

Industry was also hard-hit. In machine tools, for example, new demands fell by 50 per cent in 2009, compared to the previous year, and it is expected that this trend continued in 2010. The daily working shifts have consequently been reduced from two or three to only one.[59]

In distribution, EROSKI observes that in 2010, consumption continued to fall, although with lesser intensity, and did not expect any change in the short term.[60]

What the group is doing to counter the effects of the crisis

Mondragon Corporation's current president Jose Maria Aldekoa distinguishes three components in the reaction of the group to the crisis:

> First, there is what I would call the 'attitude', the way you face the problem. This is extensively shared among all of us. This means having a responsible attitude that faces the fact that there is a problem affecting us: with trust, for which we need to remain calm because the problem affects the whole world, and there will be winners and losers; with solidarity (I mean solidarity as equals, as peers), because it is not the guilt of any actor in particular but all, it is not a question of managers or workers, the bad times can affect anyone at any point; with flexibility, because there can be great changes for worse or for better; and in a proactive manner. We believe that we have a strong capacity to adapt.[61]

Second are the short-term measures, which are mainly conjunctural. And third the middle- to long-term measures, which are more structural. We will now consider the three components separately.

Attitude

Part of the 'attitude' comes from the cooperative model itself: 'Our internal management is based on people and is in constant adaptation. In this sense, there is no crisis in our enterprises', considers Jose Ignacio Garate, previously in charge of the Corporation's institutional relations, and with a record of leadership positions within Mondragon for 30 years. He adds: 'The cooperative model based on transparency and wealth distribution has more capacity to respond because it legitimizes the difficult decisions that have to be taken in a situation of crisis'.[62] Constan Dacosta, the president of EROSKI, affirms for his part that 'the social control in our cooperatives avoids the craze of the managers and the frenzy of the casino. We have competitive advantages in terms of management. We are engaged in the real economy for the long term, we look at future sustainability'.[63]

Another part of the 'attitude' comes from the Mondragon group's structure itself: 'By being united, we can anticipate tendencies and have a vision that other enterprises of equal size (SMEs) cannot easily have', says Garate.[64] 'In times of crisis, the dynamic of change is greater, and our coordination mechanisms become more efficient, but they are not new in themselves. The mechanisms used in previous crises have helped'.[65] Garate continues:

> As early as October 2008, the Corporation disseminated news on the crisis to all cooperatives, and, in November, it issued recommendations on how to manage it. Each year, in November, there is an annual meeting with all directors of all cooperatives, about 150 people in all, which issues guidelines for the management plans. We were aware that we would be facing a big crisis. Some cooperatives, such as those producing capital goods, had an excellent 2008 and a very good 2009. So those which did not apply the recommendation then may do so in 2010. Instead, cooperatives in the automobile sector began to apply them immediately in November 2008.[66]

Short-term measures

Financial measures. According to most of the Mondragon leaders interviewed, the financial measures have been fundamental, be they internal (such as cash flow management) or regarding relations with the banks, or other.

Internally, the systematic capitalization system in Mondragon, including both indivisible reserves but also the capitalization of the surpluses which, as we saw above, are distributed to members only when they retire, has proved to be invaluable in facing the cooperatives' financial needs under the crisis.

The measures being implemented at the individual cooperative level include a reduction of expenditure to the absolute minimum (including heating), a 30 per cent decrease in investments between 2008 and 2009, systematic sales of unnecessary assets, drastic reduction of stock, rigorous recovery of payments, the utilization of all possible public resources and tax rebates, and a democratically approved decrease of remunerations by 8 per cent.[67]

In addition, a number of measures are being taken among the cooperatives of the group, such as common purchasing: 'If all purchasing takes €5 billion, lowering only 1 per cent gives us better conditions than trying to lower the salaries by 3 per cent'.[68] The central solidarity funds are also being activated to help the cooperatives experiencing the greatest financial difficulties.

As an anti-crisis measure, some cooperatives have decided to merge. In the Danobat machine tool division, a merger has been carried out among two cooperatives, and another four are under study. How is this kind of cooperative merger implemented? The president of the Danobat division, Rafael Barrenechea, explains:

> The division makes a proposal after a study. The proposal must then be debated and approved first by the Governing Council, and then by the General Assembly of both cooperatives. The two must vote at the same time. And there must be good economic reasons for it. If some worker members must leave the new cooperative, they will be placed outside either within the division or elsewhere within the Mondragon group.[69]

On the external front, assets have been used as guarantees to obtain bank loans. This has been vital for the EROSKI distribution system, which had built very solid assets: 'We behave like the old traditional neighbourhood shop, so we generally operate in buildings we own'.[70] The Danobat machine tool division has also been using common guarantees among its constituent cooperatives for middle-term bank loans. EROSKI has issued bonds without voting rights, which around 18,000 small investors have purchased, for a total of €600 million.

The reform of the pension system. Thirty-five per cent of worker-members' labour costs are paid by the cooperatives to Lagun Aro (including 11 per cent for the State's social security system), while the worker-members contribute an additional 6.6 per cent from their own pay. This contribution covers a pension made up of a public and a complementary private part, sickness leave, and the mechanism of redundancy and redeployment of worker-members.

The pension system is well managed, costs less and gives more benefits than in ordinary businesses. However, Lagun Aro's 2010 General Assembly approved a modification in the mix of pensions. Up until then, 70 per cent came from the private sector through Lagun Aro investments, and 30 per cent from the public system. It was decided to change the percentage for those 50 years old or less, to 60 per cent for the public system and only 40 per cent from the private one. Indeed, 'Lagun Aro was affected by the crisis, and we all saw that we had taken too much risk with our own pensions', considers Garate.[71]

Employment. Mondragon Corporation president Aldekoa explains how the group views the issue of unemployment:

> We never talk in terms of managing unemployment, but in terms of managing *employment*. First of all, all non-productive employment has to be eliminated. The right of worker-members to a specific amount of working hours and the corresponding pay remains unchanged under the crisis, but those hours are used only on demand. We thus flexibilize the calendar.[72]

Aldekoa goes on: 'Furthermore, whereas the right to work remains unchanged, namely the right to a workplace of a specific level, we never consider that anyone has the right to a particular job. During periods of crisis, members have to work where and when they can be productive, within a geographical range of 50 kilometres'.

The mechanisms regarding redeployment work as follows. An employment committee at the level of the Corporation made up of six people meets regularly to evaluate the redundancy prospects of the cooperatives. It defines whether redundancy is conjunctural (up to three years) or structural (irreversible).

Then, the Lagun Aro system coordinates the redeployment of the worker-members to other cooperatives. If there are re-training or transport costs, these are covered according to the distributive differential between the two cooperatives. The Lagun Aro payment is co-financed with each cooperative. Apart from the regular contributions of the cooperatives to Lagun Aro, the cost of redeployment is co-financed as a function of the level of remuneration. If remuneration in the cooperative of destination is higher than in the cooperative of origin, Lagun Aro pays; if it is the other way round, the cooperative of origin pays. Redundant workers that cannot be redeployed stay at home, their cost being covered by Lagun Aro and the cooperative for a maximum period of two years. If the problem is structural, early retirement is the option, as of 58 years of age, with two years' unemployment until retirement.

How many redundant workers have been involved during this crisis? 'In 2009 we had 600 persons redeployed, and in 2010 we have about 400', says Mondragon president Aldekoa.[73] These include 35 workers from an industrial cooperative that had to be closed down. Virtually all the other few job losses have taken the form of voluntary pre-retirement. Fortunately, not all redundancies take place exactly at the same time: 'For example, in automobiles, 300 workers were sent to other sectors at the end of 2008. In 2009, automobiles not only got them back but also received another 300 from other cooperatives which had less activity that year'.[74] In the Danobat machine tools division, 'in 2009, we had a peak of 160 people redeployed. Now 120 of them are back, and some have gone in early retirement'.[75] In the EROSKI distribution chain, the staff of the central offices work 10 per cent more without additional pay, while others from the offices go to work in the shops as part of the workforce.

Long term measures

Mondragon corporation president Aldekoa spells out the main elements of the long term strategy:

> For the long term, the emphasis is on innovation. For this, we will have to undergo structural changes too, and everything must be better connected

to our university, our producer cooperatives and our research centres. We will have to strengthen our promotion and internationalization efforts in the USA, the BRICs [Brazil, Russia, India and China] and Germany, where we are already active. We are a sum that is more than the parts. We will have to transform the model of activity and negotiate the changes in a matrix fashion, being also aware that there cannot be one single model for all cooperatives to apply.[76]

Approach to innovation. With the crisis, the discussion on innovation within the group has intensified: 'we are in full debate on the concept of innovation. Basically, we look at how we can take advantage of the knowledge we have in order to bring about a change capable of generating added value through a high service component to the product', says Ignacio Garate.[77] This focus on innovation is also mind-opening: 'The crisis is obliging us to be more serious in looking better at all the literature, there is an emerging new thinking, and we must navigate it', considers Javier Sotil, the new Corporation vice president in charge of innovation and new sectors.[78]

Product strategy. According to Javier Sotil:

Many activities were designed in the 1960s (household goods, automobiles, metallic transformers, etc.) that unfortunately are not the leading ones today. We already knew it but we did not change it when things were going alright. The crisis is accelerating the process and is making obvious that such activities will not become profitable again and will no longer be engines of growth and job creation in tune with the local environment. We need to change fast, we cannot wait. We have strongly invested in technology, but we did it in those business activities that are no longer the growth engines of today. For example, in household goods, we invested a lot and we created many jobs (8,000 at present). It was profitable, but the sector belongs to the past.[79]

Javier Salaberria, who spent part of his career as one of the directors of the FAGOR grouping active in household goods, comments:

In the 1960s, people came from the rest of Spain to Mondragon by bus to find a job. Now the Basque labour force has a much higher educational level than ever before. They go to university, or they attend vocational education, which is the best in the whole of Spain. The Basque region has all these strong points today. Thus assembling refrigerators does not make any more sense, even if we improve distribution, quality, technology and innovation. Today we must produce refrigerators in other countries and in the Basque Region we must concentrate on design, marketing, services or activities of higher added value.[80]

The Danobat machine-tool division is also updating its products: 'we are working to make our products more sophisticated, and we are also changing our product strategy by putting together the product, the service, more value added and an integral solution for the client'.[81]

New ideas to develop for the future are the electric car, plastics, aluminium, health, services to the third age, energy, engineering, the production of turnkey factories. 'We are looking at products that have more added value and more coordination elements, so that one plus one equals more than two', says Mondragon Corporation president Aldekoa.[82]

Market strategy. Another central set of long-term measures is the repositioning on the market: 'We must position ourselves in the value chains, because globalization will continue for at least 20 years', says Jose Ignacio Garate.[83] In machine tools for example:

> we are looking for new markets. We started this process 20 years ago, China which then was our fourteenth market is now the second. Germany is the first. In 1993, there was a world crisis in our sector of machine tools with a 50 per cent fall in activity. It affected all businesses active in the sector and we had to take adjustment measures. But today it is different because we have been investing heavily and we are working on new markets. We have new plants and new models, and we have world-level platforms which we use to sell, but also to teach about our models, buy, assemble, design. It reduces costs and increases adaptation and proximity to our client. We work in the language of our clients and in their own time zone and working schedule.[84]

'It is fundamental to increase the margins, namely to produce with less money in the value chain, and to go up in the chain. For all this, we will have new financial needs. Until now, our financial needs were rather conventional, but, with bigger projects, they will grow', says Javier Sotil.[85] The group's financial structure, with its own bank, its non-banking financial instruments, and its joint guarantee systems, is certainly better armed to face this challenge than many other networks of SMEs in Europe.

Institutional changes. In 2009, Mondragon Corporación Cooperativa, renamed Mondragon Humanity at Work, decided to create a new vice presidency for innovation promotion and knowledge, answerable directly to the Mondragon president. A new division was created in engineering and services, covering all that did not belong to any productive factory cooperative.

Relations with the public authorities. As a 'common-private' (see Chapter 4) economic actor, the relationship with the public administration is very important in terms of long-term strategy. Jose Ignacio Garate, who until recently was in charge of the Corporation's institutional affairs, considers that this relationship:

> is very close, and even more so during the crisis, thanks to our transparency in the sharing of information and our democratic system. For them, we are like a laboratory, and they thus take it into account for their public policies. Through a cooperation agreement with the regional government, we participate in meetings every three months, to discuss competitiveness planning, internationalization and industrial policy.[86]

Environment and a new type of growth. The Mondragon cooperatives have obtained all the necessary environmental ISO certifications. But the issue of how to produce in tomorrow's world is not limited to clean or energy-saving production methods. Mondragon is already beginning to contemplate a new type of growth. Indeed, 'the last 10 years' growth rates could hardly be sustainable, perhaps impossible to sustain. There are no resources, raw material to sustain it', says EROSKI president Dacosta. Garate considers that 'other crises will pass, there are grave errors that can be corrected, but this one is structural, and we will have to accept that we will have to lower our living standards'. Therefore, 'we need a new type of growth, this is the biggest challenge', concludes Lezamiz.

Conclusion: main lessons from the Mondragon group

The effort to create sustainable jobs

In all the interviews and conversations we have had with Mondragon leaders since 1990, the assertion that the main purpose of Mondragon is to create jobs is a constant *leitmotiv*. However, this policy needs to be understood correctly. Mondragon's effort in the employment field is to create jobs that are sustainable over the long term, and so can have a real impact on local wealth and local development. The various self-generated support institutions of the group, be they financial, educational, research-oriented or dedicated to social protection, have all along been geared towards this key mission.

In implementing the latter, the financial investment pattern led by the Mondragon support institutions has been decisive. As we saw above, in the early 1980s, Thomas and Logan had already calculated that the Mondragon job creation process was a particularly capital-intensive one.[87] We also saw that funding these jobs was co-financed by the workers themselves through contributions in share capital equivalent to one year's wages on average. The cost of establishing performing high-tech businesses, surrounded by a whole array of business support institutions, is indeed more expensive than a simple labour-intensive policy aimed at creating workplaces for the short term.

At the same time, the group has developed a particularly safe social protection system which is, however, based on work rather than redundancies at home, through sophisticated redeployment mechanisms which are launched in times of crisis.

Another reason why jobs in Mondragon are so sustainable, according to Mondragon leaders themselves, is the cooperative approach to employment. First of all, cooperatives usually do not delocalize, which Mondragon has proved since it has entered a phase of intense internationalization. Mondragon did extend its production activities to the five continents, but never laid off its workers in order to relocate activities elsewhere. Second, the Mondragon approach has always been the systematic cooperativization of *work*, namely the fact that the cooperative link is mainly with the workers, who are thereby recognized as being the main type of stakeholder within the group. Even the support institutions, which are participated in by the individual cooperatives, are partly controlled and owned by their own workers. The cooperativization of work has unleashed enormous entrepreneurial energies down to the shop floor, including in terms of production processes, which are at the antipodes of the bureaucratization and de-humanization of work in large chains and globalized business ensembles which we discussed in Chapter 3 under the 'producer function'.

The results of this distinctive employment-oriented policy are there to be seen. In good times, the support institutions of the group have been multipliers of jobs. During the years 1957 to 1959, prior to the establishment of Caja Laboral, an average of 60 jobs were created per year by the Mondragon cooperatives. By contrast, an average of 570 jobs per year, almost 10 times as many, were created in the seven years that followed the bank's establishment.[88]

In times of crisis, all the efforts of the group's support institutions are focused on maintaining the existing level of employment. Although 10 cooperatives have been liquidated in Mondragon since the beginning of its history in 1956 (the last one in 2009), job losses in the group have been minimal thanks to the redeployment of workers from one cooperative to another under the coordination of Lagun Aro and other support institutions.[89] Even the redundant workers who cannot be redeployed receive support payment by Lagun Aro for a number of months, after which most of them can reintegrate into their cooperative of origin. During the economic crisis of the early 1980s, job growth reached an unprecedented negative trend. In 1980, this negative rate was minus 4.1 per cent. Still, it was eventually offset by an almost total reabsorption of the laid-off workers (with a net result of 0.6 per cent unemployment), while the unemployment level within the region had reached 27 per cent. After another negative rate in 1983 (minus 0.6 per cent), job growth picked up again slowly. It was still moderate during the first years after

Spain joined the European Union (3.76 per cent in 1987), another difficult period for Spanish industry. But a turn for the better occurred in 1990 (4.25 per cent, i.e., 932 new jobs). In 1990, there were only 20 unemployed persons in the group, comprising only 0.08 per cent of its total workforce. During another difficult period, in 1991–3, Lagun Aro supported close to 2,000 unemployed for several months (8 per cent of the total workforce), after which all of them could be relocated in the cooperatives of the group.

In 2008, with the global crisis, job growth rate became negative for the first time since 1983 (minus 1.1 per cent). This negative trend was further aggravated in 2009 (minus 8.3 per cent), as the average number of jobs during the year went down from 92,000 to 85,066. However, 938 (namely one-third) of the industrial jobs were recovered at the end of the year. Most of the net decrease in workplaces involved early retirement, generating virtually no permanent unemployment.

Strong emphasis on education and training, leading to a societal project

A central element of the Mondragon experience is its particularly strong emphasis on education and training. Mondragon founder Arizmendiarrieta said: 'It has been said that cooperatives are an economic movement which uses educational action, but the definition could as well be reversed by saying that they are an educational movement which uses economic action'.[90] Mondragon's educational practice, in turn, has favoured the growth of a cooperative culture and vision of society that is particularly holistic. This is how a whole project of society at the local and regional level, including most social and economic aspects that one can think of, could be engineered. Mondragon is not only a democratic corporate group, but also one that believes it has a particular mission towards the community and towards local and regional development. In fact, since the beginning, one of its core principles has explicitly been 'social transformation'.

Solidarity and cooperation among enterprises, combined with a rigorous entrepreneurial approach

Another key element is solidarity: 'we mean concrete solidarity, one with common funds, the incorporation of people from other cooperatives when necessary. No isolated cooperative could have got there without this concrete solidarity, it would have been utterly impossible', affirms Javier Salaberria, president of CICOPA.

The solidarity-based approach within Mondragon, however, has always been based on rigorous entrepreneurial management. Javier Salaberria, again, comments: 'managing enterprises is not to do cheap sociology, but to be competitive. So you need good managers and directors. Cooperative democracy must be combined with professional management. The elected Board designates a group of professional directors with a lot of power and autonomy in their day-to-day management. If they do not deliver, they are replaced'.[91]

Solidarity has expressed itself through a particularly strong type of cooperation between the cooperative enterprises. According to Javier Salaberria, without cooperation within the group:

> the large investments that have been made, the quality process, and the combined offer of products to clients, all that would have been impossible. This is even more important for cooperatives that are starting up. The group also makes it possible to respond to demands in a complete and rapid fashion. The cooperatives can take advantage of the prestige of the group, which they would never get individually. This prestige makes it also possible to obtain public aid, e.g., for the university.[92]

In particular, inter-firm cooperation has been characterized by a strong correlation between three components: (i) entrepreneurial support to the businesses in terms of services, (ii) financial support to the businesses (generally loans), and (iii) (mutually agreed) intervention capacity within businesses by the providers of entrepreneurial and financial support.

This has been possible only because inter-firm cooperation has developed *trust* within the group and has relied on a very sophisticated institutional system, with many checks and balances.

Equilibrium and adaptation to change

Mondragon has always strived to attain a fine equilibrium between apparently paradoxical aspects of the cooperative business environment such as efficiency and democracy; economic and social concerns; equality and hierarchical organization; private interests (of staff and the companies) and the general interest; identification with the cooperative model and cooperation with other business models. The group's innovative approach to organization springs from the tension between the cooperative business culture and the need to constantly adapt. Innovation stems from individual cooperatives as well as from the organization as a whole.

Mondragon, while being a big productive machine, turning over billions of euros in industrial, service and consumer goods, also offers a huge forum for internal discussions and negotiations, with scores of democratically elected boards, working groups and committees. In spite of being very 'high tech', with a university and over ten R&D centres, Mondragon is no prisoner of the technification drive, which we examined in Chapter 3, in its management pattern. Joint control by the stakeholders provides the group with a capacity to manage change and deal with the unknown and the unexpected, for which technification provides no guidance.

This constant capacity to adapt to change was well expressed by Javier Mongelos, the first president of the corporation, in a conversation in Beijing in 1993: 'Probably, the essence of our experience is that we have never stopped exploring and innovating. We have always remained in a constituent stage, we never moved to the constitutive stage'.

Is the Mondragon model replicable?

A recurrent debate is the one on whether Mondragon is an ethnic or cultural exception. Javier Salaberria, who was among the leaders of FAGOR for decades and who, as president of CICOPA, the world organization of industrial and service cooperatives, is also in contact with many other cooperative realities around the world comments:

> I don't agree that the Mondragon model is an exception. Of course, we have our characteristics in the Basque country, including an industrial culture which was there before. But if we had had an economy based on cows, we would have developed animal husbandry. It is true that the Basque country was in crisis and in search of its identity and survival. It is also true that the founders have certainly been very special people: without them, it may not have happened. The autarchy of the Spanish state under Franco certainly helped us too, because it allowed us to undertake primitive accumulation of capital, copy others' technology and then innovate. But the processes of self-management do not depend on cultural or other circumstances. There are women in Africa or India who are able to develop production and commercialization activities through cooperatives in an admirable fashion, and still they are very different from us. Human beings are first of all cooperative beings. When they join together they become efficient. I think that many aspects of the Mondragon culture can be transferred, and first of all its very strong practice of cooperation among cooperatives. It is possible to create many other Mondragons, maybe smaller or even bigger.

What is certain is that, while being very original in many of its institutional elaborations, Mondragon has been extremely orthodox in implementing the cooperative system to wider institutions than simply individual cooperatives. In fact, its main originality is perhaps to have been extremely cooperative in its rationality, namely to have applied with utter coherence and at all levels the cooperative standards and their underlying rationality, which we analysed in Chapter 4, and in particular the application of democratic procedures and dynamics, including appropriate checks and balances, to a huge industrial group of over one hundred enterprises.

9

The Global Crisis: Mother of All Warnings

Introduction

For a long time, the world was perceived as a space where there was still plenty to be conquered and where one could expand. In such a process, capitalism and debt practices went hand in hand. But times have changed. Globalization has brought about a new contradiction: 'too big to fail' firms that intend to continue enlarging their business scales, and a tightly interlinked financial and economic system. In this new circular context, the generalized use of debt is no longer sustainable. Due to its interconnectedness, it can lead to systemic implosion, just as the fast depletion of the world's natural resources is bound to bring about ecological disaster. It is no coincidence that the word 'toxic' has so often been used in relation to this crisis. It is not only the environment of the planet, but also the present global financial-economic system which is getting increasingly out of balance.

In the first section below, we summarize the state of play (analysed in Chapters 1 to 3) and suggest a path which could help us re-think anew. Following our discussion on cooperatives (in Chapters 4 to 8), we consider the latter's *direct* contribution to the economy, as well as their *indirect* contribution, as inspirational elements for other economic entities and the economy at large. Indeed, we need to develop tools and mechanisms that value the generation of wealth and capital in order to gradually break free from the debt trap that is plaguing the present economic system and is changing capitalism into something we may soon nickname 'debtism'. As illustrated in the four case studies of this book, cooperatives have overall been resilient to the crisis because they have been generating long-term wealth, skills, knowledge and trust.

We end the chapter arguing that, based on recent experience, the time may be coming for changes that would have been unthinkable not so long ago.

Stepping off the trodden path

By way of the three traps explained in Chapter 2, in particular the debt trap, wealth in its wider sense is being destroyed with each crisis. Wealth needs long-term generation, and is seemingly not well served by repeated bubbles and busts in economies loaded with debt. There has recently been a great world-wide effort to draw lessons for future regulation: the Turner Review, the Larosière and Geneva Reports, as well as the reports drafted by the G20, the IMF, the Group of Thirty chaired by Paul Volcker, and the Committee on the Global Financial System at the Bank for International Settlements. Critics of economic theory are enjoying a wide audience, which will surely lead to changes in theoretical assumptions.[1] The beliefs in 'free markets' and 'perfect information' have lost allure, especially after having been so costly to all. Governments' and central banks' powers have regained favour. In 2009 the IMF advised that 'central banks should adopt a broader macro-prudential view, taking into account asset price movements, credit booms, leverage, and the build up of systemic risk in their decisions. The timing and nature of pre-emptive policy responses to large imbalances and large capital flows need to be re-examined'.[2] Better updated theory and public oversight are urgently needed. But three years on, the debt problem is still there, just like the consequences of low demand, low credit, low investment and unemployment.

On the other hand, as we saw in Chapter 3, the basic roles in the economy are changing, bringing up the key issue of control, with a significant impact on the debt trap. Large economic actors, which are leading global chains of production and distribution in much of the 'real economy' through vertically structured control mechanisms, seem to be reaching their limits in terms of socio-economic sustainability. Consumers become users, faced with choices that are actually based on standardization processes, while being induced to consume through sophisticated methods, including routine access and service streaming. Workers become sellers of services, with a decreasing control over their employment conditions. Local entrepreneurs are increasingly tied to global chains and a financialized economy. Firms have difficulty in planning for the long term and owners may not always control their venture. Stakeholders in the 'real economy' are pressed to passively adapt to ever-changing conditions. Investors become absentee controllers, a process which is facilitated by techni-cal standardization in finance and communication. Yet, many investors, active through large managerial units, may not have access to timely critical informa-tion themselves. Chapter 3 also showed how this change in control patterns was accelerating debt practices, because debt is functional to attain concrete objectives, such as developing global chains, compensating for under-funding, avoiding tax and the risks of ownership. In addition, through co-regulation, large firms directly participate in macro-economic policy-making. Therefore, a strong link exists between economic entities at the micro/meso level and the debt trap at the macro level. These trends are going on unabated. If no fresh alternatives are found, new crises are bound to flare up. Consequently, we need to seriously consider behaviour and strategies that can help us avoid falling into the debt trap.

As we can see, it would be a mistake to only focus on macro-level monitoring on the basis of transparent credit information on the one hand, and more moderate incentives for individual loans on the other. The build up of risk, the interconnectedness and debt leverage depend on how activities in the economic sphere are organized. The connection between individuals and the macro level is built through institutionalized activity in firms and organizations. We thus need to pay greater attention to economic entities and their organization and accountability, their institutionalized values and practices, and better grasp the consequences springing from the diverse types of relationship between ownership and control.

The 2009 Nobel Prize winner for economics, Elinor Ostrom, shows in *Governing the Commons* that the conventional market economy is bound to destroy common goods, while, in turn, joint control by the stakeholders involved in the management of those common goods could preserve them.

In her discussion, Ostrom focuses essentially on the management of natural spaces (irrigation schemes, fishery reserves, etc.), which more or less correspond to the traditional sense of 'commons' since the Middle Ages. However, she also includes cooperatives in her policy analysis (even though she does not pursue the analysis of the cooperatives as such), as she explicitly states:

> What is missing from the policy analyst's toolkit – and from the set of accepted, well-developed theories of human organization – is an adequately specified theory of collective action whereby a group of principals can organize themselves voluntarily to retain the residuals of their efforts. Examples of self-organized enterprises abound. Most law firms are obvious examples ... Most cooperatives are also examples ... But until a theoretical explanation – based on human choice – for self-organized and self-governed enterprises is fully developed and accepted, major policy decisions will continue to be undertaken with a presumption that individuals cannot organize themselves and always need to be organized by external authorities.[3]

The examples used by Ostrom show organizational practices that have stood the test of time, and are still in use, because they have provided sustainable and coherent solutions. What we need today is to apply equally sustainable and coherent management practices to our major economic activities so as to respond to the challenges of our time.

The *direct* contribution of cooperatives to the economy

Systemic contribution

As illustrated in Chapter 4, cooperatives are a major actor among the 'self-organized and self-governed enterprises' to which Ostrom refers, and are involved in a whole array of fundamental common goods beyond the management of natural spaces: food, employment, housing, savings, credit, water and electricity distribution, waste management, health, social services, local development and the availability of basic necessities at affordable prices. Cooperatives tend to contribute to delivering such common goods not only at a given point in time and space, but also in a long-term economic perspective. Their institutionalized practices include democratic management with checks and balances, the systematic building of common financial reserves, the development of entrepreneurial education for ordinary people, sustainable employment, the creation of business support institutions, horizontal entrepreneurial systems and cooperation dynamics. As defined in Chapter 4, these are 'common-private' economic practices. With some noble exceptions, large-scale business appears increasingly characterized by indebtedness, enterprise short-termism, economic volatility, employment uncertainty, workplace atomization and de-humanization, as well as a lack of genuine responsibility towards the community, not to mention towards the planet.

As we also saw in Chapter 4, cooperatives have demonstrated their resilience to economic crises and have proven to be a model of accumulation of productive capital. Hundreds of millions of individual socioeconomic agents in the world (workers, producers, consumers, apartment-dwellers, bank-account holders, etc.) allow hundreds of thousands of cooperative enterprises to accumulate common reserve funds aimed at providing entrepreneurial strength and development. Productive capital accumulation becomes an important part of capital reserves in the economy at large, turning into a powerful tool for socioeconomic transformation. Cooperatives appear to be better preserved from both speculation and the debt trap for the following additional reasons, among others: cooperatives' shares are not marketable; in accounting, cooperatives follow the practice of book value instead of fair value for financial reporting; and they tend to stabilize prices through the surplus redistribution to members at the end of each year.

The four empirical cases which we presented in Chapters 5 to 8 show to what extent cooperatives can be embedded within economic reality and are capable of reacting proactively and innovating both in their organizational patterns and in the added value of their products, processes and services. Two of these cases have been investigated to compare their past practices with their current ones, because they have undergone earlier crises, in one case going as far back as the 1929 Great Depression. We have observed how crises prompt internal debates on values, with a clear tendency to avoid vertical patterns of control and, instead, to reinforce horizontal ones through cooperative practices. We have also seen that, in times of crisis, rapid decisions can be taken because the degree of legitimacy is high, and that previous investments in human resources and information flows pay off by lowering the timing of reaction and control costs. Not doing so would have been far more costly.

At the same time, we have tried to introduce the world of cooperatives without portraying an idealized picture. As in all human experience, many have suffered failure, distortion and even scandals. However, these drawbacks do not, *per se*, put the cooperative business model in question. The issue here is not to take sides 'for' or 'against' cooperatives, but to acknowledge that rich and poor, right and left, rural and urban, and people belonging to all religions and ethnic groups are using the cooperative model.

Incidence in key economic activities

There are a number of concrete processes by which cooperatives directly and substantially contribute to the world economy.

The importance of cooperative banking in stabilizing the economic system cannot be overstated. This type of banking entity makes up a very substantial share of the banking market of a number of key industrialized nations, in particular the USA, Canada, Germany, France, Italy, and the Netherlands. The cooperative banks build up counter-cyclical buffers that function well in case of a crisis, as recently demonstrated once again. As we saw in Chapters 4 and 7, they tend to have a higher-than-average risk coverage and tier-1 capital, the latter being composed in great part of reserves, therefore making it safer. They tend to lend against a real capacity to repay and have very low insolvency ratios. Furthermore, they have more local outlets than other banks and provide more credit locally and to companies involved in productive activities. They lend more to local SMEs and other producing economic entities (family businesses, farms, etc.) than most other banks. And they do not lead their members and clients towards the debt trap.

In June 2009, Italian economy minister Giulio Tremonti, in his speech at the general assembly of Confcooperative (one of the three Italian cooperative confederations), acknowledged the contribution of the cooperative banks during the crisis in stabilizing the financial system in Italy, the world's seventh economy. In Canada, as seen in Chapter 7, the Desjardins group re-purchased from its own members toxic assets attached to shares, which these members had acquired from non-banking investors. By doing so, Desjardins mutualized the loss and created trust, thereby raising its influence on the national negotiations which brought about a conversion of these assets into long-term bonds, thus allowing the latter to be substantially re-valued. Canada is the only country in the world where such revaluation of previously toxic assets has taken place at the time of writing; this has been a significant factor in the high level of financial stability which Canada has managed to maintain, a phenomenon which has been praised worldwide. This has been a key contribution of cooperative banking to the financial stability of the world's ninth economy.

The various typologies of users' cooperatives (banking, retail, housing, energy distribution, etc.) provide a model where the users are the owners-controllers. As such they seem neither likely to be impelled into the consumption trap or the debt trap discussed in Chapter 2, nor to lose control of the way their service is provided (see Chapter 3). They tend to lower and stabilize the prices of delivered goods and services while maintaining and/or enhancing their quality. They also provide access to such goods and services to the remotest and poorest areas, playing a key role in combating the economic desertification of entire regions.

Housing cooperatives, whether organized around home rental or ownership, considerably contribute to avoiding housing bubbles such as that of the sub-primes in the USA, by providing decent and inclusive housing to millions of people. It is probably no coincidence that housing crises have been weaker or non-existent in countries where the housing cooperative system is particularly strong, such as Germany or Norway.

In history, agricultural cooperatives have played a key role in ensuring foodstuff availability, in particular in many developed and emerging countries during their industrialization phase. They may return to centre stage amidst ongoing rampant speculation in commodities, pointed out in Chapter 1, especially if such speculation endangers the livelihood of entire populations.

Producers' cooperatives active in industry and services, with the help of their network of dedicated support institutions, make it possible for productive activities to remain locally based, modernize themselves through long-term business strategies and organizational and technological innovation, and provide sustainable employment or income to local inhabitants, including the less well-off. They do it better when users' cooperatives are present in the locality. They have an important potential not only as start-ups, but also in terms of business transfer. In 2006, the European Commission affirmed that 'one third of EU entrepreneurs, mainly those running family enterprises, will withdraw within the next ten years. It has been estimated that up to 690,000 businesses providing 2.8 million jobs [in EU member states] will be facing the problem of transfer to a new owner each year', and pointed out that 'if no family successor can be found a transfer to employees ensures a large degree of continuity of the business'.[4]

The risk of seeing hundreds of thousands of economic entities disappear for ever is becoming even more pressing in 2011: the problem is no longer only about businesses that nobody wants to acquire, but also about businesses that may easily find an acquirer but are then indebted, eliminated from the competition, or used to transfer the know-how, before being liquidated. The 2009 UNCTAD World Investment Report estimated that while 'it is expected that a large number of private equity firms will succumb to the crisis, [t]he surviving firms may ... concentrate increasingly on smaller transactions in small and medium-sized enterprises (SMEs)'.[5] In Chapter 1, we saw that 'enterprise investment schemes' had been recently established in the UK with large tax breaks, while France is promoting private equity within SMEs. We should be concerned with the consequences of this policy, both in terms of wealth and employment, if it is not well regulated. We saw in the case of Ceralep (Chapter 6) how private equity investors could engineer the liquidation of an SME that was economically sustainable as it proved to be after being transformed into a cooperative. In France alone, 376 enterprises that were on the verge of being closed down, such as Ceralep, were transformed into cooperatives between 2000 and 2009, with a survival rate of 79 per cent.[6] This high rate of success, in view of the difficulties involved, is not only due to a highly motivated staff that becomes master of its own destiny but also to the cooperative system as a whole, accompanying the process through an array of support institutions with top-level professionals. Thousands of jobs have been saved and economic activities maintained in the territories where these enterprises are located. The potential for business transfer to employees is substantially higher than that which is taking place today, provided appropriate public policies are designed and carried out.

Several banking and consumer cooperative groups have implemented wide-ranging training programmes in financial management in the case of banking and in consumption patterns in the case of consumer cooperatives, aimed at ordinary citizens. Banking and consumer cooperatives then play a large role in the financial and consumer education of citizens, fighting against the debt trap and the consumption trap.

Horizontal peer groups working with long-term strategies can substantially improve the long-term sustainability of cooperatives already present in a given state or region. Some of these groups are now internationalizing rapidly (as seen in Chapter 8), offering a significant alternative model to the concentration of vertically controlled global businesses. However, in order to fully develop these horizontal business processes, international regulation for peer groups would be needed. Considering that the type of scale and scope attained today by Mondragon would have been very difficult to imagine only 20 years ago, it is reasonable to foresee that globalized cooperatively managed systems of production and distribution could exist within 20 years or even earlier. Mikel Lezamiz, director of Mondragon's Otalora Training Centre, has already set his eyes on the future: 'We will soon be 100,000 [in the Mondragon group]. In fifty years' time, we will be 200,000. I don't know how we will manage all that, but it will have to be based on participatory work, culture, mission and values. Our mission is to ensure wealth in society through the creation of sustainable employment for all'.

Creating shared wealth

Since cooperatives are open enterprises that are jointly owned and democratically controlled by key stakeholders present in a given locality, their accumulated financial reserves, the added value created, the jobs and the uphill and downhill economic activities they generate, also tend to remain in the locality.

Jose Maria Aldekoa, president of the Mondragon Corporation, considers that 'both work and capital need their just compensation, but capital is only a means to generate wealth. What ensures wealth in society is employment. If any enterprise has too much capital, it must be proactive in creating new activities, more value, more jobs, otherwise that money is dead'.

The creation of real wealth can only be *long-term*, which is what cooperatives do in essence, whereas economic transactions based solely on the remuneration of capital either do not create wealth or directly destroy it (as we saw in Chapter 3 and as was just avoided in the example of Ceralep in Chapter 6). This requires the development of relationships based on trust rather than 'economic war' or the 'survival of the fittest'; the cooperative rationality, as we saw in the previous chapters, is precisely one based on the generation of *trust* among economic actors, both the members-stakeholders who own cooperatives and among cooperatives themselves.

The creation of wealth also requires *openness*, which cooperatives structurally promote, whereas closedness intrinsically dries up economic dynamics and can even lead to recession, as happened to Krugman's metaphoric (and quite un-cooperative) Capitol Hill baby-sitting co-op (Chapter 2). In turn, the more cooperative systems are open, large and integrated, reproducing on wider scales the rationality and the structure of grassroots cooperatives, the more they can ensure the creation of long-term wealth, and resist an economic environment characterized by increasingly repetitive and profound crises.

The capacity to reproduce cooperatives' economic rationality within wider cooperative groups based on joint ownership and democratic control, makes it possible to develop small and autonomous economic entities at the local level in a sustainable manner, including activities that are directly part of the globalized economy, e.g. banking or spare parts for cars, while providing these activities with the necessary economies of scale and scope that enable them to efficiently face global competition without creating cartels or oligopolies.

It is probably no coincidence that regions where cooperatives are particularly dense and organized in cooperative groups, such as Emilia-Romagna in Italy or the Basque region of Spain, are among the very top European regions in terms of economic development and are also the ones with the highest GDP per capita in purchasing power parity (PPP) in their respective countries (excluding the regions of Madrid and Milan).[7]

However, as discussed in Chapter 4, the creation of wealth by cooperatives cannot be measured solely through quantifiable indicators such as turnover, reserves, profits or numbers of jobs, because it does not only have to do with quantifiable economic wealth. Cooperative systems create and maintain locally innumerable transactions that provide transparent access to flows of information, create socialized knowledge and innovation, all of which, in turn, generate collective visions, strategies and systemic capabilities. This is what Robert Putnam called 'social capital'[8] when he studied the Italian region of Emilia-Romagna, characterized, as just mentioned, by a particularly high concentration of cooperatives.

Jose Maria Arizmendiarrieta, the founder of the Mondragon experience, wrote in this respect that:

> if we had to express in only one word the most positive contribution of cooperative enterprises to overall development in our present historical conjuncture, we would say, without any hesitation: people ... A cooperative enterprise cannot be created by only one person's design or will: we usually find at its origin a genuine team of human beings, and its expansion is proportional to the capacity of these persons to mobilize other persons in their turn. Therefore, whoever wished to calculate the 'specific weight' of cooperative enterprises through their investments or sales volume would be mistaken, because the exponential of their strength and the basis for their future development is the human potential which is being constantly cultivated within themselves, through both horizontal and vertical mobility.[9]

What Arizmendiarrieta wrote in the 1970s is being reinforced by the ongoing debate launched by Joseph Stiglitz and Amartya Sen concerning the need to transcend GDP calculation in order to measure human progress, which we examined in Chapter 4.[10] New measurement tools that would evaluate the long-term entrepreneurial sustainability of economic entities, the resulting sustainability of jobs, the level of economic, financial and entrepreneurial education imparted to ordinary citizens, the degree of participation of ordinary citizens within economic decision making, the intensity of inter-enterprise cooperation, etc., would certainly provide a more faithful image of the economic contribution of cooperatives to the generation of wealth than GDP growth does.

The economic phenomenon created by cooperatives may still be ignored for some time, but not for long. Just as policy makers all over the world have had to recognize the reality of climate change (a gigantic step forward compared to the 1990s), we believe that the contribution of cooperatives as one of the pillars of sustainable economic development, as an engine for creating shared and intergenerational wealth, will be recognized sooner than later.

The *indirect* contribution of cooperatives to the economy as a source of inspiration

Whereas cooperatives are, as we just saw, important to the economy for what they directly contribute in terms of common goods, wealth, jobs, resilience, sustainability and fair redistribution of resources, they are perhaps even more important for their *indirect* role, as concrete sources of inspiration for policy making and economic practice.

First, through their systematic accumulation of common reserves, combined with participatory dynamics, cooperatives provide a model for firms not to fall into the 'debt trap'. Whenever they have to borrow substantially in order to make the investments needed to raise their competitiveness, the risk-taking is jointly decided by the owners-members, who debate on the strategy and legitimize the decisions, thereby entailing a real shouldering of responsibility of the stakeholders towards debt. In addition, all costs in the enterprise can be better controlled when they are the result of democratic will and legitimacy. Capital accumulation and cost control strategies combined with some form of democratic legitimacy can be an inspiration for other types of economic entities. The practice of common reserves also ensures the enterprise stakeholders' freedom, in the sense that they may leave the enterprise (under agreed rules) or the enterprise may receive newcomers without experiencing disruption. The enterprise can thus be passed to many new generations of stakeholders.

As far as concrete democratic practices are concerned, the inspiration that can be drawn from cooperatives is not only about democratic control by assemblies of members as in the Athenian *agora*, but also, and perhaps more importantly, about 'republican' style democratic institutions providing checks and balances (which we explained in Chapter 4 and which we saw in the four empirical cases in Chapters 5 to 8). In turn, the prevalent view about economic democracy in an enterprise is based on the 'general assembly' model (even if generally based on the one-share-one-vote type of 'democracy', which in fact is similar to the nineteenth-century census vote). Democratic checks and balances are fundamental in the cooperative *modus operandi*, and this is why cooperatives can function as both performing and democratic enterprises. As became particularly tangible in the case of large cooperative groups such as Desjardins or Mondragon, democratic checks and balances, if properly managed, have proven not to be a cost but, quite to the contrary, a long-term strategic investment.

The experience of producer cooperatives in generating mutualized support institutions (non-banking financial instruments, common guarantee systems, etc.) could be used among SMEs at large, through mutualized structures in a clustering process. Cooperatives of small businesses, with important productivity gains and economies of scale, have interesting models to share in a number of countries. This horizontal model can also be used by artisans and professionals (including architects, lawyers, doctors, etc.). On a different scale, horizontal business groups such as Mondragon, working with long-term strategies, are showing an alternative model to the chain economy based on vertical command seen in Chapter 3: effective control can be built in a different manner within and among economic entities.

As we can see, taking stock of some elements of the cooperative experience does not necessarily imply that each economic entity should become a cooperative. We need a variety of economic forms sharing a common set of values, from new versions of co-decision (where the systems of participation in worker cooperatives provide an invaluable experience) to innovative clusters of SMEs.

In the mid-1990s, Cowling and Sugden, in proposing a European industrial strategy (a topic which is somehow coming back on to the agenda), already emphasized the need to promote the involvement of local communities in firms in order to ensure the sustainability of economic and social development and reduce the principal-agent problems arising from information asymmetry. They envisaged three possible strategies: broadening the membership of joint-stock companies to include the various stakeholders, namely employees, suppliers and local communities, through a trust system; a transfer of ownership to a group of workers and producers (as in worker cooperatives); or a new type of public enterprise, based on local community control, which, however, would become a kind of jointly owned firm.[11] But, as we saw in Chapter 3, ownership boundaries are changing, and may not *per se* hold the key to the future. Joint control, rather than joint ownership, is increasingly appearing as being even more fundamental.

More widely, the horizontal and democratic approach of cooperatives, sometimes involving a substantial ratio of the adult population in a given country or locality, raises the issue of how citizens could have more say in economic and entrepreneurial decisions that directly concern their future. While exceeding the scope of this book, this discussion should be raised at some point, as the cooperative experience has revealed the capacity of ordinary citizens to take weighed economic decisions, act against bubble-type and erratic economic behaviour, and contribute to the stability and long-term development of real-economy activities that generate wealth.

Change may well be on the horizon

The world over the last thirty years has seen a succession of dramatic developments which nobody dared to predict with certainty in such a short time frame: the end of all Latin American military regimes, the fall of the Berlin wall and of the planned economic regimes of central and Eastern Europe, the democratizing of large parts of Africa and South East Asia and, more recently, the push towards democracy in the Arab world. At the same time, the last decades have also been characterized by a contrast between the spectacular advance of political democracy across the world and substantial steps backwards in real stakeholders' choice. Political democracy loses part of its substance when there is no real choice in the economic sphere. Our difficulty in imagining an alternative to the ongoing state of affairs may be proportional to the extent to which we tend to unconsciously repeat archaic frames of mind and behaviour, even though, by so doing, we may be risking implosion.

Although the Argentinean collapse of 2001 was foreseeable, what was difficult to foresee was the very moment and precise fashion in which it would take place. The scale of the 'ya basta!' ('now it's enough!') upheaval against probably the best example of failed policy, surprised everybody. The Argentinean case is a strong warning, because it was the first big popular upheaval of the beginning of the twenty-first century and, at the same time, marked the closure of the stream of economic crises that began in 1997, followed by policies that, in order to avoid deflation, paved the way for the housing bubble and the present global crisis. Allowing the present economic system to remain unreformed (or worse, insufficiently reformed) may lead to similar phenomena but, this time, on a much wider scale. While many other steps and policies need to be carried out, falling outside the scope of this book, we argue that a key step will be to build control within economic entities. While it is possible to wait and see, it would be far less costly to try some elements of real democratization in the economic sphere – checks and balances, transparency of information, citizens' education – sooner rather than later. In any case, if another crisis arises, those who know the path of joint ownership and democratic control have more chances to fare better.

Claude Béland, president of the Desjardins group between 1989 and 2000, observes that:

> in democratic countries, we boast the merits of democracy, but when capital becomes more important and dictates its rules of the game onto governments, people will have to decide whether they want to live in a democracy or not, with a proper balance between the political, economic and civil society spheres. This is precisely the type of balance which we have in cooperatives: the political dimension cannot dominate the economic dimension nor vice versa, and the civil society dimension must be the arbiter between both.[12]

This crisis is about debt in its underlying mechanisms and, without a change in trajectory, we are most probably bound to get more booms and busts through indebtedness. As we mentioned in Chapter 1, this may not be the mother of all crises, but it may well be the mother of all warnings.

In the end, if we must respond to the question: 'what is the economy for?', can the answer be anything else than to generate wealth and enjoy it equitably in a sustainable way?

Postscript

The main purpose of this postscript, drafted two years after the first edition of the book was published,[1] is to see how the contents of the previous pages and chapters, and mainly the explanation of the global crisis that broke out in 2007, as well as the relatively high level of resilience and continued wealth generation of cooperatives, stand up to the test of time. In the first part, we take a look from the point of view of the crisis in general. In the second part, we analyse it from the point of view of cooperatives and their resilience. In the third and last part, we discuss in which way the present system continues to be unsustainable and implosion-prone, and to what extent cooperatives continue to be a source of inspiration to solve the world's needs in the 21st century including, briefly, in relation to environmental sustainability.

The global crisis: where are we now?

Almost six years since the beginning of the global crisis, it begs asking why this crisis is unending and how we can grow out of it.

It has been argued that the crisis may now be over, at least in certain countries. China, for example, had a better trade surplus in 2012 than in 2009. However, although countries such as China, Brazil and Mexico have suffered less this time than in previous debt crises and have, for a while, continued to grow at rates that can arouse the envy of developed countries, both the economic activity and capital inflows sustaining their rates of growth have slowed down, in some cases seriously. Meanwhile, in the epicentre of the crisis, namely the developed economies, the efforts to overcome it show growing internal divergence: in terms of recovery policy between the USA and Japan on the one side and the European Union on the other, as well as in terms of competitiveness and policy between the North and the South of the European Union. In the latter, policy incoherence rules as far as public debt is concerned, with countries receiving varying treatments.

As has correctly been formulated by Prof. Maria de Conceição Tavares from Brazil (see quote at the end of Chapter 1), this global crisis has left us with a system of *disorder*, with sub-crises appearing here and there. This explains partly why this crisis is unending. Upcoming sub-crises are detected regularly, as with the refinancing by the Bank of England of privately invested firms planned for 2014. Indeed, in March 2013, the Bank of England warned of a systemic threat posed by private equity buyouts as from 2014, given the 'need over the next year to refinance firms subject to heavily leveraged buyouts'.[2] Acquired firms are given as collateral to the loans used to buy them, loans that are refinanced every five to seven years. In the current context, refinancing is harder and could trigger a new phase of this global crisis. This is, however, by no means certain as new surprises, but also new solutions, can come up.

Thus, without an outright collapse in sight, global economic restructuring goes on along the lines of the highly financialized and technified system described in Chapter 3. Seven years after the beginning of the crisis, some initiatives in global restructuring that had become temporarily stalled at that time are being re-launched, such as the transatlantic negotiations between the USA and the European Union, or the globalization and consolidation of stock markets, both discussed in Chapter 1.

As far as the 'debt trap' is concerned, the possible drift of the so-called 'capitalism' towards 'debtism', discussed in the book, remains pertinent. The recent difficulties of the Italian bank Monte dei Paschi di Siena (MPS) are more than symbolic in this respect.[3] Far from being the only case, it is paradigmatic because MPS is the oldest bank in the world, founded in 1472 as a mount of piety by the authority of the then city-state of Siena. Nowadays present in the USA, Russia, China and European countries among others, it became the third bank of Italy in importance at the start of the crisis after acquiring Banca Antonveneta. This acquisition, though, was the straw that weakened MPS's capital. Previously a safe institution dedicated to the development of the real economy, and having survived through centuries, it was brought into turmoil by the unregulated and shadowy financialized system of which most executives and staff of the bank seemed to be unaware. Local authorities have been taking part in the MPS Foundation, which was established in 1995 and is steering the bank. Yet, other shareholders have actually called the shots. In 2001 the bank entered the derivative frenzy with JP Morgan, Nomura, Deutsche Bank, Goldman Sachs, Bank of America and Mediobanca, in order to mask losses with derivatives by building swaps with them. With the crisis, the EU required a higher Tier 1 capital just when the MPS Foundation was discovering how some of its managers engaged in risky financial dealings and losses that had been placed off the balance sheet until then. The balance could not be approved; the internal shareholder base entered a phase of conflict linking money and politics; the municipality could not help at a time when its own resources were downsized. The bank received state aid after approval by the European Commission for fear that if MPS fell Italy would have to request EU financial aid. But the state aid from the Monti government was in fact a loan that worsened MPS's situation. And the loan came with strings attached, requesting the MPS Foundation to relinquish any limits to outside or foreign investors, with the expectation that the bank may be bought out soon. Who are the losers? Not only Siena and its region but Italy as a whole, since the bank was one of the keys to the famous development model known as the 'Third Italy'. Last but not least, being the third Italian bank in importance, its poor situation makes Italy's economy more uncertain.

The disconnection between ownership and control discussed in Chapter 3 as a deeper cause feeding the 'debt trap' continues to figure prominently as a carrier of systemic risk. Some initiatives try to confront it, such as the UK government's announcement that it will require the country 'to ensure that all companies know who ultimately owns and controls them and to require them to obtain and hold adequate, accurate and current information on their beneficial ownership' through a central registry.[4] It is not clear, though, whether the registry will be accessible to the public, which should logically be the case given the government's endorsement of transparency and accountability.

The trend described in the book by which finance receives most of the attention persists, although it is now widely recognized that global demand remains low and unemployment across the world is rising to unacceptable levels. The grand decision-making frameworks set out to handle the crisis, namely the G20 and Basle III, continue to focus on financial issues although they appear somewhat subdued, as the G20 meetings in Mexico in June 2012 and Moscow in 2013 and the doubts concerning the implementation of Basle III reflect.[5] On the other side, the decision on tax evasion and illicit finance by the 2013 G8 meeting in Northern Ireland mirrors the OECD's tax information exchange agreements and dialogue and the G20 report of 2011. Indeed, the G20 had entrusted the OECD to consider changes to tax law as from 2014, which will restrict such negotiations to OECD members. In turn, the IMF, which had become almost irrelevant, with very little capital in 2003, has received a new life with large inflows of fresh capital and a series of new countries to supervise.

In accounting, unilateralism remains strong even though the drive towards financial reporting described in Chapters 1, 2 and 3 goes on unchanged. The United States has postponed the implementation of the International Financial Reporting Standards (IFRS), designed by the IASB [International Accounting Standards Board]. The latter reworked its definition of equity for the first time in 2011 and, for the first time, dedicated a draft to equity in 2013.

Other trends foreseen in the book, like trade and capital measures, are on the rise, as low global aggregate demand makes countries worry about their access to foreign markets and their trade deficit. While surplus countries try to reinforce their surplus, some try to safeguard their domestic market with policies like the US 'Buy American', and others take strong action to promote exports. Many countries have begun to protect themselves from wild capital outflows that could be destabilizing; even the IMF now affirms that regulating capital outflows is good. In order to avoid deflation, the USA has engaged in the so-called 'quantitative easing', a policy that may be reaching its limits after its third round, while similar measures are being implemented in Japan and the UK. This type of policy has released enormous masses of money almost free of charge (at zero or very low interest rates) that are being injected across the rest of the world through asset acquisition, with emerging markets fearful of asset bubbles and their vulnerability to rapid reversal of financial flows. Indeed, the buzz word in countries where it is known that growth rates will not be high again for years to come is to 'go out': export, consolidate and acquire foreign assets. This phenomenon brings back faded memories of the 1880s and the 1890s, in the wake of the big financial crises of that period. Differently from that time, though, fast electronic trading makes one word from the US authorities sufficient for vast sums to suddenly change course and exit emerging and less developed economies.

We thus observe that the analysis of the global crisis developed in the book remains accurate, providing not only a good explanation of the crisis itself but also useful clues as to what has been unfolding over the last two years.

Have cooperatives maintained their resilience?

At the time of drafting these lines, in mid-2013, the four empirical cases studied in the book (Natividad, Ceralep, Desjardins and Mondragon) are doing well and are weathering the crisis, like indeed cooperatives in general. This does not mean that they do not experience difficulties, but they are strong enough to find the right solutions and keep going forward. We cannot delve further into this, as it would require a fully updated version of the book, but it confirms the resilience and the innovation capacity of cooperatives throughout the crisis. By now, other studies, surveys, declarations, newspaper articles and documentary films have also confirmed this trend.[6] The potential of cooperatives to develop the real economy and promote non-predatory, inclusive, equitable and sustainable development is there to be seen, in spite of inherent limitations as we will see below.

Beyond the issues of resilience and sustainability coming to the fore, one of the main arguments in the book is that cooperatives are part and parcel of a new trajectory to be built, not only because they are resilient and dynamic, but also because they steer away from debt traps, freeing up social and economic forces for embedded community development and for generating long-term general wealth. Cooperatives' general trend two years since the first edition of the book was published reinforces this argument.

The cases studied in the book have continued to show that without delocalization and with a member-based character, cooperatives can maintain and even increase employment levels in times of crisis, with shared flexibility. In order to maintain jobs, they continue to focus on how to recreate themselves swiftly, restructure, start new activities, diversify and enter new markets. Their common funds may seem limited in the beginning but, after time, they become significant and work as an anchor of mutual trust and solidarity. With a rather healthy equity base and capital reserves, they continue to stand up to the shocks of the crisis and rethink their long-term strategies.

Furthermore, the cases of cooperatives studied in the book show that resilience to a crisis is best built in advance, and the two years that have passed since the first edition have widely confirmed this observation. Cooperatives are not resilient and innovative just by having good ideals and values (although this is certainly vital to organizational success) but by building mechanisms and dynamics that can deliver legitimacy, rapidity, flexibility and responsibility, so that they are ready to confront the difficulties and maintain their orientation in the face of a crisis.

Cooperatives' democratic framework of joint control and ownership (which is part of the very definition of a cooperative, as seen in Chapter 4) has continued to prove its prime importance in their resilience capacity, because such a framework makes it possible to prevent high leverage and indebtedness in the first place. As explained in Chapter 3, the issue of control, beyond the one of debt, has been at the root of this global crisis. It is therefore central to the solution; control must be rooted, embedded and jointly exercised.

Yet, the last two years have also shown that the resilience of cooperatives has its limits in the face of decisions that affect entire economies and bring about deflation or recession, or increasing levels of poverty, inequality, social exclusion and vulnerability among the population.[7] This is particularly true in the case of cooperatives that have been providing goods or services to the state in countries like Italy where the state has years of arrears in paying its bills. Cooperatives are no economic islands, and they cannot be expected to survive eternally if they do not receive payment for what they produce.

The problems which the UK Co-operative Bank has been facing in 2013 deserve a few words because its misfortune may affect the image of cooperatives in the UK. It should be mentioned that this is a commercial bank, a wholly owned subsidiary of the Co-operative Group, a consumer cooperative. Thus, it is not *in itself* a cooperative composed of members like the Desjardins *caisses* described in Chapter 7. Besides, the bank has its origins in the consumer movement while in the rest of Europe the origins of cooperative banking can be traced back to the locally based credit unions.[8] It is a specific case linked to the general discussion in the book, and we await with interest studies under way in the UK.

At any rate, the cooperatives' strong trend towards resilience, sustainability and innovation which we have seen in the second part of the book still holds two years after the first edition. Thus, their potential as a source of inspiration, as also suggested in the book, remains as valid as two years ago.

Cooperation in the 21st century

Instead of a collapse of 'capitalism', we continue to observe the consequences of 'the mother of all warnings' explained in Chapter 9, namely of a system that has become unsustainable.

As the book explains, this particular crisis is unique in its reach and interconnectedness. On the one hand, large segments of all major actors in the advanced economies are highly indebted both in the financial and real economy: banks, firms, households and public authorities from local to national and beyond. A large part of the economy has been financed through debt mechanisms. We have used the term 'debt trap' because it runs deeper than an ordinary public debt crisis. Secondly, as explained in Chapter 3, we are entering a new economic system based on stream access and high-frequency computerized trading in finance that by now channel most financial flows (more than 60% in the USA in 2013) while lenders continue to lend to each other and to bet against each other's default. Working in a constantly interconnected loop, the emerging system carries systemic instability. At the same time, as the book also brings forward, some current practices dealing with labour and debt are reminiscent of the Victorian times or even the *Ancien Régime*, as in Cyprus where citizens risk prison once they lose their jobs.[9] The trajectory of the last 30 years that we call 'capitalism' is increasingly prone to implosion. Even the common citizen acknowledges this faster than governing authorities do, as shown by Brazil's 2013 protests against public indebtedness brought about by lavish and ostentatious expenditure. Citizens are not only well aware of the risks involved but are also vocal about their priorities based on equity, growth and jobs.

Ongoing debates in economic theory focus on growth and inequality. In 2012, both the growing gap in income distribution and that in income concentration were recognized by the IMF as one of the major causes of instability and household indebtedness, with macroeconomic consequences. Besides, mathematical and statistical models that did not include the possibility of downturn trends, thereby creating systemic risk, are under the spotlight. And we observe that monetary policy *per se* is ceding the ground to institutionalist theories, which may bear fruit in the next decades.

But the crisis and its consequences call for a more rapid response. We observe a growing sentiment of fatigue and outrage among a large part of the population in many countries, as can be observed in elections, for example leading to three-party winners struggling to form a government, like in Italy in 2013. Disaffection of citizens towards supranational institutions including the EU is also on the rise. Yet, the nation-state faces its own limitations. This confirms what the book argues, namely that this global crisis is bringing about historical discontinuity and that there is an urgent need to rebuild governance within institutions.

Some lessons from late 19th century and early 20th century, when cooperatives played a critical role in freeing ordinary citizens and entire regions from vicious cycles of debt, poverty and vulnerability, deserve attention for their relevance today. For example, the origins of the experiences of the Desjardins group in Quebec, the Raiffeisen group in Germany and the Slovene cooperatives had to do with the state of generalized indebtedness that was keeping people in the vicious cycle of poverty in their respective country or region.[10] Freedom from debt mechanisms and predatory practices through cooperatives triggered the potential for well-being in those communities, regions and countries. Such observations can make us re-think the role of cooperatives in the light of the present crisis.

The case studies of cooperatives discussed in the book prove that it is possible to sustain job security at times of crisis thanks to flexible arrangements based on solidarity and built in advance. In order to open up the debt trap on the one hand and restart healthy demand on the other, there is a need for sustainable jobs accompanied by decent working conditions and coverage for illness and old age. It is no coincidence that state-led welfare policy began to take root in the 1930s. We believe that, in the end, this time will not be different. There is already discussion around a minimal income for the unemployed and most vulnerable in Germany and Italy. Yet, to build a future of more security with solidarity, the promotion of clustering and cooperation among SMEs, artisans and liberal professions will need to function on the basis of stakeholders in the real economy and not on financial ones.

Cooperation can be lived not only within organizations but among the multiplicity of stakeholders that are present on the territory. By multiplying on the ground, cooperatives can remain rather small and embedded across the territory and society. Through cooperative networks and consortia they are able to mutualize support resources. Through spin-offs and upper level cooperatives they can innovate, specialize in specific activities, enter new ones or upgrade skills and knowledge. This path may leave behind individualistic assumptions while, in turn, placing the individual, the person, at the centre. This non-individualistic individual can be conceived as co-operator, co-author, co-owner and co-controller. Indeed, we cannot expect all-round comprehensive solutions from only one stakeholder, and cooperatives can replicate their model with various stakeholders.

Two years after its first edition, the cases of cooperatives discussed in the book have continued to show their capabilities not only to cooperate in order to innovate and respond to prospective needs and aspirations of citizens and communities, but also to generate further specialization. It would be highly desirable to undertake more studies on these capabilities, because such knowledge could be very useful not only to other cooperatives themselves, but also to SMEs, social movements, NGOs and local communities. We move here from the micro level towards the idea of building meso-economies, hinted at in Chapter 9, with sustainable pools of resources, flows and affinities that both respond to the needs and aspirations of local people and communities and are able to enhance the sustainability of all life on the planet.

The need to rethink growth has never been more pressing, in order to respond to both the ecological overshoot and increasing inequality and unemployment levels that limit the recovery and leave a large part of the population vulnerable. The need for real-economy development that is sustainable, with a long-term vision, embedded, equitable and transparent, is pressing. Growth could be reframed in terms of the 'Commons' and the generation of general wealth, overcoming the purely financial notion of private riches. The discussion, therefore, should not limit itself to Rogoff and Reihart's threshold level of debt used to justify austerity that is self-defeating: job loss and pay cuts with high taxes for the common citizen, leading to increasing poverty and precariousness, making citizens vulnerable and prey to further indebtedness, while many firms are not being duly paid for their services by state authorities.[11]

The focus of efforts should be on building a new path, like an arrow of time, towards lowering vulnerability to indebtedness, from a new type of industrial policy connecting sustainability and innovation with values of ethics and solidarity, to internalizing the value of nature, and calling for new investment into social organizations based on trust, transparency and accountability. To jump onto such path, financialization and technification, as discussed in Chapter 3, shall have to be re-embedded and remain comprehensible to human beings. Debt reduction and restructuring are necessary but cannot be done successfully when all actors are weary of increasing consumption and investment. Neither can they be implemented under rigid ideological or self-regarding positions. Finally, consumption and investment patterns must be transformed as well. The debt trap may be seen as similar to the ecological overshoot. To avoid it, we must first imagine and chart a new trajectory. There is a need to focus on how to generate genuine value that brings about general wealth in a sustainable manner. To achieve this, critical awareness of how we organize among ourselves will be fundamental.

On environmental sustainability, Chapter 5 on the Mexican Natividad Cooperative remains highly relevant and surprising because this cooperative enterprise engaged in a path of de-growth since the very beginning by avoiding predation and taking up a scientist as a member. Yet, nature's rewards were so significant that the cooperative could consequently engage in industry, exports, tourism and nature conservation activities. With its success also came responsibility and the cooperative had to prevent others' predatory practices. This case study presents a very interesting approach to the debate on growth and de-growth, to climate change, dwindling fishing stocks and environmental concerns.

As in other grand crises in history, recovery is likely to be uplifted by new energy sources followed by new types of transportation. This time, energy sources are likely to take more micro forms and thus function in an interconnected way. The type of energy that will predominate will certainly have a dramatic impact on the world's sustainability and peace. This, in turn, will lead to changes in the location and structure of industries, units of production and their social organization. The need for cooperation will be greater, and the 200 years of experience of cooperatives across the world can prove highly relevant in this respect. The call is to apply organizational innovation in the field of horizontal coordination, together with the cooperative values and principles, in responding to the challenges of the 21st century.

Claudia Sanchez Bajo
Bruno Roelants
8 August 2013

Notes

1 The Mother of All Crises?

1. Trichet, J.C., 9 October 2009. For the USA, see Jickling, M., 29 January 2009.
2. See the excellent chronology in the 'Timeline of the crisis', http://timeline. stlouisfed.org/. The Fed St. Louis is one of the 12 decentralized regional banks that make up one of the three parts of the Federal Reserve System of the USA. For a good explanation of the crisis in the USA, see the paper by Julie Stackhouse, Senior Vice President, Federal Reserve Bank of St. Louis 'The Financial Crisis: What Happened?' updated September 21, 2009.
3. 'Freddie Mac Announces Tougher Subprime Lending Standards To Help Reduce The Risk Of Future Borrower Default', for immediate release, 27 February, 2007, http://www.freddiemac.com/news/archives/corporate/2007/20070227_ subprimelending.html.
4. Blinder, Alan S. and Mark Zandi, 2010.
5. Geither, Timothy F., 'Welcome to the recovery', op-ed contribution, 2 August, 2010, *New York Times*.
6. 'Economists spar on effectiveness of US stimulus response', 3 August, 2010, at http://bloomberg.com/news/2010-08-03/taylor-contests-blinder-zandi-study-that-stimulus-spurred-strong-recovery.html.
7. On 17 August, 2010, Moody's AAA Sovereign Monitor affirmed that the United Kingdom, France and Germany, the largest triple-A rated European countries 'have already started implementing fiscal tightening... In the US, a strategy for debt stabilization is still in the early stages of being developed... with Moody's highlighting growth revival as the first challenge'. The four countries were investigated closely by Moody's, which had only downgraded Ireland thus far. As fiscal tools were no longer at the countries' disposal, Moody's called for credible medium-term fiscal adjustment programmes and policies to further labour supply and cut costs due to ageing populations, noting that 'another consequence of the crisis is the reduced time available for governments to confront those challenges'. By Moody's: US, UK, France, Germany 'Distance to Downgrade' reduced, on http:// marketnews.com, 17 August 2010.
8. 'Eurozone austerity takes toll on growth', 24 August, 2010, *Financial Times*, p. 1.
9. 'Wall Street slips on fears data point to weak recovery', Reuters, 24 August, 2010.
10. Bosworth, B. and A.Flaaen, 2009, p. 2.
11. 'This paper shows that there is no obvious explanation for a sudden increase in the relative demand for housing which could explain the price rise. There is also no obvious explanation for the increase in home purchase prices relative to rental prices. In the absence of any other credible theory, the only plausible explanation for the sudden surge in home prices is the existence of a housing bubble. This means that a major factor driving housing sales is the expectation that housing prices will be higher in the future. While this process can sustain rising prices for a period of time, it must eventually come to an end... The Japanese economy experienced simultaneous bubbles in its housing and stock markets in the late

eighties. The collapse of these two bubbles has left Japan's economy nearly stagnant for more than a decade. The United States faces the same sorts of risk from the collapse of its stock market and housing bubbles'. Dean Baker, 2002, 'The run-up in home prices: is it real or is it another bubble?' (pdf), Center for Economic and Policy Research, briefing paper.

12. Dean Baker, 'Adjustable rate mortgages reached 35 % of all mortgages in 2004–06, often starting with very low interest rates in the first 2 years, jumping after to high levels even if interest rates did not. "2–28" mortgages were especially common in the subprime segment, the latter booming from less than 9 per cent of the market in 2002 to 25 per cent of the market by 2005. Besides, the "Alt-A" mortgages were loans to buyers without complete documentation, many for investment, that covered the full price or even more. In 2005–2007, many of the latter carried payments for at least five years only on the interest and not the principal debt. These two categories, subprime and Alt-A, made 40 % of all loans at the peak of the bubble'. http://www.paecon.net/PAEReview/issue46/Baker46.pdf.

13. Bosworth, B. and A. Flaaen, 2009, *ibid*, p. 2.

14. Demyanyk, Yuliya and Otto Van Hemert, 2008.

15. http://www.nytimes.com/2010/04/25/business/25goldman.html?scp=4&sq=gold man%20sachs&st=Search.

16. Demyanyk, Yuliya and Otto Van Hemert 2008.

17. 'Why economists worry about who holds foreign currency reserves', Frederick Kempe, http://online.wsj.com/public/article/SB114710757447146758-[cont url] vgS6pBo_YDBwbCu5e9LjfsSVBgg_20070508.html?mod=blogs.

18. Bank of Spain 2006 Annual Report, 'The revaluation of financial and real estate assets, although, in the latter case, it was lower than in the previous year, as a result of the continuing profile of a slowdown in the housing price, which grew by... almost 4 pp (in the last quarter). In the early months of 2007...the growth of this variable was reduced by almost 2 per cent', p. 22 (translation by the author), http://www.bde.es/webbde/Secciones/Publicaciones/PublicacionesAnuales/ InformesAnuales/06/inf2006.pdf.

19. Banco de España, April 2006, Boletín Económico, Informe trimestral de la economía española, Madrid, p. 16, http://www.bde.es.

20. 'En décembre 2006, le "mortgage desk" de Goldman Sachs, la section chargée d'acheter et de vendre des titres de prêts immobiliers, avait affiché de lourdes pertes dix jours d'affilée. En secret, le directeur financier, David Viniar, responsable du contrôle des risques, avait ordonné le délestage progressif de ces actifs toxiques. Parallèlement, l'établissement avait continué de les vendre comme si de rien n'était à ses clients. Lorsque la bulle avait éclaté, Goldman avait empoché des bénéfices substantiels, tandis que les acheteurs de ses CDO y avaient laissé leur chemise.' 17.04.10 http://www.lemonde.fr/economie/ article/2010/04/17/le-systeme-goldman-sachs-en-accusation_1335177_3234. html. The fall in prices continued in 2010. It 'probably will rise this year for the first time since 2006, boosting homeowners' equity. The median US home price likely will increase to $177,200 in the second quarter from $167,600 in the current period, according to the National Association of Realtors.' US home prices fell 13 per cent last year to a median of $172,500, the largest annual drop since the 1930s, according to the National Association of Realtors. The decline followed a 9.5 per cent drop in 2008, NAR said. 'The people who bought in 2006 and 2007 have seen their equity wiped out because of falling prices, but if you bought in 2003 or 2004, you probably still have enough of a "stake" to

qualify for a home equity loan, said Lafakis', http://www.businessweek.com/print/lifestyle/content/mar2010/bw20100311_624208.htm.

21. Taylor, John B., 2008.

22. 'About That Free Trade', Spiegel Online, May 15, 2006, http://service.spiegel.de/cache/international/0,1518,416217,00.html.

23. The World Trade Organization is holding its first major ministerial meeting since Hong Kong in 2005 as it seeks to find some way to get the Doha Round back, in http://blogs.telegraph.co.uk/finance/edmundconway/100002355/trade-a-tragedy-in-the-making/.

24. 'Why economists worry about who holds foreign currency reserves', Frederick Kempe, http://online.wsj.com/public/article/SB114710757447146758- [cont url] vgS6pBo_YDBwbCu5e9LjfsSVBgg_20070508.html?mod=blogs

25. 'The two new elements in the global financial constellation that I have been stressing – the US current account deficits mirrored primarily by surpluses outside of the traditional industrialized nations, and the staggering accumulation of reserves by emerging market countries, both suggest the obsolescence of the G7/G8 as the dominant forum for international financial discussion.' Lawrence H. Summers, 24 March, 2006, 'Reflections on Global Account Imbalances and Emerging Markets Reserve Accumulation', L.K. Jha Memorial Lecture, Reserve Bank of India, Mumbai, India, http://www.hks.harvard.edu/fs/lsummer/speeches/2006/0324_rbi.html.

26. Roubini Global Economics, 'Global Imbalances Outlook, Q3 2009', http://www.roubini.com/analysis/96789.php.

27. Frederick Kempe, 9 May, 2006, 'Why economists worry about who holds foreign currency reserves', *Wall Street Journal*, p. A8.

28. 'In July 2005, China adopted a new exchange rate regime for the Yuan (CNY), scrapping its peg to the USD and replacing it with a managed float against a basket of currencies. The Yuan appreciated initially from CNY 8.28 to CNY 8.11 per USD and then to CNY 7.87 per USD by November 2006', OECD, 2007, 'Agricultural Policies in Non-OECD Countries, Monitoring and Evaluation 2007', p. 4.

29. 'NYSE chief aims for global empire after striking $10bn merger deal with Euronext', *The Guardian*, 3 June, 2006.

30. 'We do have the ability to offer new products through Liffe into the US', Mr John Thain said. 'We also have the opportunity to acquire a US futures exchange, and I wouldn't rule out either of those', http://business.guardian.co.uk/story/0,,1801033,00.html.

31. http://business.guardian.co.uk/story/0,,1789532,00.html He is member of the French-American Foundation, the Trilateral Commission and the international board of British American Business.

32. 'Il évite l'isolement de la zone Euro par rapport à Londres et New York en créant un pont avec la zone dollar. Il permettra aux investisseurs Européens de diversifier leurs actifs sur le marché américain et élargira considérablement les possibilités de financement des entreprises Européennes. Les sièges internationaux du nouvel ensemble resteront à Paris et à Amsterdam pour les marchés au comptant et à Londres pour les dérivés... inciter les entreprises des nouveaux pays émergents (Brésil, Chine, Inde, Russie) à choisir Paris pour leur cotation plutôt que Londres', François Bujon de l'Estang est ambassadeur de France, président de Citigroup France.Citigroup conseille le NYSE pour cette transaction, in article 'Paris, future capitale financière',. 27 June 2006, http://www.lemonde.fr/web/article/0,1-0@2-3232,36-788239,0.html.

33. In December 2005, the LSE rejected a £1.5 billion takeover offer from the Australian Macquarie Bank. It then received a bid in March of 2006 for £2.4 billion from NASDAQ, which was also rejected. On April 12, 2006, the Nasdaq bought a 15 per cent stake in LSE, raising later to almost 30 per cent. See the story in 'NASDAQ OMX Group', on http://en.wikipedia.org/wiki/NASDAQ_OMX_Group.

34. 'Nasdaq in driving seat as LSE studies options' 16 April 2006, http://observer.guardian.co.uk/business/story/0,1754478,00.html.

35. 'London Stock Exchange cuts jobs as recession hits revenues', http://www.telegraph.co.uk/finance/markets/5832006/London-Stock-Exchange-cuts-jobs-as-recession-hits-revenues.html, 15 Jul 2009.

36. It is worth mentioning that this process of concentration towards a seamless stock market picked up again in 2010.

37. The European Union Heads of State and Governments and the President of the United States met on 22 February 2005 in Brussels, followed by a EU-US Summit on 20 June 2005 in Washington. The US Congress passed a Draft House Resolution 77 on Transatlantic Relations on 9 February 2005 and the European Commission its Communication – COM(2005)0196 – on 18 May 2005 entitled 'A stronger EU-US Partnership and a more open market for the 21st century'. In, 8 May 2006, the European Parliament Rapporteur Elmar Brok handed out its final report (2005/2056(INI) Committee on Foreign affairs) The US-EU partnership aims at a liberalized free market, the harmonization of many sectors and coordinated action in regard to other countries such as China, Russia and Ukraine. The Transatlantic Partnership Agreement has other dimensions than purely commercial, with political, regulatory and security goals such as ensuring the security of energy and raw material supplies. In November 2005, working groups were established to guarantee their intellectual property rights, border enforcement cooperation, public-private partnerships and coordinated technical assistance. There is a Transatlantic Legislators' Dialogue that has proposed the idea of setting a transatlantic assembly with legislators' summits and the European Parliament has proposed to have a permanent representation in Washington.

38. 'Europe remains the number one geographical location for US overseas investment, with 60% of US corporate assets abroad located in the EU, and with Europe providing nearly 75% of all foreign investment in the US in the last 5 years... Whereas the European and US capital markets account for 68% of the global bond and stock market capitalisation and the two are each other's main export markets for financial services, with EUR 85 000 million worth of transactions by EU investors in US equities in 2003–4 and EUR 40000 million worth in the other direction... However, corporate scandals such as those surrounding WorldCom and Parmalat underline the need for the EU and the US to step up cooperation on improving transatlantic auditing and governance policies... Welcomes the April 2005 US-EU agreement on a "roadmap" toward equivalence of accounting standards as progress toward the use of one single accounting standard in the EU and the US; Notes, however, that the full potential of open, deep, and dynamic transatlantic financial markets and services is far from reached and highlights that dismantling existing investment barriers could yield significant economic rewards to the transatlantic economy in the shape of higher liquidity, cheaper access to capital and lower transaction and trading costs (a 9% decline in the cost of equity capital, 60% lower trading costs, and a consequent 50% increase in trading volumes, according to the Commission); points to the need to address

anomalous ownership restrictions on the US side, particularly in the defence, aviation and media sectors, and to develop a structured dialogue aimed at achieving a mutually fair and adequate competition policy... 4. Believes that cooperation and dialogue on corporate governance could assist in avoiding the adoption of discriminatory legislation such as the Sarbanes-Oxley Act of 2002 with its damaging consequences for EU companies'. Source: European Parliament Rapporteur Elmar Brok report 8 May 2006 (2005/2056(INI) Committee on Foreign affairs, European Parliament.

39. Voltaire, *Candide*.
40. Robin Blackburn, 'The Subprime Crisis', *New Left Review 50*, March–April 2008, p. 63.
41. Blackburn, 2008, *ibid.*
42. Van Denburgh, William and M Harmelink, Philip J, 'Accounting Implications of the Subprime Meltdown', *The CPA Journal*, 1 December 2008, http://www.allbusiness.com/trends-events/audits/11729624-1.html. On page 4 of the article: 'In late 2007, billion-dollar subprime exposures were reported by Countrywide Financial Corp. (subsequently taken over by Bank of America), Wells Fargo & Co., Citigroup Inc., HSBC Finance Corp., and Thornburg Mortgage Inc. In the case of Citigroup, it reported $55 billion in direct subprime exposure with up to $11 billion in potential revenue exposure. bank failures ... Washington Mutual's failure on September 25 being the largest but even this track record grossly understates the severity of the financial market crisis. One indication of the overall impact of the subprime problems can be seen in the fact that the Nasdaq Bank index as of October 2008 was down about 50% when compared to June 2007. The September 2007 $2.5 billion failure of NetBank, Inc. and the subsequent takeover by the Federal Deposit Insurance Corp. (FDIC) should dispel the myth once and for all that accounting earnings do not matter'.
43. http://www.spiegel.de/international/business/0,1518,692007,00.html#ref=nlint.
44. 'Bear Stearns was the first Wall Street bank to blow up in the recent crisis, caught in the credit crunch in early 2008 and foreshadowing the cascading financial meltdown in the fall of that year. Two of Bear Stearns's hedge funds failed in June 2007 as a result of bad bets on the sub-prime mortgage market, costing investors $1.8bn (£1.2bn) and touching off the domino chain that brought the firm to the brink in March 2008... Cayne was a flamboyant character ... As the two hedge funds melted down, he reportedly managed to spend 10 of 21 workdays out of the office... for regular golf games and skipping work to play in bridge tournaments. Cayne recounts in his prepared testimony that amid "unfounded" concerns and "rumours" in the market about Bear Stearns's solvency in the week of 10 March 2008, the firm's brokerage customers pulled out assets and other firms cancelled special loans known as repurchase agreements.' http://www.guardian.co.uk/business/2010/may/05/bear-stearns-credit-crunch-inquiry.
45. Bear Stearns' Cayne concedes leverage was too high, http://www.reuters.com/article/idUSTRE64420N20100505.
46. Wall Street cae tras la quiebra de Lehman Brothers y la venta de Merrill Lynch 15/09/2008 http://www.eleconomista.es/mercados-cotizaciones/noticias/751842/09/08/Wall-Street-cae-tras-la-quiebra-de-Lehman-Brothers-y-la-venta-de-Merrill-Lynch.html.
47. 'EEUU-Tesoro inyecta 200.000 mln usd para Fannie Mae y Freddie Mac', 8 September 2008, http://www.eleconomista.es/empresas-finanzas/noticias/739114/09/08/EEUU-Tesoro-inyecta-200000-mln-usd-para-Fannie-Mae-y-Freddie-Mac.html.

48. The case is 'Lehman Brothers Holdings Inc, U.S. Bankruptcy Court, Southern District of New York, No. 08-13555', http://uk.biz.yahoo.com/11032010/325/lehman-examiner-report-public.html Reuters. Filed in February under seal, it was withheld because much of the information was subject to confidentiality agreements. Some changes were thus made for the public view, in particular 12 pages related e.g. to the Chicago Mercantile Exchange parent CME Group Inc.

49. Lehman Brothers: Repo 105 and other accounting tricks; http://www.guardian.co.uk/business/2010/mar/12/lehman-brothers-repo-105-enron.

50. Lehman Brothers Holdings Inc. case at the United States Bankruptcy Court Southern District of New York, Report by Anton Valukas, http://lehmanreport.jenner.com/VOLUME%203.pdf, page 740.

51. 'It is not that they sold them to off-balance-sheet vehicles, it is that they subsequently were forced to buy them back. It was dubious in accounting terms', Greenspan said, http://www.guardian.co.uk/business/2010/apr/07/blame-Europe-alan-greenspan-tells-congress.

52. http://www.guardian.co.uk/business/2008/apr/08/creditcrunch.useconomy.

53. 'The FDIC took over Washington Mutual on September 25, 2008 – the largest bank failure in history – then almost immediately sold all of the bank's deposits, loans and branches to JP Morgan Chase for $1.9 billion. All accounts were transferred to Chase, regardless of the size, even if they were above the FDIC limits. Nobody lost any money on deposits at Washington Mutual', in 'What the WaMu collapse means for its customers', http://www.washingtonpost.com/wp-dyn/content/article/2008/09/30/AR2008093000803.html.

54. 'Senate panel finds major fraud at Washington Mutual', AP, Associated Press, 13 April 2010, *Washington Post.*

55. 'Floyd Norris accountants misled us into crisis', 13 September 2009, blog at nytimes.com/Norris.

56. FASB chairman Robert Herz, declaration to the US House Financial Services Committee, 19 April, 2010, http://www.fasb.org/cs/ContentServer?c=Document_C&pagename=FASB%2FDocument_C%2FDocumentPage&cid=1176156813156

57. Regulation 1602/2002, amended by Regulation 297/2008 governs the terms and the EU Commission powers concerning the adoption of IFRS. Article 3 grants full powers to the Commission unless there is incompatibility with the European public interest or with Directives 78/660 and 83/349.

58. 'Freddie Mac annonce une perte nette de 21,5 milliards en 2009' LEMONDE and AFP 24.02.10 http://lemonde.fr/economie/article/2010/02/24/freddie-mac-annonce-une-perte-nette-de-21-5-milliards-en-2009_1310866_3234.html.

59. Michiel Bijlsma and Gijsbert Zwart, Ch. 2 'The Great Recession: CPB about the credit crisis', http://www.degroterecessie.nl/ chapter02.htm, website of the Centraal Planbureau.

60. http://www.nytimes.com/2008/10/19/world/Europe/19hungary.html.

61. http://www.dw-world.de/dw/article/0,,3721020,00.html.

62. Krugman, P., 23 December, 2008 'Latvia is the new Argentina (slightly wonkish)', *New York Times*, http://krugman.blogs.nytimes.com/2008/12/23/latvia-is-the-new-argentina-slightly-wonkish/.

63. Mark Weisbrot and Rebecca Ray, February 2010, 'Latvia's recession: the cost of adjustment with an internal devaluation'; Center for Economic and Policy Research http://www.cepr.net/documents/publications/latvia-recession-2010-02.pdf.

64. http://www.straightstocks.com/hungary/and-so-it-ends-hungarys-government-announces-foreign-currency-loan-wind-up-package.

65. Hungary closing embassies due to economic crisis, 17 June 2009, http://euobserver.com/9/28315.
66. 'La crise selon Patrick Artus'. interview with Mr. Artus, Director of Natixis, 13 February 2010, *Le Monde.*
67. Enderle. 2007.
68. Joseph Schumpeter's *Capitalism, Socialism and Democracy* (1942) talked of a 'process of industrial mutation that incessantly revolutionizes the economic structure from within, incessantly destroying the old one, incessantly creating a new one'. This was achieved through entrepreneurial innovation in the real economy.
69. According to Strietska-Ilina, member of the European Commission's expert group that drafted the 'New Skills for New Jobs' report, 'some companies shift from offering sure employment and become less inclined to invest in training, according to Olga Strietska-Ilina, a skills policy specialist at the International Labour Organisation (ILO) in an interview, she said this is leading to a further deterioration in skill levels in the workforce..., highlighting the need for investment in IT competence, languages and training for green jobs', in 'As crisis bites, companies wind down training programmes', 24 March 2010, http://www.euractiv.com/en/enterprise-jobs/crisis-bites-companies-wind-down-training-programmes-news-372425.
70. http://www.guardian.co.uk/business/2010/feb/11/banks-crisis-commercial-property-loans.
71. 'Le système Goldman Sachs en accusation', 18 April 2010, http://lemonde.fr/economie/article/2010/04/17/le-systeme-goldman-sachs-en-accusation_1335177_3234.html.
72. 'US banks facing $1.4tn crisis over commercial property loans', http://www.guardian.co.uk/business/2010/feb/11/banks-crisis-commercial-property-loans, 11 February 2010.
73. 'Fears of credit card crisis as bank write-offs double', *The Daily Telegraph,* UK, 30 November 2009, http://www.telegraph.co.uk/finance/newsbysector/banksandfinance/6694719/Fears-of-credit-card-crisis-as-bank-write-offs-double.html.
74. 'Fears of credit card crisis as bank write-offs double', *The Daily Telegraph,* 30 November 2009, http://www.telegraph.co.uk/finance/newsbysector/banksandfinance/6694719/Fears-of-credit-card-crisis-as-bank-write-offs-double.html.
75. December consumer credit down for 11th straight month, Feb 5, 2010, http://www.reuters.com/article/idUSTRE61450A20100205.
76. Dean Baker, 'The housing bubble and the financial crisis', in *Real-world Economics Review* no. 46, p. 75. Statement based on the comparison of data from January 2008 and data from October 2007 in the Case-Shiller 20 City Indexes at http://www2.standardandpoors.com/portal/site/sp/en/us/page.article/0,0,0,0,1145923002722.html.
77. 'One in five homeowners with mortgages under water', 31 October 2008, Reuters.
78. 'Home repossessions hit record high; new foreclosure filings level off', April 16 2010, http://www.palmbeachpost.com/money/real-estate/home-repossessions-hit-record-high-new-foreclosure-filings-567071.html?cxtype=rss_news.
79. 'Program to modify loans loses steam', August 23 2010, the *Wall Street Journal.*
80. Explanation by Chief Executive Officer Brian Moynihan, in 'Home equity lending that fuelled consumer spending to recover', March 11, 2010, http://www.businessweek.com/print/lifestyle/content/mar2010/bw20100311_624208.htm. In October 2010, 50 US states and their highest courts began a joint investigation into whether mortgage firms were wrong to repossess homes. The main issue at

stake is ownership rights: a lender must prove it owns the note underlying the property for the foreclosure to be legal. When loans were bundled into securities, the chain in ownership was neglected. 'US October 2010 wide probe into home repossessions', 13 October 2010, http://www.bbc.co.uk/news/business-11535939.

81. 'The decrease in net worth for each quintile from 2004 to 2009 is even larger among homeowners than non-homeowners. In the lowest quintile, homeowners are projected to average net debt of $1,600–$14,000 while other households in the bottom fifth have wealth of between $2,000–$2,400... As a percent of 2004 net wealth, the losses are much heavier at the lower end of the wealth ladder. The bottom 20 percent of households aged 45–54 in 2004 had little wealth — only $3,500 on average. Five years later, the bottom fifth of that age group are projected to have average net wealth of negative $2,300. The second quintile is expected to have 54 percent less net wealth than in 2004, the middle quintile 42 percent, and the fourth quintile 35 percent. The top quintile, averaging $2.5 million in 2004, is expected to have net wealth 35 percent lower in 2009 — almost $900,000 less per household', in 'The wealth of the baby boom cohorts after the collapse of the housing bubble', by David Rosnick and Dean Baker, February 2009, Center for Economic and Policy Research, PDF on www.cepr.net.

82. Testimony of Dean Baker Before the Senate Special Committee on Aging, 25 February, 2009, http://aging.senate.gov/events/hr204db.pdf.

83. 'Considering price inflation effect on households' expenditures, the purchasing power of the gross available income (RDB or Revenu disponible brut) slowed down strongly (only 0,6% compared to 3,1% in 2007). The purchasing power by household actually decreased by 0.8 % in 2008, close to the 1980 fall of 0.7 % and the worst since 1960', source: http://www.insee.fr 'Revenu disponible ménages et évolution du pouvoir d'achat'.

84. lemonde.fr/societe/article/2010/03/13/manifestations-en-france-pour-appuyer-un-moratoire-des-expulsions-locatives_1318605_3224.html.

85. Le commerce mondial n'avait pas connu un niveau aussi bas depuis 1945 lemonde.fr avec AFP, 24 february 2010.

86. 'US jobless rate hits 5-month low but payrolls fall', http://www.reuters.com/article/idUSN1416882220100206.

87. 'Home Equity Lending That Fueled Consumer Spending to Recover, March 11, 2010, http://www.businessweek.com/print/lifestyle/content/mar2010/bw20100311_624208.htm.

88. http://www.guardian.co.uk/business/2009/oct/05/financial-job-losses-cbi.

89. http://www.guardian.co.uk/business/2009/oct/05/financial-job-losses-cbi.

90. Source: General Election 2010: Tories' public sector savings 'could cost 40,000 jobs'.

91. http://www.guardian.co.uk/commentisfree/2009/jul/15/rebalancing-economy-unemployment-figures.

92. 'La grogne sociale monte discrètement', *Le Monde*, 16 April 2010.

93. Faillites : une année record en Belgique, 5 April 2010, http://www.lalibre.be/economie/actualite/article/580325/faillites-une-annee-record-en-belgique.html.

94. http://www.rtbf.be/info/belgique/politique/la-fgtb-manifestera-vendredi-a-bruxelles.

95. On Caterpillar job cuts in August 2010 – 4,000 blue collar workers, 7,500 white collar and 8,000 temporary workers, see http://www.lavenir.net/article/detail.aspx?articleid=244037 On the trade union FGTB position see http://www.econosoc.be/files/memorandumFGTB-rw.pdf.

96. 'Global trade union network established at Caterpillar', http://www.imfmetal. org/index.cfm?c=22885&l=2.

97. http://www.liberation.fr/economie/0101619029-deux-nouveaux-suicides-chez-france-telecom.

98. 'Commercio: in un anno 20.000 negozi in meno', La Repubblica, 20 gennaio 2010, http://www.repubblica.it/economia/2010/01/20/news/meno_negozi-2014542/.

99. http://www.repubblica.it/cronaca/2010/03/28/news/suicidi-confindustria-2959194/index.html?ref=search.

100. 'Un paysan français se suicide chaque jour', 27 April, http://www.lefigaro.fr/ actualite-france/2010/04/26/01016-20100426ARTFIG00654-un-paysan-francais-se-suicide-chaque-jour-.php.

101. 'Le Coopérateur Agricole', July–August 2010, Vol 39, No 6, on http://www. lacoop.coop/cooperateur/articles/2006/09/p26.asp.

102. Doran, Kathryn Hopkins and David Gow, *The Observer*, Sunday 26 April 2009, http://www.guardian.co.uk/business/2009/apr/26/unions-direct-action-employment.

103. Sources on the crisis' impact on China and China's measures:

    1 'How the bubble burst – and why 10 bourses have bucked the downturn", David Teather, *The Guardian*, 5 August 2008, http://www.guardian.co.uk/business/2008/ aug/05/stockmarkets.creditcrunch. Impact on China's stockmarket;

    2 'Loans path eases for China s farmers' by Olivia Chung 30 May 2008, http:// www.atimes.com/atimes/China_Business/lC21Cb01.html, on rural credit and Agricultural Bank of China restructuring;

    3 'Beijing Bank Bailout May Help Farmers', Tschang, correspondent in BusinessWeek's Beijing bureau., http://www.chinaeconomicreview.com/ partnercontent/info/Beijing_Bank_Bailout_May_Help_Farmers.html;

    4 'How the financial crisis is changing China', by Geoff Dyer, 22 October 2008, http://www.ft.com/cms/s/0/e5d48044-a04c-11dd-80a0-000077b07658,dwp_ uuid=9c33700c-4c86-11da-89df-0000779e2340.html;

    5 'China pushes SDR as global super-currency', 23 March 2009, Reuters, http:// www.reuters.com/article/marketsNews/idINPEK18455820090323?rpc=44& pageNumber=1&virtualBrandChannel=0;

    6 'Government revealed 4-trillion yuan stimulus package, CITIC Pacific will be bailed out by its parent company CITIC Group, both PPI and CPI declined in October', 10 to 14 November 2008, *Caijing Magazine*, http://english.caijing. com.cn/2008-11-14/110028661.html;

    7 'Financial crisis China's factories try to weather the economic storm'; December 2008, http://www.chinaeconomicreview.com/cer/2008_12/ Chinas_factories_try_to_weather_the_economic_storm.html;

    8 'Labor Lawsuits in China Rise as Factory Closings Continue', Associated Press, http://online.wsj.com/article/SB123610779112521363.html, Researchers Crissie Ding in Yiwu and Liu Liu in Beijing contributed to this report;

    9 'In China, Despair Mounting Among Migrant Workers', by Ariana Eunjung Cha, Washington Post Foreign Service, 4 March 2009; A10, *Washington Post*, http://www.washingtonpost.com/wp-dyn/content/article/2009/03/03/ AR2009030303287.html;

    10 'Asian economies feel the pull of protectionism', by Jamil Anderlini in Beijing, 24 June 2009, *Financial Times*, http://www.ft.com/cms/s/0/

8f5898d8-6057-11de-a09b-00144feabdc0.html. On tax rebates raised for Chinese exporters and fears of the 'American buy' clause by the US;

11 'China and the global financial crisis: implications for the United States', Wayne M.Morrison, CRS Report for Congress, 9 February 2009, U.S. Congressional Research Service, www.crs.gov. On the impact of the crisis on China; the latter's contribution to world economic growth and a mention to 20 million migrant workers (p. 1);

12 'China and the Global Crisis, The Trillion Dollar Club', Nicholas R. Lardy, 10 March 2009 Senior Fellow Peterson Institute for International Economics, Washington, DC. The crisis' impact on China in tables and figures, PDF;

13 'Southern China to shed millions of jobs as economic crisis bites', 23 October 2008 AFP http://afp.google.com/article/ALeqM5hc2rYiyODxC0j7fWnn6maL 2W0Rcg.

104. 'Le commerce mondial n'avait pas connu un niveau aussi bas depuis 1945', 24 February 2010 Le Monde and AFP.

105. 'The Great Depression in the 1930s showed that protectionism in the face of a global crisis can deepen and lengthen a crisis. While WTO members have an unchallenged right to use contingency measures that are consistent with WTO rules, at a time of global crisis the proliferation of such measures among trading partners would have adverse economic effects with few of the positive offsetting effects that are invoked to justify such measures', 2009 WTO Trade Report, p. 159, http://www.wto.org/english/res_e/booksp_e/anrep_e/world_trade_report09_e.pdf.

106. Supachai Panitchpakdi's statement, 4 May, 2009, 'Investment, Enterprise and Development Commission', UNCTAD World Investment Prospects Survey 2009–2011 http://www.unctad.org//Templates/webflyer.asp?docid=11479&intlte mID=3549&lang=1. See also 'Crisis slows North-to-South Investment', September 2009, http://ipsnews.net/columns.asp?idnews=48636.

107. McKinsey Global Institute, 'Mapping global capital, entering a new era', http://mckinsey.com/mg/publications/gcm_sixth_annual_report/slideshow.

108. Declaration (under the heading 'An Open Global Economy') G20 Summit Declaration, 'A Framework for Strong, Sustainable, and Balanced Growth', Pittsburgh, 25 September 2009.

109. G20 Summit Declaration, 'A Framework for Strong, Sustainable, and Balanced Growth', Pittsburgh, 25 September 2009.

110. 'Investment, Enterprise and Development Commission', S. Panitchpakdi's state-ment, 4 May, 2009, UNCTAD World Investment Prospects Survey 2009–2011, http://www.unctad.org//Templates/webflyer.asp?docid=11479&intItemID=3549 &lang=1.

111. http://www.guardian.co.uk/business/2010/jan/01/us-bails-out-gmac-general-motors, 1 January 2010, 'US bails out General Motors-related company GMAC with further $3.8bn'.

112. 'Les conditions d'une vraie reprise ne sont pas réunies', Le Monde; 12 February 2010.

113. 'L'économie française a rétréci de 2,2% en 2009, la plus importante baisse depuis l'après-guerre', 12 February 2010, AP, http://fr.news.yahoo.com/3/20100212/tbs-france-croissance-2009-synthese-50976bf.html.

114. In 2009, French GDP fell only by 2.2%, the worst year since the WWII, according to the National Statistical Institute INSEE. due to lower internal demand (minus

0.6 point), lower stocks (minus 1.4 point) and declining foreign trade (minus 0.2 point). Good news were due mainly to stocks and secondly to car consumption sustained by government temporary 2009 subsidies. http://www.lefigaro.fr/conjoncture/2010/02/13/04016-20100213ARTFIG00188-la-croissance-francaise-resiste-mieux-que-celle-de-ses-voisins-.php.

115. http://www.lemonde.fr/economie/article/2010/02/19/le-benefice-net-de-carrefour-en-chute-de-74-en-2009_1308284_3234.htm.

116. 'Imprese, crisi avvertita di più nel Nord-Ovest e nel Centro', http://www.repubblica.it/economia/2009/12/27/news/imprese_crisi_avvertita_di_piu_nel_nord-ovest_e_nel_centro-1820670/.

117. Rabobank, monthly update Germany, 3 August 2010, http://overons.rabobank.com/content/images/cbge-2010-08-EN_tcm64-124605.pdf.

118. 'Italian deficit nearly doubles as GDP shrinks', in 2 March, 2010, http://www.smh.com.au/business/world-business/italian-deficit-nearly-doubles-as-gdp-shrinks-20100302-pdww.html. Also http://fr.news.yahoo.com/4/20100212/tbs-italie-pib-7318940.html.

119. http://www.repubblica.it/economia/2010/01/12/news/default_bond_societari-1918062/.

120. http://www.repubblica.it/economia/2010/01/19/news/bini_smaghi_crescita-2001188/.

121. Joseph E. Stiglitz , 'Towards a new global economic compact, principles for addressing the current global financial crisis and beyond', address to the United Nations, http://www.un.org/ga/president/63/commission/principles_current_global_fcrisis.pdf.

122. 'Mexico Expomanagement 2009', presentation at a conference press, *Periódico La Jornada*, 19 November 2009, p. 24, www.jornada.unam.mx/2009/11/19/index.php?section=economia&article=024n1eco.

123. 'Money trickles north as Mexicans help relatives', by Marc Lacey, *New York Times*, 15 November, 2009, 'At one small bank in Chiapas that used to see money flowing in from the United States, more money is going out than coming in. "I'd say every month 50,000 pesos are sent from here to there," said Edith Ramírez Gonzalez, a sales executive at Banco Azteca in San Cristóbal de las Casas. "And from there, we'd receive about 30,000 pesos." Fifty thousand pesos is $3,840. With nearly half its population living in poverty, Mexico is not well placed to prop up struggling citizens abroad. Mexico could lose as many as 735,000 jobs this year and its economy may decline 7.5 per cent, government economists predict, making the country one of the worst affected by the global recession', http://www.nytimes.com/2009/11/16/world/americas/16mexico.html.

124. Denmark's new Development Aid Minister Søren Pind wants to cut back on aid recipient countries, http://politiken.dk/newsinenglish/article928560.ece For the Netherlands, http://www.nrc.nl/international/opinion/article2463024.ece/An_imminent_revolution_in_Dutch_foreign_aid.

125. 0.7 refers to the repeated commitment of the world's governments to commit 0.7% of rich-countries' gross national product (GNP) to Official Development Assistance. First pledged 35 years ago in a 1970 General Assembly Resolution, the 0.7 target has been affirmed in many international agreements over the years, including the March 2002 International Conference on Financing for Development in Monterrey, Mexico and at the World Summit on Sustainable Development held in Johannesburg later that year. In Paragraph 42 of the Monterrey Consensus, world leaders reiterated their commitment, stating that 'we urge developed countries that

have not done so to make concrete efforts towards the target of 0.7 percent of gross national product (GNP) as ODA to developing countries'. In: 'What is the 0.7% target?' http://www.unmillenniumproject.org/press/07.htm.

126. Three reports provide a good view of the situation: UNIDO's Machiko Nissante 2010, 'The global financial crisis and the developing world: Transmission channels and fall-outs for industrial development', Vienna, http://www.unido.org/fileadmin/user_media/Publications/RSF_DPR/WP062009_Ebook.pdf. For Africa, see UNECA March 2009, 'Africa and the global financial crisis: towards a "just bargain" at the G20 summit', a background paper for the 2 April, 2009 G20 Summit in London http://www.uneca.org/trid/financing/crisis/ECA%20G20%20Paper.pdf. And for the least developing countries, landlocked developed countries and small islands, see UN-OHRLLS June 2009 John Serieux report 'The impact fo the global financial and economic crises on the development prospects of the landlocked developing countries', http://www.unohrlls.org/UserFiles/File/LLDC%20Documents/LLDCs%20and%20the%20Crises%20-%20UNOHRLLS%20%5BJune%202009%5D.pdf.

127. Martin Khor, 'Six key issues in the UN conference on economic crisis', South Centre Bulletin Reflections and Insights Issue 38, 7 July 2009.

128. SDRs are the the monetary unit of the reserve assets of the International Monetary Fund (IMF).

129. BBC news 'Poor countries get "$1 trillion"', http://news.bbc.co.uk/2/hi/business/7445489.stm.

130. This is not to defend those who continue to act as if nothing happened, like Fortis' feast on 10 October in Monaco, and AIG's 5-star hotel massages for directors, after being saved with public money.

131 On 13 October 2008, the then UK Prime Minister Gordon Brown called for a 'new Bretton Woods' international agreement. Source: 13 Oct 2008, 'Financial Crisis: Gordon Brown calls for "new Bretton Woods"', by Robert Winnett, Deputy Political Editor, http://www.telegraph.co.uk/finance/financetopics/financialcrisis/3189517/Financial-Crisis-Gordon-Brown-calls-for-new-Bretton-Woods.html

On 13 October, the European Union leaders met in Paris to coordinate their actions. The 13 October agreement had four parts: (1) Measures for banks to obtain new capital by guaranteeing the banks' issuance of new medium-term debt; (2) banks' recapitalization; (3) a pledge by governments to buy preferred shares; and (4) an urgent EU request to the IASB to relax the mark-to-market accounting rules. The EU agreement adopted many of the measures taken by the United States a few days previously. The Paris meeting of the 15 eurozone countries was in fact the first formal meeting since the launch of the Euro in 1999. Source: Financial Crisis Timeline, Page 3, July–December 2008, University of Iowa Centre for International Finance & Development, Jason Cox and Laurie Glapa, Last updated: July 1, 2009. http://www.uiowa.edu/ifdebook/timeline/timeline3.shtml.

132. de la Dehesa, G., 2009, p. 22.

133. Fontaine, 2008.

134. http://business.timesonline.co.uk/tol/business/industry_sectors/banking_and_finance/article7034454.ece.

135. http://www.ustreas.gov/press/releases/tg65.htm and http://www.ustreas.gov/press/releases/reports/ppip_fact_sheet.pdf.

136. 'SEC vows to launch more actions over crisis', 27 August 2010, *Financial Times*, p. 1.

137. 17 October 2008, UBS and Credit Suisse secure $70bn, http://business.timesonline.co.uk/tol/business/industry_sectors/banking_and_finance/article4959175.ece.

138. http://www.sbpost.ie/commentandanalysis/nama-is-highway-robbery-44915.html and http://www.ifss2009.com/Leading%20economists%20disagree%20over%20NAMA%2021.10.09.pdf.

139. http://www.nrc.nl/international/opinion/article2457326.ece/Iceland_needs_international_debt_management.

140. Jakob von Weizsäcker and David Saha, 2009, 'Estimating the size of the European stimulus packages', Policy Contributions 276, Bruegel, Briefing Paper for the Annual Meeting of the Committee on Economic and Monetary Affairs with the National Parliaments on 11–12 February 2009 at the European Parliament in Brussels.

141. 'China, worried by slowing growth and widespread reports of factory closures, is to step up support for manufacturers by raising the export tax rebates paid on more than 3,700 types of goods... it was also decided... to scrap duties on some steel products, chemicals and grain exports', in tax rebates raised for Chinese exporters, 12 November, 2008, http://www.ft.com/cms/s/0/821df3c4-b0db-11dd-8915-0000779fd18c.html.

142. China had a nearly 30% increase in foreign capital investment between July 2009 and July 2010, and 6.9 bill US$ only for July 2010, according to the Ministry of Commerce. Further, tertiary industry investment grew year on year by 37,6% with 26,31 bill US$, http://english.cntv.cn/program/bizasia/20100820/104489.shtml.

143. On the use of yuan in cross-border trade, http://www.china-briefing.com/news/2010/06/29/china-expands-pilot-areas-for-rmb-settlement-of-cross-border-trade-transactions.htm.On liberalizing the use of foreign capital, http://www.china-briefing.com/news/2010/08/23/china-encourages-further-use-of-foreign-capital.htm. On investing freely abroad http://www.china-briefing.com/news/2010/08/25/pilot-program-allows-enterprises-to-deposit-export-revenues-overseas.html.

144. Banks sell switch to renminbi payments for trade with China, 27 August 2010, *Financial Times*, p. 1.

145. Measures included (a) the reduction of down payment on housing, tax cuts and exemptions for home buyers; (b) a land reform act allowing farmers to earn money by subletting, leasing, or transferring the rights of their farmland to others, even factories; (c) rural villages were allowed to organize their own credit cooperatives to finance farmers; (d) there was a new government subsidy of 13% of the retail price for household appliances; (e) the extension of rural credit after the restructuring the Agricultural Bank of China, as the other state-owned banks now listed overseas and in Shanghai had closed branches in the countryside, leaving a vacuum in financial services. The Agricultural Bank had to shed its bad loans and to be recapitalized. ABC's nonperforming loan ratio was to fall from 23.5% at the end of 2007 to only 4.1%. On 21 October ,2008, Beijing approved the restructuring plan and the biggest bailout ever for a Chinese bank; (f) the government procurement price for all grain products rose by 13 %, to 120 billion Yuan in 2009 compared to 102.9 billion Yuan in 2008.

146. See discussions about US economic stimulus plans on http://bx.businessweek.com/us-economic-stimulus/.

147. Reinhart and Rogoff, 2010.

148. Carmen M. Reinhart and Kenneth S. Rogoff, 7 January 2010, pp. 23 and 24.

149. Rabobank, monthly update Germany, 3 August 2010, http://overons.rabobank. com/content/images/cbge-2010-08-EN_tcm64-124605.pdf.

150. UN World Economic and Social Survey 2010: 'a new global reserve system could be created, one that no longer relies on the United States dollar as the single major reserve currency. The dollar has proved not to be a stable store of value, which is a requisite for a stable reserve currency', overview, p. XXII, http:// www.un.org/esa/policy/wess/wess2010files/wess2010.pdf. The IMF proposed: 'A global currency, bancor, issued by a global central bank (see Supplement 1, section V) would be designed as a stable store of value that is not tied exclusively to the conditions of any particular economy. As trade and finance continue to grow rapidly and global integration increases, the importance of this broader perspective is expected to continue growing'. The proposal appeared in the document 'Reserve Accumulation and International Monetary Stability' prepared by the Strategy, Policy and Review Department, in collaboration with the Finance, Legal, Monetary and Capital Markets, Research and Statistics Departments, and consultation with the Area Departments, in April 13 2010, http://www.imf.org/ external/np/pp/eng/2010/041310.pdf.

151. 'Uh-oh. The ECB Is Buying Bonds Again', 23 August 2010, http://blogs.wsj.com/ marketbeat/2010/08/23/uh-oh-the-ecb-is-buying-bonds-again/.

152. 'We don't classify the United Kingdom (whose long-term sovereign note is AAA, but with a negative perspective) among the least risky banking systems of the world', UK's AAA credit rating in danger, S&P, Monday, 29 March 2010, http:// www.guardian.co.uk/business/2010/mar/29/uk-aaa-credit-rating-warning.

153. 'L'Europe sommée d'assainir au plus vite ses banques', *Le Monde*, 12 June 2009.

154. 'Greece's spending cuts are making debt crisis worse, says national bank', 22 March 2010, http://www.guardian.co.uk/business/2010/mar/22/greek-cuts-make-debt-crisis-worse.

155. On February 11th, at an informal European Council, Germany promised to support Greece if need be, were the latter to adopt an austerity package (which indeed happened). Two days later, Merkel renounced the promise and added that Greece could even be excluded from the Eurozone. Why was Merkel stuck? The state election of North Rhine-Westphalia can install a new majority in Germany's lower parliamentary house. Business leaders want the CDU coalition to retain power in order to further fiscal consolidation and austerity measures, necessary for their competitiveness. and they are firmly opposed to helping Greece. Merkel even said that the option of expelling a member of the Eurozone could be envisaged. In Juncker's opinion, this would necessarily need a counterpart clause allowing a voluntary exit option. In his view, Merkel's idea would eventually destabilize the currency zone. But way before the 2010 state election, Merkel kept changing tack. On 5th October 2008, she opposed a European plan to help banks because in her view German banks were not affected. With the fall of Real Hypo Estate, one week later, she allowed the Eurogroup summit to adopt a European plan. She was also against a European plan to relaunch the European economy, changing position once Germany began to suffer, three weeks later. She also opposed the French plan to help the European automobile sector, leading to the adoption of various European countries, including her own country, of national uncoordinated plans to promote the purchase of new cars.

156. 'A paralyzing state election, the man who could take down Merkel', *Der Spiegel*, http://www.spiegel.de/international/germany/0,1518,675759,00.html 02/05/2010.

157. More than €3bn (£2.6bn) of deposits held by Greek households and companies left the country in February, while in January about €5bn of deposits were moved out, according to the latest figures available from the Bank of Greece. Switzerland, the UK and Cyprus have been the largest recipients of the money, with the wealthiest Greeks looking to move their deposits to Swiss bank accounts to escape the more punitive tax measures many fear will be introduced in the wake of the country's economic crisis, http://www.telegraph.co.uk/news/worldnews/Europe/greece/7557213/Greek-banks-hit-by-wealthy-citizens-moving-their-money-offshore.html Greek banks hit by wealthy citizens moving their money offshore 05 Apr 2010.

158. Juncker EPRef-68929 on 22/03/2010 – live recording of European Parliament Committee on Economic and Monetary Affairs, exchange of views with Jean-Claude Juncker, President of the Eurogroup, http://ec.Europa.eu/avservices/player/streaming.cfm?type=ebsplus&sid=157252.

159. http://www.euractiv.com/en/future-eu/opinion-stability-growth-pact-focus-public-debt/article-134932.

160. Charles Wyplosz, professor of economics at the Graduate Institute of International Studies in Geneva, 'How to rebuild the stability pact',1 February 2005, http://www.ft.com/cms/s/0/b20bfa32-73f8-11d9-b705-00000e2511c8.html.

161. http://www.nytimes.com/interactive/2010/04/06/business/global/European-debt-map.html?ref=global.

162. http://www.lefigaro.fr/conjoncture/2010/03/23/04016-20100323ARTFIG00418-les-etats-unis-inquiets-a-propos-de-la-grece-.php.

163. Expectations of adjustment policies and lower consumption, impacted on largely indebted large enterprises, like the construction group Ferrovial, 'L'angoisse gagne les marchés boursiers', *Le Monde*,6 February 2010.

164. http://www.project-syndicate.org/commentary/eijffinger2/English 2010-02-08.

165. Susan Strange. 1996.

166. Richard Wilkinson and Kate Pickett, 2010.

167. Bosworth and Flaaen, 2009: pp. 2–3.

168. http://business.timesonline.co.uk/tol/business/industry_sectors/banking_and_finance/article7034454.ece.

169. lemonde.fr/economie/article/2010/01/20/en-cedant-ses-assurances-vie-l-americain-aig-poursuit-sa-cure-d-amaigrissement.

170. 'Waterland to acquire MetLife', 20 April 2010, Taiwan, http://www.taipeitimes.com/News/biz/archives/2010/04/20/2003471035.

171. Testimony of Michael W. Masters, Managing Member Portfolio Manager of Masters Capital Management, LLC before the Committee on Homeland Security and Governmental Affairs of the United States Senate: May 20 2008 hsgac.senate.gov/public/_file052008Masters.pdf.

172. 'An EIS investment can be used to defer CGT liabilities as follows. Suppose you made a £20,000 profit by selling shares, and owe the Revenue £3,600 in CGT. If you put the £20,000 into an EIS, you will not need to hand over the £3,600 until you sell your investment in the EIS, when you may have more of your annual CGT allowance available', http://uk.biz.yahoo.com/12032010/399/tax-benefits-draw-investors-start-ups.html Tax benefits draw investors to start-ups 20100312.

173. Christian Gomez, 2008, 'Pour une réforme radicale du système bancaire', *LeTemps, Economie & Finance*, 11 October 2008.

174. See Shore, B.: *EU finance ministers agree new hedge fund curbs*, 19 October 2010, BBC News, Brussels http://www.bbc.co.uk/news/business-11577887, and rapporteur Paul Gauzès' speech on 10 November at European Parliament http://www.

europarl.europa.eu/sides/getDoc.do?type=CRE&reference=20101110&secondRef=ITEM-016&format=XML&language=EN, and MEP Jean-Luc Mélanchon's comments http://www.europarl.europa.eu/sides/getDoc.do?type=CRE&reference=20101111&secondRef=ITEM-009&format=XML&language=EN.

175. 'Equity investors move into overseas funds', 20100312http://uk.biz.yahoo.com/12032010/399/equity-investors-move-overseas-funds.html.

176. http://www.telegraph.co.uk/finance/newsbysector/banksandfinance/4298973/GLG-buys-rival-as-funds-consolidate.html, 20 Jan 2009.

177. http://www.telegraph.co.uk/finance/newsbysector/banksandfinance/5759938/Hedge-funds-post-best-monthly-performance-for-10-years.html.

178. 'Groups turn to private placement for funding', 24 August 2010, *New York Times*, p. 11.

179. http://uk.biz.yahoo.com/12032010/325/uk-consider-state-investment-fund-mandelson.html.

180. A counter-party (sometimes contraparty) is a legal and financial term, meaning a party to a contract. Also within financial services, counterparty can refer to brokers, investment banks, and other securities dealers that serve as the contracting party when completing 'over the counter' securities transactions. http://en.wikipedia.org/wiki/Counterparty.

181. 'Countercyclical capital buffer proposal – consultative document', July 2010, draft for comments by September 2010, http://www.bis.org/publ/bcbs172.pdf.

182. 'Light touch', 24 September 2010, The Economist Intelligence Unit, http://gfs.eiu.com/Article.aspx?articleType=wif&articleId=315.

183. 'Dodd-Frank Bill's Volcker rule a win for big banks', 25 June 2010, http://www.theatlantic.com/business/archive/2010/06/dodd-frank-bills-volcker-rule-a-win-for-big-banks/58747/, Rules take effect 15 months to two years after a law is passed, banks would have two years to comply, with three one-year extensions after that and could seek another five years for 'illiquid' funds such as private equity or real estate.

184. 'Upbeat jobs data overshadowed by FED speech', 27 August 2010, *Financial Times*, p. 24.

185. Bank of International Settlements, 28 June 2010, 22009-2010 Annual Report, http://www.bis.org/publ/arpdf/ar2010e.htm.

186. 'Banks told to hoard up to £130bn in case of crisis: G20 hammers out deal to avoid future bail-outs', 29 June 2010, http://www.dailymail.co.uk/news/article-1290152/G20-SUMMIT-Banks-told-hoard-130bn-case-crisis.html.

187. Available on the website of ECLAC (Economic Commission for Latin America and the Caribbean) http://www.eclac.cl/cgi-bin/getProd.asp?xml=/prensa/noticias/comunicados/1/39481/P39481.xml&xsl=/prensa/tpl/p6f.xsl&base=/tpl/top-bottom.xsl.

188. http://www.itamaraty.gov.br/sala-de-imprensa/notas-a-imprensa/xxxiiio-periodo-de-sessoes-da-cepal-2013-brasilia-30-de-maio-a-1o-de-junho-de-2010-1.

2   Causes and Mechanisms

1. Bosworth, B. and A. Flaaen 2009.

2. Taleb, 2007.

3. We found the following to be particularly useful: Gramlich (2007), Baily and Litan (2008), Gorton (2008), and Hatzius *et al.* (2008).

4. Shiller, R., 2001, pp.5–6, see Figure 1.1.

5. Forrester Research, Net Investing Goes Mainstream, 1999, http://www.forrester. com/ER/Research/Report/Analysis/0,1338,5876,FF.html.
6. US Securities and Exchange Commission, Special Study 'On-Line Brokerage: Keeping Apace of Cyberspace', http://www.sec.gov/news/studies/cyberspace.htm.
7. 'Quick recovery? Wall Street is losing hope', *New York Times*, 1–2 September 2001, pp. 1 and 5.
8. Baker, Dean. 2002, 'The run-up in house prices: is it real or is it another bubble?', Washington, DC: Center for Economic and Policy Research http://www.cepr. net/index.php/publications/reports/the-run-up-in-home-prices-isit-real-or-is-it-another-bubble/.
9. Shiller, 2001, p. 4.
10. Dirk Müller is nicknamed 'Mister DAX' and works for broker ICF in Frankfurt. He published 'Crashkurs' and appears regularly on German media.
11. In 'The Chinese Literati', Weber talks of patrimonial bureaucratic structures connected to 'interventions (that) were monopolistically or financially determined, and ofter they were quite incisive. They were partly mercantilist regulations and partly in the nature of regulations of status stratification... made for bureaucratic meddling in everything', pp. 440 and 441 in Gerth and Wright Mills, 1991. Although the concept of patrimonialism has been criticized as vague, Weber used it in contraposition to 'citizenry or professional bureaucracy', see John Love, 'Max Weber's Orient', pp. 196–197 in Turner, 2000.
12. Arendt, H., 2006: p.278.
13. Veblen, T., 1899.
14. Alan Greenspan's Financial Crisis Inquiry Commission Testimony, http://www. fcic.gov/hearings/pdfs/2010-0407-Greenspan.pdf.
15. Raines and Leathers, 2008, pp. 35–7.
16. Greenspan, in Raines and Leathers 2008, p. 19.
17. R. Christopher Whalen, March 2008, 'The subprime crisis, cause, effect and consequences', in Policy Brief 4, Networks financial institute, Indiana University.
18. Greenspan, A., 19 September 1996.
19. John B.Taylor, 2008; and United Nations, 2009.
20. Chart 3 produced by staff at the International Monetary Fund (IMF) in 2005, showing that the global savings rate – world savings as a fraction of world GDP – was very low. in the 2002–04 period, especially when compared with the 1970s and 1980s.
21. European Central Bank President Jean Claude Trichet, Venice, 9 October 2009, 'The crisis and its lessons', lecture at the University of Venice.
22. Raines and Leathers, 2008, pp. 26–7.
23. In 2002, there was an over-supply of rental housing, with vacancy rates rising to near record levels beyond 9.0 per cent, compared to 7.5 per cent in the mid-90s. The record vacancy rates switched from the rental side to ownership units in 2006. By the fourth quarter of 2006, the vacancy rate on ownership units was almost 50 per cent above its prior peak. Fourth quarter of 2007 is available at http://www.census.gov/hhes/www/housing/hvs/qtr407/q407press.pdf, cited by Dean Baker, Real-world economics review no. 46, 'The housing bubble and the financial crisis', http://www.paecon.net/PAEReview/issue46/Baker46.pdf, p. 74.
24. Cassidy John, 2009, 'How markets fail: the logic of economic calamities', (New York: Farrar, Straus and Giroux, 2009). See also the article 'What was really behind last year's market crash?', in which John Cassidy explains how salary incentives led to a culture that helped trigger the financial crisis, published in *The Guardian* on 25 November 2009, p. 4 of section G2, UK.

25. Casper van Ewijk and Coen Teulings, 2009, 'The Grote Recessie, het Centraal Planbureau over de kredietcrisi', The Hague, Netherlands, (in English: The Great Recession: CPB about the credit crisis) http://www.degroterecessie.nl.

26. Loan originations increased from $14 billion in 2002 to $60 billion in 2006. At the same time, there was an 'alarming and steady increase in early payment default'. There were increasing amounts of loan 'kickouts' for a variety of reasons. Over $800 million in loans from 2004 and 2006 were rejected by investors simply because of missing documentation, New Century did not have adequate internal controls. New Century's management repeatedly exerted concerted and continued pressure on KPMG engagement teams. The New Century controller, a former KPMG manager, avoided producing requested documents by emailing the audit engagement partner a response which said that he was not a 'training center'.

27. VanDenburgh, William M. and Harmelink, Philip J., 'Accounting implications of the subprime meltdown', *The CPA Journal*, 1 December 2008, http://www.allbusiness.com/trends-events/audits/11729624-1.html.

28. 'A lender failed. did its auditor?' 13 April 2008, http://www.nytimes.com/2008/04/13/business/13audit.html?pagewanted=4.

29. European Central Bank President Jean Claude Trichet, speech given in Venice on 9 October 2009.

30. Anna Katherine Barnett-Hart, 2009.

31. http://www.spiegel.de/international/business/0,1518,692007,00.html#ref=nlint.

32. 'Rating agency data aided Wall Street in deal', Gretchen Morgenson and Louise Stor, April 23 2010, http://www.nytimes.com/2010/04/24/business/24rating.html?ref=business.

33. Bank of International Settlements, 'Triennial and semi-annual surveys on positions in global over-the-counter derivatives markets as of the end of June, 2007', Table A available at http://www.bis.org/publ/otc_hy0711.pdf?noframes=1].

34. John B.Taylor, 2008, 'The financial crisis and the policy responses, an empirical analysis of what went wrong'. Also see *World Economic Situation and Prospects 2010, Global outlook*, United Nations, New York, 2009.

35. Bancel interview.

36. Lord Mandelson, Mansion House Speech, 1 March 2010, http://www.allbusiness.com/economy-economic-indicators/economic-conditions-recession/14018387-1.html.

37. Boyer and Drache, 1996.

38. Chenais, 1996.

39. Dockès, P., 'Croissance, adaptation ou rupture?' in Dockès and Lorenzi, 2009, pp. 49–71.

40. 'The IMF can work to try to ensure that financial and current account imbalances are addressed rather than ignored – and that they are addressed by policies that are not destructive of global prosperity', Nouriel Roubini and Brad Setser, October 2005 updated September 2006, 'The future of the IMF', paper for the 2007 World Economic Forum http://www.weforum.org/pdf/initiatives/IMCP_RoubiniSetser.pdf. Russian private actors borrowed at least 490 billion dollars from abroad and spent it handsomely. Government support gave them contracts, subsidies and tax breaks, while local banks became good partners. Foreign banks and investors were happy. Corruption and other ills were unheard of. Until it blew up. Eventually, the government had to 'squeeze at least some of its oligarchs'. In 1997, Indonesia and Thailand families fought to see who could save their banks.

If the government breaks the relationship with some oligarchs, the regime may fall. In Indonesia, it led to the fall of the Suharto regime. According to Simon Johnson, the countries got into trouble because their powerful elites took on too much debt. Credit was given to them since they were tightly knit and supported by their governments. And the fact is, as with the origin of Argentina's debt in 1982, or Russia's in 1998, someone at the government will suddenly move that private debt into the state sphere and place it on the shoulders of the ignorant citizens. The guess is that governments will save their debt collection if need be.

41. Dockès Pierre, in Dockès and Lorenzi 2009, pp. 65–9.
42. Philippe Douroux, 10 February 2010, 'La crise financière en 4 ou 5 chiffres, 2 temps et 3 mouvements', http://blog.slate.fr/phdx/2010/02/10/la-crise-financiere-en-4-chiffres-2-temps-et-trois-mouvements.
43. Raines and Leathers, 2008 , p. 35.
44. Greenspan, 2002a, December.
45. Greenspan, 1999, in Raines and Leathers, 2008, p. 36.
46. Greenspan, 2002b, November.
47. Bernanke, B.S., July 2003.
48. Raines and Leathers, 2008, p. 33.
49. Papadimitriou, *et al.* 2002 in Raines and Leathers, 2008, p. 37.
50. Raines and Leathers, 2008, p. 19.
51. Bush, M.L., 2000 and Fontaine, 2008.
52. Atkins, Charles and Susan Lund, March 2009, 'The economic impact of increased US savings', The McKinsey Quarterly, Economic Studies, McKinsey Global Institute, http://www.mckinseyquarterly.com/The_economic_impact_of_increased_US_savings_2327.
53. Greenspan, Alan and James Kennedy, March 2007, p. 2.
54. Krugman, 2008, pp.158–62.
55. 'About £1bn of debt from the first two years of the scheme will probably never be recouped', http://uk.news.yahoo.com/25042006/140/families-hit-tax-credit-fiasco.html.
56. Mauss, 1923–4.
57. For Mauss, social exchange could not be isolated from values that provided overall social cohesion. Contrary to some who think that Mauss criticized all use of money, Mauss was rather against systems based on patrimonialism, speculation and usury. His phrase 'personal security that the noble guaranteed' bears no relation to any monetary payment.
58. Mauss, 1923–4.
59. Langlois, 2006.
60. Bauman, Z. *Consuming Life* (Cambridge: Polity. 2007)
61. Moati, 2001.
62. Baudrillard, 2006.
63. Veblen, [1899] 2005.
64. Galbraith, 1958.
65. See Bourdieu 1977 and 1992.
66. Langlois, 2006, p. 37.
67. Mundis, 1990.
68. Sanctions include taxes on products which cause obesity or legal claims for monetary compensation against firms selling harmful products. Studies on the traceability of products and the organized action of groups of consumers have

had interesting developments, heightening concerns related to interconnectedness, in the environmental, social and financial spheres. These actions stimulate the evolution of regulation as well as studies of legal and regulatory aspects of consumption.

69. McKinsey Charles Atkins and Susan Lund, March 2009, 'The economic impact of increased US savings', *The McKinsey Quarterly*, Economic Studies, McKinsey Global Institute, http://www.mckinseyquarterly.com/The_economic_impact_of_increased_US_savings_2327.

70. Today China's thrifty households tuck away a quarter of their after-tax income – one of the highest saving rates in the world (National Bureau of Statistics of China Household Income and Expenditure Survey, China Statistical Yearbook, 2004. Household saving rate is measured as a percentage of household disposable income)... A McKinsey survey indicates that the top two reasons for high saving rates in China are concerns about healthcare and retirement. (Kevin P. Lane and Ian St-Maurice, 'The Chinese consumer: to spend or to save?' *The McKinsey Quarterly*, 2006, no. 1, pp. 6–8). (http://www.mckinseyquarterly.com).

71. Tsai. 2002.

72. 'Since, however, Keynes says that the liquidity trap is only a theoretical possibility, but had not happened to his knowledge; this is clearly a mistake on the part of those who used his argument to dismiss the efficacy of ever using monetary policy', in Backhouse, Roger and Bateman Bradley, W., 2006, p. 289.

73. See the interesting comparison between Japan's crisis and the recent one by Robert Madsen, in 'Comparing crises, worse and worser', in his response to Richard Katz, in *Foreign Affairs* May/June 2009, vol. 88, no. 3. Robert Madsen works at the MIT Center for International Studies, http://www.foreignaffairs.com/articles/64917/robert-madsen-richard-katz/comparing-crises.

74. Skidelsky, Robert, 2009.

75. 'The Savings and Loans bailout with US taxpayers money for $300 billion dollars, much more than if the problem had been revealed earlier', see Susan Strange, 1996, p. 144.

76. Friedman, Milton, 1971,

77. Lebonte, Marc, 'US economy in recession: similarities to and differences from the past', 5 February 2009, Congressional research service, www.crs.gov.

78. 'Nouriel Roubini sees double dip risk at over 40%', 26 August 2010, http://www.bi-me.com/main.php?id=48044&t=1&c=62&cg=4&mset=1011.

79. Krugman, Paul, 2008.

80. *Ibid.*, p. 17.

81. *Ibid.*, pp. 16–20.

82. *Ibid.* p. 70.

83. Krugman, P. (1999), 'Balance sheets, the transfer problem and financial crisis', in Isard P., Razin, A. and Rose, A. (eds) *International Finance and Financial Crises*.

84. 'Latvia: Europe's most extreme, dramatic economy', 15.02.2009, http://www.dw-world.de/dw/article/0,,4025197,00.html.

85. BIS Quarterly Review, December 2008, 'International banking and financial market developments', http://www.bis.org/publ/qtrpdf/r_qt0812.pdf.

86. Stiglitz, 2001.

87. Banque de France, 15 February 2006, http://www.banquedefrance.fr/fr/stat_conjoncture/telechar:stat_mone/edcb_presentation1.pdf, in Holbecq André-Jacques and Philippe Derudder, 2008, 'La dette publique, une affaire rentable: a qui profite le système ?', editions Yves Michel, Gap, France.

88. 1988 Nobel Prize of Economic Sciences winner, Maurice Allais, published his ideas first on12, 19 and 26 October 1998 in the French newspaper *Le Figaro* and reprinted the text in Allais, 1999.
89. Skidelsky, Robert, 2009, pp. 176–7.
90. Fontaine, 2008.
91. *Ibid.*, pp. 278–9.
92. *Ibid.*, p. 289.
93. Report by Geneviève de Gaulle-Anthonioz to the Social and Economic Council, 1995, France, cited by Jean-Michel Servet, 'Banquiers aux pieds nus, La microfinance' (Paris: Odile Jacob, 2006, p. 160), cited by Fontaine 2008, p. 312.
94. Fontaine. 2008, p. 300.
95. *Ibid.*, pp. 301.
96. *Ibid.*
97. Fischer, Irving, 1933, pp. 337–557.
98. *Ibid.*
99. Dirk H. Ehnts, 2008, 'Revisiting Keynes' general theory – lesson learned?', Faculty of Economics, University of Oldenburg, Germany November, mimeo.
100. *Ibid.*
101. Irvin, George , Research Professor at SOAS in London , 'EU growth can offset the US debt crisis', 11 September 2006, http://euobserver.com/9/22308.
102. 'The cost of maintaining ownership in the current crisis: comparisons in 20 cities', Dean Baker, Danilo Pelletiere and Hye Jin Rho, April 2008, http://www.cepr.net/documents/publications/ownrent_2008_04.pdf.
103. Strange, 1996, p. 185.
104. CAS – Centre d'analyse stratégique, 2009.
105. http://www.lejdd.fr/Economie/Actualite/Tapie-veut-prendre-le-Club-Med-73626/.
106. The International Accounting Standards Board issued IFRS 9, includes the revised set of rules dealing with the classification and measurement of financial assets.
107. Kempf, 2009, p. 18.
108. Andrew Ross Sorkin, 2009 p. 4: 'Big brokerage firms had been bolstering their bets with enormous quantities of debt. Wall Street firms had debt to capital ratios of 32 to 1'.
109. Summary debt schedule, http://www.treasurydirect.gov/govt/govt.htm.
110. Congressional Budget Office Federal Debt and the Risk of a Fiscal Crisis, July 27, 2010, Economic and Budget Issue Brief: 'Although deficits during or shortly after a recession generally hasten economic recovery, persistent deficits and continually mounting debt would have several negative economic consequences for the United States. Some of those consequences would arise gradually: A growing portion of people's savings would go to purchase government debt rather than toward investments in productive capital goods such as factories and computers; that "crowding out" of investment would lead to lower output and incomes than would otherwise occur. In addition, if the payment of interest on the extra debt was financed by imposing higher marginal tax rates, those rates would discourage work and saving and further reduce output. Rising interest costs might also force reductions in spending on important government programs. Moreover, rising debt would increasingly restrict the ability of policymakers to use fiscal policy to respond to unexpected challenges, such as economic downturns or international crises. Beyond those gradual consequences, a growing level of federal debt would also increase the probability of a sudden fiscal crisis, during which investors would lose confidence in the government's ability to

manage its budget, and the government would thereby lose its ability to borrow at affordable rates', http://www.cbo.gov/doc.cfm?index=11659.

111. 'China announced a long-awaited exchange rate reform in July 21, allowing the renminbi to appreciate by 2 per cent and linking the currency to a basket of foreign currencies instead of the US dollar alone... The renminbi has been on an upward trend against the dollar since the reform', *China Daily* 12/28/2005 p.10, http://www.chinadaily.com.cn/english/doc/2005-12/28/content_507256.htm.

112. Bernanke, 2003 in Raines and Leathers, 2008 p. 37.

113. Hyman P. Minsky, 1992 and 2008.

114. Veblen 1904; Schumpeter 1934 and 1939.

115. Joseph E. Stiglitz , 2001.

116. Bush, M.L., 2000, p. 41.

117. *Ibid*. p. 59.

118. *Ibid*.

119. Those in temporary debt bondage learnt about different life-styles before returning to their original background. They also learnt about intensive monoculture, and tended to reproduce it eventually. During the past decades, however, such crises were seen as events affecting only developing and emerging countries, from Asia to Russia, Turkey, Brazil and Argentina, to name a few.

120. Bush, M.L., 2000, p. 240, 'Bonded labour systems ... were finally phased out by ... on the other hand by ... family farms emerged seeking self-subsistence through the cultivation of a cash crop'.

3   Shifting Control *versus* Ownership

1. On financialization, for example, Dominique Plihon, 1996. On technification, for example, Jeremy Rifkin, 2001.

2. In 1994, a Brazilian economist proposed the concept of quasi-firms to define those firms whose business rationale is highly curtailed by a low degree of autonomy (Oliveira, 1994). Quasi-firms do not belong to the core business or the core interests. They are peripheral to the main strategy, 'part of the global resources that the primary firm disposes of to finance its [final] strategy' (Oliveira, 1994: 38).Oliveira bases his notion on 'specially those [obstacles] that impede the full and autonomous exercise of the process of capital accumulation' (Oliveira, 1994: 35). Those of financial nature would impede the use of profits and/or capture resources in order to augment the business' assets and sale. The firm as a locus of internal capital accumulation would be overall limited. From a different context, we can observe the notion of an economic entity endangered by distant controllers, as the firm cannot exercise full autonomous capabilities.

3. Mayntz, Renate, 1998.

4. European Commission, 2001, p. 8 (footnote). Since 2000, the EU Commission had governance as one of its 4 priorities. 'Governance' was then the object of a White Book to reform the manner in which European public policy was done.

5. *Ibid*. pp. 23–34.

6. Razeen, 1995.

7. Schmitter, 2001.

8. Abbott and Snidal, 2000.

9. 'Ownership is an accredited discretionary power over an object on the ground of a conventional claim; it implies that the owner is a personal agent who takes thought for the disposal of the object owned. A personal agent is an individual,

and it is only by an eventual refinement – of the nature of a legal fiction – that any group of men is conceived to exercise a corporate discretion over objects. Ownership implies an individual owner. It is only by reflection, and by extending the scope of a concept which is already familiar, that a quasi-personal corporate discretion and control of this kind comes to be imputed to a group of persons. Corporate ownership is quasi-ownership only; it is therefore necessarily a derivative concept, and cannot have preceded the concept of individual ownership of which it is a counterfeit. It is difficult to see how an institution of ownership could have arisen in the early days of predatory life through the seizure of goods, but the case is different with the seizure of persons. The captives taken under rude conditions are chiefly women... This ownership – marriage seems to be the original both of private property and of the patriarchal household. Both of these great institutions are, accordingly, of an emulative origin'. Thorstein Veblen, 'The Beginning of Ownership', *American Journal of Sociology*, vol. 4 (1898–9), http://socserv2.socsci.mcmaster.ca/~econ/ugcm/3ll3/veblen/ownersh.

10. Fontaine, 2008.
11. In this sense, what women suffered in the past and continue to suffer in some countries is similar to today's discourses on workers' incapable of being in control of a firm.
12. Stiglitz. 2001.
13. *Ibid.*, p. 513.
14. O'Hara, 2002.
15. Veblen, 1923, pp. 430–31 and p. 445.
16. Lord Mandelson, 'One year on', 1 March 2010, Trade and Industry Dinner, Guildhall, London, http://www.bis.gov.uk/news/Speeches/mandelson-mansion-house.
17. On Weber and patrimonialism, see Gerth. and Wright Mills, 1991, pp. 298 and 440–1. Also see Love, 2000, pp. 196–7.
18. Chandler, Alfred, 1994.
19. It was this situation that gave rise to the recent International Financial Reporting Standard number three (IFRS3) on mergers and acquisitions, with the idea of aligning ownership along control. The world of accounting recognized that this was not that easy to obtain.
20. 'EU seeks to end bias among shareholders', 16 October 2005, *Financial Times*, http://www.ft.com/cms/s/0/ae17a66e-3e6f-11da-a2cb-00000e2511c8.html.
21. de Beaufort, 2006.
22. http://www.fasb.org/project/cf_phase-b.shtml.
23. http://www.fasb.org/action/aa103008.shtml.
24. Veblen, 1923.
25. Apart from Veblen institutionalist hypothesis, other main theories to explain the profit squeeze on the firm came from Marxian and radical economists. See Fred Moseley, 'The rate of profit and the future of capitalism', *Review of Radical Political Economics*, December 1997.
26. Needham, 1956.
27. Husserl, 1970; Habermas, 1971; Heidegger, 2000.
28. Severino, 2002.
29. Galimberti, 2002, p. 712.
30. Shiller, 2001.
31. Mandelbrot and Hudson, 2008.
32. Skidelsky, 2009, p. xvi.
33. Strange, 1996.

34. UK Financial Service Authority, http://www.fsa.gov.uk/pages/Library/Communication/PR/2009/037.shtml.
35. Chandler, 1994.
36. Philippe Gaud, Martin Hoesli and Andre Bender, May 10, 2004, 'Further evidence on debt-equity choice', HEC – University of Geneva and FAME – International Center for Financial Asset Management and Research Paper, no 114.
37. BVCA and PriceWaterhouseCoopers, 'A guide to private equity', June 2003.
38. Thiess Buettner and Georg Wamser, August 2009, 'Internal debt and multinational's profit shifting, empirical evidence from firm-level panel data', WP 09/18, Ifo Institute and Munich University, and the Oxford University Centre for Business Taxation.
39. Stiglitz, 2001, p. 513.
40. Watt and Galgóczi, 2009.
41. Useem, 1996.
42. *Ibid.*, p. 266.
43. 'Banking, money, and finance', in *American Decades*, 2001, Encyclopedia.com, http://www.encyclopedia.com/doc/1G2-3468303335.html.
44. *Ibid.*
45. 4 February 2010, http://www.complianceweek.com/blog/whitehouse/2010/02/04/fasb-iasb-ready-comprehensive-income-requirements/.
46. Lord Mandelson, 'One year on', 1 March 2010, Trade and Industry Dinner, Guildhall, London http://www.bis.gov.uk/news/Speeches/mandelson-mansion-house.
47. Stiglitz, 2001.
48. Blackburn, 2008.
49. www.dgtpe.minefi.gouv.fr/TRESOR_ECO/tresoreco.htm. Source alternatives, *economiques*, no, 288, February 2010 p. 60.
50. Baker and Wurgler, 2000.
51. Monica D'ascenzo, 25 July 2010, 'Più banche in azienda dopo la crisi', Il Sole 24 Ore, http://www.ilsole24ore.com/art/finanza-e-mercati/2010-07-25/banche-azienda-crisi-080606.shtml?uuid=AYJlfuAC.
52. Ruigrok and Van Tulder, 1995.
53. *Ibid.*, pp. 36–62.
54. Mittelman, 1996 pp. 237–41.
55. Pang, A. (2010), 'Toyota off the cliff?' Research paper provides lessons in leadership http://reliableplant.com/Read/23080/Research-paper-Toyota-leadership.
56. http://www.guardian.co.uk/business/2010/feb/14/mobile-world-congress-phones-networks.
57. http://www.7sur7.be/7s7/fr/1536/Economie/article/detail/1073003/2010/02/26/L-aide-financiere-a-Carrefour-bloquee.dhtml.
58. http://www.franchise.be/content.php?lng=fr&news_id=1343.
59. http://www.7sur7.be/7s7/fr/1536/Economie/article/detail/1073276/2010/02/27/Carrefour-avait-deja-voulu-quitter-la-Belgique-en-2008.dhtml.
60. Lachmann, H., Ch. Larose and M. Penicaud, February 2010, 'Bien-être et efficacité au travail – 10 propositions pour améliorer la santé psychologique au travail', report carried out at request by the French Prime Minister, Paris, available on http://www.ladocumentationfrancaise.fr/rapports-publics/104000081/index.shtml?xtor=AL-850&r=Crise. The report on workers' welfare and productivity, undertaken between November 2009 and February 2010, is a report of 'practioners' showing the linkages between the changes in both the economic system worldwide and the firm or enterprise, and the impact on human behaviour of both managers and workers.
61. *Ibid.* p. 7.

62. De Weghe (SETCa) déplore que 'les représentants du personnel ne soient une fois de plus pas tenus au courant de cet énième réaménagement au sein du groupe. Carrefour ignore ainsi à nouveau les principes de base les plus élémentaires du dialogue social'. The last French manager sent in July 2009, Gérard Lavinay, faced increasing tensions since trade unions requested explanations on September's restructuring Paris plan (http://www.rtbf.be/info/les-syndicats-de-carrefour-sindignent-du-enieme-changement-de-pouvoir-gva-122698.
63. Rifkin, 2001.
64. Ostrom, 1990.
65. Allais, 1953.
66. Allais, 1947.
67. International Monetary Fund Public Investment and Fiscal Policy, 12 March 2004 para 36, http://www.imf.org/external/np/fad/2004/pifp/eng/PIFP.pdf.
68. David Hall, October 2008, 'Public–Private partnerships (PPPs) summary paper' Public Services International Research Unit (PSIRU) www.psiru.org.
69. Denis Dessus, 'L'endettement caché de la France', *Le Monde* 27 April 2010 http://www.lemonde.fr/opinions/article/2010/04/27/l-endettement-cache-de-la-france-par-denis-dessus_1342858_3232.html#xtor=AL-32280340.
70. 'New decision of Eurostat on deficit and debt treatment of public-private partnerships', 11/02/2004, http://europa.eu.int/rapid/pressReleasesAction.do?reference=STAT/04/18&format=HTML&aged=0&language=EN&guiLanguage=en.

4   Cooperatives

1. Ostrom, 1990, p. 25.
2. Côté, 2001, pp. 395–8.
3. Harte, 1997, p. 44.
4. *Ibid.*, p. 41.
5. Hansmann, 2000, p. 78.
6. *Ibid.*, p. 89.
7. Williamson, 1985 Chapter 9.
8. Schediwy, 2001 p. 106.
9. Hansmann, 2000 p. 81.
10. Koulitchisky and Mauget, 2001, p. 81.
11. Chaves and Monzón 2001, p. 72, and Koulitchisky and Mauget, 2001 p. 81.
12. Harte, 1997, pp. 31–53, and Côté, 2001, pp, 395–6.
13. Hansmann, 2000, p. 103.
14. Harte, 1997, p. 56.
15. Communication, Bruno Busacca, Legacoop, at Cooperatives Europe's State Working Group meeting, 3 July 2008.
16. Schenk, M. (2009) Commercial Banks and Credit Unions – Facts, Fallacies and Recent Trends. CUNA, ppt presentation.
17. Credit Union National Association (CUNA), http://advice.cuna.org/download/uscu_profile_yearend09.pdf.
18. According to the European Grouping of Cooperative banks (EACB), see http://www.eurocoopbanks.coop/GetDocument.aspx?id=cd5c2f96-5298-4aad-a941-e817f3eec7cb.
19. According to the site of the International Cooperative and Mutual Insurance Federation (ICMIF), at http://www.icmif.org/index.php?option=com_content&view=article&id=210&catid=20&Itemid=96&lang=en.

20. http://www.copa-cogeca.be/Main.aspx?page=CogecaHistory&lang=en.
21. European Commission Communication on the Promotion of Cooperative Societies in Europe, COM(2004)18. Beyond the similarity between the ILO and the EU titles, the two texts have explicit interlinkages, the latter mentioning that the former had been approved by the governments of all EU countries.
22. *Ibid.*
23. According to the ICA, see www.ica.coop.
24. Brazil–Arab News Agency, 2 February 2007, http://www.anba.com.br/ingles/noticia.php?id=13698.
25. New Zealand Cooperative Association, 2007, quoted by the ICA www.ica.coop.
26. http://www.wisc.edu/uwcc/icic/orgs/copac/member/un/int-day/950701/pub-info.html.
27. Communication, Indian Farmers Fertilizer Cooperative Ltd. (IFFCO).
28. ICA, see www.ica.coop.
29. Communication, Eurocoop.
30. Co-op 2007, Facts and Figures, Japanese Consumers' Co-operative Union.
31. *GNC Newsletter*, no. 348, June 2007.
32. New Zealand Cooperative Association, 2007, quoted by the ICA on www.ica.coop.
33. www.icahousing.coop.
34. European Commission Communication on the Promotion of Cooperative Societies in Europe, COM(2004)18.
35. ICA, see www.ica.coop.
36. Communication, International Cooperative Alliance.
37. 2008 Revision of World Population Prospects, Population Division of the Department of Economic and Social Affairs of the United Nations Secretariat, June 2009, http://esa.un.org/unpp/.
38. Communication, Cooperatives Europe.
39. Communications from the All China Federation of Supply and Marketing Cooperatives and from the All China Federation of Handicraft Industry Cooperatives.
40. University of Wisconsin: Research on the Economic Impact of Cooperatives, see http://www.uwcc.wisc.edu/.
41. Communication, Indian Farmers Fertilizer Cooperative Ltd. (IFFCO).
42. Communication, Cooperatives Europe.
43. According to Universidade Estadual de Santa Cruz http://www.uesc.br/cursos/pos_graduacao/especializacao/eco_cooperativas/index.php?item=conteudo_mercado.php.
44. Communication, André Chapleau, director for relations with the media, Desjardins Federation.
45. Communication, Indian Farmers Fertilizer Cooperative Ltd. (IFFCO).
46. DGRV: The German cooperatives in Europe (mimeo, 2008).
47. *Ibid.*
48. Communication, David Rodger, president of ICA-Housing, 24 May 2010. The estimate takes account of the total number of cooperative members in Europe (6.8 million), and an estimated average of 4 persons per dwelling.
49. ISTAT (2007) *Le cooperative sociali in Italia – Anno 2003–2006.* Rome: ISTAT.
50. Communication, André Chapleau, Communication Director of the Desjardins Group.
51. See ICA Global 300 website at http://www.global300.coop/Global300List.aspx.
52. Hesse, Heiko and Martin Čihák, 2007, *Cooperative Banks and Financial Stability,* IMF Working Paper, p. 19.

53. Paradis, G., Notes for the brainstorming session, United Nations Expert Group Meeting on 'Cooperatives in world in crisis', 28–30 April 2009, New York.
54. According to the European Grouping of Cooperative banks (EACB), see http://www.eurocoopbanks.coop/GetDocument.aspx?id=cd5c2f96-5298-4aad-a941-e817f3eec7cb.
55. According to the National Rural Electric Cooperative Association, see http://www.nreca.org/AboutUs/Co-op101/CooperativeFacts.htm.
56. Hassan Masum, Stiglitz and Sen, 'Manifesto on measuring economic performance and social progress', 30 September2009 at http://www.worldchanging.com/local/canada/archives/010574.html.
57. Birchall J. and Ketilson H.K., 'Responses to the global economic crisis – resilience of the cooperative business model in times of crisis', Geneva: ILO, 2009, p. 19.
58. According to the Credit Union National Association, see http://advice.cuna.org/download/uscu_profile_yearend09.pdf.
59. *Ibid.*, p. 23.
60. EACB, 'European cooperative banks in the financial and economic turmoil – first assessments', research paper, 2010, p. 8, at http://www.eurocoopbanks.coop/GetDocument.aspx?id=f235ed2e-3a13-4ce8-9262-4fcd25df1155.
61. *Ibid.*, p. 10.
62. http://www.easybourse.com/bourse/article/10362/credit-agricole-une-perte-nette-de-309me-au-t4.html.
63. EACB, European cooperative banks in financial and economic turmoil – Expert Group Meeting on 'Cooperatives in a world in crisis' and the International Year of Cooperatives, United Nations, New York, 28–30 April 2009.
64. European Association of Cooperative Banks (EACB): European co-operative banks in financial and economic turmoil – Expert Group Meeting on 'Cooperatives in a world in crisis' and the International Year of Co-operatives, United Nations, New York, 28–30 April 2009. Using another calculation, Rabobank reaches a result of 9.2 per cent of Tier 1 ratio for European cooperative banks, see: EACB: 'European cooperative banks in the financial and economic turmoil – first assessments', research paper, 2010, p. 8, at http://www.eurocoopbanks.coop/GetDocument.aspx?id=f235ed2e-3a13-4ce8-9262-4fcd25df1155.
65. Communication, Gérard Leseul, Fédération Nationale du Crédit Mutuel.
66. Michael Stappel, *Nach der Krise*, in *Die deutschen Genossenschaften 2009*, Wiesbaden: Deutscher Genossenschafts-Verlag eG, 2009, pp. 22–3.
67. See Rabobank website: http://www.annualreportsrabobank.com/downloads/Key_figures_2009.xls.
68. Rabobank faced walkout after cutting bonuses, nrchandelsblad,19 January 2010 http://www.nrc.nl/international/article2462577.ece/Rabobank_faced_walkout_after_cutting_bonuses.
69. A 'building society' in the UK is a type of mutual, akin to a cooperative.
70. Alan Coles (DG of the Building Societies Association), 'Demutualisation: what happened, why and where now?' Presentation at the UK Cooperative Forum, Manchester, 21 March 2006, and personal communication by Mervyn Wilson (Principal, Cooperative College UK).
71. Communication, Rodrigo Gouveia, general secretary of Eurocoop.
72. Communication, Stefania Marcone, international relations director, Legacoop.
73. Communication, David Rodger, President of ICA-Housing.

74. Hachmann, C:.,'The impact of the financial crisis on housing cooperatives in Europe', PPT presentation available on www.icahousing.coop.
75. Available on www.cicopa.coop.
76. *Ibid.*
77. Patchy but real historical evidence shows that cooperatives – or enterprises organized as such – had already begun to exist a few decades earlier in the UK and elsewhere in Europe as well as North America.
78. An example is a French book, of 1839, explicitly discussing cooperatives among other types of self-help institutions as a well-developed phenomenon, found at the private library of Heudicourt's castle in France. It mentions 400 cooperatives in one specific region of France. Another example is the first cooperative in the United States called the Contributorship of Philadelphia (an insurance company against fire) created by Benjamin Franklin in 1752, which still exists today under cooperative statute, more than 250 years later.
79. Since the cooperatives are not a constituent part of the ILO, cooperative participants had been accredited in the ad hoc commission either under government, trade union or employers' delegations.
80. Among which, one of the two authors of this book.
81. In the discussions, proposals for totally different world standards were proposed by some governments and by the employers' delegation. The ILO was not bound by the ICA standards, and the possibility that other standards could have been approved was real.
82. Roelants, 2003.
83. A cooperative is 'an autonomous association of persons united voluntarily to meet their common economic, social and cultural needs and aspirations through a jointly owned and democratically controlled enterprise', ILO Recommendation 193/2002, available on *www.ilo.org.*
84. Fourth principle, 'autonomy and independence': 'Cooperatives are autonomous, self-help organizations controlled by their members. If they enter into agreements with other organizations, including governments, or raise capital from external sources, they do so on terms that ensure democratic control by their members and maintain their cooperative autonomy', *ibid.*
85. First principle, 'voluntary and open membership': 'Cooperatives are voluntary organizations, open to all persons able to use their services and willing to accept the responsibilities of membership, without gender, social, racial, political or religious discrimination', ILO Recommendation 193/2002 on the Promotion of Cooperatives, annex, available on *www.ilo.org.*
86. Seventh cooperative principle, 'concern for community': 'Cooperatives work for the sustainable development of their communities through policies approved by their members', *ibid.*
87. Sixth cooperative principle, 'cooperation among cooperatives': 'Cooperatives serve their members most effectively and strengthen the cooperative movement by working together through local, national, regional and international structures', ILO Recommendation 193/2002, available on *www.ilo.org.*
88. General Assembly of the United Nations, fifty-fifth session: 'Resolution adopted by the General Assembly – 56/114 – Cooperatives in Social Development', 19 December 2001. This excerpt was also inserted in the preamble of ILO Recommendation 193/2002 on the Promotion of Cooperatives.
89. We can mention, among others, Crédit Mutuel and Banques Populaires in France, the Raiffeisen banking group in Germany, Coopitalia (distribution)

CCPL (industry), CCC-ACAM (construction), CNS (services) and CGM (social services and work integration) in Italy, UNIMED in Brazil, Amul and IFFCO in India, SANCOR in Argentina, Cruz Azul in Mexico.

90. Second cooperative principle, 'democratic member control': 'Cooperatives are democratic organizations controlled by their members, who actively participate in setting their policies and making decisions. Men and women serving as elected representatives are accountable to the membership. In primary cooperatives members have equal voting rights (one member, one vote) and cooperatives at other levels are also organized in a democratic manner', ILO Recommendation 193/2002 on the Promotion of Cooperatives, annex, available on *www.ilo.org*.

91. Fifth cooperative principle 'education, training and information': 'Cooperatives provide education and training for their members, elected representatives, managers, and employees so they can contribute effectively to the development of their cooperatives', ILO Recommendation 193/2002 on the Promotion of Cooperatives, annex, available on *www.ilo.org*.

92. Stiglitz, J., 2001.

93. Cooperativa Obrera, Bahia Blanca, Argentina, http://www.cooperativaobrera. com.ar/consumidores/circulo_consumidores.jsp.

94. Scuola Coop is an educational consortium launched by the Italian consumer cooperative group Coopitalia, see http://www.scuolacoop.it/.

95. Third cooperative principle 'members' economic participation': 'Members contribute equitably to, and democratically control, the capital of their cooperative. At least part of that capital is usually the common property of the cooperative. Members usually receive limited compensation, if any, on capital subscribed as a condition of membership. Members allocate surpluses for any or all of the following purposes: developing their cooperative, possibly by setting up reserves, part of which at least would be indivisible; benefiting members in proportion to their transactions with the cooperative; and supporting other activities approved by the membership', ILO Recommendation 193/2002, available on *www.ilo.org*.

96. Part of the third cooperative principle 'members' economic participation', available on *www.ilo.org*.

97. Some cooperative legislations make it possible to have a limited ratio of external investor–members, e.g. in France and Italy. But in fact, the financial motivation being low, the external investors–members are usually either 'mother' cooperatives engineering spin-offs, or clients, suppliers, foundations or other actors involved as stakeholders in the business.

98. Part of the third cooperative principle, ILO Recommendation 193/2002, available on *www.ilo.org*.

99. *Ibid*.

100. *Ibid*.

101. Roelants, 2009.

102. Part of the third cooperative principle, ILO Recommendation 193/2002, available on *www.ilo.org*.

103. ILO Recommendation 193 on the Promotion of Cooperatives, annex.

104. 1997 edition.

105. The Mutuals Manifesto 2010, available at: http://www.icmif.org/images/stories/ MutualsManifesto.pdf.

106. http://www.amice-eu.org/today.aspx?lang=en#A_unique_legal_concept.

107. There is much debate on when and how globalization began. For the purpose of this book, we consider two major waves, one between mid-nineteenth century and the start of the twentieth, and the other since the 1960s and still ongoing.
108. Polanyi, 1957.

5 Natividad Island Divers' and Fishermen's Cooperative

1. Fraire interview 2010.
2. Vincent Perazio: *La isla de la Natividad – un sanctuaire protégé*; documentary film from the *Le document sauvage* series, broadcast on France 5 Channel on 3 November 2009.
3. *Ibid.*
4. *Ibid.*
5. *Ibid.*
6. *Ibid.*
7. *Ibid.*
8. Fraire interview 2010.
9. *Ibid.*
10. Vincent Perazio: *La isla de la Natividad – un sanctuaire protégé*; documentary film from the *Le document sauvage* series, broadcast on France 5 Channel on 3 November 2009.
11. http://www.cobi.org.mx/?pag=r-pbc-isla-natividad&idioma=esp.
12. Ostrom, 2000.
13. Petrella, 2001.

6 Ceralep Société Nouvelle

1. This chapter is based on, and further develops, a chapter on Ceralep in Roelants *et al.* 2011.
2. http://www.riversidecompany.com/.
3. Mottin interview, 2010.
4. Artaud interview, 2010.
5. 'Ceralep: un sursis de six mois', *Le réveil*, 19 September 2003, p. 27.
6. Mottin interview, 2010.
7. *Le réveil*, 19 September 2003, p. 27.
8. Nicaise and Iglicki interviews, 2010.
9. Valla interview, 2010.
10. *Ibid.*
11. Chanterac interview, 2010.
12. Iglicki interview, 2010.
13. Nicaise and Iglicki interviews, 2010.
14. France Inter programme *Là bas si j'y suis* and France 2 documentary film for *Complément d'enquête*.
15. France Inter programme *Là bas si j'y suis*.
16. Robert Nicaise interview, 2010.
17. Robert Nicaise interview, 2010.
18. Communication, Robert Nicaise, 2 August 2010.

7   The Desjardins Cooperative Group

1. Desjardins website (www.desjardins.com) and personal communication from Desjardin executive Ann Lavoie.
2. *Ibid.*
3. Poulin. 2000, pp. 3–8.
4. Béland interview, 2010.
5. Poulin, 2000, p. 2.
6. Poulin and Tremblay, 2005 p. 7.
7. http://www.desjardins.com/fr/a_propos/profil/histoire/dorimene-desjardins.jsp#ref3#ref3.
8. *Ibid.*
9. http://advice.cuna.org/download/uscu_profile_yearend09.pdf.
10. Poulin. 2000, pp. 37–9 and Poulin, 2009.
11. Poulin, 2000, p. 41; Poulin 2009, p. 16.
12. Poulin. 2000, p. 43.
13. The Quebec government terminated this subsidy in 1970: personal communication from Pierre Poulin, main historian of the Desjardins group.
14. *Ibid.* p. 44.
15. Poulin, 2000, pp. 48–50; Poulin and Tremblay, 2005, p. 6; Poulin, 2009, p. 16.
16. Poulin, 2000, pp. 65–6.
17. Poulin, 2000, p. 71.
18. *Ibid.*, pp. 71–8. The Desjardin system organizes regular congresses, which are an occasion for all delegates from all the *caisses* from the system to debate current issues. Although the Desjardins congresses have no decision-making powers (differently from the annual general assemblies), they have a very important role in the debates leading to democratic decision making.
19. *Ibid.*, p. 81.
20. Poulin and Tremblay, 2005, pp. 23–5.
21. *Ibid.*, p. 28.
22. *Ibid.*, pp. 31–6.
23. *Ibid.*, p 48.
24. *Ibid.*, pp. 49, 56.
25. Poulin, 2000, pp. 89–90.
26. Poulin and Tremblay, 2005, p. 68.
27. Béland interview, 2010.
28. Poulin and Tremblay, 2005, pp. 49–52.
29. *Ibid.*, p. 79.
30. *Ibid.*, p. 57.
31. *Ibid.*, pp. 65–6.
32. *Ibid.*, pp. 65–7.
33. Brideault interview, 2010.
34. Béland interview, 2010.
35. 'Les fonds de placement, une carte maitresse pour Desjardins', *La Revue Desjardins*, 5 (1998), pp.14–15.
36. Poulin and Tremblay, 2005, p. 118.
37. *Ibid.*, pp. 118–19.
38. *Ibid.*, p. 41.
39. *Ibid.*, p. 84.
40. *Ibid.*, p. 90.

41. *Ibid.*, p. 92.
42. Re-engineering also implied a transformation of the service offer characterized by the development of advisory services and increased automation in ordinary transactions (personal communication by historian Pierre Poulin).
43. *Ibid.*, p. 125.
44. *Ibid.*, pp. 127–8.
45. *Ibid.*, pp. 129–30.
46. *Ibid.*, pp. 137/138.
47. *Ibid.*, pp. 144–5.
48. *Ibid.*, pp. 155–7.
49. Ibid., p. 169, completed by Albans D'Amours through e-mail communication.
50. *Ibid.*, p. 187.
51. Communication, Pierre Poulin, August 2010.
52. D'Amours interview, 2010.
53. Alban D'Amours personal e-mail communication, 5 August 2010.
54. *Ibid.*
55. *Ibid.*
56. D'Amours interview, 2010.
57. Desjardins, Communiqué de Presse, 2 March 2009, http://www.desjardins. com/fr/a_propos/salle_presse/la_une/communiques/resultats-financiers-2008. pdf.
58. René Vézina, 'Desjardins termine la plus importante transformation de son histoire depuis la fusion des fédérations régionales. Le pouvoir revient aux caisses; lesaffaires.com, 01–11–2009, http://www.dev-mm.com/lesaffaires/web/archives/ commerce/la-revolution-desjardins/504917.
59. Communication, Pierre Poulin, August 2010.
60. 'Desjardins amorce 2009 sous le signe du changement', http://www.newswire. ca/en/releases/archive/March2009/28/c5166.html.
61. Chapleau interview, 2010.
62. Monique Leroux, 'Coopérer pour créér l'avenir', preparatory document to the Desjardins 2009 Congress.
63. Since 1995, all the elected officers receive a remuneration, and, since 2003, the presidents as well (communication Pierre Poulin, August 2010).
64. Poulin, 2000, pp. 123–5.

8 The Mondragon Cooperative Group

1. This chapter is based on, and further develops, a chapter on Mondragon in Roelants *et al.* 2010.
2. Sanchez Bajo, 2007b.
3. Thomas and Logan, 1982, pp. 43–8.
4. Thomas and Logan, 1982, pp. 31–2.
5. Interview, Lezamiz 2010.
6. Ormaechea, 1991, pp. 44–52.
7. Ormaetxea, 1998, p. 97.
8. *Ibid.*
9. *Ibid.*, p. 99.
10. Sanchez Bajo, 2007b.
11. Sanchez Bajo, 2007b; Whyte and Whyte, 1991, p. 64.

12. Whyte and Whyte, 1991, pp. 69–71.
13. Ormaechea, 1991, p. 101.
14. Ormaechea, 1991. pp. 96–101.
15. Thomas and Logan, 1982, pp. 43–8.
16. MCC, 2007, p. 8; Whyte and Whyte 1991, p. 55.
17. Thomas and Logan, 1982, p. 126.
18. Whyte and Whyte, 1991, ,p. 74
19. Salaberria interview, 2010.
20. *Ibid.*
21. Whyte and Whyte, 1991, pp. 181–92
22. See MCC annual report, 1998.
23. Whyte and Whyte, 1991, pp. 179–81.
24. Whyte and Whyte, 1991, p. 192.
25. Salaberria interview, 2010.
26. Sanchez Bajo, 2007a.
27. Salaberria interview, 2010.
28. Sanchez Bajo, 2007a.
29. Whyte and Whyte, 1991, pp. 197–200.
30. Ormaetxea, 1998 p. 553.
31. Salaberria interview, 2010.
32. Ormaetxea, 1998, pp. 553–4.
33. Gorroñogoitia interview, 1992.
34. Ormaetxea, 1998, p. 569.
35. *Ibid.*
36. Ormaetxea, 1998, p. 570.
37. Salaberria interview, 2010.
38. *Ibid.*
39. MCC, 1995.
40. *Ibid.*
41. Plants can be found in 17 countries: Brazil, China, Czech Republic, France, Germany, India, Italy, Mexico, Morocco, Poland, Portugal, Romania, Thailand, Turkey, the UK, and Taiwan. Corporate offices can also be found in Chile, Russia, the USA and Vietnam; see http://www.mondragon-corporation.com/language/ en-US/ENG/Mondragon-in-the-World/Corporate-Offices.aspx.
42. Sanchez Bajo, 2007a.
43. Gallastegui 1994, p. 19 and communication Mikel Lezamiz.
44. Garate interview, 2010.
45. Sanchez Bajo, 2007a.
46. Dacosta interview, 2010.
47. Sotil interview, 2010.
48. http://www.mondragon.edu/home/view?set_language=en.
49. Sanchez Bajo, 2007b.
50. Lezamiz interview, 2010.
51. Aldekoa, Dacosta, Lezamiz, Garate, Goitexea interviews, 2010.
52. http://www.mondragon-corporation.com/language/en-US/ENG/Economic-Data/ Most-relevant-data.aspx.
53. http://www.mondragon-corporation.com/ENG/Press-room/articleType/ ArticleView/articleId/1475.aspx.
54. Lezamiz interview, 2010.
55. Garate interview, 2010.

56. Caja Laboral, *Informe economico y social 2009*, https://www.cajalaboral.com/clweb/pdf/sobre_nosotros/informes/2009/es/Informe_Economico_y_Social.pdf.
57. Lezamiz interview, 2010.
58. See Lagon Aro's 2009 annual report on http://www.seguroslagunaro.com/corporativa/secciones/informacion_corporativa/quienes_somos/memorias.php?idioma=es.
59. Barrenechea interview, 2010.
60. Dacosta interview, 2010.
61. Aldekoa interview, 2010.
62. Garate interview, 2010.
63. Dacosta interview, 2010.
64. Garate interview, 2010.
65. Aldekoa interview, 2010.
66. Garate interview, 2010.
67. Aldekoa, Lezamiz, Garate interviews, 2010.
68. Aldekoa interview, 2010.
69. Barrenechea interview, 2010.
70. Dacosta interview, 2010.
71. Garate interview, 2010.
72. Aldekoa interview, 2010.
73. *Ibid.*
74. Goiketxea interview, 2010.
75. Barrenechea interview, 2010.
76. Aldekoa interview, 2010.
77. Garate interview, 2010.
78. Sotil interview, 2010.
79. *Ibid.*
80. Salaberria interview, 2010.
81. Barrenechea interview, 2010.
82. Aldekoa interview, 2010.
83. Garate interview, 2010.
84. Barrenechea interview, 2010.
85. Sotil interview, 2010.
86. Garate interview, 2010.
87. Thomas and Logan, 1982.
88. Roelants, 2001.
89. Ormaechea, 1991, p. 101.
90. Arizmendiarrieta, 1984, p. 68.
91. Salaberria interview, 2010.
92. *Ibid.*

9 The Global Crisis

1. See, for example, Smith, 2010.
2. IMF, 2009.
3. Ostrom, 1990, pp. 24–5.
4. Commission Communication 'Implementing the Lisbon Community Programme for Growth and Jobs: Transfer of Businesses – Continuity through a new beginning', COM (2006) 117 final.

5. UNCTAD (1999) *World Investment Report* (Geneva: UNCTAD – United Nations Conference on Trade and Development) , p. 27.
6. Communication Pierre Liret, communication director of CGSCOP (French Confederation of Producers' Cooperatives).
7. Eurostat, regional GDP per inhabitant in 2007, 18 February 2010.
8. Putnam, 1993.
9. Arizmendiarrieta, 1984, p. 106.
10. Hassan Masum, Stiglitz and Sen, 'Manifesto on Measuring Economic Performance and Social Progress', September 30,2009 at http://www.worldchanging.com/local/canada/archives/010574.html.
11. Cowling and Sugden, 1994, pp. 44–5.
12. Claude Béland interview, 2010.

Postscript

1. See reactions and critique at http://www.capital-and-the-debt-trap.com/. There is a 2013 Spanish translation of the book, plus Chinese and Slovene ones in the making. The research was presented at the Imagine 2012 International conference on Cooperative Economics in Quebec City, 6–8 October.
2. See Private Equity and Financial Stability, Bank of England, Quarterly Bulletin 2013 Q1, http://www.bankofengland.co.uk/publications/Documents/quarterly-bulletin/2013/qb130104.pdf and 'Private equity crash could trigger next wave of financial crisis, Bank warns', by Larry Elliot, The Guardian, 14 March 2013, http://www.guardian.co.uk/business/2013/mar/14/private-equity-financial-crisis-bank-of-england
3. Sources on Monte dei Paschi case:

    1) Monte dei Paschi Siena Foundation, http://www.fondazionemps.it/eng/introduzione.asp?id=1
    2) Wikipedia website, http://en.wikipedia.org/wiki/Monte_dei_Paschi_di_Siena;
    3) Finance: Entangled in Tuscany, by Rachel Sanderson, http://www.ft.com/cms/s/0/7809ab88-7541-11e2-b8ad-00144feabdc0.html#ixzz2UQY3fJJZ, 13 February 2013
    4) Monte dei Paschi : scandalo o prassi normale delle banche?, http://www.lastampa.it/Page/Id/1.0.1193132872, 26 January 2013
    5) Caso Mps, Monti bacchetta il Pd ma candida ex membro del Cda di Mps, http://www.ilsole24ore.com/art/notizie/2013-01-25/caso-monti-bacchetta-candida-162723.shtml?uuid=AbTIS4NH, by Antonio Larizza, 25 January 2013, and
    6) Mps, lotta contro il tempo si punta sulla vendita di filiali, by Adriano Bonafede, 28 May 2012, http://www.repubblica.it/mobile-rep/affari-e-finanza/2012/05/28/news/mps_lotta_contro_il_tempo_si_punta_sulla_vendita_di_filiali-36304669

    For similar cases, see Derivatives: The Unregulated Global Casino for Banks, bank case by case in the US, http://demonocracy.info/infographics/usa/derivatives/bank_exposure.html.
4. http://www.belfasttelegraph.co.uk/news/g8-summit/g8-summit-world-leaders-reach-deal-on-tackling-tax-avoidance-and-money-laundering-29354299.html
5. The G20 Summit held in Los Cabos, Mexico, on 18–19 June 2012 was very light in results, and the G20 meeting of finance ministers and central bankers in Moscow, Russia, in mid-February 2013, had a heated debate about exchange rates being utilized to further exports.

6. See, for example, the International Labour Organization, Birchall and Ketilson, Resilience of the Cooperative Business Model, Sustainable Enterprise Programme, Geneva: ILO, 2009. See also Oliver Wyman's Report '*Outlook for Co-operative Banking in Europe 2012*' at http://www.oliverwyman.com/the-outlook-for-cooperative-banking-in-europe-2012.htm#.UbctP82Ezdw and The Banker, 2 January 2013 at http://www.thebanker.com/Banking/The-co-operative-lesson.
7. See EU Employment and Social Situation Quarterly Review, March 2013 at http://ec.europa.eu/social/main.jsp?langId=en&catId=89&newsId=1852&furtherNews= yes, and ILO Global Employment Trends 2013 executive summary at http://www.ilo.org/wcmsp5/groups/public/---dgreports/---dcomm/---publ/documents/publication/wcms_202215.pdf.
8. See 'The six executives responsible for Co-op Bank's troubles', by Simon Bowers, 17 June 2013 at http://www.guardian.co.uk/business/2013/jun/17/coop-bank-six-executives-responsible. See also http://www.guardian.co.uk/business/2013/jun/17/co-operative-bank-stock-market-listing#show-all and http://www.guardian.co.uk/politics/2011/oct/07/moodys-downgrade-osborne-british-banks.
9. 'The problem of unpaid debts and fines is adding to the already existing issues of overcrowding and our aging buildings where we cannot separate the inmates completely, which is a problem for us ... The majority of the 12 Cypriots, Tryfonides said, were unemployed persons who were unable to pay-off their debts but he said their family members were trying to reach an agreement with the attorney-general to gradually pay-off their debts'. P. Stevenson, at http://cyprus-mail.com/2013/07/23/rise-in-debtors-adds-to-prison-overcrowding/, 23 July 2013.
10. This was, again, confirmed by history experts from these movements at a series of conferences on cooperatives in 2012 where we presented this book.
11. Rogoff K. et Reinhart C., 2009, This Time is Different: Eight Centuries of Financial Folly. Princeton University Press.

List of Interviewees

Aldekoa, Jose Maria, president of the Mondragon Corporation, Mondragon/Arrasate, 30 March 2010.

Artaud, Dominique, member of the Board of the Ceralep cooperative (Saint-Vallier, France), ex-human resources director at Olivetti, ex-general director of Coca Cola France, ex-CEO of Steelcase Strafor Europe, ex-CEO of Cash-In-Transit Company Brinks for France and North Africa, Saint-Vallier, 1 April 2010.

Bancel, Jean-Louis, president of the International Banking Cooperative Association, chairman of Crédit Coopératif, Paris, 17 March 2010.

Barrenachea, Rafael, president of the Danobat Machine-Tools group, Mondragon Corporation, Elgoibar, 29 March 2010.

Béland, Claude, president of the Desjardins Confederation between 1989 and 2000, telephone interview, 16 April 2010.

Brideault, Alain, president of the Canadian Worker Cooperative Federation, chairman of Orion Cooperative, Quebec, telephone interview, 30 March 2010.

Chanterac, Bernard de, branch director of Credit Cooperatif, ex-director of the Valence branch, Lyon, 2 April 2010.

Chapleau, Alain, general director for relations with the media, Desjardins Federation, telephone interview, 14 April 2010.

Cheval, Jacques, mayor of Saint-Vallier, Saint-Vallier, 2 April 2010.

D'Amours, Alban, president of the International Federation of the People's Banks, president of the Desjardins Federation between 2000 and 2008, telephone interview, 20 April 2010.

Da Costa, Constan, president of the EROSKI consumer cooperative group, Mondragon Corporation, Elorrio, 31 March 2010.

Detilleux, Jean-Claude, president of the Groupement National de la Coopération, deputy chairman of Crédit Coopératif, Brussels, 2 March 2010.

Fraire, Esteban, president of the Baja California Divers' and Fishermen's Cooperative, Natividad Island, Mexico, telephone interview, 26 July 2010.

Garate, Jose Ignacio, former Institutional Affairs director of Mondragon Corporation, former head of the Technical Secretariat for Strategic Planning of Mondragon Corporation, former head of the Intervention Directorate of Caja Laboral, Aretxabaleta, 29 March 2010.

Genthon, Alain, president of the General Council of the Drôme Département, Anneyron, 1 April 2010.

Goiketxea, Jose Ramon, president of the Automotion Division, Mondragon Corporation, Mondragon/Arrasate, 30 March 2010.

Iglicki, Karine, ex-member of the staff of the Rhône-Alpes Regional Union of Worker Cooperatives URSCOP-R-A, Lyon, 2 April 2010.

Kharchouf, Driss, worker and trade union representative at Ceralep cooperative (Saint-Vallier, France), Saint-Vallier, 1 April 2010.

Lezamiz, Mikel, director of Otalora training centre of the Mondragon Corporation, Aretxabaleta, 28 and 29 March 2010.

Nicaise, Robert, president of the Board of the Ceralep cooperative (Saint-Vallier, France), Saint-Vallier, 1 April 2010.

Ouellet, Paul, general coordinator, Quebec Service Center, Caisse d'Economie Solidaire Desjardins, telephone interview, 3 May 2010.

Pellegrini, Jean Marie, worker representative at Ceralep cooperative (Saint-Vallier, France), Saint-Vallier, 1 April 2010.

Pflimlin Etienne, president of Cooperatives Europe, chairman of the Fédération du Crédit Mutuel, Paris, 17 March 2010.

Salaberria, Javier, president of the International Organisation of Industrial, Artisanal and Service Producers' Cooperatives (CICOPA) and former legal director at Fagor Electrodomesticos, Brussels, 18 May 2010.

Sotil, Javier, vice president of Mondragon Corporation for innovation and new sectors, president of the new Engineering and Services Division, ex-director of LKS Consulting, Mondragon Corporation, Mondragon/Arrasate, 30 March 2010.

Valla, Bernard, consultant at the Rossignol business consulting firm, Lyon, 2 April 2010.

Zelaia, Adrian, president of Ekai Center, former secretary general of the Mondragon Corporation, Aretxabaleta, 29 March 2010.

Bibliography

Abbott, K. and Snidal, D. (2000) *International 'Standards' and International Governance*, Chicago Working papers, htttp://harrisschool.uchicago.edu/about/publications/working-papers/pdf/wp_00_18.pdf.

Ahamet, L. (2009) *Lords of Finance – 1929, the great depression, and the bankers who broke the world* (London: Windmill Books).

Albert, M. *Kapitalismus contra Kapitalismus*, (Frankfurt: Campus, 1992).

Alchian, A. and Demsetz, H. (1972) 'Production, Information Costs, and Economic Organization', *American Economic Review*, 62 (December) pp. 777–95.

Allais, M. [1947] (1998) *Economie et intérêt* (2nd edn) (Paris: Editions Clément Juglar).

Allais, M. (1953) 'La généralisation des théories de l'équilibre économique général et du rendement social au cas du risque', in: *les Actes du Colloque: Fondements et Applications de la théorie du risque en Econométrie*, (Paris: CNRS).

Allais, M. (1999) *La Crise mondiale d'aujourd'hui. Pour de profondes réformes des institutions financières et monétaires* (Paris: Editions Clément-Juglar).

Allen, W. (1992) 'Our schizophrenic conception of the business corporation', *Cardozo Law Review*, 14 (2), pp. 621–81.

Amromin, G. and Sharpe, S. (2008) *Expectations of Risk and Return Among Household Investors: Are Their Sharpe Ratios Countercyclical?* Board of Governors of the Federal Reserve System, Finance and Economics Discussion Series 2008–17, April.

Arendt, H. (1999) *The Human Condition* (2nd rev edn) (Chicago: Chicago University Press).

Arendt, H. (2006) *Eichman in Jerusalem: a report on the banality of evil* (New York: Penguin Classics).

Arizmendiarrieta, J.M. (1984) *La empresa para el hombre* (Bilbao: Alkar).

Backhouse, R. and Bateman, B.W. (2006) *The Cambridge Companion to Keynes* (Cambridge: Cambridge University Press).

Baily, M.N. and Litan, R.E. (2008) *A Brief Guide to Fixing Finance*, The Brookings Institution, 22 September, http://www.brookings.edu/papers/2008/0922_fixing_finance_baily_litan.aspx.

Baker, D. (2008) *The Housing Bubble and the Financial Crisis* (Washington: Center for Economic and Policy Research).

Baker, M.P. and Wurgler, J.A. (2000) 'The Equity Share in New Issues and Aggregate Stock Returns', *Journal of Finance*, 55(5), October.

Barnett-Hart, A.K. (2009) *The Story of the CDO Market Meltdown: An Empirical Analysis*, Presented to the Department of Economics in partial fulfilment of the requirements for a Bachelor of Arts degree with Honors, Harvard College Cambridge, Massachusetts, 19 March, http://www.hks.harvard.edu/m-rcbg/students/dunlop/2009-CDOmeltdown.pdfc.

Basun, S. (1977) 'The investment performance of common stocks relative to their price-earnings rations: a test of the efficient markets', *Journal of Finance*, 32(3), pp. 663–82.

Baudrillard, J. (2006) *The System of Objects* (London: Verso).

Beaver, W. (1981) 'Market Efficiency', *The Accounting Review*, LVI (1), January, pp. 23–37.

Berle, A. and Means, G. (1932) *The Modern Corporation and Private Property* (New York: Commerce Clearing House).

Bernanke, B.S. (2003) 'An Unwelcome Fall in Inflation?' Remarks before the Economics Roundtable, University of California, San Diego, La Jolla, California, 23 July, http://www.federalreserve.gov/boarddocs/speeches/2003/20030723.

Bhagat, S., Shleifer, A. and Vishny, R. (1990) 'Hostile Takeovers in the 1980s', Brookings Papers on Economic Activity – Microeconomics, pp. 1–72.

Blackburn, R. (2008) 'The subprime crisis', *New Left Review* 50, March–April, pp. 63–106.

Blair, M. (1995) *Ownership and Control: Rethinking Corporate Governance for the Twenty-First Century* (Washington DC: Brookings Institution).

Blinder, A. S. and Zandi, M. (2010) 'How the Great Recession was brought to an end', July 27, http://www.economy.com/mark-zandi/documents/End-of-Great-Recession.pdf.

Bosworth, B. and Flaaen, A. (2009) 'America's Financial Crisis: the End of An Era', The Brookings Institution, Paper presented at ADBI Conference 'Global Financial and Economic Crisis: Impacts, Lessons and Growth Rebalancing', 22–3 April, Tokyo, Japan, http://www.brookings.edu/papers/2009/0414_financial_crisis_bosworth.aspx.

Bourdieu, P, (1977) 'Outline of a Theory of Practice', *Cambridge Studies in Social and Cultural Anthropology* 16, (Cambridge: Cambridge University Press).

Bourdieu, P. (1992) *The Logic of Practice* (Cambridge: Polity Press).

Boyer, R. and Drache, D. (1996) *States against Markets: the limits of globalisation* (London: Routledge).

Brunnermeier, M., Crocket, A., Goodhart, C. and Shin, H. (2009) 'The Fundamental Principles of Financial Regulation', Geneva Reports on the World Economy 11.

Buettner, T. and Wamser, G. (2009) 'Internal debt and multinational's profit shifting, empirical evidence from firm-level panel data', WP 09/18, Ifo Institute and Munich University, and the Oxford University Centre for Business Taxation, August.

Bush, M.L. (2000) *Servitude in Modern Times, Themes in History* (Oxford: Blackwell Publishing).

BVCA and PriceWaterhouseCoopers, (2003) *A Guide to Private Equity*, June.

Caballero, R. and Krishnamurthy, A. (2008) 'Musical chairs: a comment on the credit crisis', Banque de France, *Financial Stability Review*, 11, February.

Caprio, G. and Klingebeil, D. (2003) *Episodes of Systemic and Borderline Financial Crises*, World Bank, January.

CAS – Centre d'analyse stratégique (2009) *Nouveau monde, nouveau capitalisme?* Colloque nouveau capitalisme, 8 and 9 January, Paris, mimeo.

Chandler, A. (1977) *The Visible Hand* (Cambridge: Harvard University Press).

Chandler, A. (1990) *Scale and Scope: the dynamics of industrial capitalism* (Cambridge: Harvard University Press).

Chatriot, A., Chessel, M.E. and Hilton, M. (2004) *Au nom du consommateur – Consommation et politique en Europe et aux Etats Unis au XXe siècle* (Paris: La Découverte).

Chaves, R. and Monzón, J.L. (2001) 'Les groupes d'économie sociale: dynamiques et trajectoires', in: Côté, D. (ed.) *Les holdings coopératifs: évolution ou transformation définitive?* (Brussels: De Boeck) pp. 53–76.

Chenais, F. (1996) *La mondialisation financière, genèse, coût et enjeux* (Paris: Alternatives économiques, Syros).

Coase, R. (1988) *The Firm, the Market, and the Law* (Chicago: University of Chicago Press).

Collombat, B. and Servenay, D. (2009) *Histoire secrète du patronat de 1945 à nos jours* (Paris: La découverte).

Committee on the Global Financial System (2009) *Report of the Working Group on Capital flows to Emerging Market Economies*, Chairman: Rakesh Mohan, Bank for International Settlements, Basel.

Côté, D. (ed.) (2001) *Les holdings coopératifs: évolution ou transformation définitive?* (Brussels: De Boeck).

Cowling, K. and Sugden, R. (1994) 'Industrial strategy – Guiding principles and European context', in Bianchi, P., Cowling, K. and Sugden, R. (eds) *Europe's economic challenge – analyses of industrial strategy and agenda for the 1990s* (London: Routledge).

de Beaufort, V. (2006) 'One Share - One Vote, the new Holy Grail for a good corporate governance?' Essec Research Center, DR-07009B January, ESSEC Business School, France.

de la Dehesa, G. (2009) 'Banking Rescue and Economic Recovery Plans in the EU', in Economic Recovery Packages in EU Member States, Compilation of Briefing Papers by the European Parliament European Parliament's Economic and Monetary Affairs Committee, Policy Department Economic and Scientific Policy, IP/A/ECON/RT/2008-30, January, http://www.europarl.europa.eu/activities/committees/studies/download.do?file=24251.

de Larosière J. (2009) *Report of the High-Level Group on Financial Supervision in the EU*, chaired by Jacques de Larosière, Brussels.

De Long, J.B. and Summers, L.H. (1986) 'Is Increasing Price Flexibility Stabilizing?' *Journal of Money, Credit and Banking*, 21, pp. 481–97.

Demyanyk, Y. and Van Hemert, O. (2008) *Understanding the Subprime Mortgage Crisis*, Federal Reserve Bank of St. Louis and New York University, draft of 5 December.

DiMaggio, P.J. and Powell, W.W. (1983) 'The Iron Cage Revisited: Institutional Isomorphism and Collective Rationality in Organizational Fields', *American Sociological Review*, 48(2), pp. 147–60.

Dockès, P. and Lorenzi, J.H. (2009) *Fin de monde ou sortie de crise?* (Paris: Editions Perrin).

Ellerman, D. (1984) 'Entrepreneurship in the Mondragon Cooperatives', *Review of Social Economy*, XLII, December, pp. 272–94.

Enderle, G. (2007) 'Business ethics and wealth creation: conceptual clarifications and research questions', 23 April, Conference on Creation of Wealth, http://www.nd.edu/~ethics/wcConference/.

Ericson, R. (1991) 'The classical Soviet-type economy', *Journal of Economic Perspectives*, 5(4), Fall, pp. 11–27.

Ernst and Young (2008) 'How do private equity investors create value? a study of 2006 exits in the US and Western Europe', http://www.ey.com/Global/assets.nsf/International/ TAS_PE_CreateValue/$file/EY_TAS_PE_Create_Value_07.pdf, 2008.

European Commission, (2001) *White Paper "European Governance"*, Brussels, 25 July, COM(2001) 428 final.

Federal Reserve Bank of St. Louis (2009a) *Monetary Trends*.

Federal Reserve Bank of St. Louis (2009b)*The Financial Crisis: What Happened.*

Fisher, I. (1911) *The Purchasing Power of Money* (New York: Macmillan).

Fisher, I. (1929) *Booms and Depressions.* (New York: Adelphi).

Fischer, I. (1993) *The Debt-Deflation Theory of Great Depressions; Econometrica, Volume 1*, pp. 357–77.

Fontaine, L. (2008) *L'économie morale, pauvreté crédit et confiance dans l'Europe preindustrielle* (Paris: Gallimard).

Friedman, M. (1971) *A Monetary History of the United States 1867–1960* (Princeton: Princeton University Press).

Fukuyama, F. (1992) *The End of History and the Last Man* (New York: Free Press).

G20 Working Group 1 on Enhancing Sound Regulation and Strengthening Transparency, Final Report, 25 March 2009, http://www.g20.org/Documents/g20_wg1_010409.pdf.

Galbraith, J.K. (1958) *The Affluent Society* (London: Penguin Books).

Galimberti, U. (2002) *Psiche et techne, l'uomo nell'età della tecnica* (Milan: Feltrinelli).

Gallastegui, I. (1994) *El Movimiento Cooperativista de Mondragon: el papel jugado por Caja Laboral*; Congresso 'Competencia y Participación: formas organizativas emergentes; Barcelona: 22-24 June, mimeo.

Gaud, P., Hoesli, M. and Bender, A. (2004) *Further Evidence on Debt-Equity Choice*, HEC – University of Geneva and FAME – International Center for Financial Asset Management and Research Paper No 114, 10 May.

Gerth, H.H. and Wright Mills, C. (eds) (1991) *From Max Weber: essays in sociology* (London: Routledge).

Gorton, G. (2008) *The Panic of 2007*, Yale School of Management and NBER, draft, 4 August.

Gramlich, E.M. (2007) 'Booms and busts: the case of subprime mortgages', *Economic Review*, Federal Reserve Bank of Kansas City, issue Q IV, pp. 105–13.

Greenspan A, (1996) Remarks by Chairman Alan Greenspan, 'Regulation of electronic payment systems', at the US Treasury Conference on Electronic Money and Banking: The Role of Government, Federal Reserve Board, Washington DC, 19 September, http://www.federalreserve.gov/boarddocs/speeches/1996/19960919.htm.

Greenspan, A. (2002a) 'Issues for Monetary Policy', remarks by Chairman Alan Greenspan before the Economic Club of New York, New York City, 19 December, http://www.federalreserve.gov/boarddocs/speeches/2002/20021219/default.htm.

Greenspan, A. (2002b) 'The economic outlook', testimony of Chairman Alan Greenspan before the Joint Economic Committee, US Congress, 13 November, http://www.federalreserve.gov/boarddocs/testimony/2002/20021113/default.htm.

Greenspan, A. and Kennedy, J. (2005) 'Estimates of Home Mortgage Originations, Repayments, and Debt on One-to-Four-Family Residences', Finance and Economic Discussion Series 2005-41, Federal Reserve Board. Washington DC, September.

Greenspan, A. and Kennedy, J. (2007) 'Sources and Uses of Equity Extracted from Homes', Finance and Economics Discussion Series, 2007-20, Divisions of Research and Statistics and Monetary Affairs, Federal Reserve Board, Washington DC, March.

Group of Thirty, (2009) 'Financial Reform: A Framework for Financial Stability', chaired by Paul A. Volcker, Washington DC.

Habermas, J. (1971) 'Technology and science as "ideology"', in *Toward a Rational Society: student protest, science, and politics* (Boston: Beacon Press).

Hansmann, H. (2000) *The Ownership of Enterprise* (Cambridge, MA: Harvard University Press).

Harte, L. (1997) 'Creeping Privatisation of Irish Co-operatives: A Transaction Cost Explanation', in Nilsson, J. and van Dijk, G. (eds) *Strategies and Structures in Agro-Food Industries* (Assen, The Netherlands: Van Gorcum & Comp).

Hatzius, J., Greenlaw, D., Kashyap, A.K. and Shin, H.S. (2008) 'Leveraged Losses: Lessons from the Mortgage Market Meltdown', US Monetary Policy Forum Report No. 2, Rosenberg Institute, Brandeis International Business School and Initiative on Global Markets, University of Chicago Graduate School of Business.

Heidegger, M. (2000) 'The Question Concerning Technology' in S.F. Krell (ed.) *Basic Writings of Martin Heidegger* (London, Routledge).

Held, K. (2003) 'Husserl's phenomenological of the life-world', in Donn Welton (ed.) *The New Husserl: a critical reader, studies in continental thought* (Bloomington, Indiana: Indiana University Press) pp. 32–62.

Hobsbawn, E. (2003) *The New Century: in conversation with Antonio Polito* (London: Abacus).

Husserl, E. (1970) *The Crisis of European Sciences and Transcendental Phenomenology: an introduction to phenomenological philosophy* (Chicago: Northwestern University Press).

IMF, (2009) *Initial Lessons of the Crisis*, February.

Irvin, G. (2006) *Regaining Europe* (London: Federal Trust), http://www.imf.org/external/np/pp/eng/2009/020609.pdf.

Isard P., Razin, A. and Rose, A. (eds) (1999) *International Finance and Financial Crises* (Norwel: Kluwer).

Jensen, M. (1989) 'The Eclipse of the Public Corporation', *Harvard Business Review*, 67, October, pp. 323–9.

Jickling M. (2009) 'Causes of the Financial Crisis', (29 January version), Congressional Research Service, CSR report for Congress R40173, www.csr.gov.

Johnson, S. (2009) 'The quiet coup', testimony submitted to the Joint Economic Committee hearing on 'Too big to fail or too big to save? Examining the systemic threats of large financial institutions', April 21, http://www.scribd.com/doc/14490679/BaselineScenario-TestimonyJECApril202009FINAL.

Kaplan, S. and Stein, J. (1993) 'The Evolution of Buyout Pricing and Financial Structure in the 1990s', *Quarterly Journal of Economics* 108, May, pp. 313–57.

Kempf, H. (2009) *Pour sauver la planète, sortez du capitalisme* (Paris: Seuil).

Keynes, J.M. [1931] (1963) *Essays in Persuasion* (New York: Norton).

Keynes, J.M. [1936] (1964) *The General Theory of Employment, Interest and Money* (New York: Harcourt Brace).

Kindleberger, C.P. [1973] (1986) *The World in Depression 1929–1939* (Berkeley: University of California Press).

Koulytchizky, S. and Mauget, R. (2001) 'Mutations et valeurs dans les groupes coopératifs', in Côté, D (ed.) *Les holdings coopératifs: évolution ou transformation définitive?* (Brussels: De Boeck) pp. 103–14.

Krugman, P. (1998) 'Its Baaack! Japan's Slump and the Return of the Liquidity Trap', Brookings Papers on Economic Activity, pp. 137–87.

Krugman, P. (2007) 'Introduction to an anniversary edition of John Maynard Keynes' *The General Theory of Employment, Interest, and Money* (Basingstoke: Palgrave Macmillan).

Krugman, P. (2008) *The Return of Depression Economics and the Crisis of 2008* (London: Penguin Books).

Langlois, S. (2006) *Consommer en France, Cinquante ans de travaux scientifiques au Crédoc* (Paris: Éditions de l'Aube).

Love, J. (2000) 'Max Weber's Orient', in Stephen Turner, (ed.) *The Cambridge Companion to Weber* (Cambridge: Cambridge University Press) pp. 196–7.

Mandelbrot, B. and Hudson, R.L. (2008) *The (Mis)Behaviour of Markets: a fractal view of risk, ruin and reward*, (London: Profile books).

Marx, K. and Engels, F. [1848] (1971) *Manifesto of the Communist Party* (New York: International Publishers).

Mauss, M. (1923–4) 'Essai sur le don. Forme et raison de l'échange dans les sociétés archaïques', online document in the collection: 'Les classiques des sciences sociales', http://www.uqac.uquebec.ca/zone30/Classiques_des_sciences_sociales/index.html.

Mayntz, R. (1998) 'New challenges to governance theory', European University Institute, Jean Monnet Chair Paper RSC 98/50.

MCC (1995) *Compendio de Normas en Vigor del Congreso de MCC* (Arrasate: MCC).

MCC, (2007) *Historia de una experiencia* (Arrasate: MCC).

McNally, D. (1993) *Against the Market: Political Economy, Market Socialism, and the Marxist Critique* (London: Verso).

Minsky, H.P. (1975) *John Maynard Keynes* (New York: Columbia University Press).

Minsky, H.P. (1982) *Can 'It' Happen Again?* (New York: Armonk).

Minsky, H.P. (1992) 'The Financial Instability Hypothesis', Bard College,The Levy Economics Institute, The Jerome Levy Economics Institute Working Paper no. 74.

Minsky, H.P. (2008) *Stabilizing an Unstable Economy* (Columbus, OH: McGraw-Hill).

Mittelman, J.H. (1996), How Does Globalization Really Work', in James H. Mittelman (ed.) *Globalization: Critical Reflections*. (Boulder: Lynne Rienner Publishers).

Moati, P. (2001) *L'avenir de la grande distribution* (Paris: Odile Jacob).

Mundis, J. (1990) *How to Get Out of Debt, Stay Out of Debt, and Live Prosperously* (New York: Bantam).

Needham, J. (1956) *Science and Civilisation in China, Volume II, History of Scientific Thought* (Cambridge: Cambridge University Press).

Nilsson, J. (2001) 'Modèles organisationnels pour coopératives laitières', in Côté, D. (ed.) *Les holdings coopératifs: évolution ou transformation définitive?* (Brussels: De Boeck) pp. 161–75.

O'Hara, P. A. (2002) 'The Contemporary Relevance of Thorstein Veblen's Institutional-Evolutionary Political Economy', *History of Economics Review*, No. 35, Winter, pp. 78–103, http://www.hetsa.org.au/pdf/35-A-7.pdf.

Oliveira, J.C. de (1994) '*Firma e Quase-Firma no setor industrial – o caso da Petroquímica Brasileira*', Doctoral Thesis defended at the Institute of Industrial Economics of the Federal University of Rio de Janeiro.

Ormaechea, J.M. (1991) *La experiencia cooperativa de Mondragón* (Mondragón: Otalora).

Ormaetxea, J.M. (1998) *Origenes y claves del cooperativismo de Mondragón* (Arrasate: Saiolan).

Ostrom, E. (1990) *Governing the Commons* (Cambridge: Cambridge University Press).

Petrella, R. (2001) *The Water Manifesto: arguments for a world water contract* (London: Zed Books).

Plihon, D. (1996) 'Déséquilibres mondiaux et instabilité financière: la responsabilité des politiques libérales', in François Chesnais (ed.) *La mondialisation financière, genèse, coût et enjeux* (Paris: Syros) Chapter 4, pp. 97–141.

Polanyi, K. (1957) *The Great Transformation: the political and economic origins of our time* (Boston: Beacon Press Paperback).

Poulin, P. (2000) *Desjardins, 100 ans d'histoire* (Lévis: Dorimène).

Poulin, P. (2009) 'Des moments difficiles dont Desjardins a su tirer profit', *Revue Desjardins*, 75(1), February–March and (2) April–May.

Poulin, P. and Tremblay, B. (2005) *Desjardins en mouvement* (Montreal: HEC).

Putnam, R. (1993) *Making Democracy Work: civil traditions in modern Italy* (Princeton: Princeton University Press).

Raines, J.P. and Leathers, C.G. (2008) *Debt, Innovations, and Deflation: the theories of Veblen, Fisher, Schumpeter, and Minsky* (Cheltenham: Edward Elgar Publishing).

Razeen, S. (1995) *States and Firms: Multinational Enterprises in Institutional Competition* (London: Routledge).

Reinhart, C.M. and Rogoff, K.S. (2010) 'Growth in a Time of Debt', paper for the American Economic Review Papers and Proceedings; 7 January.

Rifkin, J. (2001) *The Age of Access: The New Culture of Hypercapitalism, Where all of Life is a Paid-For Experience* (New York: Ken Tarcher/Putnam).

Roe, M. (1991) 'A Political Theory of American Corporate Finance', *Columbia Law Review*, 91, January, pp. 10–67.

Roelants, B. (2001) 'Profilo storico del movimento Cooperativo di Mondragon', *La Cooperazione Italiana*, first issue.

Roelants, B. (2003) 'La première norme mondiale sur les coopératives – la recommandation 193/2002 de l'Organisation mondiale du travail', *RECMA, Revue des Études Coopératives. Mutualistes et Associatives*, no. 289, July.

Roelants, B. (ed.) (2009) *Cooperatives and Social Enterprises – Governance and Normative frameworks* (Brussels: CECOP Publications).

Roelants, B and Sanchez Bajo, C. (2002) 'Cooperatives in the world: reality and perspectives', Geneva, paper for the World Commission on the Social Dimension of Globalisation, ILO.

Roelants, B., Pellirossi, V. and Biron, O. (eds) (2010) *Cooperatives, Territories and Jobs* (Brussels: CECOP Publications).

Roubini, N. (2007) 'Asia is learning the wrong lessons from its 1997–98 financial crisis: the rising risks of a new and different type of financial crisis in Asia', *Roubini Global Economics*, May.

Roubini, N. (2009) 'Latvia's currency crisis is a rerun of Argentina's', *Roubini Global Economics*, January.

Roubini, N. and Mihm, S. (2010) *Crisis Economics – a Crash Course in the Future of Finance* (London: Allen Lane).

Ruigrok, W. and Van Tulder, R. (1995) *The Logic of International Restructuring* (London: Routledge).

Sanchez Bajo, C. (2001) *The Political Economy of Regionalism – Business Actors in Mercosur in the Petrochemical and Steel Industrial Sectors* (Maastricht: Shaker Media).

Sanchez Bajo, C. (2005) 'Visionen der sozialen und solidarischen Okonomie zu Beginn des 21. Jahrhunderts in Europa und im Mercosur – ein Vergleich', in Clarita Muller-Plantenberg *et al. Solidarische Okonomie in Brasilien und Europa, Wege zur konkreten Utopie* (Kassel: Kassel University) pp. 25–58.

Sanchez Bajo, C. (2006) 'Union Européenne et Mercosur: processus d'intégration régionale et politiques sur les coopératives', in Munoz, J., Radrigin, R. and Regnard, Y. (eds) *La Gouvernance des entreprises cooperatives* (Rennes: Presses Universitaires de Rennes).

Sanchez Bajo, C. (2007a) 'Mondragon – a cooperative experience', lecture at Kassel University.

Sanchez Bajo, C. (2007b) 'Education in Mondragon', lecture at Kassel University.

Schediwy R. (2001) 'Vers une théorie du cycle de vie des fédérations de coopératives et d'autres groupes similaires', in Côté, D. (ed.) *Les holdings coopératifs: évolution ou transformation définitive?* (Brussels: De Boeck) pp. 53–76.

Schmitter, P.C. (2001) 'What is there to legitimize in the European Union... And how might this be accomplished?' working document Jean Monnet No.6/01, symposium: 'Mountain or Molehill?' A critical evaluation of the White Paper of the European Commission, 2001, http://www.jeanmonnetprogram.org/papers/01/011401.rtf.

Schumpeter, J. A. [1939] (1982) *The Theory of Economic Development: An Inquiry into Profits, Capital, Credit, Interest, and the Business Cycle* (Piscataway, NJ: Transaction Publishers).

Schumpeter, J.A. [1942] (1984) *Capitalism, Socialism and Democracy* (London: HarperCollins).

Schumpeter, J.A. [1934] (1989) *Business Cycles: A Theoretical, Historical and Statistical Analysis of the Capitalist Process* (Philadelphia: Porcupine Press).

Sen, A. (1999) *Development as Freedom* (New York: Alfred A. Knopf).

Severino, E. (2002) *Techne, le radici della violenza* (Milano: Rizzoli).

Shiller, R. J. (2001) *Irrational Exuberance* (Princeton: Princeton University Press).

Shleifer, A. and Summers, L. (1988) 'Breach of Trust in Hostile Takeovers', in Auerbach, A. (ed.) *Corporate Takeovers: Causes and Consequences* (Chicago: University of Chicago Press).

Skidelsky, R. (2009) *Keynes: the return of the master* (London: Penguin Books).

Smith, A. [1776] (1937) *An Inquiry into the Nature and Causes of the Wealth of Nations* (New York: Modern Library).

Smith, Y. (2010) *Econned: how unenlightened self interest undermined democracy and corrupted capitalism* (Basingstoke: Palgrave Macmillan).

Sorkin, A.R. (2009) *Too Big to Fail: Inside the Battle to Save Wall Street* (London: Allen Lane).

Stiglitz, J.E. (2001) 'Information and the change in the paradigm in economics', Nobel Prize Lecture, 8 December, http://nobelprize.org/nobel_prizes/economics/laureates/2001/stiglitz-lecture.pdf.

Strange, S. (1996) *The Retreat of the State: the Diffusion of Power in the World Economy* (Cambridge: Cambridge University Press).

Taleb, N. (2007) *The Black Swan: The Theory of the Highly Improbable* (New York: Random House).

Taylor J.B. (2008) 'The financial crisis and the policy responses, an empirical analysis of what went wrong', Bank of Canada, a festschrift in honour of David Dodge, November.

Thomas, H. and Logan, C. (1982) *Mondragon: an Economic Analysis* (London: Allen & Unwin).

Trichet, Jean Claude, (2009) ECB President, '*The crisis and its lessons*', lecture at the University of Venice, 9 October, http://www.ecb.int/press/key/date/2009/html/sp091009.en.html.

Tsai, K. (2002) *Back-Alley Banking: Private Entrepreneurs in China* (Ithaca: Cornell University Press).

Turner Review (2009) 'The Turner Review: A Regulatory Response to the Global Banking Crisis', chaired by Lord Turner, Financial Services Authority, UK.

Turner, S. (ed.) (2000) *The Cambridge Companion to Weber* (Cambridge: Cambridge University Press).

United Nations (2009) *World Economic Situation and Prospects 2010, Global outlook* New York: UN).

Useem, M. (1996) *Investor Capitalism: how money managers are changing the face of corporate America* (Jackson: Basic Books).

Veblen, T. [1904] (1920) *The Theory of Business Enterprise* (New York: Charles Scribner's Sons).

Veblen, T. [1899] (1994) *The Theory of the Leisure Class*, unabridged, Dover Thrift editions (New York: Dover publications).

Veblen, T. [1899] (2005) *Conspicuous Consumption* (London: Penguin Books).

Veblen T. [1923] (2007) *Absentee Ownership, Business Enterprise in Recent times: the case of America* (New Brunswick and London: Transaction Publishers).

Vitols, S. (2009) 'The growing crisis in private equity: binding regulation and an action plan are needed', ETUI Policy Brief, European Economic and Employment Policy, 3/2009: http://www.etui.org/research/Media/Files/EEEPB/2009/3-2009/.

Voltaire, F. (2006) *Candide* (London: Penguin Classics).

Watt, A. and Galgóczi, B. (2009) 'Financial capitalism and private equity – a new regime?' in *Transfer* 2/09 15 (2), Summer, pp. 189–208.

Weitzman, Martin (1974) 'Prices vs. Quantities', *Review of Economic Studies* 41(4) October, pp. 477–91.

Whyte, W. and Whyte, K. (1991) *Making Mondragon* (Ithaca: ILR Press).

Wilkinson, R. and Pickett, K. (2010) *The Spirit Level: Why More Equal Societies Almost Always Do Better* (London: Penguin Books).

Williamson, O.E. (1981) 'The Modern Corporation', *Journal of Economic Literature*, December, pp. 1537–68.

Williamson, O.E. (1985) *The Economic Institutions of Capitalism* (New York: The Free Press).

World Economic Forum (2009) 'Report, A Near-Term Outlook and Long-Term Scenarios', co-ordinated by David M. Rubenstein, Co-Founder and Managing Director of The Carlyle Group and John A. Thain, President of Global Banking, Securities and Wealth Management of the Bank of America Merrill Lynch, p. 7.

Wray, R. (2007) 'Lessons from the Subprime Meltdown', Levy Institute Working Paper No. 522, December.

Yellen, J. (2008) 'The Financial Markets, Housing, and the Economy', FRBSF Economic Letter, April.

Index

Printed and bound in the United States of America